DEBATING THE SLAVE TRADE

Ashgate Series in Nineteenth-Century Transatlantic Studies

Series Editors: Kevin Hutchings and Julia M. Wright

Focusing on the long nineteenth century (ca. 1750–1900), this series offers a forum for the publication of scholarly work investigating the literary, historical, artistic, and philosophical foundations of transatlantic culture. A new and burgeoning field of interdisciplinary investigation, transatlantic scholarship contextualizes its objects of study in relation to exchanges, interactions, and negotiations that occurred between and among authors and other artists hailing from both sides of the Atlantic. As a result, transatlantic research calls into question established disciplinary boundaries that have long functioned to segregate various national or cultural literatures and art forms, challenging as well the traditional academic emphasis upon periodization and canonization. By examining representations dealing with such topics as travel and exploration, migration and diaspora, slavery, aboriginal culture, revolution, colonialism and anti-colonial resistance, the series will offer new insights into the hybrid or intercultural basis of transatlantic identity, politics, and aesthetics.

The editors invite English language studies focusing on any area of the long nineteenth century, including (but not limited to) innovative works spanning transatlantic Romantic and Victorian contexts. Manuscripts focusing on European, African, US American, Canadian, Caribbean, Central and South American, and Indigenous literature, art, and culture are welcome. We will consider proposals for monographs, collaborative books, and edited collections.

Debating the Slave Trade

Rhetoric of British National Identity, 1759–1815

SRIVIDHYA SWAMINATHAN
*Long Island University,
Brooklyn Campus, USA*

ASHGATE

© Srividhya Swaminathan 2009

All rights reserved. No part of this publication may be reproduced, stored in a retrieval system or transmitted in any form or by any means, electronic, mechanical, photocopying, recording or otherwise without the prior permission of the publisher.

Srividhya Swaminathan has asserted her moral right under the Copyright, Designs and Patents Act, 1988, to be identified as the author of this work.

Published by
Ashgate Publishing Limited
Wey Court East
Union Road, Farnham
Surrey, GU9 7PT
England

Ashgate Publishing Company
Suite 420
101 Cherry Street
Burlington, VT 05401–4405
USA

Ashgate website: http://www.ashgate.com

British Library Cataloguing in Publication Data
Swaminathan, Srividhya.
 Debating the slave trade : rhetoric of British national identity, 1759–1815.
 – (Ashgate series in nineteenth-century transatlantic studies)
 1. Antislavery movements – History – 18th century. 2. English language –18th century – Rhetoric. 3. Rhetoric – Political aspects – Great Britain – History – 18th century.
 4. National characteristics, British – History – 18th century.
 I. Title II. Series
 326.8'014–dc22

Library of Congress Cataloging-in-Publication Data
Swaminathan, Srividhya.
 Debating the slave trade : rhetoric of British national identity, 1759–1815 / Srividhya Swaminathan.
   p. cm. – (Ashgate series in nineteenth-century transatlantic studies)
 Includes bibliographical references and index.
 ISBN 978–0–7546–6767–4 (alk. paper)
 1. English literature – 18th century – History and criticism 2. Slavery in literature.
 3. Antislavery movements – Great Britain – History – 18th century. 4. Antislavery movements – Great Britain – History – 19th century. 5. English literature – 19th century – History and criticism. 6. English language – 18th century – Rhetoric.
 7. English language – 19th century – Rhetoric. 8. Antislavery movements in literature.
 9. Slave trade in literature. I. Title.

PR448.S55S93 2009
820.9'358–dc22   2009003047

ISBN 978–0–7546–6767–4

Printed and bound in Great Britain by
TJ International Ltd, Padstow, Cornwall.

To my family
To Mahalakshmi (Pati)

Contents

List of Figures ix

Chronology of the British Slave Trade and Empire xi

Acknowledgements xv

Introduction 1

1 Building a Common Vocabulary: The Language of Reform and the Slave-Trade Debates 11

    Cultural Shifts and the Language of Reform 14
    Surveying the Terrain: Major Points of Argument in the Debates 30
    Overview of Scholarship and Methodology 38

2 Converging Arguments in British Resistance: Writing from the Colonies to Great Britain, 1759–1776 47

    Contentious Quakers: Anthony Benezet and Colonial Activism 49
    Slavery, Granville Sharp, and English Civil Law 61
    Beginnings of a "British" Resistance to Slavery 76

3 Proliferating Antislavery Arguments and the Creation of an Activist Community, 1772–1789 83

    Interpreting Mansfield through the Logos of Liberty 86
    Pathos Appeal and the Politics of Oppression 100
    Claiming a (Protestant) Christian Ethos: Black Voices and British Identity 110

4 The Proslavery Rebuttal: Developing New Strategies of Defense, 1770–1789 127

    Invalidating Antislavery Interpretations of the "Mansfield decision" 129
    Developing Counter-Arguments and Rhetorical Strategies 141
    Counter-Images of Identity: The Slave-Holding Briton 155

5 Whose Victory? Abolition and the Construction of British Identity, 1788–1807   171

    Proliferation of Abolitionist Rhetoric, 1785–1796   174
    Recasting Humanity in the Planter/Merchant Image, 1788–1793   191
    Abolishing the Slave Trade and Building an Empire, 1795–1807   203

Epilogue: Towards an Imperial Briton   211

Bibliography   219

Index   239

List of Figures

2.1	Anthony Benezet, title page to *A Caution and Warning to Great-Britain and her Colonies*. Philadelphia: D. Hall and W. Sellers, 1767. Courtesy of The Library Company of Philadelphia.	54
2.2a	Granville Sharp, title page, "Extract from *A Representation of the Injustice and Dangerous Tendency of Tolerating Slavery*." London: Printed 1769. Philadelphia: Reprinted by Joseph Crukshank, 1771. Courtesy of the Library of Congress, Rare Books Division.	66
2.2b	Granville Sharp, advertisement,"Extract from *A Representation of the Injustice and Dangerous Tendency of Tolerating Slavery*." London: Printed 1769. Philadelphia: Reprinted by Joseph Crukshank, 1771. Courtesy of the Library of Congress, Rare Books Division.	67
3.1	Francis Hargrave, title page, *An Argument in the case of James Sommersett a Negro, lately determined by the court of King's Bench*. London: Printed for the author, 1772. Courtesy of the Library of Congress, LC–USZ62–90721.	90
4.1	James Ramsay, title page, *An Essay on the Treatment and Conversion of African slaves in the British Sugar Colonies*. Dublin: Printed for T. Walker, C. Jenkin, R. Marchbank, L. White, R. Burton, P. Byrne, 1784. Courtesy of the Library of Congress, Rare Books Division.	149
4.2	James M. Adair, title page, *Unanswerable Arguments against the Abolition of the Slave Trade with a Defence of the Proprietors of the British Sugar Colonies*. London: J. P. Bateman, 1790. Courtesy of the Library of Congress, Rare Books Division.	156
4.3	Anonymous, "Abolition of the Slave Trade, or the Man the Master." London, 1789. Courtesy of the Library of Congress, LC–USZ62–30930.	162
5.1	Anonymous, "Stowage of the British slave ship 'Brookes' under the regulated slave trade." Created for Thomas Clarkson, 1788. Courtesy of the Library of Congress, LC–USZ62–44000.	188
5.2	Isaac Cruikshank, "The Abolition of the Slave Trade." London: S.W. Fores, 1792. Courtesy of the Library of Congress, LC–USZC4–6204.	193

Chronology of the British Slave Trade and Empire

1562–63: Sir John Hawkins sails first English ship on a private slaving voyage, disregarding Spanish and Portuguese monopolies on the slave trade.

1607: Founding of Jamestown in Virginia, the first successful English settlement in North America.

1619: First Africans sold in British colony of Jamestown.

1625–55: British establish their first West Indian colony on Barbados and continue onward to establish colonies on St. Kitts, Nevis, Antigua, Montserrat, and finally Jamaica in 1655. Sugar becomes the primary crop in the West Indies. Early colonies relied heavily on native American and indentured labor, but African slaves gradually replace both groups as the primary labor force on the islands.

1632–63: Establishment of North American colonies from Maryland to the Carolinas. Most settlers came from Great Britain and the slave population did not develop until after 1700.

1672: Royal African Company granted a new charter to control the British slave trade.

1688: Aphra Behn publishes *Oroonoko*.

1712: Richard Steele publishes "Inkle and Yarico" in *Spectator* no. 11.

1713: Granting of the Spanish *asiento*, the official right to supply the Spanish Empire in the New World with its slaves. This right was negotiated as part of the Treaty of Utrecht and provided the foundation for the Royal African Company's monopoly of the transatlantic slave trade.

1730–40: First Maroon War in Jamaica, which resulted in a community of "Cimarrons" or escaped slaves who fled into the hills of Jamaica. Slave rebellions would continue to break out on various islands throughout the century.

1756–63: Seven Years War with France; Treaty of Paris grants Great Britain the West Indian colonies of Grenada, Dominica, St. Vincent, and Tobago.

1757: Robert Clive defeats the Nawab of Bengal at the Battle of Plassey; Clive becomes Governor of Bengal in 1758.

1758–69: Anthony Benezet publishes his antislavery tracts focusing particularly on the evils of the slave trade.

1765:	Clive takes over the revenue management of Bengal and British control over Bengal established.
1771–72:	Somerset Case in Great Britain: Lord Mansfield rules that no slave can be forcibly removed from England against his or her will. Antislavery activists interpret ruling as the end of slavery in England. Correspondence begins between Anthony Benezet and Granville Sharp, introducing the idea of prompting legislative action against the slave trade.
1776–83:	American revolutionaries overturn British rule and establish the United States of America, a racially exclusive democracy, distancing antislavery efforts in the colonies and spurring anti-slave-trade efforts in Great Britain.
1783:	The *Zong* case brought to the attention of the British public. Captain Collingwood of the slave ship *Zong* accused of throwing up to 132 slaves overboard in order to collect the insurance. Great Britain recognizes the independence of the United States.
1783–85:	Quaker abolitionist societies form in London and present the first petition to abolish the slave trade to the House of Commons.
1784:	Bengal placed under the dual control of the British Crown and the East India Company.
1785:	Arrival of the first fleet in the Botany Bay penal colony in Australia; Warren Hastings resigns as Governor-General of India.
1786:	Thomas Clarkson publishes *An Essay on the Slavery and Commerce of the Human Species*, which later influences William Wilberforce to take up the abolitionist cause.
1787:	The Society for Effecting the Abolition of the Slave Trade forms in London. This organization included Quaker and Anglican activists in London. However, the antislavery cause had interested parties in all part of England, Scotland, Wales, and Ireland, so local abolitionist societies soon formed in cities across the country.
1788:	Abolitionists succeed in having the Privy Council Committee for Trade and Plantations investigate British relations with Africa. Parliament passes Dolben's bill to regulate the carrying capacity of slave ships; activists see this bill as the first step towards abolition. Trial of Warren Hastings begins in Parliament.
1788–92:	Petition campaigns and slave-trade debates gain momentum. Slave rebellion in St. Domingue (1791) causes slave revolts to spread across the West Indies.
1789:	William Pitt and William Wilberforce introduce twelve resolutions against the slave trade to the House of Commons, which begins its own inquiry. Outbreak of the French Revolution.
1789–91:	French and Haitian Revolutions stymie the progress of the anti-slave-trade campaign.

1792: A bill for gradual abolition to be completed by 1 January 1796 passes the House of Commons and is defeated in the House of Lords.

1793–98: British troops invade St. Domingue in an effort to end the civil unrest and capture the colony from France. They suffer heavy casualties and withdraw after concluding a treaty with Toussaint L'Ouverture.

1796: Wilberforce reintroduces the bill for immediate abolition of the slave trade, which is defeated in the House of Commons by only four votes.

1799–1815: Napoleonic Wars.

1805: Wilberforce's bill for abolition again defeated, but shifting political alliances make the defeat temporary.

1807: Bill to abolish the slave trade passes the House of Commons and the House of Lords, and the African Institution is formed to enforce abolition and develop African trade in other commodities besides slaves.

1808: Thomas Clarkson publishes *History of the Rise, Progress and Accomplishment of the Abolition of the African Slave–Trade by the British Parliament.*

1814: Restoration of the French monarchy prompts British subjects to submit 800 petitions to Parliament urging the Legislature to intervene with the French to dismantle their slave trade.

1815: Napoleon defeated at the Battle of Waterloo.

1819: British establish an anti-slave-trade squadron to patrol the waters off the coast of West Africa for slave-trading vessels.

Acknowledgements

No book is written in a vacuum and is always the result of creative, intellectual and emotional support from a diverse group of people. My work is no exception and I would like to acknowledge the wonderful people who made this book possible. First and foremost, I would like to thank my graduate advisers Robert Hume and Clem Hawes for reading each page of this work exhaustively and offering numerous suggestions for improvement. My writing improved greatly under Rob's tutelage and Clem's encyclopedic knowledge of later eighteenth-century scholarship is definitely reflected in the bibliography. Other scholars whose expertise contributed significantly to my analysis were Kumkum Chatterjee, John Harwood, Cheryl Glenn, and Paul Youngquist. My thanks for your insightful reading and commentary.

I would like to thank the Institute for the Arts and Humanities at the Pennsylvania State University for the summer residency fellowship in 2002. Thanks also to the Provost at Long Island University and the College of Liberal Arts at Penn State for travel grants that allowed me to research primary sources at the British Library in London. The Library of Congress Prints and Photographs Division and the Rare Books room provided the excellent images that augment my analysis. I would also like to thank the Library Company of Philadelphia for the use of an image from their extensive collection of eighteenth-century printed material.

A special thanks goes to my editor, Ann Donahue, whose warmth and wit made this process much less painful. Throughout the review and final editing process, Ann remained funny, kind, calm, and reassuring. I would also like to thank my generous reader for the glowing reader's report. I hope the improvements that I have made in the manuscript accord with your original, kind assessment.

Finally, I would like to thank my family for their emotional support. My parents, Nalini and Swaminathan, took a leap in encouraging me to pursue my dream when tradition dictated otherwise. My siblings, Vivek and Vinaya, kept me going with frequent visits and lots of laughter. My extended family in India, specifically Vimala Chithi and Swetharanyam Periappa, never failed to exhibit their pride in my accomplishments. Thanks also to my cousin, Lalitha, for her home cooking and tax help, which has kept me sane and focused over many years. Lastly, this book is really dedicated to my grandmother, Mahalakshmi Ramamoorthy. At the age of 14, she married according to tradition and her growing family kept her from pursuing an education. In spite of this limitation, she is the most intelligent, erudite, and amazing woman I know. Her unconditional support and genuine respect for education has shaped me profoundly and I will always be grateful.

Introduction

Rule, Britannia, rule the waves;
Britons never will be slaves.

James Thomson's now emblematic georgic, "Rule Britannia," perfectly encapsulates a specific moment in the evolution of British culture when the "nation" and the "Briton" began to coalesce. Written some thirty years after the Act of Union (1707) which bound England, Scotland, and Wales into Great Britain, the poem simultaneously celebrates and delineates a common sense of "Britishness" that binds the nation and provides a sense of national imperative. The "charter of the land" impels "Britons" not only to "rule the waves" but also to "never be slaves."[1] This pairing of commerce and freedom becomes a lightning rod for poets, writers, and revolutionaries. The "blest isle" withstands all challenges from "tyrants" and rises triumphant to the "dread and envy of them all." The glorious destiny of Britain is to be an exemplar of freedom to other nations through a sense of divine purpose coupled with supremacy over the seas. Though the specific historical context for the poem involved the trade war with Spain, Thomson's language establishes a more far-reaching image of Britishness. The poem introduces succinctly the most significant rhetorical construct of the later eighteenth-century—national identity.

Thomson's use of the term "Briton" reflects a developing, unified sense of national identity intended to move beyond the regional identities of "Welsh," "English," and "Scottish" that divided the island. Though the term "Briton" dates to the end of the thirteenth century, it came into common use during the eighteenth century. The *Oxford English Dictionary* defines the term since the Act of Union to mean "a native of Great Britain, or of the British Empire." The question of who qualifies as "native" becomes central to the idea of the Briton, and this question is addressed directly in the debate to abolish the slave trade in the latter half of the century. While many different strains of thought contributed to the construction of national identity during this time, no other cause brought so clearly into conflict Britain's "charter" of commerce and freedom.

The voluminous scholarship on slavery and the slave trade seems to leave little room for new or interesting analyses. For many years, historians monopolized the field and finely parsed the economic, social, and political implications of African slavery on Europe, Africa and the Americas. Older historical studies tended to

---

[1] The poem, first printed in 1740, was part of a masque, titled "Alfred," written by Thomson and Mallett. It quickly became popular and was set to music by the most famous composer of the time, Thomas Arne. For a history of the poem, see Edward Rimbault Dibdin's "The Bi-Centenary of 'Rule Britannia'" in *Music and Letters*, 21.3 (1940): 275–290.

divide the African slave trade by national participants and compartmentalize abolitionist thought. American scholars wrote about slavery in the United States, British scholars focused on slavery in Britain and her colonies, and so on. The multi-national interconnectedness of movements for and against slavery and the slave trade demanded closer attention. The newest books by David Brion Davis and Christopher Leslie Brown offer readings specifically of Britain's and America's successive antislavery campaigns. Davis's *Inhuman Bondage* seeks to situate American slavery in the "larger contexts of the Atlantic Slave System." The scope of his analysis extends far beyond a study of British slavery so there is little opportunity to investigate the subtleties of the first abolitionist campaign. Brown's analysis provides a clearer trajectory for the development of antislavery thought in Britain from the "haphazard" to the moment at which the movement "coalesced."[2] His careful research on the strands of argument and how they came together, however, lacks close reading of the primary texts.

Literary scholars have opened the field of slavery studies to a different sort of scrutiny in order to examine the extent to which "slavery" provided powerful literary tropes. Romanticists like Peter Kitson and Debbie Lee have firmly placed British abolition and writings about slavery within the Romantic period.[3] Recent studies by Markman Ellis, Deirdre Coleman, Debbie Lee, Suvir Kaul, and Srinivas Arvamudan examine the poetry and prose of the abolitionist movements in relation to sentimental or Romantic literary trends of the later century.[4] However, these scholars tend to focus on abolitionist rhetoric to the virtual exclusion of proslavery response, an approach which fails to appreciate the dialogue between proslavery and antislavery that actively captured public interest in the later century. A more recent study by Brycchan Carey does a noteworthy job of tracing the influence of sentimental rhetoric on British abolitionism.[5] He uses a broader variety of sources including pamphlet and newspaper accounts; however, his study and the others

---

[2] David Brion Davis, *Inhuman Bondage* (Oxford: Oxford University Press, 2006), 2; Christopher Leslie Brown, *Moral Capital* (Chapel Hill: University of North Carolina Press, 2006).

[3] Kitson and Lee co-edited the now landmark reprint series *Slavery, Abolition and Emancipation: Writings in the British Romantic Period* (London: Pickering & Chatto, 1999). This excellent, if highly selective, survey of antislavery texts helped to launch a new wave of fruitful literary scholarship.

[4] Markman Ellis, *The Politics of Sensibility: Race, Gender and Commerce in the Sentimental Novel* (Cambridge: Cambridge University Press, 1996); Deirdre Coleman, *Romantic Colonization and British Anti-Slavery* (Cambridge: Cambridge University Press, 2005); Debbie Lee, *Slavery and the Romantic Imagination* (Philadelphia: University of Pennsylvania Press, 2002); Suvir Kaul, *Poems of Nation, Anthems of Empire: English Verse in the Long Eighteenth Century* (Charlottesville: University Press of Virginia, 2000); Srinivas Aravamudan, *Tropicopolitans: Colonialism and Agency, 1688–1804* (Durham, NC: Duke University Press, 1999).

[5] Brycchan Carey's *British Abolitionism and the Rhetoric of Sensibility: Writing, Sentiment, and Slavery, 1760–1807* (New York: Palgrave Macmillan, 2005).

view antislavery language as a product of Romanticism, which limits the reading of other influences on the arguments. Abolitionist and proslavery writing shape socio-cultural trends; therefore, they utilize a number of literary and non-literary forms of persuasion to present each case.

Another dynamic field of scholarship that has entered into the study of slavery is the study of rhetoric. This field, well nigh totally dominated by American scholars, focuses on American antislavery and proslavery almost to the exclusion of all other influences. Excellent recent works on proslavery rhetoric in the South by Patricia Roberts-Miller and antislavery rhetoric by Jacqueline Bacon and Glen McClish examine the different strains of argument evident in poetry and prose.[6] Jacqueline Bacon's study of the relationship between rhetoric and empowerment of white women and African Americans in antebellum America "recovers" the marginalized voices in a movement that is ironically about marginalization. However, these studies either ignore or only give passing acknowledgement to the influence of British abolitionists and slavery advocates in crafting many of the rhetorical strategies that American abolitionists later used. The gap my study seeks to address occurs at the nexus of these three disciplines. Through close reading and the application of rhetorical theory, I trace a trajectory of the development of British abolitionist and proslavery thought as being concomitantly focused on the development of national identity and the issue of slavery.

How does the language of a social movement and its opposition utilize rhetorical strategies to draw upon and contribute to the construction of British national identity? The first abolitionist campaign in Great Britain targeted the African slave trade and described it as a venture designed to corrupt and degrade the morals of the nation. The process by which the slave trade became the focus of "moral action" is detailed in Brown's *Moral Capital*. I extend his overview to a more direct interrogation of how arguments emerged to target the slave trade. In the development of the image of the Briton, no other issue could have established the rhetorical terrain of national identity as effectively. In the course of arguing for abolition, writers engaged in constructing a new sense of "native"—not as primitive but as civilized and British—and also questioned who had legitimate claim on the term. Through the latter portion of the eighteenth century, antislavery writers organized and focused their efforts on abolishing the slave trade by waging a successful campaign in print. The proslavery response, while initially less prolific, also grew to combat the increasingly serious accusations by abolitionists and proposed its own reforms to address the issues. Ultimately, the idea of "native" character and interests became the most consistent rhetorical topos on which

---

[6] Patricia Roberts-Miller, "Robert Montgomery Bird and the Rhetoric of Improbable Cause," *Rhetoric Society Quarterly* 35 (Winter 2005): 73–90; Jacqueline Bacon and Glen McClish, Descendents of Africa, Sons of '76: Exploring Early African-American Rhetoric," *Rhetoric Society Quarterly* 36 (Winter 2006): 1–29; Jacqueline Bacon, *The Humblest May Stand Forth: Rhetoric, Empowerment, and Abolition* (Columbia: University of South Carolina Press, 2002).

both camps chose to present their individual cases for either the abolition or the preservation of the slave trade.

A complete catalog of all printed materials relating to slavery and the slave trade in the later eighteenth century is beyond the purview of this study. Such a catalog, while of infinite value as a list of materials, offers little by way of analysis. Nor does this study claim to be an exhaustive survey of all printed and manuscript documents produced during the time. Given the sheer volume of material, I have been deliberately selective in the documents chosen for analysis. I have not incorporated any manuscript sources as it is almost impossible to determine distribution. Some private letters have been consulted in order to trace the transatlantic influence in defining the opposition to the slave trade in particular. As my study is a reflection on audience perception, I have chosen documents with the widest known circulation and where possible I have included publication information for each. I have also generally avoided literary periodization and not classified these works according to any one period of literary trends. In other words, the arguments for national identity emerge from a brilliant mishmash of ideas that can be classified as products of the "Enlightenment" of "sentimentalism" of "Romanticism" and even of the "Age of Reason." I maintain that the confluence of all such ideas allowed for the development of nationalist rhetoric from this particular social, political, moral movement.

The slave-trade debates that took place over a roughly fifty-year time span captured public interest and became the *cause célèbre* by the end of the century.[7] These debates were well-known and closely followed by the reading public, which allowed writers to disseminate ideas that extended beyond opposition or support of the slave trade. Slavery, more specifically the slave trade, was a *national* problem that demanded a solution from the people of the nation. Rhetorical strategies used by each side relied upon particular constructions of nationhood and national character to make the respective arguments. Each side claimed to have a "truer" sense of the nature of the "Briton" and crafted appeals to propagate this perception. The slave-trade debates played a pivotal role in the emerging discourse of national identity and contributed to public understanding of Great Britain and her empire.

My study extends rhetorical, literary, and historical analyses of abolition to trace the repercussions of slave-trade rhetoric on the growing sense of British nationhood at the turn of the century. Historians have traced in painstaking detail the trajectory of abolition, beginning with Great Britain's initial involvement with African slavery. Their studies focus primarily on why the antislavery campaigns succeeded and what factors influenced the success of abolition. Through historical reconstruction, we know that the movement against the transatlantic slave trade arose out of a favorable confluence of cultural and political factors. In the late eighteenth century, Great Britain was the site of multiple reform movements that

---

[7] While the most active period of these debates occurred between 1788 and 1792, the arguments that came into common usage during that time developed much earlier in both Great Britain and the colonies.

sought to address inequalities within British society. These movements questioned aspects of society, like the rigid social hierarchy, the uneven distribution of wealth, and what "natural rights" should belong to all citizens of the Crown. Each social movement proposed particular changes to ameliorate current conditions, and they created a dynamic cultural climate that encouraged clearer definitions of the nation and the character of its citizens. This atmosphere of reform, as detailed in Chapter 1, drew upon philosophical, social, and economic theories to create a common vocabulary on which both proslavery and antislavery writers built their arguments. Abolitionists contributed to the emerging discourse of national identity in hopes of shaping a moral, Christian Briton for whom the slave trade would be anathema. By contrast, proslavery writers offered the image of an affluent, commercially savvy Briton, who understood the value of trade and would seek a more moderate solution. Both camps responded to and appropriated elements of the other's arguments to advocate their particular vision of the "Briton."

This analysis focuses on how the rhetorical strategies used in the slave-trade debates helped to shape the identity and character of the "Briton." Both sides produced canny arguments that responded to public perceptions of the morality and legality of the slave trade. These arguments can be read as a series of dialogues among diverse groups, consisting of proponents, opponents, and the greater reading public in Great Britain. Denouncing or advocating the slave trade on legal and moral grounds required a common conceptual framework that appealed to all audiences. Antislavery crusaders delineated this conceptual framework in the 1770s when their ideas first began to receive serious attention from the reading public. Since the proslavery contingent initially had stronger support, their arguments for slavery relied upon biblical justification and commercial value as insuperable rationale. Antislavery writers first had to establish that a specific problem existed before pushing for reform. Slavery as a general evil could not be successfully argued to a public that had little if any direct understanding of the institution. While audiences in the mother country had little understanding of the institution, colonials were much savvier. The transatlantic exchange of ideas proved invaluable in helping to define both the exact danger of slavery and how to focus the cause against slavery.

Concrete examples that emphasized the humanity of the African while simultaneously questioning the humanity of the European proved more effective than blustering condemnations from the pulpit. Early activists like Anthony Benezet and Granville Sharp proposed an alternate understanding of the institution of slavery as one that tainted the high ideals of the nation and corrupted the character of the Briton. As the public began to accept this view of slavery and the slave trade, the balance of power shifted and proslavery writers found they could no longer rely upon the standard defenses of slavery. The common rhetorical battlefield of the debates was the concept of a shared British national identity, which became central to both abolition and anti-abolition. Over the course of the debates, writers proved highly responsive to their audiences and their opposition in crafting their respective set of attributes comprising national character.

Investigating the debates entails a "mapping" of the changes in the rhetoric used by both proslavery campaigners and antislavery/abolitionists. Each side develops arguments that respond to a complex mixture of factors such as geographical location, legal decisions, and publications with opposing viewpoints. Understanding the relationship between these factors necessitates a systematic plotting of the shifts in argument over the roughly sixty-year time span covered in this analysis. The chapters span discrete time periods during which significant "transformations" in arguments take place and discuss both the antislavery/abolitionist and proslavery perspectives. "Transformations" produce evolving constructions of national identity that respond to changes in political and social climate over time. The earliest emergence of the debates in the 1760s and '70s focuses on defining the problem, consolidating support and changing legal decisions within Great Britain. Writers from both camps initially address audiences in specific geographical locations (for example, London, Philadelphia, and so on) and generally appeal to regional identities. However, these regional identities are highly complicated by the interaction of the mother country and the colonies. By the 1780s, writers begin to develop arguments that focus less on regional distinctions such as English or Pennsylvanian and more on divisions between mother country and colonies. With the formal organization of the abolitionist movement at the end of the 1780s, the rhetoric of both camps includes discussions of who qualifies as legitimate citizens of Britain and what characteristics those citizens should embody. By the 1790s, the most dynamic period of the debates, the public demonstrates a strong engagement with the arguments and their constructions of British identity. Both proslavery and abolitionist rhetoric found sympathetic audiences, and by the first decade of the nineteenth-century the "victory" could not be simplistically handed to the abolitionists. Instead, I argue for a more complex reading of this seeming triumph by contending that a synthesis occurs in the claims of both camps and a combined identity, one that leads naturally to imperialism and a sense of global superiority, emerges.

To trace the significant "transformations" in the debates, I employ rhetorical analysis and theory in order to establish the importance of each shift in strategy. The slave-trade debates exerted a singular influence on the British public precisely because the battles were waged openly in print rather than behind the closed doors of Parliament. At their height between 1788 and 1792, the variety of publications numbered in the hundreds, spanned every genre from fiction to non-fiction to poetry, and circulated throughout the empire. Using the classical Aristotelian "modes" of rhetoric as organizing principles, I illustrate how arguments for and against abolition made successive use of ethos, logos, and pathos appeals. Mapping the debates requires an understanding of the motives driving each shift in argument and the meaning produced by these transformations. Kenneth Burke's focus on "transformations" as productive of meaning in *A Grammar of Motives* will be utilized in my discussion of proslavery and antislavery/abolitionist appeals to "Britons" in their respective arguments. His discussion of "circumference" and his dramatic pentad prove particularly useful in exploring shifts in rhetorical arguments within and between each camp. Writers participating in the slave-trade debates develop arguments that define territorial boundaries and the metaphysical nature of national character. Identifying a writer's "circumference," a concept which refers to the cosmology constructed by the writer for the reader, allows for an understanding of the particular assumptions made about the audience. The changes in "circumference" occur with the writers' negotiations of identity and their audience's access to that identity. Finally, the dramatic pentad offers a framework for a nuanced examination of rhetorical changes within a piece of literature and over the course of a single activist's career.

Analysis of this dialogue reveals that writers continuously revised the predominant characteristics of the "Briton" in response to audience and opposition. The position of the author in relation to his or her audience directly influenced the shape and tone of the arguments advanced, a significant nuance that is ignored when looking for general literary or historical trends. In the 1770s, the issue of slavery began to attract more attention from a larger audience that spanned two continents. Writers in both Great Britain and her Colonies produced numerous documents that sought to represent the "true" nature of slavery to their particular audiences; however, the type of slavery under discussion differed according to geographic location. Among early antislavery activists, a divide appeared between authors located in Great Britain and authors located in the Colonies. Writers in Great Britain who had little direct contact with African slaves tended to advocate the total abolition of slavery, but colonial writers sought a more gradual abolition that would begin by outlawing the transatlantic slave trade. Chapter 2 discusses the impact of antislavery crusaders who provided an initial template for abolitionist rhetoric against the standard defenses of slavery. The colonial Quaker activist, Anthony Benezet, inspired the London activist Granville Sharp to refine his arguments and set particular goals. Both writers approached their topics as though slavery was commonly accepted as a problem, but their arguments differed sharply in terms of providing a concrete solution. Their "circumferences" clearly emerged from geographic location and personal experiences of slavery. While Sharp focused on the issue primarily with respect to the mother country, he found Benezet's descriptions of colonial atrocities compelling. He eventually understood that immediate emancipation would not be a feasible solution and accepted the strategy of his colonial counterpart. Ironically, the development of the anti-slave-trade movement came from the American colonies, which then proceeded to sever its ties with the mother country. The interaction between these crusaders influenced the arguments of other writers who took up the task of getting a broader segment of the population to acknowledge the evils of slavery.

Chapter 3 discusses how other activists brought more diverse perspectives and expanded the form of abolitionist writing after Benezet and Sharp. More women began to take an active part in manipulating public sympathies and created works of poetry and fiction that incorporated images of the atrocities of slavery. Diversity in writers prompted a diversity in forms of writing as the anti-slave-trade appeals expanded into fiction and poetry. These other genres enabled writers to dramatize the experience of slave trading and slave holding more effectively. Poetic appeals to the "compassionate" and the "moral" Briton often preceded detailed depictions of the horrors of slavery. Poets identified the traits that characterized a British conscience and portrayed the horrors endemic to the condition of slavery as antithetical to British character. Some of the most effective translators of the slave experience to poetry were British women who expanded the image of the Briton to include members of their sex. The 1770s and '80s were marked by the publication of literature by former slaves. Slave narratives dictated or written by Ukawsaw Gronniosaw (1770), Ottobah Cugoano (1787), and, most importantly, Olaudah Equiano (1789) disproved theories of African racial inferiority. The *Letters of Ignatius Sancho* (1781) provided an intimate glance into the life of a middle-class Afro-British man who successfully blended antithetical aspects of his personal identity. Perhaps the most inspiring publication came in the form of verse by the young Phillis Wheatley, which was first published in London in 1773. The excellence of her poetry resonated on several levels by defying stereotypes of race and gender and providing abolitionists like Granville Sharp with powerful evidence against racial stereotypes of African slaves.

The proponents of the slave trade initially regarded antislavery writers as mere nuisances; over forty years, however, a significant shift in power occurred. Chapter 4 outlines the gradual changes in argument and tone of proslavery rhetoric as writers respond to an increasingly powerful opposition and an unsympathetic public. Initially, the slave trade and slavery had the tacit approval of an apathetic public because most antislavery tracts published prior to the 1770s barely elicited a response from proponents and were not perceived as threatening planter and trader livelihoods. However, public sentiment forced both traders and planters gradually to assume a defensive rhetorical position and refute the growing list of abolitionist claims. The harsh and profoundly disturbing nature of abolitionist accusations expanded proslavery arguments in significant ways, and many writers countered the push for abolition by proposing their own reforms. These writers, who were primarily from the West Indies, had to carve a place for themselves within the nation that was consistent with the "civilized" qualities of national character. They sought to reconcile images of the Briton as moral and Christian with the importance of trade and respect for property upheld by British law. Elements of their arguments resonated with the public and instigated an organized abolitionist rebuttal.

The most dynamic period of the debates resulted from the active engagement between proslavery and abolitionist writers regarding the nature of the British empire. Arguments from each camp coalesced during the four years following the introduction of the bill for abolition. From 1788 to 1792, each side solidified its image of the Briton and began to discuss the implications of these competing images for the rest of the world. Chapter 5 examines the last stages of the debates from the first inquiry into the slave trade in 1788 to abolition in 1807. During this time, both proslavery and abolitionist "circumferences" broadened to include a more global perspective. Abolition would have implications not only for Great Britain, but the whole "civilized" world. The elements of national character advocated by each side began to take on an increased significance because each side also sought to claim for Great Britain the top place in the international arena. By the conclusion of the debates a synthesis of characteristics had occurred that produced an image of the globally aware and morally superior Briton. The form of national identity that emerged from the slave-trade debates of the late eighteenth century directly contributed to British imperialism in the nineteenth and twentieth centuries.

By the early twentieth century, the British empire spanned the globe and included an array of races, religions, and cultures, unified by a sense of "Britishness" which came into being in the eighteenth century. The campaigns for and against the slave trade contributed significantly to this sense of unified British imperial identity. To see the first abolitionist movement only in terms of its immediate goal limits our understanding of this dynamic instrument of cultural change. This dialogue was an integral part of public discourse in its time and commanded the interest of a considerable segment of the reading public. Historical analyses take an overarching perspective that sometimes subsumes the vibrant and rigorous nature of the debates to a specific teleology. More recent historical study has challenged this view, but the studies still offer limited close reading, which can flatten the nuances of argument. Literary analyses tend to view only some of the writing of abolitionists that conform to specific literary movements, such as Romanticism and sentimentalism. Close reading of the shifts in the debates reveals that writers of the time were concerned with more than immediate abolition. The rhetorical appeals of these writers reflected multiple transformations in social composition and strains of thought. Analyzing the debates from the perspective of rhetoric offers a fresh approach and an opportunity for nuanced reading. First and foremost, this debate attempted to persuade the public into participating in the idea of a collective national, commercial, moral identity, and understanding this mode of persuasion requires a careful study of the shifts in argument of this dynamic movement.

Chapter 1
Building a Common Vocabulary: The Language of Reform and the Slave-Trade Debates

The slave-trade debates in Great Britain both shaped and reflected the changes in culture over the last decades of the eighteenth century.[1] In 1808, Thomas Clarkson published a history of abolition that characterized the success of the movement as inevitable because "liberty" could not be stifled indefinitely. This teleological reading of the abolitionist movement successfully prejudiced two centuries of historical scholarship to follow. Even while historians debated the actual contribution of abolitionist societies in effecting change, their analyses posited a specific trajectory of the nation, reinforcing the belief that abolition was inevitable given the particular economic and political trends. Though this teleology is less accepted in current scholarship, a systematic examination of the movement as a dialogue with implications for shifts in culture is still lacking.[2] This study re-evaluates the purpose and function of the abolitionist movement during the time of its emergence. While the stated goal was abolition, the process of attaining this goal contributed to a secondary cascade of critical transformations in British culture. The slave-trade debates occurred during a period of multiple reform movements whose putative purpose was the "betterment" of society. The well-crafted language of reform appealed to and, in essence, created a society that could be "improved" by attention to particular causes. The slave-trade debates offered an ideal issue—combining the language of reform and the rhetoric of nation—to develop a particular vision of British society.

Reform writers inundated the reading public with essays, pamphlets, poetry and fiction that challenged the status quo and instigated changes in public perceptions. The principal characteristic of the reform movements of the eighteenth century was their use of print to build and organize public support. The increased literacy of the public allowed for greater involvement in the shaping of culture by different social groups within British society. No longer was cultural character reflective only of aristocratic or elite interests. Instead, the emerging sense of public culture

---

[1] Since this study focuses on the geographic boundaries drawn by nationalist rhetoric, I use "Great Britain" to refer only to England, Scotland, Wales, and Ireland. All other parts of the "empire" are referred to as the colonies.

[2] Christopher Brown's *Moral Capital* begins to address this oversight; however he takes a broader perspective as social history rather than a detailed examination of rhetoric.

at the end of the eighteenth century reflected a larger cross-section of society.³ The expansion of "print culture" in the late eighteenth century enabled writers to effect significant changes or "transformations" within society. Perhaps the most profound transformation to occur in this period was the cohesion of the "modern" nation-state whose origin can be traced through the development of an "imagined political community."⁴ Benedict Anderson, who first advanced this theory, described the nation as "*imagined* because the members of even the smallest nation will never know most of their fellow-members, meet them, or even hear of them, yet in the minds of each lives the image of their communion ... the nation is always conceived as a deep, horizontal relationship" (6, 7). He further argued that "nation-ness," a "cultural artefact" that came into being in the late eighteenth century, was disseminated through the vehicle of print, which had a profound effect on the increasingly literate European societies. In the particular case of Great Britain, this sense of national identity emerged, not from the pens of the existing power structure, but from those challenging it.

Reform movements in the eighteenth century developed a shared vocabulary to challenge the status quo and shift the balance of power. The writers from both camps in the slave-trade debates drew upon this vocabulary to craft their appeals to varying audiences. In the process, they helped to shape particular nationalist tropes that contributed to the emerging discourse of British identity. Linda Colley's *Britons* examines the "patriotism" of the British people and locates the "forging" of national identity primarily from external pressures.⁵ The multiple and expensive wars waged against France during the course of the eighteenth century inspired a "mass allegiance" in people who subsequently "invented Britishness." However, I would argue that British identity emerged more from internal pressures, originating in the metropole and spreading throughout the empire. Other critics, like Srinivas Aravamudan, have contested Colley's "parthenogenetic" account of nationalism; however, they also posit broadly defined concepts (for example, "Orientalism") to identify elements outside of the metropole as critical to identity.⁶ A closer analysis

---

³ I do not claim that previously disenfranchised groups were easily or successfully integrated into the power structure as a result of print culture. However, the language of reform depicted and made visible the varying conditions within British society in a fresh and innovative manner. See Kathleen Wilson's *The Sense of the People* (Cambridge: Cambridge University Press, 1995) and Raymond Williams, *The Long Revolution* (New York: Columbia University Press, 1961).

⁴ Benedict Anderson, *Imagined Communities: Reflections on the Origin and Spread of Nationalism* (1983; London: Verso, 1991). While historians have critiqued and added to Anderson's theory of nation, his text continues to be the foundational study on which other theories of nationhood are based.

⁵ Linda Colley, *Britons: Forging the Nation, 1707–1837* (New Haven: Yale University Press, 1992).

⁶ Aravamudan, *Tropicopolitan.* "While staying on literary terrain, *Tropicopolitans* indirectly contests Colley's parthenogenetic account of eighteenth-century British nationalism.

of a more discrete period of time reveals multiple strains of thought that merged to construct a vision of national identity. The slave-trade debates provide the perfect test case for "forging" a national identity that set Britons apart from other Europeans and created a place for British colonial identity. Twentieth-century critic Ernest Gellner emphasized the importance of a "similarity of culture" as "the basic social bond."[7] He states, "In its extreme version, similarity of culture becomes both the necessary and the sufficient condition of legitimate membership: *only* members of the appropriate culture may join the unit in question, and *all of them* must do so" (3-4). Since slavery was an inherently "British" issue, affecting the English, Scots, Welsh, and Irish equally and without regard to regional identity, participants in the slave-trade debates looked beyond regional loyalties to forge a shared national culture. Thus the "social bond" created in this literature proposed a common morality, worldview, and the idea of a national code of conduct applicable both at home and abroad. Through print, the public kept informed of social issues, negotiated positions, and actively fashioned a shared cultural identity.

This chapter investigates significant shifts in cultural context that occurred prior to and during the course of the British slave-trade debates. Many more shifts have been identified by historians, but I cover only those that have direct relevance to the language of reform and its implications for national identity formation. Burkean analysis allows for a mapping of the changes in rhetoric decade by decade with particular attention to the developing images of the Briton presented by each side. By identifying changes in social, philosophical, and economic theory, I identify the most significant factors that influenced antislavery/abolitionist arguments in both the planning phase and the active phase of the organized movement against the slave trade. Prior to the formation of the first abolitionist society in 1787, most writers focused their critiques on the problematic nature of slavery without necessarily proposing feasible solutions. I use the terms antislavery and abolitionist to indicate distinct periods in the movement against the slave trade. Antislavery refers to the period of gathering public support and abolitionist refers to the official, organized movement. Writers did not develop their arguments in a cultural vacuum; instead, they freely appropriated the discourse of concurrent movements in crafting their rhetoric. Examining the evidence of these varying rhetorical strains in the debates provides an overview of the principal arguments advanced by each side. The debate over the slave trade, which took place over roughly sixty years, represents a transformative period in British culture. Rather than argue for the inevitability of abolition, a topic that has been amply discussed in historical surveys and analyses, I wish to complicate this narrative by arguing that the interchange between proslavery and antislavery/abolitionist writers precipitated transformations in culture that exceeded the goal of abolition. I propose an alternate teleology for abolition, one

---

Xenophobia, colonialism, orientalism, and racism had just as large a role to play in the constitution of national identity as the admittedly important category of religion" (10).

[7] Ernest Gellner, *Nationalism* (New York: New York University Press, 1997) 6.

that succeeded in critiquing, delineating, and restructuring the concept of both the colonial and the metropolitan "Briton."

Cultural Shifts and the Language of Reform

In the final decades of the eighteenth century, British culture underwent significant changes both in structure and ideology. A host of structural factors, such as shifts in the economy, redistribution of wealth, and alterations in social composition, upset the established hierarchies and precipitated subtle shifts in the balance of power.[8] Great Britain was moving from an agrarian to an industrial economy, which steadily valued manufactured goods over raw materials. This move diminished the clout of landed interests of the aristocracy and placed more emphasis on trade. The acquisition of colonial property in both the East and the West allowed merchants to increase the scope of their trade and their consumer base. However, the nature of colonization differed between the New World and the East Indies, a fact which would become increasingly important in antislavery arguments. The rising merchant class possessed vast and rapidly expanding economic resources that increased its social power. These shifts in social infrastructure helped to form a growing body politic that rigorously and passionately questioned the status quo. Along with these transformations, social theorists developed new ideologies to accommodate and facilitate the changes in their worlds. They reconfigured the nature of man along more optimistic and individualistic lines and scrutinized the workings of society.[9] These beliefs began to proliferate throughout all levels of British society, albeit in distilled forms, and shaped the appeals of many reform movements at the end of the century. David Brion Davis commented on "the social functions of ideology" in which "shifting patterns of thought and value focused attention on new problems" and "defined new conceptions of social reality."[10]

---

[8] While every century in British history can claim a certain manipulation of the established power structure, the serious threat to aristocratic landed interests posed by the rise of the merchant class was unheard of prior to the eighteenth century. For a historical analysis of this phenomenon see E. P. Thompson's *The Making of the English Working Class* (New York: Pantheon Books, 1964) and Margaret R. Hunt's *The Middling Sort: Commerce, Gender, and the Family in England, 1680–1780* (Berkeley: University of California Press, 1996).

[9] The purpose and efficacy of these re-imaginings of society have been seriously critiqued by twentieth-century social theorists, like Theodore Adorno. My study neither reinforces nor contradicts the motives behind eighteenth-century "liberal progressivism"; rather, I seek to highlight the function of this rhetoric in shaping both antislavery and proslavery arguments at the end of the century.

[10] David Brion Davis, *The Problem of Slavery in the Age of Revolution, 1770–1823* (Ithaca: Cornell University Press, 1975) 349.

By the late eighteenth century, the issue of slavery became a new and troubling social reality that came into focus because of important changes in ideology.

Another significant development involved the shifts and changes in class hierarchy in British society. Over the course of the seventeenth and eighteenth centuries, the great divide between privileged and under classes narrowed in perceptible ways. Studies like Thompson's *The Making of the English Working Class* and Hunt's *The Middling Sort* trace the various social and economic changes that opened class structure to a new and empowered middle class. Kathleen Wilson's *The Sense of the People* adds the development of "urban political culture" that "mitigated the harsher aspects of oligarchy" (13). Additionally, the accessibility of new political ideas and propaganda to the greater public allowed more citizens to challenge the "customs and values of patrician society"(13). Politics was no longer a practice confined to the Houses of Parliament and a social elite. "Cultural objects and practices were, in a word, polysemic, and their meanings were contingent upon the social environments in which they were used" (13). The social environment of the time produced a dynamic cultural intervention by defining the issue of slavery as anathema to the general public.

One "new problem" that needed to be established involved the institution of slavery, which was tacitly accepted by society in the early part of the eighteenth century. The British public had an awareness of the institution of slavery before any concerted and organized resistance mobilized the nation. Objections to and apologies for slave holding and slave trading had been published prior to the 1770s; however, the reading public was relatively unconcerned with either argument. Subjects in Great Britain, such as the day laborer, domestic servant, and farm worker, had limited contact with the actual practice of slavery. In fact, the African-English population in Great Britain was comparatively small and confined largely to major cities like London, Bristol, and Liverpool.[11] Estimates place the population at about 15,000–20,000 in London—enough to be visible but not enough to inspire political change. These African-English existed in widely varying circumstances; however, the "labor" they performed did not differ in nature from the labor performed by white English citizens. Most slaves who accompanied their masters to England mainly performed the duties of domestic servants, so the back-breaking labor of colonial plantation life appeared only in testimonial and fiction. Early antislavery protest fell on deaf ears as the public tacitly condoned the practice of slavery in the colonies through a lack of interest in the antislavery cause. Meanwhile, proslavery interests in Parliament ensured that the institution would survive regardless of the meager antislavery protest. In the perception of slave holders and slave traders, slavery was accepted by the public

---

[11] Though many Britons were aware of slave labor, they witnessed black slaves performing tasks and holding positions similar to white laborers. The atrocities of slavery were rarely seen. For a more complete discussion see Peter Fryer, *Staying Power: The History of Black People in Britain* (London: Pluto Press, 1984) and Gretchen Gerzina, *Black London: Life before Emancipation* (New Brunswick, NJ: Rutgers University Press, 1995).

as a "necessary evil" to be tolerated because of the valuable products exported from the colonies.

What factors induced decisive transformations in ideology that made the general reading public more receptive to appeals for reform? A perceptible change in receptivity occurred in the late 1760s that provided incentive for the movement against slavery and the slave trade and influenced the language of reform. Interestingly, this change came from the American colonies to the mother country. No appreciable change in public thought or public perception of slave holding and slave trading came about in the decades before this shift: Theological debates over the validity of African slavery had not been resolved; the black population in Great Britain did not significantly increase to form a more visible presence in the public eye. The changes that took place involved critical shifts in thought about the nature and responsibility of man to his society. Philosophers, economic theorists, and social reformers disseminated their ideas, and these ideas—albeit in a distilled form—encouraged the general reading public to question the hierarchies and institutions that structured British society. Antislavery ideology emerged from the nexus of significant social changes that transformed the public's attitudes about individuality, social responsibility, labor, and humanity.

Historians have investigated the dynamic cultural climate of the late eighteenth century and isolated significant influences on public thought.[12] These influences constitute the ideological precursors to effective antislavery arguments and the development of a language of reform. Histories of British slavery and abolition generally credit three important factors for the shift in cultural climate: Enlightenment philosophy, economic theory, and revolution. The social philosophy of the Enlightenment, states Ernest Gellner, "consisted, basically, of a repudiation of this world: notoriously, its ambition was to see the last king throttled with the entrails of the last priest" (19). This overturning of the *ancien régime* opened new dialogues between social groups and instigated a critical rethinking of tradition and identity in Great Britain. The writings of political and social philosophers demonstrated the most consistent challenge to societal structures. Beginning with Locke's *Two Treatises on Government* (1690), political theorists built upon the

---

[12] Several comprehensive histories on slavery discuss the influence of cultural factors on the development of the antislavery argument. The landmark studies are David Brion Davis' *The Problem of Slavery in Western Culture* (Ithaca: Cornell University Press, 1973), *The Problem of Slavery in the Age of Revolution, 1770–1823*, and *Slavery and Human Progress* (Oxford: Oxford University Press, 1984). For general histories, see Michael Craton, *Sinews of Empire: A Short History of British Slavery* (Garden City, NY: Anchor Books, 1974), James Walvin, *Black Ivory: A History of British Slavery* (London: HarperCollins, 1992), and Robin Blackburn, *The Making of New World Slavery* (London: Verso, 1997). For specific studies of the slave trade, see Herbert S. Klein, *The Atlantic Slave Trade* (Cambridge: Cambridge University Press, 1999), James A. Rawley, *The Transatlantic Slave Trade: A History* (New York: W. W. Norton, & Company, 1981), and Hugh Thomas, *The History of the Slave Trade: The Story of the Atlantic Slave Trade, 1440–1870* (New York: Simon and Schuster, 1997).

concept of certain "natural rights" shared by all men. Locke stated, "To understand Political Power right, and derive it from its Original, we must consider what State all Men are naturally in, and that is, a *State of perfect Freedom* to order their Actions, and dispose of their Possessions, and Persons as they think fit, within the bounds of the Law of Nature, without asking leave or depending upon the Will of any other Man."[13] He emphasized man's ability to reason and credited rational thought as a true marker of humanity. While he acknowledged great inequalities amongst men in their capacity to reason, he believed in a basic equality of access for the rational man to participate in society. John Locke was by no stretch of the imagination an abolitionist and he would have had serious reservations about applying his social theories to slave trading and slave holding.[14] However, his theory of civil government contributed to an emerging discourse about "natural rights" and liberties shared by *all* men. Other social theorists had no qualms about applying Locke's philosophies to larger and more diverse populations. Social reform movements of the late eighteenth century occurred as a result of serious philosophical questioning of the capabilities of man.

Enlightenment thinkers redefined man's role in society and fostered a conviction in progressive social change based on innate human capabilities. Locke articulated a belief in man's inherent ability to reason that guaranteed a "Freedom from Absolute, Arbitrary Power." His contention carried forward into the work of other Enlightenment thinkers who collectively began to construct a new narrative of man's position and role within society. This new narrative stressed the merits of individual autonomy and enterprise, encouraging first men then women to pursue self-interest. As the ideas began to develop, the notion of civil society broadened to include a more diverse class, gender, and racial composition. A sense of humankind's "progress," meaning "a belief in the movement over time of some aspects of human existence, within a social setting, toward a better condition," emerged from the writings of both philosophy and religion.[15] Rather than viewing men and women as naturally degraded or steeped in original sin, writers of the progress narrative placed them on a linear path moving forward and improving life conditions. This optimistic view of society contributed to the development of humanitarian ideals that advocated the amelioration of all suffering in human existence. Social inequalities engendered by class, labor conditions,

---

[13] John Locke, "An Essay Concerning the *True Original, Extent, and End* of Civil Government," *Two Treatises of Government*, ed. Peter Laslett (Cambridge: Cambridge University Press, 1967) 287.

[14] I do not contend that Locke is antislavery, a claim clearly contradicted by the constitution that he wrote for the Carolina colony. Rather, I argue that his treatise offered effective arguments against slavery. For an analysis of these contradictory documents, see David Armitage's "John Locke, Carolina, and *Two Treatises of Government*," *Political Theory*, 32.5 (2004): 602–627.

[15] David Spadafora, *The Idea of Progress in Eighteenth-Century Britain* (New Haven: Yale University Press, 1990) 6.

and enslavement came under heavy scrutiny by social reformers. The progress narrative fostered a commitment to the belief that the existing conditions within society could be ameliorated through collective effort that would appeal to the higher sensibilities of a rational public.

While secular theories of progress gained credibility, Protestant theologians reconfigured a Christian progress narrative. Many philosophers denounced Christianity as outdated and an obstacle to the progress of society, primarily because of its doctrine of original sin and cyclical construction of history.[16] Original sin belied the rational person's ability to function honorably within society, and the cyclical view of history did not allow for advancement.[17] Secular critiques of Christianity viewed it as stagnant, backward, and incapable of participating in this new and inherently optimistic strain of thought. Though traditional Protestants (particularly within the Church of England) dismissed these philosophical critiques outright, "progressive" thinkers, such as John Wesley and Thomas Clarkson, took the opportunity to reinterpret religious doctrine. These "progressive" religious figures de-emphasized original sin; instead, they lauded the Christian's commitment to the welfare of his fellow man. This "ethic of benevolence" reconstituted the moral fabric of the practicing Christian to stress an obligation to the downtrodden within society. Man became an instrument of God whose divine plan for the betterment of civilization allowed for a Christian spin on the Enlightenment progress narrative. "In eighteenth-century Britain, then, there were Christian doctrines of progress that depicted religious knowledge as advancing, the true faith as spreading, and, in more general terms, Christianity as improving" (Spadafora 97). These humanitarian and "true" Christian impulses reached a highly sympathetic audience in the British public. They responded positively to the more optimistic view of human nature, and strove to reconcile the pursuit of self-interest with the "ethic of benevolence."

Secular theorists faced similar challenges in attempting to reconcile the doctrine of individualism with the desire for "social good." The work of social and cultural historians has accurately depicted eighteenth-century British society as being in the midst of significant transitions—transitions that led to reformations of religious beliefs, cultural attitudes, and perceptions of self. People from all social levels began to view society as perfectible; they responded favorably to the doctrine of individualism and the goal of always striving for personal fulfillment. The expansion and increasing success of colonial ventures, both east and west of Great Britain, attested to the application of the doctrine of individualism.

---

[16] Davis, *Slavery and Human Progress*, 129.

[17] This summary of the Enlightenment critique of Christian doctrine is necessarily reductive for the purposes of my analysis. No uniform critique of Christianity emerged in this time period just as the term "Enlightenment" masks the many debates taking place amongst philosophers of this time. For a thorough and nuanced analysis of the Christian notions of progress in the context of Enlightenment critique, see David Spadafora's *The Idea of Progress in Eighteenth-Century Britain*.

Of course, the colonial venture benefited the colonizer at the expense of the colonized, a fact that became increasingly problematic over the last decades of the eighteenth century. While colonial adventurers were not always regarded in a wholly positive light, their actions were generally considered to be a benefit to the kingdom. These perceptions often resulted in clashing impulses that set social good opposing self-interest. The expansion of colonial ventures over the course of the eighteenth century began to have a noticeable impact on subjects in the mother country. Increased variety in goods and their availability to a larger segment of the population provided a daily reminder of overseas enterprises. The often fabulous sums accumulated by the colonial elite brought out the contempt of the aristocracy and the jealousy of the poor. Periodicals and newspapers began to publish more news from the colonies, and the reading public developed a tentative awareness or sense of a British "empire."

With this tentative awareness, eighteenth-century social critics extended their analyses to the colonial societies that necessitated interactions between European and non-European peoples. The American, West Indian, and East Indian colonies each functioned according to differing principles of government that challenged the singular construction of "civil society" that had prevailed in Locke's time. Each colony operated under unique conditions that had no precedent in the government of the mother country. The extension of Britain to the east and the west introduced a new relationship with "foreign" people that went far beyond the trading relationship. Secular and religious scholars strove to make sense of these changes and understand the connections between European and non-European peoples. As Britain extended her dominion beyond her shores, the very idea of the "English" and then "British" subject underwent continuous reassessment. With colonial acquisition, British society took on a new composition accompanied by new obligations for people who neither resembled the average Briton nor behaved in a familiar manner. These topics pervaded the print culture of the later eighteenth century and fostered an awareness in all levels of metropolitan society.

A parallel concern that influenced public receptivity at the time of the slave-trade debates involved the actions of the East India Company in their newly acquired territory. The "conquest" of Bengal in 1757 created an unprecedented situation in British mercantile history—a trading company with political control. The responsibility of administering East India affairs required employees of the company to have a more extensive understanding of the culture and traditions of its newly established colonies. Orientalists, like Sir William Jones, theorized and researched complex genealogies that linked Indians and Europeans through common language.[18] Religious scholars investigated Hindu texts and formulated

---

[18] Jones and his colleagues noted similarities of structure between Sanskrit and Latin, which they believed descended from the same language. The Indo-European language family connected Indic, Romance, Germanic, and Slavic languages pointing to a common ancestry for all these peoples.

a Hamitic line of descent for East Indians.[19] The fascination with India entered a new phase in British cultural understanding as those who studied "Indian" culture also attempted to justify British political incursions into that country. British political presence in the East Indies came under intense scrutiny during the highly visible trial of Warren Hastings in 1788.[20] Hastings' actions as governor of Bengal earned him the scathing denunciations of Edmund Burke, who spoke eloquently against Hastings' abuses of the "begums of Oudh" and the "prestige" of the "British nation." His trial for mismanagement of colonial affairs reinforced emerging convictions about the nature of British national character and echoed abolitionist arguments. Burke and his supporters spoke of a "reformed" imperial presence in the East and a West that reflected the superior qualities of the British as "responsible" rulers.

The philosophical shifts that initiated a reconfigured understanding of society and the individual did not occur smoothly or seamlessly. The efforts of activists in the late eighteenth century who attempted to resolve the discordance between philosophy and practice attest to this fact. In *The Problem of Slavery in the Age of Revolution*, Davis encapsulated the contradictions inherent in Enlightenment beliefs and the position of antislavery in reconciling, albeit tenuously, these beliefs. He states:

> At the risk of gross over-simplification, it can be said that the Enlightenment was torn between the ideal of the autonomous individual and the ideal of the rational and efficient social order ... Both major and minor thinkers of the Enlightenment strove to reconcile some notion of individual liberty with some notion of a rationally functional state. Negro slavery dramatized the difficulties of any synthesis; antislavery provided an illusory means of resolution (263).

Antislavery ideology proved "illusory" in that access to "individual liberty" could not be guaranteed with abolition. Paradoxically, the rhetoric of the slave-trade debates encouraged a more rather than less stratified society, particularly in terms of hierarchizing "non-white" communities.

A second major influence on the language and reception of the slave-trade debates was the swiftly changing nature of the British economy and the economic theory that accompanied these changes. Twentieth-century economic historians, such as Seymour Drescher, have typically characterized the eighteenth century

---

[19] See Thomas R. Trautmann, *Aryans in British India* (Berkeley: University of California Press, 1997).

[20] For a history of this trial, see Prince J. Marshall's *The Impeachment of Warren Hastings* (London: Oxford University Press, 1965). For a more recent analysis, see Jeremy Bernstein's *Dawning of the Raj: The Life and Trials of Warren Hastings* (Chicago: Ivan R. Dee, 2000).

as moving from a mercantilist to a capitalist mode of economic production.[21] The reasons for this shift involved both market forces and the influence of important economic theorists. The mercantile system functioned by relying on royally sanctioned monopolies of trade and market prices set by government rather than consumer demand. Merchant capital became an increasingly contested form of investment in the mercantilist mode of production. By the 1750s, economists began to criticize the inefficiency of mercantilist trade, particularly with respect to the colonies. Many economists wrote against the mercantile system and cited the colonies as an excessive drain on British capital that would be more usefully invested in the metropole.[22] Scholars of economic history explain that this phenomenon resulted from contradictory forces: "Historically, merchant capital proved a proverbial Janus, looking at once forward and backward. It bound within the market system both archaic and revolutionary social relations."[23] The idea that an individual could exercise more autonomy with investment fit neatly into the revolutionary spirit developing at the time. Free-market and free-trade capitalism proved an attractive concept to an increasingly "liberty" oriented public.[24]

The mercantilist system proved highly susceptible to criticism in the atmosphere of increased belief in personal autonomy that characterized the late eighteenth century. Government subsidies and price-fixing of commodities, such as sugar, incited economists to a flurry of critique. The most influential of these economists was Adam Smith whose *Wealth of Nations* (1776) revolutionized public perceptions of the market and of labor. His vision for Great Britain's future involved a greater emphasis on trade and commerce, with minimal governmental restrictions. Smith favored a capitalist economy that would allow for the free and "unfettered" play of market forces in setting prices for commodities. He strongly denounced price-fixing and advocated the more equitable economics of supply and demand, which would allow commodity prices to stabilize without government interference and according to the demands of consumers. In a sense, Smith's theories threatened

---

[21] See, for example, Seymour Drescher, *Econocide: British Slavery in the Era of Abolition* (Pittsburgh: University of Pittsburgh Press, 1977).

[22] Richard B. Sheridan, *Sugar and Slavery: An Economic History of the British West Indies, 1623–1775* (Barbados: Caribbean Universities Press, 1974) 9.

[23] Elizabeth Fox-Genovese and Eugene D. Genovese, *Fruits of Merchant Capital: Slavery and Bourgeois Property in the Rise and Expansion of Capitalism* (Oxford: Oxford University Press, 1983) 36.

[24] The relationship between the antislavery cause and emerging capitalist economic system in Great Britain has been thoroughly discussed in historical scholarship. The first historian to make a connection between the movement and capitalism was Eric Williams, *Capitalism and Slavery* (1944, reprinted Chapel Hill: University of North Carolina, 1994). Though his work is considered dated, his thesis set off a debate that continues in historical scholarship today. For a more recent consideration of this question, see Thomas Bender, ed., *The Antislavery Debate: Capitalism and Abolitionism as a Problem in Historical Interpretation* (Berkeley: University of California Press, 1992).

the class structure of British society by de-valuing traditional landed interests. The prosperity of the nation lay in the hands of the independent consumer, not the aristocratic landowner. His work appealed both to the working classes and to the rising middle class in British society.

The main arguments advanced by the *Wealth of Nations* proposed an evolutionary model of economy as progressing through four social stages: hunting, pasturage, farming, and commerce. In book five, Smith detailed the difference between each stage and illustrated how civilizations advanced in complexity and sophistication when moving through each stage. Hunting and pasturage characterized the most primitive (nomadic) of societies whose simple economic systems precluded the acquisition of land and the formation of civil government. Once societies moved to the farming stage, land became the primary commodity of exchange and ownership of this form of property instituted an imbalance of power based on the subordination of non-landowners. However, the fourth stage of economic progress re-established the balance of power in favor of merchants and laborers by diminishing the importance of landed interests. Smith argued that Great Britain had progressed to the most advanced form of economic structure—commerce. This structure surpassed the more "primitive" barter economy and caused a fruitful division of labor within the realms of agriculture and manufacture. Regarding the efficiency of specialized labor, he wrote,

> When the division of labour has been once thoroughly established, it is but a very small part of a man's wants which the produce of his own labour can supply. He supplies the far greater part of them by exchanging that surplus part of the produce of his own labour, which is over and above his own consumption, for such parts of the produce of other men's labour as he has occasion for. Every man thus lives by exchanging, or becomes in some measure a merchant, and the society itself grows to be what is properly a commercial society.[25]

Citizens exchanged money for necessities and other goods, which freed them from the task of being responsible for every aspect of their sustenance. For example, if a householder wished to provide the family with food and clothing, the householder no longer needed to grow crops and livestock to satisfy those needs. Nor did the householder need to supply other goods for a direct exchange. Instead, as Smith argued, the householder could fulfill all needs by way of wages earned through a specialized division of labor.

The larger repercussions of this economic theory not only placed greater emphasis on labor, but redefined the concept of "value" as well. *Wealth of Nations* opened with a paean to labor: "The greatest improvement in the productive powers of labour, and the greater part of the skill, dexterity, and judgment with which it is anywhere directed, or applied, seem to have been the effects of the division

---

[25] Adam Smith, *An Inquiry into the Nature and Causes of the Wealth of Nations, Books 1–3* (1776), ed. Andrew Skinner (London: Penguin Books, 1970) I.iv.126.

of labour" (I.i.109). Smith recounted the number of specialized tasks contained within the manufacture of a single pin and credited this specialization with increased productivity and quality of product. The division of labor gained more significance because of Smith's redefinition of "value." He differentiated between two forms—"value in use" and "value in exchange." He focused on the "value in exchange" since a characteristic of commercial society was that no one man could produce everything necessary for his use. Money had typically been regarded as the standard "value in exchange"; however, Smith's emphasis on the division of labor re-envisioned the actual value of money. He proposed that both money and manufactured goods be measured in labor as a truer marker of "value in exchange." In praising labor, Smith de-valued the commodities of exchange as intrinsically inferior to human capacity. In other words, he viewed positive social change as stemming from reconfigured forms of labor rather than commodities. Smith, in a sense, refuted the total commodification of human beings (particularly in the case of enslavement) as an effective strategy for production. His ideas became a rhetorical commonplace in refuting proslavery views of Africans as property, and they provided economic justifications for the wisdom of antislavery arguments for "humane" labor conditions.

While Smith analyzed the prevailing conditions of the British economy in minute detail, he advanced two revolutionary ideas that had a significant impact on abolitionist rhetoric. He contended that the true value of a commodity rested in the labor required to produce the commodity, and that free labor was the most efficient mode of production because it worked on the principle of self-interest. Smith distinguished between the nominal and real price of commodities, claiming that the "value in exchange" of most goods was estimated by the nominal price—money. Unfortunately, money or cost was never stable and fluctuated with market conditions, whereas labor provided a real price and a "real measure of the exchangeable value of all commodities" (I.v.133). With the division of labor, a man's effort was not sufficient to provide him with the "necessaries, conveniences, and amusements of human life." Instead, people had to rely increasingly on the efforts of others to produce these goods. "The value of any commodity, therefore, to the person who possesses it, and who means not to use or consume it himself, but to exchange it for other commodities, is equal to the quantity of labour which it enables him to purchase or command" (I.v.133). Smith shifted value from money (nominal) to labor (real) as an efficient method of contesting the mercantilist system and the practice of "unnaturally" inflating market prices. If true value rested in the ability to purchase or command labor, then artificially fixing prices of commodities cheated the consumer. The amount of labor commanded by the cultivation or manufacture of the commodity was not reflected in the price.

Smith's challenge to the mercantile system by identifying labor over money as the true measure of value had a considerable effect on the perception of labor. By esteeming the effort expended to produce a commodity, Smith believed that wages should reflect the influence of the market over the whims of the master. This compensation, rather than draining the economy, would actually contribute to the overall growth and affluence of the nation. He stressed that if the market were left unchecked by external forces, as in a capitalist structure, then the value of commodities and labor would find a "natural" price through the fluctuation of supply and demand. He theorized that when demand for a particular commodity was high then the labor used to manufacture the commodity would be commensurately valued in the form of higher wages. Surplus, in the form of revenue or stock, would lead to the creation of more wage-earning positions, which would contribute directly to the increased prosperity of a nation. "The liberal reward of labour, therefore, as it is the necessary effect, so it is the natural symptom of increasing national wealth" (I.viii.176). Thus, nations maintained a healthy economy through the fair reimbursement of labor, which led to increased wealth and national prosperity.

By emphasizing the importance of fair reimbursement for labor and the accompanying rise in national wealth, Smith extended his analysis to a strong critique of the slave system. The system bred inefficiency, promoted indolence, and drained resources. He contrasted the costs of free versus slave labor to argue that free labor provided the greatest return, both moral and economic, to the nation. The free laborer managed his own needs, whereas the slave's needs were managed by "a negligent master or careless overseer." The "strict frugality and parsimonious attention" of the free laborer was completely absent in the slave for logical reasons. Smith based his assertions about the greater benefits of free labor on the inherent self-interest of the laborer. Indeed, he defined the primary motivation for all labor as located in "self-love." Since man's primary motivation was to act in his own best interest, his interactions with society would have to be reciprocal in nature. The exchange of goods and services did not stem from a person's benevolence; instead, the bargain focused on mutual benefit. Perhaps the most quoted sentence in Smith's tracts involved this doctrine of self-interest: "It is not from the benevolence of the butcher, the brewer, or the baker, that we expect our dinner, but from their regard to their own interest" (I.ii.119). Thus, man's desire to better his own existence affected his labor in substantial ways. Smith linked the amount of effort a person put into individual labors with the amount of reward he or she expected to gain from those labors. Since slaves could expect no reward for their labor, they had very little motivation to work. Even fear could not provide the same impetus for labor as self-interest. The system of slave labor used in the colonies could not contribute fully to the economy because of the conflicting interests of the slaveowner and the slave.

Slavery proved to be the greatest challenge to the doctrine of self-interest for how could colonial planters claim to find greater benefit in slave labor over free labor? Since the wealth of the nation rested in labor rather than commodities or coinage, Smith seriously questioned both the efficiency and productivity of slave labor. The conditions of enslavement worked against self-interest, and, since the slave was only permitted to labor in service to his master, all his material needs (food, clothing, shelter, and so on) had to be provided for him. The slave represented a double drain on the resources of the owner. Smith pointed out that "[a] person who can acquire no property, can have no other interest but to eat as much, and to labour as little as possible" (III.ii.488–489). Smith's comments equally derided the slave holder stating, "the pride of man makes him love to domineer" (III.ii.418). Given the choice, Smith argued that pride provided the impetus to choose slave labor over free *whenever the work could afford it*. Though this qualifier tacitly reinforced the Caribbean, sugar-based, slave economy, which could "afford it," Smith's condemnation of planter "pride" opened a new space for antislavery critique.

Smith's analysis supplied ample avenues of argument for abolitionists by illustrating the inefficiency and the costliness of the slave system. He discredited the proslavery argument that claimed a necessity for slave labor by recasting the public's perception of agriculture. His analysis illustrated that particular crops supported the system of labor used rather than necessitating the system of labor. For proof, he turned to the West Indian and American colonies to compare specific crops—sugar, tobacco, and corn—against the number of slaves required to raise them. He concluded: "Both can afford the expense of slave-cultivation, but sugar can afford it still better than tobacco" (III.ii.489). Smith used colonial abolition efforts as an added support to his contentions by commenting on the relative ease with which the Quaker community eliminated slavery among their congregants.[26] Smith further maintained that replacing slave labor with free labor would increase the output of the colonies and contribute positively to national wealth. His "productivity critique" translated into convincing and useful lines of argument used by abolitionists to combat proslavery claims of economic security in slavery.

A third factor that significantly affected British cultural perceptions in the period of the slave-trade debates was the rhetoric of revolution that pervaded the publications of the late eighteenth century. This period of political turmoil prompted serious re-evaluation and questioning of the legitimacy of the various components of English, and later British, identity. The ideological claims of revolution challenged the status quo and in some sense co-opted the language of the governing body by guaranteeing better conditions under a new regime. The three revolutions that had the greatest impact on the cultural climate in Great Britain were the American (1776), the French (1789), and the Haitian (1791). Though each one had a specific list of grievances motivating its respective cause, the one common ideological principle that connected all three was the belief in liberty. These revolutions reconfigured how the British public understood and valued the concept of liberty, and they had a profound impact on British perceptions of

---

[26] This line of argument both anticipates and supports Williams' thesis connecting the abolition of slavery and the rise of capitalism. Of course, Smith glosses over the struggle and turmoil attached to abolition within the Quaker community, which took almost 150 years to rid its members of slavery. In some cases, West Indian Quakers split with the church rather than give up their livelihood.

self and the stability of their system of government.[27] Revolutionary ideology transformed the conceptual questioning of Enlightenment thinkers into real and immediate action intended to implement the changes advocated by those thinkers. The rhetoric of revolution violently challenged government and its ability to meet the needs of its people, questioned the existence of oppressive social hierarchies, and questioned each citizen's access to the rights owed them by their sovereign nation. The varying threads of these arguments pervaded the rationale for revolution and profoundly affected the language of reform.

The rebellion of the American colonies introduced a critique of the colonial enterprise to the public and threatened strongly held beliefs in British character. This revolution set off a re-evaluation of Great Britain's relationship to her colonies and the obligations of the government to all its citizens. Unlike Cromwell's bloody overthrow of Charles I, this civil war was fought solely in the colonies. The battles that occurred in Great Britain were waged primarily in print as liberals and conservatives debated the legitimacy of colonial claims. American territories started out as a lucrative extension of Great Britain's financial interests, and now their denizens repudiated the connection to the mother country in favor of self-government. American colonists criticized the British parliamentary system as disenfranchising a significant portion of the population. They also charged the Crown with willfully trampling on individual and "inalienable" rights guaranteed to all British citizens. These charges seriously challenged the public's understanding of the relationship between Great Britain and her colonies. Historians have rightly pointed out that the American colonists were by no means united in their declaration of war. Many loyal colonials pledged support for the King and Parliament and fought against the revolutionaries. However, the situation was equally conflicted on the other side of the Atlantic. As Linda Colley points out, "what mattered most at the time was that responses [to the American war] were neither overwhelmingly pro-war nor uncompromisingly anti-war, but instead profoundly mixed" (137). The competing ideological claims of the American war forced British citizens to think in deeper, more complex ways about ideological concepts, such as liberty and the function of change within society.

Though the responses to the American war were conflicting, the loss of the American colonies had a profound impact on British cultural climate. The most threatening cry uttered by the warring colonists, ideologically speaking, was the cry for liberty. Writers began to inundate the public with definitions of and theories about liberty—who had the correct understanding of the concept and which country's citizenry truly enjoyed liberty to the fullest extent. The idea came to be the defining characteristic of civil society and was used as a gauge of the

---

[27] Historians have analyzed each revolution in great detail to reveal the complex confluence of forces that prompted the violent uprisings in each country. To undertake a similarly detailed survey is beyond the scope of this book. While I acknowledge the multiple influences of revolution on British politics, economics, and social structure, my argument is necessarily reductive to focus on the impact revolution has on the rhetoric of reform.

"progress" made by "advanced" (read European) civilizations. For the majority of the British public, the rebellion of the American colonies barely registered until the 1780s. However, when prominent public leaders like Edmund Burke began to speak out in favor of the American cause, they prompted intense scrutiny of how the British people understood themselves. Perhaps the most threatening result of the American Revolution was that Great Britain lost. More than the economic loss, the ideological loss, as Linda Colley points out, affected British society in powerful ways. For the American Revolution to succeed on the platform of "liberty," albeit one more concerned with freedom from unfair taxation, meant that citizens in the mother country needed to reassess the extent to which they enjoyed their own liberty. The enormous support for the American cause by other European countries jostled the metropolitan public from its complacent belief in British superiority and contributed new arguments to the growing climate of change.

The violent and bloody overthrow of the monarchy in France raised another set of fears and doubts in every stratum of British society. The French revolt had repercussions throughout Europe, but for the British it resurrected painful memories of the past. Great Britain had already beheaded a king, reinstated the monarchy, and thwarted several challenges to the throne.[28] This revolution threatened the social order in much more tangible ways because of Great Britain's proximity to France and its own tumultuous history with civil war. Reports of the bloodshed and the persistent calls to action traveled quickly across the English Channel. The visible presence of aristocratic refugees offered a vivid and constant reminder of the powerful belief in liberty that instigated treasonous actions. This attack against the French oligarchy contributed, as Linda Colley has noted, to a growing dissatisfaction in Great Britain with the "landed interest" and the "legitimacy of the power élite." Using the ideological principles of "liberté, égalité, and fraternité" to justify the bloody overthrow of the French monarchy horrified the British aristocracy who fully recognized the tenuousness of its own position. While the American Revolution threatened the mother country's conceptions of her own superiority, the French Revolution confronted the hierarchical structure of British society—a confrontation that would explode in print form.

The French Revolution provided fodder for both radical and conservative publications that focused on the rights of man and the "natural" order of government. The political and philosophical tracts of the 1790s created a dynamic environment for debate that invigorated the social movements of the time. Along with the debate about liberty, analysis of the French Revolution interrogated the concept of citizenship and what a government owed its citizens. These questions were intensely debated in the public sphere and tended to divide politically along conservative and radical lines. The conservative faction denounced the revolution as the work of discontented rabble who severely destabilized an accepted way of life. The American Revolution represented a considered and logical rebellion of

---

[28] For a discussion of the Jacobite challenges to the throne and their impact on British national identity, see Colley, *Britons*, 74–79.

people who had been uniformly deprived of rights promised by the government, but the French Revolution was sheer anarchy and chaos. Edmund Burke, who had eloquently supported American independence, vehemently opposed the methods and claims of the oppressed French citizenry. At the other end of the political spectrum, the radical faction applauded the bloody and dramatic reappropriation of unfairly deprived rights Social theorists like Thomas Paine and Mary Wollstonecraft argued for natural, inherent rights to which every citizen had access, regardless of class or gender. Conservative and radical alike offered the general public a mélange of theories about liberty, citizenship, and natural rights. These debates had a direct impact on the rhetoric of reform because the social change advocated by various movements utilized conservative and radical redefinitions of liberty and citizenship. The malleability of these arguments also allowed proslavery interests to make use of them in the debates in order to advocate for more moderate reforms that would not completely overset the status quo.

The uproar in France and the chaos that immediately followed inadvertently served as the catalyst for another, more serious revolution that had a direct effect on the slave-trade debates—the Haitian revolution. This bloody rebellion, which realized the worst fears of all colonial European slave holders, had a significant effect on the economic, political, and social workings of Great Britain and the Americas.[29] Haiti, or Saint Domingue, was only slightly larger than the colony of New Jersey and contained almost two-thirds of the number of slaves in the entire American South by 1790. This richly productive French colony dominated the Caribbean sugar trade, accounting for more than 30 percent imported by North Atlantic economies.[30] The racial tensions on the island had resulted in minor rebellions in the past, but nothing on the scale of what was to erupt in 1791. The talk of liberty and natural rights encouraged the newly formed Société des Amis des Noirs (1788) to appeal to the Estates General regarding the status of slaves in French colonies.[31] Their first goal was to abolish the slave trade and they invited British abolitionist Thomas Clarkson to speak on this issue in 1789.[32] However, French merchant interests prevailed to block any discussion

---

[29] For an excellent account of the events of the Haitian revolution and its effects on other Caribbean colonies, see C.L.R. James, *Black Jacobins: Toussaint L'Ouverture and the San Domingo Revolution*, 2nd ed., rev. (New York: Vintage Books, 1989).

[30] Davis, *Slavery and Human Progress*, 78.

[31] Davis, "A Calendar of Events Associated with Slavery, the Slave Trade, and Emancipation, 1770–1823," *The Problem of Slavery in the Age of Revolution*, 23–36. The summary of events regarding the Haitian revolution are drawn from Davis' concise timeline. For a thorough discussion of the French antislavery movement see Lawrence C. Jennings, *French Anti-Slavery: The Movement for the Abolition of Slavery in France, 1802–1848* (Cambridge: Cambridge University Press, 2000).

[32] A number of countries, including the newly formed and supposedly liberty-loving United States of America, intervened to quell the unrest in Haiti. Since my analysis focuses

of the slave trade. By the following year, the unrest in Haiti had grown and royal troops put down an uprising in 1790. In 1791, when the French assembly extended suffrage to all free blacks in the colonies, mass insurrection broke out among the slave population. The resulting civil war, fought along clear racial lines, beggared Haiti and incited fear among the planter elite of surrounding West Indian colonies.

The effect of the Haitian revolution on British politics was almost immediate. Reports of this bloody revolt excited hysterical debates both in the colonies and Great Britain, and dealt a severe blow to the abolitionist movement. Even moderate abolitionists who advocated a gradual end to the slave trade could not overcome the genuine fear engendered by the mass destruction of Haiti. Reports of the race wars contributed greatly to the proslavery arguments, which had long predicted the dire consequences of freeing slaves. The timing of the revolution severely impeded discussion of the anti-slave-trade bill and convinced Parliament to delay the dismantling of the slave trade for almost fifteen years. The thought of a slave rebellion was profoundly disturbing to the upper echelons of British society. They were no longer complacent about the state of the West Indian slaves as the British slave owners' greatest fear was that the uprising in Haiti would be repeated in Barbados, Jamaica, or any of the other British colonies. However, the slave uprising also undermined certain proslavery arguments as well. Proslavery writers had a more difficult time asserting the relative happiness of slaves in the colonies and could no longer convincingly argue that African slaves did not value liberty. The Haitian revolution and brief freedom gained by the slaves graphically illustrated to the British public that the conditions of enslavement could not compensate for the loss of freedom.

The dynamic environment of the late eighteenth century created possibilities for transformation in British culture and identity. Multiple and significant changes in the socio-political arena allowed a greater segment of the public to participate in shaping their society. Not only did literacy increase over the century, but the public awareness of events—local, regional, national, and international—increased exponentially. Accompanying this newfound awareness was the belief that members of all social classes could participate in "positive" change. The development of reform movements in this time was predicated on the assumption that the literate, concerned, political subjects could be mobilized to effect social action. These movements served to create both a socially conscious body politic and a language of reform to influence their views. This possibility for transformation motivated the abolitionist movement, and the language of reform shaped the arguments of both antislavery and proslavery writers. The construction of this politically and socially aware public pushed the slave-trade debates onto the rhetorical terrain of national identity.

---

on reconstructing the British cultural climate, I will not discuss other countries' involvement with Haiti. See James' *Black Jacobins* for a comprehensive analysis.

Surveying the Terrain: Major Points of Argument in the Debates

The conflicting ideologies of the pro-slave-trade and anti-slave-trade factions took shape amidst larger ideological shifts in the condition and understanding of Western civilization. The late eighteenth century was a time when most of the major European colonial powers experienced a crisis of conscience regarding the practice of African slavery. New World agriculture was based primarily on imported African labor, and chattel slavery seemed to be an integral, if not inseparable, part of colonial interests. Though the practice of slavery differed depending on the European power, the status of Africans remained subordinate to European interests.[33] These powers, specifically the French and the English, evinced a growing discontent with the slave culture of the New World, which initiated powerful social movements across the Continent and Great Britain. David Brion Davis summarized the problem of slavery in Western culture as a critical shift in European beliefs:

> In the 1760s there was nothing unprecedented about chattel slavery, even the slavery of one ethnic group to another. What was unprecedented by the 1760s and early 1770s was the emergence of a widespread conviction that New World slavery symbolized all the forces that threatened the true destiny of man.[34]

Emancipation efforts swept the colonies and the Continent; however, each country addressed the issues surrounding the practice of New World slavery in differing ways.

Prior to the 1770s, the debate over slavery in Britain occurred primarily amongst theologians who argued over Biblical definitions of servitude and slavery. Both colonial and metropolitan clergymen delivered and published sermons regarding the licit or illicit practice of enslaving a non-Christian population and holding them in perpetual slavery. These theological musings initiated ancillary arguments about the nature of the "true Christian," which strongly influenced future antislavery rhetoric. Religious scholars posed several questions regarding the validity of slave holding. Could the institution of slavery coexist with the belief in Christian benevolence? Did the Bible sanction slavery? What responsibilities did the Christian slave holder owe to his heathen slaves? Clergy who participated in slave holding and slave trading offered arguments for the legality of the institution based on biblical text. Even the Society for Propagating the Gospel unashamedly touted their slave-derived income from the colonies. These proslavery clergy

---

[33] For example, Spanish practices of slave holding were often vehemently criticized by the English and French because of growing Spanish *mestizo* populations. Both European powers decried the unconsidered habits of Spanish slave holders who fostered a large population of "half-breeds" by sleeping with their slave women. The French and English believed this population would compete with the "pure" Spanish for colonial interests.

[34] Davis, *The Problem of Slavery in Western Culture*, 41.

pointed to the enslavement of the Israelites in Egypt and the laws governing slave holding as stipulated in the Bible. These advocates identified the African peoples as descendents of Ham, who looked upon the nakedness of his father and was cursed with dark skin. An additional consequence of this curse was that Ham's descendents were to be enslaved as punishment for the sins of their progenitor.[35] Proslavery clergy supported the conversion of slaves, but they were quick to assert that conversion did not provide a just cause for manumission.

Opposition to slavery dismissed Old Testament validations and provided a common field of discussion that united many Protestant sects. Antislavery clergy emphasized the doctrine of Christian benevolence found in the New Testament and argued that Christ's teachings were antithetical to slave holding. They disdained Old Testament lineage as justification for enslavement, choosing to rely on New Testament denunciations of slavery in their rebuttals. They also questioned proslavery claims that African heathens were better off with Christian slave-masters than in their native countries. When these Christian masters actively resisted converting their slaves, what benefit did the slave derive from his or her relocation? The primary duty of every Christian was to convert the heathens, not enslave them. Many slave holders were very reluctant to allow their slaves to be converted to Christianity because they felt that slaves would then claim their freedom.[36] Antislavery clergy blasted the British slave holders from their pulpits, accusing them of "unChristian" behavior. Rebutting biblical justifications for slavery provided a useful platform for different denominations of Christianity to unite in their denunciations. While the Quakers were most noted for their early involvement in antislavery efforts, Anglican clergy also condemned the institution for its corrupting influence on Christian morality. In spite of their combined eloquence, these religious communities addressed a largely apathetic public on the question of slavery in the early part of the century. The issue was neither pertinent to the life of the average Briton nor a common sight among the laboring classes.

By the end of the century, the various strains of political, economic, and social thought began to question the concepts of national character and conscience. The emerging discourse of national identity not only allowed Britons to transcend

---

[35] Work of Orientalist scholars like William Jones also attempted to trace East Indian ancestry back to Ham; however, Indians were not believed to have inherited the burdens of slavery. Few scholars during the eighteenth century noted or addressed this contradiction. For a discussion of Orientalist constructions of biblical ancestry, see Trautmann's *Aryans in British India*.

[36] Records do not indicate that many slaves sued for their freedom after converting to Christianity; however, the slave holders fear of such an act prompted the Yorke-Talbot opinion of 1729; see Granville Sharp's *Representation of the Injustice and Dangerous Tendency of Tolerting Slavery* (London: Printed for Benjamin White and Robert Horsfield, 1769). This opinion stated that neither baptism nor coming to England resulted in manumission for a slave. This decision was partially contradicted by Lord Mansfield in 1772, but conversion to Christianity never became sufficient cause for manumission.

regional interests, but initiated discussion about the relationship of the Briton to the rest of the world. Active engagement with print culture broadened access to numerous debates about improving society, and the reading public felt empowered to effect change in an unprecedented manner. The most visible example of this new sense of social participation occurred with the multiple petitioning campaigns that included signatures representative of all classes, both genders, and even multiple races. By the end of the century, specific critical transformations had taken place to give the reading public a better sense of British national character and identity. No one social movement accomplished this feat; rather, the multiple movements and reform ideology combined to shape this discourse. The slave-trade debates both contributed to and utilized nationalist discourse in constructing its arguments.

Antislavery and proslavery writers responded to the growing public awareness of the issue by introducing new and innovative appeals into their tracts. As arguments for each side evolved, they drew heavily upon the complex ideological shifts to appeal to their audiences in a more persuasive manner. Each of the major influences identified in the section above shaped the discussion regarding the slave trade in specific and useful ways by providing ideas, concepts, and terms around which to build arguments. While I locate the debates in the consolidation of public support, I argue that consolidation began as early as the 1750s. Prior to this time, both antislavery and proslavery writing was sporadic and, in the case of antislavery, conflicted regarding practical solutions to the problem of slavery. While most writers agreed on the depravity of the institution, they could not reach a similar consensus with respect to emancipation. Proslavery writing began as purely reactive and writers expended little effort to formulate their own critiques of antislavery/abolitionist rhetoric. However, as the public's interest developed, both sides felt pressure to delineate their positions, advance their arguments, and offer practical methods for either dismantling or ameliorating the institution.

Each decade signaled a change in the debates and a gradual shift in the balance of power from proslavery to antislavery interests. This study posits three distinct stages for the slave-trade debates: first, the converging of the colonial and metropolitan argument; second, the proliferation of antislavery and anti-slave-trade sentiment; and third, the battle for control over the definition of the Briton. Writers in the 1770s problematized the issues of slavery and the slave trade to the extent that the public became more responsive to the idea of change. The dialogue that opened between activists in the mother country and in the American colonies shaped the goals of the nascent movement. Proslavery interests still felt secure enough in their position that they mounted a totally reactive campaign. In the 1780s, public support built to such a degree that demands for feasible and realistic changes resulted in the creation of an abolitionist society. Slavery apologists began to perceive a real and persistent threat to the institution and countered antislavery/anti-slave-trade accusations with increasing sophistication. The 1790s became the most dynamic time for the debates as both abolitionist and proslavery writers attacked each other with new arguments. Each group competed to make their vision of the Briton acceptable to the reading public. Thus, the impetus to engage in public debate came from the responsive, interested, and sympathetic audience.

Antislavery and proslavery writers defined their arguments by drawing upon the dynamic cultural currents of reform to appeal to the broadest audience possible. Enlightenment philosophy, economic theory, and revolutionary ideology proliferated through print culture, so many writers modeled their arguments on these critical strains of thought. Writers from both sides of the debates were able to employ reform language with consummate skill. They combined the language of reform with the emerging discourse of national identity both to shape national awareness of the issues and to shape the citizens of the nation. The most significant by-product of these arguments was the delineation of a British national identity that originated from particular constructions of character, conscience, and obligation. This identity did not emerge in a neat and uniform fashion out of a consensus over the primary attributes of the Briton. Indeed, during the initial stages of the debate, proslavery writers evinced a greater consensus amongst their interests than antislavery writers. As public sympathies began to shift from one camp to the other, authors had to determine how best to appeal to their audiences and motivate them to change. By the end of the 1780s, proslavery writers acknowledged the serious threat posed by abolitionist organizations and they proposed regulation and other such reforms as a more feasible solution to immediate abolition. Advocating change was not the province of one side alone; proslavery writers did not merely defend the status quo. The main sites of debate focused on the nature of humanity, the nature of commerce, and the nature of liberty. They employed a language and logic that was both familiar and accessible to the general reading public, and each side adapted the rhetorical strategies of philosophers, economists, and revolutionaries to advance their cause.

Social theorists of the eighteenth century recognized multiple sites of ideological transformation within British society, and slavery became a prominent issue of communal change. Enlightenment philosophers, such as Locke, Rousseau, and Montesquieu, theorized a new set of values necessary to social order and instituting those values made certain British practices obsolete. In order for society to achieve greater development in civilization, citizens should be prepared to cast off all vestiges of primitive practices (for example, slavery). The progress narrative offered a compelling and logical premise from which to question slavery and the slave trade. Did the practice of chattel slavery in the New World provide a necessary source of labor or impede progress in the development of British civilization? The nature of humanity came to be defined in specific terms that were to be applied universally, though some nations applied with greater rigor than others. The contradictions inherent in claims for "natural rights" emerged when the public began to take a closer look at colonial slave practices. Arguments for and against slavery considered the concept of "natural rights" that theoretically belonged to all humans. The debates over the slave trade extended philosophical dialogue to encompass other factors such as religion, race, and nationality in trying to justify or argue against the stratification of humanity.

In contrast to the utility of secular Enlightenment beliefs, Christian doctrine proved to be a highly contentious source used by both sides in their developing arguments. Writers appropriated theories about civilized society, "natural rights," and progress and argued them from a "Christian" perspective. Antislavery came from multiple sources both within and without the established Church of England. While the Quakers were most noteworthy for their early efforts, other groups such as Evangelicals (for example, Thomas Clarkson) and Methodists (for example, John Wesley) contributed greatly to abolitionist claims. Proslavery writers relied on what had become the traditional Anglican justification for slavery as found in the Old Testament and in the New Testament doctrine of St. Paul. Both camps mined the stories of the Bible for justifications and refutations of the New World's practices. Each side debated the religious obligations that the Christian slave holder owed to his slaves. Though the Bible justified ancient slave practices, writers debated the relevance of these practices in the "modern" and "more civilized" time. They also argued over the obligations of enlightened Christians towards their heathen (African) "brethren." The focal question of Christian responsibility within the institution of slavery involved a deeper consideration of the "true" nature of the Christian. Proslavery and antislavery advocates professed to have a better and more progressive understanding of Christianity that was deeply bound up with the experience of slavery. Each side sought to lay claim to greater piety and "real" Christianity.

A central question informing the conversion of slaves and their position in the colonies involved constructions of humanity and the awareness/construction of global stratification of cultures. Was the African a man in the same sense as the European and thereby guaranteed the same "natural rights"? The slave-trade debates took up the concept of "natural rights" by constructing and delineating theories of race. Sources as deeply opposed as the Bible and "scientific" observation provided numerous reasons why Africans were singularly well-suited to New World slavery. Proslavery advocates made racial suitability an integral component of their arguments and responded to the continual challenges to the necessity of slave labor by referring to race. European immigrants to the West Indian and American colonies were unable to survive the combination of climatic conditions and the grueling toil demanded by sugar, tobacco, and cotton crops on plantations. Their inability to do so forced plantation owners to look elsewhere for stronger workers. Though African slaves provided a "solution" to the labor problems, the perception of their humanity proved to be a cause for concern.

Under increasing pressure from antislavery activists, slave owners and traders resorted to explanations of slavery that centered on the nature of the slave. They dehumanized slaves and used racial characteristics as validation—the innate qualities of the African justified both his suitability for and the enterprise of slavery. From the antislavery perspective, racial theories proved equally complex in balancing the conflicting desires to humanize and to hierarchize. While most writers were willing to grant the African slave equal status as a human being, they were reluctant to place him or her on par with the "white" race. To reconcile these needs, abolitionists qualified that native societies in Africa exhibited the potential for advancement, but they required the instruction of Europeans to realize the highest level of civilization. Their enslaved brethren also possessed the innate intelligence to appreciate the benefits of British standards of civilization. The real challenge to the doctrine of "natural rights" espoused by the antislavery cause occurred in this recognition of difference.

A second major argument in the slave-trade debates reconsidered the nature of commerce to enable a serious critique of the supposedly unchangeable aspects of colonial cultivation. Commercial enterprise was the lifeblood of English and then British colonialism, and the produce of the colonies was highly valued by the public. The mercantilist system ensured price stability for colonial crops that enabled slave traders and planters to maintain high profit margins. From the introduction of the first African into the colonial plantation system, traders and planters claimed that slave labor was a necessary component of New World colonialism. Their rationale drew upon the failed attempts to use indentured servants and Native Americans for the more labor-intensive crops. For over a century, the merchant argument for the necessity of slave labor provided the strongest justification for slavery. Proslavery advocates grew complacent in their belief that no citizen in Great Britain would wish to sacrifice his or her own comfort for the sake of an unknown and largely unseen people. However, the introduction of new economic theories that critiqued every aspect of mercantilism upset planter and trader complacency. Adam Smith's interrogation of the mercantilist system raised serious objections to the current workings of commerce and perceptions of labor. His direct attack on the necessity of slave labor provided antislavery/anti-slave-trade advocates with powerful questions to challenge the proslavery lobby.[37] Smith's detailed descriptions of the superiority of free labor threatened the very foundations of trader and planter beliefs. The nature of commerce came under intense scrutiny, which forced slavery advocates to reconsider their assertions about necessity. Disputing the efficacy of the mercantilist system helped dismantle the most effective contentions about the direct link between slave labor and the success of the colonies.

Questioning the mercantilist system also provided the anti-slave-trade movement with another form of social action—the organized consumer boycott. In a targeted form of protest, women were encouraged to eschew the consumption of West Indian sugar. Just as the proslavery interests confidently believed that the British public could be controlled through its desire for colonial goods, anti-slave-trade organizers recognized the value of commerce in effecting change. Though abstaining from sugar may not have had any real effect on the decision for abolition, organizers managed to amass enough support for the sugar protests to feature prominently in political cartoons and the popular press. Writers infused

---

[37] Before the formation of abolitionist societies, most tracts focused their critique of the institution on slavery; thus, my use of both terms. The proslavery lobby understood that an attack on the slave trade could lead to an attack on the entire institution. Their arguments did not only involve a defense of the slave trade, so I use the term proslavery throughout the periods being covered.

their economic arguments against slave labor with moral dicta indicting the user of tainted goods. Sugar provided the most effective target since no other colonial crop required the same amount of labor in cultivation. The public associated sugar with the most horrid abuses of slavery primarily because anti-slave-trade writers included detailed statistics about the mortality rate on sugar plantations. Activists organized several movements against the consumption of West Indian sugar in the early 1790s to protest the use of slave labor in growing the product. Many proposed that the British public only use sugar grown in the East Indies to demonstrate support for "free labor," as East Indian sugar did not rely on African slaves. Sugar became a contentious symbol of slavery and an appropriate economic target for manipulation. While the actual success of these protests is unclear, the rhetoric of the appeals demonstrated definite changes in public perceptions that anti-slave-trade writers facilitated.[38] They challenged the belief in the power of demand in maintaining status quo, and they shaped a kind of public morality by advocating that the public should be responsible consumers.

A third major strain of argument drew upon the volatile rhetoric of revolution to define superior national characteristics and advocate reform. The common stated goal of each revolution that affected Great Britain was the pursuit of "liberty," and this concept had long been considered an integral aspect of English and British identity. The value and impact of this belief in "liberty" on British culture cannot be overstated. With each revolution—American, French, and Haitian—seeking to advance its own conception of liberty, British writers sought to reclaim and establish their country's superior grasp of the idea. This contested term served as the primary marker of all free, moral, and highly developed cultures. Certainly the country that represented the purest form of liberty gained a particular advantage in a world of growing Western European domination. The basis of imperial ideology emerged from entitlement to the governance of "uncivilized" societies and superiority over other civilized societies. The pinnacle of civilization was the reverence for and proper exercise of "liberty." Participants in the slave-trade debates quickly understood the importance of this idea to Western culture and incorporated revolutionary rhetoric in their writings. Though antislavery may have advanced stronger arguments for liberty, both sides of the debate capitalized on the idea for specific ends. Liberty, or freedom, involved the ability to live one's life to the fullest without interference from others. For antislavery, this freedom entailed an eventual elimination of bondage, beginning with the dismantling of the trans-Atlantic slave trade, that would eliminate the hypocrisy in British assertions of liberty. For proslavery, this freedom guaranteed protection for planter/trader property and commercial interests by upholding the rights guaranteed in British law.

---

[38] For a discussion of sugar boycotts see Keith Sandiford, *The Cultural Politics of Sugar: Caribbean Slavery and the Narratives of Colonialism* (Cambridge: Cambridge University Press, 2000) and Sidney W. Mintz, *Sweetness and Power: the Place of Sugar in Modern History* (New York: Viking, 1985); for a detailed history of the relationship between sugar and colonial slavery see Sheridan, *Sugar and Slavery*.

Revolutionary ideology combined two highly valued cultural precepts—reform and progress—creating powerful arguments for both antislavery and proslavery. Scholars such as David Spadafora have illustrated the importance of the progress narrative in British culture. One way progress could be achieved was through reform, the most extreme example of which was revolution. While conditions in Britain did not reach this extreme, the multiple reform movements of the latter part of the century created a highly volatile cultural climate. The push for restructuring gained momentum from a belief in the importance of progress for the further evolution of the culture. Societies engaged in a continual quest for increasing sophistication that came from the positive application of reform. The question that emerged from the maelstrom of ideas regarding reform was what constituted a "civilized" society? The dialogue about racial characteristics transcended the anti-slave-trade and antislavery movements to become an increasingly significant characteristic of the "civilized." Writers in public discourse also used the standards of other countries to measure the state of British society. Calls for revolution in the American colonies unsettled British self-perceptions about a superior sense of liberty, just as cries of revolution in France and Haiti threatened the stability of British social structures. However, the most useful attributes of "civilized" society consisted of a belief in the betterment of society and the desire to effect this improved state of being. Thus, progress and reform joined to create a compelling formula for the success of national endeavors.

The commitment to reform and progress had a noticeable impact on the main arguments of the slave-trade debates. Antislavery groups denounced the entire slave system as a corrupting influence on society as a whole. The idea of having absolute power over a group of people could only result in the degradation of all human qualities and create petty tyrants. They used proslavery arguments about the laziness of slaves to prove that the institution destroyed a naturally industrious nature. They indicted slave traders for inciting rebellions in African countries as a method of procuring their slaves. They also published detailed reports about the gross injustices perpetrated by slave holders in every level of society. Antislavery advocates critiqued colonial laws from the administration of individual plantations to the administration of entire colonies and used them as exemplars of abuse. Since proslavery writers, specifically colonial planters, could do little more in defense than promise a careful review of the laws, they turned the language of reform in another direction. They critiqued the operations of the Royal African Company and the blatant favoritism involved in choosing representatives to administer the slave trade and enforce slave laws. In the mid-eighteenth century, merchants from Liverpool, Bristol, and London controlled much of the trade and ensured the appointment of representatives who would be sympathetic to their interests.[39] "Reform" tracts published by proslavery writers in the 1770s and 1780s detailed

---

[39] James Rawley's extensive research on the port of London and its connection to the slave trade is useful. He has proven conclusively that London maintained a large number of slaving vessels and vied with Bristol as the second most popular slaving port

the abuses of these "corrupt" businessmen.[40] Slavery advocates conceded that the institution had serious flaws, but they pushed for restructuring over abolition as an equitable solution.

Both camps drew upon the language of reform to construct their arguments, producing numerous publications that are a rich source for cultural analysis. The movements for and against slavery evolved from the occasional sermon and rebuttal to heated debates in print that focused on the issue of the slave trade. During the course of this evolution, writers wrote for and responded to an actively engaged public whose members gained a different kind of self-awareness. The complex process of delineating the main points of debate and arguing them persuasively in print resulted in a growing cohesion within each group of writers. Antislavery/abolitionist writers began to organize their critique of slavery along specific arguments designed to appeal to a broad audience. Understanding the horrors of slavery and agitating for change transformed into a moral imperative affecting the character of the British people. Meanwhile, proslavery writers waged a campaign that offered a competing image of the moral Briton who condoned slavery. They sought to defuse the abolitionist accusations by advocating humane improvements to the existing system. The concern for the prosperity of the Briton superseded any fear of moral degradation. The push for reform instigated a battle in print over the true character of the Briton, and the national identity that emerged contained elements of each side's claims.

Overview of Scholarship and Methodology

Most of the scholarship on the institution of slavery in Great Britain and her colonies has originated from the discipline of history. Historians have examined the antislavery debates for economic, political, and social trends. The issue of slavery evoked widespread interest across the British Isles and her colonies through the latter portion of the eighteenth century and continues to be a rich subject for investigation. Recent studies, like Hugh Thomas' *The History of the Slave Trade* and Herbert Klein's *The Atlantic Slave Trade*, provide comprehensive overviews of European involvement with the slave trade, while an excellent study by Stephanie Smallwood theorizes many new details about the possible experience of the middle passage based on ship's records.[41] Most historians contend that

---

after Liverpool. See his *London, Metropolis of the Slave Trade* (Columbia: University of Missouri Press, 2003).

[40] An excellent example of this detailed recounting is John Roberts' *Extracts from an account of the state of British forts, on the Gold Coast of Africa, taken by Captain. Cotton, of His Majesty's ship, Pallas, in May and June, 1777. To which are added, observations by John Roberts, governor of Cape Coast Castle* (London: Printed for J. Bew, 1778).

[41] Stephanie Smallwood, *Saltwater Slavery: A Middle Passage from Africa to American Diaspora* (Cambridge, MA: Harvard University Press, 2007).

abolition occurred because of a complex mixture of financial and cultural factors, and the extent to which the social movement contributed to this change continues to provoke conversation. Given the extensive body of secondary criticism, what new knowledge can be gained through a systematic analysis of the debates? Historical scholarship has focused primarily on the question of why abolition occurred during this particular time period. Eric Williams' ground-breaking study *Capitalism and Slavery* (1944) contends that economic forces, rather than any organized movement, facilitated abolition. As Seymour Drescher described Williams' thesis: "economic interest giveth, economic interest taketh away."[42] When the slave system ceased to be profitable, the slave trade and then slavery were systematically abolished. Drescher contests this theory with extensive research proving that the slave trade and slavery were abolished while still financially viable.[43] Historians then turned to social and political trends for explanations regarding the timing of abolition; unfortunately, the cultural implications of antislavery/anti-slave-trade rhetoric have not yet been thoroughly explored. Examining the language deployed during the first abolitionist campaign will provide historians and literary scholars with new insight into the development of key cultural concepts, like race, national identity, and imperialism.

A recent spate of interest in the creative output of abolition has also produced a series of studies by literary scholars. By creative output I mean the almost exclusive focus on the poetry and fiction of the later eighteenth century. Scholars like Deirdre Coleman, Peter Kitson, Debbie Lee, Brycchan Carey, and Markman Ellis view abolitionist writing and writing about slavery as products of Romantic ideals or sentimental rhetoric. Suvir Kaul does an excellent reading of abolitionist poetry and its connection to empire.[44] In *Poems of Nation, Anthems of Empire*, he discusses the "imposing edifice of antislavery" that built upon "elaborate nationalist foundations" (233). However, Kaul's genre-based study ignores the contribution of proslavery poetry that also employs nationalist tropes. These studies are thorough and considered works that sidestep the larger cultural implications of the social movement. By giving only a passing analysis to the pamphlets and other essays produced in the same period, these theorists tend to miss significant turns of argument in their desire to slot these texts into a specific literary mode. Brycchan Carey, who does study these less popular texts in the oeuvre of abolition, also grounds his research in illustrating how "sentimental rhetoric" is constructed in and by these texts. To date, no studies cross the disciplinary divide to examine the

---

[42] Seymour Drescher, *Econocide: British Slavery in the Era of Abolition* (Pittsburgh: University of Pittsburgh Press, 1977) 5.

[43] A number of historians have since meticulously disproved most of Williams' thesis regarding abolition; however, scholars still acknowledge and address his work as the foundation of economic analysis of British slavery.

[44] Suvir Kaul, *Poems of Nation, Anthems of Empire: English Verse in the Long Eighteenth Century* (Charlottesville: University Press of Virginia, 2000).

intersection of culture and rhetoric, particularly with a focus on the first abolitionist campaign.

Historical scholarship does acknowledge the contributions of the abolitionist movement to the shaping of British culture, though no systematic study of the language of abolition exists.[45] Howard Temperley makes an important connection between antislavery agitation and "cultural imperialism."[46] Davis's exhaustive study of slavery and its connection with Western progress documents the anxiety of reconciling conflicting notions of moral and economic progress. Christopher Brown's study *Moral Capital* purports to be "a meditation on the chasm that distinguishes moral opinion from moral action" (2). Brown does an excellent study of how particular figures and historical events shaped the abolitionist movement. He identifies the American Revolution as the primary motivation behind delineating the movement and the new "imperial" drive of the country. Once again, however, the proslavery response becomes a footnote in the larger struggle to define a "moral" and "imperial" nation.

Linda Colley characterizes abolition of the slave trade and slavery as precipitating "an extraordinary revolution in sensibility and ideas, one that revealed as much if not more about how the British thought about themselves, as it did about how they saw black people on the other side of world" (351). This astute statement invites more detailed investigation to understand the scope of the "extraordinary revolution." Though Colley attributes abolition to the will of Parliament and the ruling classes, she recognizes that the antislavery/abolitionist movement mobilized unprecedented numbers of people who came from all walks of life and from widely differing class, regional, and racial backgrounds. It also invited the active participation of women. Abolitionists and anti-abolitionists predicated their arguments on the good of the entire British nation, with good defined in moral or commercial terms. The debates contributed to the formation of British national identity and abolition became as Colley put it, an "emblem of national virtue."

Colley's brief synopsis of the impact of antislavery ignores the rich rhetorical and cultural implications of the debates. She identifies one reason for the success of the cause as coming from its "uniquely uncontroversial and eclectic appeal." She labels the various arguments used by abolitionists as "uncontroversial" because they do not challenge the developing British national identity. Instead,

---

[45] Perhaps the only exception is Moira Ferguson's *Subject to Others: British Women Writers and Colonial Slavery, 1670–1834* (New York: Routledge, 1992), an impressive study analyzing the participation of women and their writing in both abolitionist movements. Since Ferguson focuses mainly on women's writing and the bulk of her study examines the second abolitionist campaign, I continue to assert that the language of abolition in the first campaign requires a closer and more nuanced critique.

[46] Howard Temperley, "Anti-Slavery as a Form of Cultural Imperialism," *Antislavery, Religion, and Reform: Essays in Memory of Roger Anstey*, ed. Christine Bolt and Seymour Drescher (Folkestone, Kent: W. Dawson & Sons, 1980): 335–350.

these appeals work within the framework of developing nationalism that she outlines. Far from "uncontroversial," the publications, when examined, reveal a heated dialogue between advocates and opponents of the slave trade. Both camps utilized highly sophisticated rhetorical arguments that reflected the finer changes in cultural climate over the decades. While our twenty-first-century sympathies support abolition, we should acknowledge that proslavery writers produced valid arguments against the plan. Their accusations of "dangerous idealism" were not without justification, and they correctly pointed to laborers and the British poor as also being in need of "liberty." Social histories pay little or no attention to the differences within abolitionist and anti-abolitionist writing, so Colley's summation is an oversimplification of abolitionist and anti-abolitionist documents. How would an examination of these differences enhance our understanding of the time period?

Colley's contentions are incomplete because they assume the eventual success of the abolitionist movement, ignoring the highly contested nature of the issue during its time. Proslavery and antislavery activists responded to each others' arguments, changing their appeals to address shifting audiences with differing interests. In the process, each group developed ideas about national character, the value of commerce, race, and liberty to use in support of its specific agenda. Abolition was a series of *debates* in which writers from both camps engaged in an ongoing dialogue about competing versions of morality, Christianity, and national character. At the beginning of the eighteenth century, colonial planters and slave traders had the open support of Parliament and the indifferent support of public opinion. However, by the end of the century a serious change in public sentiment occurred to strip proslavery advocates of both kinds of support.

Each side in the debates produced lengthy tracts to prove how their position remained true to the ideals of the "British" nation. If abolition is used as the marker of success, then the simplest conclusion would be that abolitionist writers more successfully propagated their vision of identity to the general reading public. The error in this reasoning lies in viewing the formation of identity as an either/or prospect. Proslavery rhetoric also left an indelible mark upon the perception of nationhood and national character. The forging of attributes came about from a *synthesis* of arguments that incorporated qualities described in both proslavery and abolitionist rhetoric. The debates transformed and transcended their initial purpose once they captured serious public attention at the end of the 1780s. Abolition became a vehicle for advancing particular visions of the Briton, and proslavery rebuttals not only defended planter/merchant livelihood but their very place within the nation. How did this transformation occur? What impact did each stage of the debate have on the version of national identity that emerged in the beginning of the nineteenth-century? These questions can only be answered by studying the language and strategies used by both sides of the movement and their engagement with cultural contexts of their time.

My study identifies and explicates the differences within abolitionist writing, the interaction between abolitionist and anti-abolitionist tracts, the scope of each group's argument, and the construction of culture that emerges from the literature. This movement produced the first organized committees for abolition and represented the beginning of the campaign to abolish slavery throughout the British empire. The writing disseminated by advocates also drew upon the emerging discourse of national identity and defined a vision of the "Briton" to suit particular moral, social, political ends. Essentially, I am interested in how the slave-trade debates defined and appealed to a "British" (by which I mean both colonial and metropolitan) audience during the first organized campaign against slavery. Different disciplines have partially addressed this question without a detailed analysis of the power and function of language. Historians isolate the trends in culture that produced the abolitionist impulse. Economists focus on the numbers of slaves transported and the quantifiable business transactions that took place. Political theorists analyze the shifts in Parliament and the monarchy, locating the power for change primarily in the government. While these studies offer valuable insight, they deal primarily with the success of the movement. In other words, analysis of antislavery plots a linear narrative from inception of an organized society to the successful abolition of the slave trade and slavery.

The transformative power of this social movement has been well-documented in sociological studies. In an examination of cultural formation, Leo d'Anjou finds a strong correlation between social movements and the social construction of meaning. Using the London Abolitionist Society as a case study, he traces this correlation through the campaign to abolish the slave trade in Great Britain.[47] The "collective action" taken by anti-slave-trade activists functions for the immediate goal of outlawing the slave trade, but the long-term implications of the campaign serve to effect cultural change. "Movements play this role of signifying agents in interaction with the media, the state, countermovements, and other actors in society and are thus part of the social processes in which meanings are constructed."[48] In this analysis, d'Anjou demonstrates how the public understanding of the meaning of "slave" and "slavery" changed in the wake of the first abolitionist campaign. He uses sociological "action theory," located in the "behavior of human beings," to relate how the composition of the anti-slave-trade societies and their resultant platform brought about a crucial shift in public understanding. The "actors" are authors whose political and religious affiliations contribute to the shape of the social movement and the meanings it constructs. Using the premise of social movement constructing social meaning, my argument expands the terms being negotiated. In addition to changing public definitions of "slave" and "slavery," the first abolitionist movement and its opposition attempted to construct a singular

---

[47] The Society for Effecting the Abolition of the Slave Trade was founded in London in 1787. By 1788, similar societies had been organized throughout major cities in England, Scotland, and Ireland, each using the same title. Though there was no "London Abolitionist Society," I use the title for the sake of simplicity and accuracy.

[48] Leo d'Anjou, *Social Movements and Cultural Change: The First Abolition Campaign Revisited* (New York: Aldine de Gruyter, 1996) 5.

national identity amidst competing social discourses that delineated race, class, and gender in new ways.

To develop common cultural concepts, writers of this social movement continuously defined and redefined the attributes of nation and national character throughout the campaigns. The movement to abolish the slave trade in many ways had greater implications for the British public than for the African trade, especially since historians have proved the trade continued for many years after it was legally dismantled. Public opinion shifted during the course of the debates, and during the course of these shifts the British public gained a new awareness of a collective self. In Benedict Anderson's terms, the slave-trade debates helped establish an "imagined community" of "Britons." Since competing rhetoric targeted different audiences across Great Britain and her colonies, the "imagined community" alternately expanded and contracted to include or exclude groups (for example, former slaves, English laborers, women). Certain arguments held greater appeal for the general public and authors proved very sensitive to which of their arguments successfully captured their audience(s). The authors of tracts, pamphlets, essays, periodical and newspaper articles, poems, and short stories brought individual perspectives to serve collective ends. In the cohesion of these perspectives, we can see how societal beliefs and self-perception undergo several transformations.

I rely mainly on rhetorical analysis to explicate the use of various appeals by the different camps in the debates, to map the changes in audience, and to trace identity construction through their respective arguments. Both antislavery/ abolitionist and proslavery writers negotiated between colonial, metropolitan, elite, and common-born audiences in crafting their arguments. They strategically employed ethical, legal, and pathetic appeals to capture public interest and shape public perceptions of both their respective causes and opposition. Examining the shifts in rhetorical strategy offers valuable information about the nature of British audiences over the course of the debates and the constraints faced by writers in each camp. The complex motives of each group involved persuading audiences to accept not only their perception of slavery, but their perception of British character as well. Tracing the development and changes in these motives requires a more nuanced and sophisticated method of analysis beyond standard explication.

In order to carry out my examination of the debates, I have chosen to use Kenneth Burke's *Grammar of Motives* because of its helpful critical terminology.[49] Burke posits a "dramatic pentad" in which he offers five "principles" of investigation: Act, Scene, Agent, Agency, and Purpose. The Act refers to "what took place" and Scene refers to the "background of the act or the situation in which it occurred" (xv). Agent and Agency, respectively, answer by whom and how an act was committed, and Purpose posits the "why." The interplay of these five terms illustrates "*the strategic spots at which ambiguities necessarily arise*" (xviii). Burke's "pentad" offers a basic structure in which each element interacts

---

[49] Kenneth Burke, *A Grammar of Motives* (1945; Berkeley: University of California Press, 1969).

with another element, scene with act, act with agent, agent with purpose, and so on. These interactions are set up as ratios with emphasis on the first element of the ratio enhancing or diminishing the second element. The "pentad" ratios provide a vocabulary for understanding motives. Burke states:

> At every point where the field covered by any one these terms overlaps upon the field covered by any other, there is an alchemic opportunity, whereby we can put one philosophy or doctrine of motivation into the alembic, make the appropriate passes, and take out another. From the central moltenness, where all the elements are fused into one togetherness, there are thrown forth, in separate crusts, such distinctions as those between freedom and necessity, activity and passiveness, cooperation and competition, cause and effect, mechanism and teleology (xix).

One abolitionist document may characterize the nature of slave *trading* as inherently corrupting; whereas, another abolitionist document may view the slave *trader* as inherently depraved. Each document stresses a different aspect of the ratio in locating motive. In the first document, the act–agent ratio places the motive in the realm of the act; that is, the act corrupts the agent. In the second document, the act–agent ratio shifts and the motive stems from the "corrupt" nature of the agent. The elements of the pentad offer a systematic method with which to study the changes within the rhetorical strategies of each camp as well as the strategies of rebuttal between each camp.

Kenneth Burke's notion of "circumference" provides a useful tool to understand the strategic positioning of the writers and their audiences over the course of the debates. The term refers to the scope and context in which "acts" take place and "agents" operate. Circumference defines a cosmology in which the motives of acts and agents and the depiction of scenes are derived from the world shared by the author and reader. By establishing circumference, the writer erects boundaries for human action and rules for human behavior. He or she delineates the relationship between circumference and the "circumfered" prior to the creation of acts, scenes, and agents. Thus, circumference provides a set of organizing principles according to which the "ambiguities" that produce transformations can be analyzed. Delineating circumference establishes variable motivational contexts in which the dramatic pentad can be used to analyze the "circumfered." The choice of circumference could influence the scene–act and scene–agent ratios by placing greater emphasis on the scene in defining both act and agent; thus, the scene will have an immediate influence on the putative motive of the act and the nature of the agent. Burke states that "when 'defining by location,' one may place the object of one's definition in contexts of varying scope … the choice of circumference for the scene in terms of which a given act is to be located will have a corresponding effect upon the interpretation of the act itself" (77). Thus, the "scenic scope" of a given act shapes the audience's view of agent and agency. With abolitionist writing, the acts, which involve the institution of slavery, take place in varying "scenic scopes" that indicate critical shifts in circumference. The nationality and immediate goals of the author influence these changes. For example, American antislavery writings draw separate circumferences for the practice of slavery in the American colonies versus the West Indian colonies. For British writers, these distinct circumferences overlap in the general description of "colonial" slavery.

Circumference encompasses each element of the pentad and offers a framework for understanding the relationship between author and audience. The term also provides a useful method of "stylizing" the conversation.[50] The audience is able to make specific judgments about act, agent, and motives based on the parameters or horizons established by the author. As Robert Wess puts it, "Circumference thus makes the constructionist point that representations of reality are never simply reproductions of reality without any intervention on our part" (150). The writer's description of circumference, whether implicit or explicit, is designed to direct the audience's perceptions of a mediated reality. This conscious and "stylized" reality serves the particular ends of the writer in persuading his or her audience to accept the message of the work.

This study analyzes how the writers of abolitionist and anti-abolitionist texts "select a circumference" that poses a particular image of the practice of slavery and the slave trade. I expand Burke's term to include the writer and the audience in the "circumfered" because they are implicitly represented in the language of the tracts. By examining the drawing and redrawing of circumference in the texts, we can see how identities are formed and reformed according to shifts in cultural and historical moments. Initially, these shifts can be mapped geographically according to the location of the author. Colonial publications differ from metropolitan publications in tone and circumference to accommodate the colonial audience for whom slavery is a visible practice. As the movement becomes organized and gathers strength, additional variations occur based on the race or gender of the writer. Each shift opens a gap of "ambiguity" in which a "transformation" of cultural meaning emerges.

A final critical component of analysis will be the application of David Theo Goldberg's race theory to understand the emerging concept of race at this time. The slave-trade debates initiated a significant change in British perceptions of racial hierarchies and characteristics. While other groups, such as Orientalist researchers, participated in this discourse, the struggle between proslavery and abolitionist writers over the position of Africans within humanity directly shaped modern understandings of race. In the slave-trade debates, the arguments for "natural rights" and "liberty" demanded further discussion of the position of African slaves within the British empire. The participation of Afro-British writers transformed the perceptions of British citizenship by demonstrating both the inherent capabilities of Africans and their ability to adapt to the European lifestyle. Race proved to be an integral concept in every stage of the debates, and discussions of race informed the construction of national identity in important ways.

---

[50] Robert Wess, *Kenneth Burke: Rhetoric, Subjectivity, and Postmodernism* (Cambridge: Cambridge University Press, 1996) 149.

The contribution of the slave-trade debates to the construction of national identity is noteworthy in the development of British imperialism, and its influence has only been selectively studied in past scholarship. Both abolition and nation-building have generated copious and valuable scholarship without necessarily overlapping in scope. By viewing the two as discourses that mutually influence each other, I offer a fresh and more subtly inflected reading of the manner in which social reform influences the construction of national identity. The controversy over the slave trade contains precisely the right mixture of elements—liberty, morality, and humanity—to create a national character, whose primary attributes were antithetical to colonial practices but an exemplar for the world. Great Britain, by abolishing the slave trade and sacrificing her trade to higher moral ends, proves to the "civilized" world her greater capacity for humane and just dominion. Success of this social movement represents a defining moment in British cultural formation in which a common vision of the (imperial) Briton emerged.

Chapter 2

Converging Arguments in British Resistance: Writing from the Colonies to Great Britain, 1759–1776

The public reaction to African slavery underwent a critical change from general apathy to growing support over the course of the eighteenth century. Britain's involvement in the slave trade and colonial slavery was firmly established by the mid-century; however, most Britons had only a peripheral awareness of colonial activities and a limited understanding of the practices on plantations. The "civilized" European nations participating in the slave trade maintained colonies in the New World that relied upon African slave labor.[1] The institution provided valuable goods for the British consumer and generated considerable profits that contributed to "national prosperity"—as proslavery writers maintained throughout. Traders and merchants insisted that slavery was a necessary evil to be tolerated in order for the nation to continue reaping the benefits of commerce. Antislavery clergy preached vigorously about the corrupt nature of the institution, but their constituents had little sense of what they could do to effect change or even why it mattered. This apathetic attitude began to change in the 1760s and transformed gradually over the course of the 1770s. The impetus for this change came from several significant shifts in the antislavery argument that precipitated transformations in the public understanding of slavery.

Prior to the 1770s, most attacks on slavery came from clergy who argued against it based on Christian doctrine. Their sermons usually countered the biblical justifications that had become a standard element in justifying slavery by the end of the century. Antislavery ministers framed the question of slavery in terms of a Christian moral dilemma, and directed their comments primarily to their own constituency. Divisions between Anglicans, Dissenters, Presbyterians, and other sects in England and Scotland translated into divided antislavery sentiments.[2] Records from the mid-century do not indicate that clergymen from differing sects

---

[1] The Ottoman Empire also engaged in an active slave trade that captured East African labor. The Eastern, Islamic slave trade became a kind of measuring stick against which more sophisticated antislavery writers compared European practices.

[2] Records from the early eighteenth century do not indicate that antislavery sentiment flourished in Ireland. However, once abolitionist societies organized by 1788, Dublin was the site of active campaigning against the slave trade. See Nini Rodgers, *Ireland, Slavery, and Antislavery: 1612–1865* (New York: Palgrave Macmillan, 2007).

collaborated to persuade their constituents of the ills of slavery. Their writing remained primarily defensive as it sought to correct the "misinterpretations" of the Bible used by proslavery ministers. When published, antislavery sermons had small print runs and were confined to local areas of distribution. The finer points of theological explication did not capture the interest of the larger reading public in Great Britain. Various ministers may have had limited success in persuading members of their congregations, but antislavery sentiment was neither widely known nor very successful.

The Quakers proved most successful in abolishing the practice of slavery amongst their members. In 1727, the Society of Friends condemned the institution of slavery in the Colonies, and by 1776 the Society had abolished slave trading and slave holding within its congregation, much to the distress of the West Indian Friends.[3] The Friends campaigned vigorously in the 1740s and '50s to persuade their brethren in the American and West Indian colonies to emancipate their slaves. The area of the most concentrated resistance to slavery was the Delaware Valley, specifically Pennsylvania and New Jersey. Quaker publishing houses in Philadelphia began to print and distribute pamphlets to Friends in the area. The Delaware Valley members evidenced radical beliefs in the capabilities of "Negroes," going so far as opening schools for them and providing the same instruction as white children received.[4] A shift occurred among the antislavery activists within the Society and they began to look beyond the actions of their own members. The activities of Pennsylvania Quakers, especially Anthony Benezet, in the 1760s helped to extend the condemnation of slavery beyond the concerns of their particular community. They began to print tracts and essays arguing that slavery was a concern for all humanity. This Quaker "humanitarianism" instigated a rethinking of antislavery sentiment as Quakers on both sides of the Atlantic took up the cause against the slave trade.[5] The concept of "British" as it evolved from the slave-trade debates actually originated in the American colonies. Colonial writers developed a bridge between their concerns as residents of slave-holding colonies and subjects of Great Britain. Their works had a significant impact on

---

[3] Opposition to slavery in the Quaker community began with its founder, George Fox, in 1671. In a visit to Barbados, Fox urged Friends to free and educate plantation slaves, stating that slavery was antithetical to Quaker philosophy. Unfortunately, another hundred years would pass before Fox's pronouncement would be taken up by all members of the community. For an excellent discussion of the rise and progress of Quaker abolitionist struggles, see Jean R. Soderlund's *Quakers and Slavery: A Divided Spirit* (Princeton: Princeton University Press, 1985).

[4] Henceforth I will use the term Negroes without quotation marks when making reference to the terminology used at the time of the debates.

[5] The rhetoric of humanitarianism strongly influenced the antislavery movement and shaped the language of both campaigns for abolition. For a complete analysis of this connection, see Frank J. Klingberg, *The Anti-Slavery Movement in England: A Study in English Humanitarianism* (1926; reprinted Hamden, CT: Archon Books, 1968).

the mother country and set in motion events which culminated in the formation of multi-sectarian abolitionist societies.[6]

This chapter traces the transformations in antislavery rhetoric in the works of early activists who encouraged growing public support for an organized movement. Two major writers in the 1770s, Anthony Benezet and Granville Sharp, reframed the arguments against slavery in secular and nationalist terms. Their prolific writings on the cause influenced the writing of subsequent activists and helped mobilize public opinion against proslavery interests. I illustrate how shifting circumferences over this period of time ultimately defined the rhetorical topoi of national identity used in later stages of the debates. Over the course of the 1760s, Benezet honed his arguments against slavery and narrowed his focus to the slave trade. As his writing became more sophisticated, he began to distribute his work to wider audiences. He used innovative rhetorical techniques and relied on a combination of religious and secular arguments in problematizing slavery. The arguments of Granville Sharp, whose antislavery work in England also evolved over a decade in response to a growing awareness of the larger implications of slavery, developed in part from Benezet's influence. Sharp's rhetorical circumference shifted significantly after he began to correspond with Anthony Benezet, and his arguments transformed to incorporate colonial perspectives and a wider "British" audience. To chart the evolution of the antislavery argument in this early work is to see the narrowing and increased focus on the slave trade. The gradual unification in purpose of colonial and metropolitan activists opens the possibility of a resistance movement that envisions a "British" response to the slave trade. In transcending regional concerns regarding slavery, these "pre-abolitionist" texts established the terrain of national identity as a critical component in the resistance to the British slave trade.

Contentious Quakers: Anthony Benezet and Colonial Activism

The focus on the slave trade that became the purpose of the first abolitionist campaign was neither accidental nor a foregone conclusion. Part of the teleological perspective too often utilized by historians and other scholars posits a natural progression from the abolition of the slave trade to the abolition of slavery in the British Empire. While abolition of the slave trade obviously could not have occurred *after* emancipation, I argue that the decision to concentrate on the slave trade developed out of a dialogue between the American colonies and the mother country. The antislavery writing of the 1740s and '50s in Great Britain reveals a general disgust with the institution of slavery and puts forth impassioned

---

[6] The use of the term "multi-sectarian" is intended to acknowledge the many Protestant sects who participated in the movement. Religion, specifically Christianity, was an integral component of the argument against slavery and later the slave trade, but in this cause the differences between sects of Christianity appear to have been leveled.

arguments against continuing the practice. Colonial arguments of that same period concentrate on the slave trade as the most egregious part of the institution. The term "colonial" refers specifically to the northern American colonies, which began to produce antislavery tracts very early because of the efforts of the Quakers.[7] Over the course of the 1760s and '70s, these differing foci converge and develop into a set of foundational contentions that structured abolitionist appeals. The initial step in this convergence occurs in the innovations in argument employed by Anthony Benezet, whom I characterize as the first "crusader" of the organized movement.

The abolitionist movement in Great Britain actually began a century earlier on another continent with the activities of the Pennsylvania Quakers.[8] As early as 1688, a group of Friends signed an appeal to Parliament calling for the dismantling of the slave trade on grounds of corruption and its promotion of anti-Christian behavior.[9] Five years later, an anonymous group published *An Exhortation and Caution to Friends Concerning Buying or Keeping Negroes* (New York, 1693). The growing sentiment against slavery in the northern Quaker meetings met serious opposition from southern and West Indian Quakers who flourished under the plantation system. The conflict amongst the members resulted in rather lukewarm declarations advising against participation in the trade. By 1715, factions within Pennsylvania were appealing to the London meeting in an effort to discourage all American Quakers from participating in the slave trade and slavery. However, the reform movement stalled until the 1750s when activists gained control of the American meetings and began to rally once again against the slave trade. Though the Society of Friends would debate for another twenty years, they eventually came to the decision to ban slave trading and slave holding among their membership.

The significance of these early struggles amongst the Quakers was their crafting of particular arguments that influenced the antislavery movement in Britain. Sentiment against the institution of slavery began in the Pennsylvania meetings because they had a higher concentration of non-slave-holding members. The Quakers who did own slaves tended to have them work as farm laborers and domestic servants. Though northern slave holders did not have the same degree of investment as southern and West Indian slave holders, they were still reluctant to free their slaves.[10] In the 1740s and '50s, many antislavery writers suggested that

---

[7] I can find no evidence of any antislavery or abolitionist tracts published in the West Indies, or the southern American colonies prior to start of the revolution in 1776 during the entire period of the debates.

[8] All facts are derived from Soderlund's *Quakers and Slavery*.

[9] Known as the "Germantown Protest," this document stands apart as a progressive and forward thinking objection to the slave trade. The full text of the protest can be found in Derek Hughes, *Versions of Blackness* (Cambridge: Cambridge University Press, 2007).

[10] See Soderlund, "Slavery: Temptation and Challenge," chapter 3 in *Quakers and Slavery*. The critical difference in slave-holding patterns occurred when Africans dominated the labor force in southern and West Indian plantation culture. Northern slave holders purchased fewer slaves and could make do with family labor and indentured servitude.

individuals refrain from purchasing new slaves as the first step towards removing slavery from their lives. These activists focused on limiting and eventually stopping the importation of slaves into their own colonies. To that end, their appeals focused on the slave trade and spoke to a localized audience. The basis of objection lay in the violation of the Golden Rule. Anti-slave-trade Quakers argued that enslaving and selling another human being was the grossest violation of Christ's dictate "To do unto all Men, as we would they should do unto us." Some activists came up with innovative and dramatic methods of illustrating this violation to their local meetings. The most famous example was Benjamin Lay who carried a book resembling the Bible that contained a "bladder of blood" into the Philadelphia Yearly Meeting in 1738. During his impassioned speech against the slave trade, he drew a sword and stabbed the book, spraying the "blood" on the people seated near him.[11] One year prior to this inflammatory incident, Lay had published a book in Philadephhia entitled, *All Slave-Keepers, That Keep the Innocent in Bondage, Apostates* (1737). While subsequent publications by other authors may not have employed such a strong indictment of slave holders, they argued that purchasing and keeping slaves were antithetical to Quaker beliefs. These abolitionists represented the suffering of African slaves to illustrate the "unChristian" behavior of "cruel" masters. They also referred to Africans as "fellow creatures," refusing to validate proslavery arguments that Africans were intended for slavery by their nature. Justifications for slavery often cited the purported African ability to withstand the harsher climate of slave territories. Many writers compared them to "beasts of burden" in order to validate the use and treatment of slaves. The basic premises of Quaker opposition to importing and enslaving Africans formed a strong foundation for other antislavery and abolitionist appeals later in the century.

While the initial push for reform concentrated within the Society of Friends, activists began to broaden the audience and scope of their arguments. The Philadelphia Friends in particular recognized the greater potential for reform outside their own members and individual writers sought to appeal to a larger audience with their rhetoric. The moral imperative for reform exceeded the members of the Society alone. By the 1750s, the city bustled with activity and included an increasing number of non-Quakers. The primary purpose of concentrating on the slave trade was to prevent the further importation of slave labor into the Pennsylvania colony. However, that goal could only be accomplished by convincing all constituents to stop participating in the trade. To that end, publications in Philadelphia began to circulate beyond Quaker members thereby broadening their appeals to wider audiences within the city. Writers in the 1750s and '60s gradually expanded their arguments from local to regional to national interests, particularly when

---

[11] Lay's "bladder of blood" was actually filled with red juice. Dressed in military garb, he announced to the "Negro masters" at the meeting "I would be as justifiable in the sight of the Almighty ... if you should thrust a sword through [your slaves'] hearts as I do through this book!" (Soderlund 16). Such theatrics proved to be too much for the Quakers and Lay was asked to leave the community.

their publications began crossing the Atlantic to the mother country. The most influential and prolific writer to demonstrate the widening of audience and shifts of argument was Anthony Benezet.

Benezet's background greatly influenced the scope and nature of his activism, and his beliefs were a radical departure from those accepted by metropolitan and colonial society.[12] His parents were French Huguenots who fled to London and then Philadelphia to escape persecution. His family spent sixteen years in London, where at the age of fourteen Benezet joined the Society of Friends. The family moved to Philadelphia when he was eighteen, and his involvement with the Quaker community prompted and encouraged his activist efforts. Thomas Clarkson immortalized Benezet as "one of the most zealous, vigilant, and active advocates which the cause of the oppressed Africans ever had."[13] Perceiving the grave wrongs committed against enslaved people, he established an evening school for Africans in Philadelphia (17).[14] He supported the radical notion that Africans were not inherently inferior in their intellect, so denying them basic education was a sin. "I can with truth and sincerity declare, that I have found amongst the negroes as great variety of talents, as among a like number of whites; and I am bold to assert, that the notion entertained by some, that the blacks are inferior in their capacities, is a vulgar prejudice" (18). While he was aware of the developing discourses of race and color prejudice, Benezet clearly believed in the Quaker characterization of Africans as "fellow creatures" and "brethren" rather than "inferiors." This belief had a strong influence on the manner in which he defined circumference, act, scene, and agent in his antislavery writing.

The circumference and act defined in Benezet's writings emerged from both his colonial and religious perspectives. While his initial concerns may have been regional, he understood the larger implications of his efforts within the "*British nation.*" His tracts reflected a colonial understanding of the interconnectedness of trade and the complex relationship between Great Britain, her colonies, and Africa. He defined a circumference on a global scale and discussed the implications of his critique for people on three different continents. This global worldview had a direct impact on the delineation of act in his writings. Benezet acknowledged the complexity of issues involved in analyzing the institution of slavery and, following the lead of his predecessors, chose to focus his critique on the slave trade. He

---

[12] All biographical material has been taken from a reprint of Benezet's memoirs, which went out of print very quickly and were poorly preserved. Wilson Armistead, *Anthony Benezet. From the original memoir: Revised with additions* (London: A. W. Bennett, 1859; reprinted Freeport, NY: Books for Libraries Press, 1971).

[13] Thomas Clarkson, *The History of the Rise, Progress and Accomplishment of the Abolition of the African Slave-Trade by the British Parliament*, 2 vols. (London: Printed by R. Taylor and Co. for Longman, Hurst, Rees, and Orme, 1808) 17.

[14] He does not give an exact date, but Benezet tutored African children in his home informally from the mid-1750s. He established the first girls' school in Philadelphia in 1755 and the first African school in 1770.

did not approve of enslavement and the current practices of southern and West Indian colonists, but he understood the first step toward eradicating the practice was to stop the flow of fresh labor from Africa. Quaker resistance to the practice of slavery amongst its members had long followed a two-step process. First, members should limit the number of their slaves by not purchasing new laborers, and second, members should educate and then manumit those currently held in bondage. Benezet sought to expand his audience beyond the Quaker community and to encourage other communities to stop supporting the trade.

His publication record over the 1760s and early '70s demonstrated his desire to disseminate his arguments to broader audiences. His work gained considerable recognition in Great Britain possibly because he relied primarily on secular appeals that targeted emotion rather than religious denomination. His first tract, *Observations on the Inslaving, importing and purchasing of Negroes* (1759) was published in Germantown, Pennsylvania, and directed to people outside of the Quaker community.[15] He published *A Short Account of that part of Africa Inhabited by the Negroes* (1762) in Philadelphia, and the tract quickly went into a second edition the same year.[16] The third edition was printed in London in 1768 by Granville Sharp, who found Benezet's description of the slave trade to be quite compelling. *A Caution to Great Britain and her Colonies, in a short representation of the calamitous state of the enslaved Negroes in the British dominions* (1766) was published first in Philadelphia and reprinted in London in 1767, 1784, and 1785 (see Figure 2.1).[17] He compiled his research from first-hand accounts of the conditions of the slave coast and published *Some Historical Account of Guinea* (1771), which was reprinted in London by Granville Sharp's publisher in 1772 and by the Quaker publisher James Phillips in 1788.[18] Benezet has also been credited with providing source material for the London Quaker meeting to craft its appeal to Parliament. *The Case of our Fellow-Creatures, the Oppressed Africans, respectfully recommended to the serious consideration of the Legislature of Great-Britain* (1783) presaged the introduction of the first petition for abolition proposed by the Quakers in 1785. While this is by no means a complete list of Benezet's publications, they represent significant moments in the evolution of his appeals to wider audiences and his

---

[15] Benezet's biographer states that he published most of his tracts himself and personally distributed them to "important" personages. He sent several copies of pamphlets to Granville Sharp who arranged to have them reprinted in London. His later tracts went to important figures in England, such as the Archbishop of Canterbury, along with personal letters.

[16] Published in Philadelphia by W. Dunlap, 1762; 2nd ed. with amendments published by W. Dunlap, 1762; and 3rd ed. reprinted in London by W. Baker and J.W. Galabin, R. Horsfield, B. White, J. Allix, 1768.

[17] Published in Philadelphia by Henry Miller, 1766, with a second printing the following year; published in London in 1767; published in Philadelphia by D. Hall and W. Sellers, 1767; and reprinted in London by J. Phillips, a Quaker publisher, 1784 and 1785.

[18] Printed in London by W. Owen and E. and C. Dilly. Sharp identified Dilly as one of the publishers of his work in a letter to Benjamin Rush dated 21 February 1774.

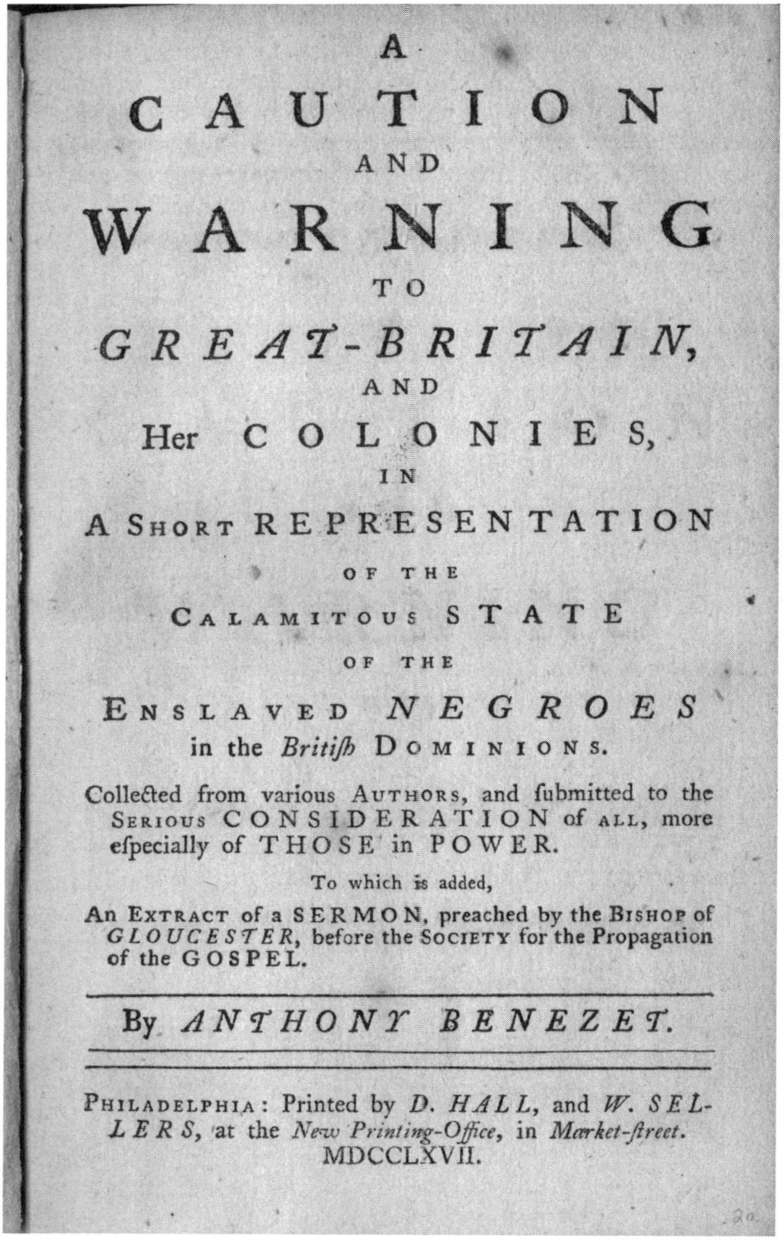

A
CAUTION
AND
WARNING
TO
GREAT-BRITAIN,
AND
Her COLONIES,
IN
A SHORT REPRESENTATION
OF THE
CALAMITOUS STATE
OF THE
ENSLAVED *NEGROES*
in the *British* DOMINIONS.

Collected from various AUTHORS, and submitted to the SERIOUS CONSIDERATION of ALL, more especially of THOSE in POWER.

To which is added,

An EXTRACT of a SERMON, preached by the BISHOP of *GLOUCESTER*, before the SOCIETY for the Propagation of the GOSPEL.

By *ANTHONY BENEZET.*

PHILADELPHIA: Printed by *D. HALL*, and *W. SELLERS*, at the *New Printing-Office*, in *Market-street.* MDCCLXVII.

Fig. 2.1 Anthony Benezet, title page to *A Caution and Warning to Great-Britain and her Colonies*. Philadelphia: D. Hall and W. Sellers, 1767. Courtesy of The Library Company of Philadelphia.

transcontinental publication record indicates a wider sphere of influence. Benezet's writings provided a strong bridge between colonial and metropolitan antislavery efforts both within and outside of the Quaker community.

The initial goal of his publications was to problematize the slave trade and persuade his audience to cease purchasing new slaves. While he considered slave holding to be equally contemptible, he evidenced a sophisticated understanding of his larger audience in his contentions. The northern colonies did not rely upon the plantation system for their economies, so the need for continuous supplies of slave labor was minimal; however, they did rely on slaves to perform farming and domestic tasks. Asking his regional, colonial audiences to emancipate their slaves would have been neither feasible nor convincing. By focusing his critique on the trade itself, he could present a more realistic appeal to stop the purchase of new slaves. Also, members of his audience who were slave holders might not feel personally indicted—and therefore antagonized—as they would have been by lengthy diatribes against slave holding. The structure of Benezet's tracts interspersed his own commentary between testimonials and passages quoted from other publications. Since he had neither purchased slaves nor participated in their capture and transportation, he established his ethos by citing the descriptions of men employed within the trade. Initially, he denounced all European slave-trading enterprises, though his audience consisted primarily of Pennsylvanians. In *Observations on Inslaving, importing, and purchasing Negroes* (1759), he quoted from a "Factor in the Dutch *African* Company," an "Agent General of the French Royal African Company," a "Person of Candour" living in Philadelphia, and "Book of Geography" printed in London. These early writings illustrate how the first priority of antislavery writers was to establish the iniquities of the trade, and directed attacks on the British slave trade in particular would come later.

Identification of audience also shifted in these tracts in an effort to connect with and capitalize upon budding patriotism among readers. Though he wrote for colonial readers, Benezet had a sense that these readers possessed a dual identification as Europeans and colonials. His first tract indicted the behavior of *Europeans* and their involvement in the trade without accusing a specific nation of being more culpable than any other. In his second tract, *A Short Account of that part of Africa inhabited by Negroes* (1762) printed in Philadelphia, he began focusing on the "guilt" of the "*English* nation" and drew upon a sense of regional loyalty in denouncing the trade. He stated "May the Almighty preserve the Inhabitants of *Pennsylvania* from being further defiled by a Trade, which is entered upon from such sensual Motives, and carried on by such devilish Means" (6).[19] Following these earlier tracts published just at the end of the 1750s and beginning of the '60s, Benezet's sense of audience changed dramatically. *A Caution to Great Britain and her Colonies* (1766) clearly demonstrated a stronger focus on the British trade and appealed to both colonial and metropolitan audiences. Subjects of "the

---

[19] The 1768 London reprint of this tract commissioned by Granville Sharp also includes the original plea on behalf of Pennsylvanians.

British Dominions" were targeted for supporting the institution of slavery and the testimonials reproduced in this later tract contained examples of atrocities committed in the West Indies and the southern colonies, as well as on African soil. For Benezet, the "British nation" encompassed much more territory than England, Scotland, Wales, and Ireland. Though he tended to conflate "English" and "British" in his writing, his appeal to *"Britons"* included readers in both the mother country and the colonies.

Benezet's tracts included multiple shifts in scene and agent as he argued for the corrupt and corrupting nature of the trade. Previous antislavery publications differed in their definition of the "act" on which to focus their critique. The act invoked to illustrate cruelty varied from enslavement to punishment to capture and sale. By defining the act as specifically the "slave trade," Benezet was able to incorporate differing scenes, ranging from the acquisition of slaves in Africa to their sale in America and the West Indies, within his publications. He devoted a great deal of attention to the manner in which slaves were procured in Africa and the painful separations within families that began at the slave forts along the coast. *A Short Account of that Part of Africa Inhabited by Negroes* focused solely on how Europeans took advantage of conflicts between African nations to procure their slaves. He refuted claims by proslavery writers that all slaves acquired were criminals who had been sentenced to death and "chose" slavery as a better option. Testimonials from participants in the trade critiqued European perceptions of "voluntary" enslavement, a concept that would also be called into question by Granville Sharp. Benezet quoted descriptions of the conditions at slave forts and on slave ships to illustrate the "inhumanity" of slavery. Through his use of first-person testimonial, a strategy that would become increasingly useful over the course of the campaign, he also identified a European agent exercising agency in each scene. Benezet's commentary countered firmly established prejudices in his audience by shifting the culpability for the trade from African to European. By the 1760s, a variety of travelers had written "geographies" and "histories" of Africa, in which they discussed the "savage wars" resulting from "mutual Animosities" of the populace. They also described the "harsh climate" that was "inhospitable" to civilized living. These depictions served to justify the enslavement and transportation of millions, based on the contention that Africans were better off outside of Africa. However, Benezet argued that the demand for slaves created and fostered the wars taking place in Africa. The anguish of mother, fathers, children, and siblings at the slave forts belied any claims for voluntary transportation. European greed fed the trade, and European agency took on a more sinister intent.

While his arguments grew out of earlier Quaker publications, Benezet incorporated a singular blend of religious and secular critique in his commentary. His tracts advocated what I would characterize as Christian humanism, blending biblical language with the precepts of humanitarianism. The slave trade and slavery violated the basic precepts of Christ's doctrine to "Do unto others." He characterized the behavior of Europeans in Africa as "unChristian" and prophesied a "Divine retribution" for the "sins of the Nation." Quakers had been warning their members for at least three decades that their behavior was in "direct violation of the Gospel-rule." Benezet extended this warning to a larger audience. He dismissed biblical justifications and pointed out that "[u]nder Mosaic Law Man-stealing was the only Theft punishable by Death."[20] He cleverly utilized Christian distinctions of "Good and Evil," seeking to "lay before the candid Reader the Depth of Evil" embodied by the trade. Every Christian subject of the Crown had a "Duty to God" to "Love our Fellow Creatures" and "deliver" them from the "iniquitous Trade." A major point in Benezet's religious commentary was to warn "nations" that continued participation in the slave trade would lead to "Divine Wrath" of some form. He cautioned, "Evils do not arise out of the Dust nor does the Almighty willingly afflict the Children of Men; but when a People offend as a Nation, or in a publick capacity, the Justice of his moral Government requires that as a Nation they be punished."[21] As his appeals became more specific, the "nations" to which he referred narrowed considerably to the "British Dominions." Benezet also stressed that "Europeans" set a very poor example for Africans by enslaving their people, thereby evoking "the utmost Scorn and Detestation of the Christian name."[22] To redeem the nation and bring the "true" spirit of Christianity to Africa, "*Britons*" needed to set aside their "greed" and give up the slave trade. However, if the Christian spirit was not incentive enough to give up the trade then the dictates of reason should prevail.

Benezet drew upon the "compassionate spirit" of his audience to argue that the slave trade was "inhuman" and unworthy of "civilized" peoples. He stated that the practice ran "contrary to the Dictates of Reason, and the common Feelings of Humanity."[23] This argument relied heavily on his belief that Africans were "fellow creatures" who experienced the same desires and suffered to the same degree as Europeans. To underscore this fact, he included testimonials in each of his tracts that attested to "tender attachment" that was often broken by the "cruel Separation" of families at the auction block. He used pathetic appeals to try and recreate the experience for his audience: "reflect ... some Parent or Wife, who had not even the Opportunity of mingling Tears in a parting Embrace ... or let any consider what it is to lose a Child, a Husband or any dear relation."[24]

---

[20] *Observations on the Inslaving, importing, and purchasing of Negroes* (2nd ed., 1760) 10. The focus of this essay was the unlawful nature of the slave trade. The reference to Mosaic law cleverly circumvented biblical validations of slavery by stating that the acquisition itself was not legal.

[21] *Observations on the Inslaving* 4. While Benezet makes references to the sins of "nations" in all of his tracts, his solution is still targeted to the individual. He does not propose a formal bill for "abolition" by the government, rather he hopes that individuals will be convinced to abjure the slave trade collectively. "Without Purchasers, there would be no Trade" (4).

[22] *A Short Account* 23.

[23] Ibid. 4.

[24] *Observations on the Inslaving* 8.

The break-up of families became a powerful and important criticism of the trade and Benezet reproduced descriptions of similar scenes of grief in all of his tracts. When Africans were "deprived of every fond and social tie," Europeans lost a bit of their own humanity and "tender sensibilities."[25] When he began to write about the atrocities of the British nation in particular, he included first-person accounts of slave tortures witnessed in the West Indies and the southern American colonies. The descriptions of mistreatment in the "West India Islands" were particularly harsh, and most of the accounts detailed the frequent whippings and grueling labor involved in plantation work.[26] Benezet also included an account of similar brutality witnessed in Georgia, thereby calling into question the benefits of the colonies. He encouraged all citizens concerned "for the civil or religious welfare of their country" to consider the implications for "Humanity" should the trade persist.[27] These practices, driven by "Prejudice, Passion, and Interest," corrupted the "Heart of Man" and destroyed "human Sentiment." The trade was "destructive of the Welfare of human Society" and defiled all those who engaged in the practice.[28]

As Benezet began to write specifically to the British nation, he utilized the discourse of "Liberty" to add a more personal dimension to his contentions. He maintained that Africans, who were "free by nature," could not be deprived illegally of their "natural liberties." The agitation in the American colonies over the "preservation of those valuable privileges transmitted to us from our ancestors" was growing steadily by the end of the 1760s.[29] Benezet framed his critical remarks about the slave trade against the emerging sense of rebellion. In the opening paragraph of *A Caution to Great Britain and her Colonies*, he asked "how many of those who distinguish themselves as the Advocates of Liberty, remain insensible and inattentive to the treatment of thousands and tens of thousands of our fellow men?" (3). To Benezet, pointing out the hypocrisy of American colonial rumblings against Great Britain presented the ideal opportunity to gain support for his own cause. He drew upon a current, compelling discourse, and, in doing so, introduced one of the most powerful concepts for the antislavery/abolitionist argument. The discontent in the American colonies evolved from the belief that "English *law ... so truly valuable for its justice*" guaranteed the fullest extent of "rights and liberties," unmatched by any other European nation (21). By using

---

[25] *A Short Account* 53, note.

[26] The "inhumane" conditions of fieldwork in the West Indies were referred to as a "seasoning" period, and only the hardiest of slaves were reputed to have survived the heat and back-breaking labor. Most slaves were worked to death and scholars estimate that the average lifespan for field slaves on the sugar plantations was seven to nine years. Depicting the harsh situation in the West Indies would become an increasingly valuable rhetorical strategy for antislavery and abolitionist writers.

[27] *A Caution* 3.

[28] Ibid. 4.

[29] Ibid. 3.

this discourse, Benezet introduced a nationalist emphasis in his argument that presaged a significant transformation in antislavery writing. Slavery was the blight of Europe that only the "pure" spirit of "English liberty" could cure.

He established this nationalist emphasis through a series of assumptions and questions about national character. His concept of nation plainly extended beyond the mother country to include the colonies; therefore, colonial corruption or degradation affected the mother country to the same extent. In *A Caution to Great Britain and her Colonies*, Benezet focused directly on the implications of the slave trade for the British empire. Though he continued to remark that the trade itself was a blight on all of Europe, English/British character was especially vulnerable to criticism because of the supposed reverence for the "rights of mankind." He contended:

> *Britons* boast themselves to be a generous, humane people, who have a true sense of the importance of Liberty; but is this a true character, whilst that barbarous, savage Slave-Trade, with all its attendant horrors, receives countenance and protection from the Legislature, whereby so many Thousand lives are yearly sacrificed? Do we indeed believe the truths declared in the Gospel? Are we persuaded that the threatenings, as well as the promises therein contained, will have their accomplishment? If indeed we do, must we not tremble to think what a load of guilt lies upon our Nation generally and individually, so far as we in any degree abet or countenance this aggravated iniquity? (42)

His language challenged readers to reconcile the totally contradictory concepts of liberty and enslavement. He urged his audience to exercise not only their compassion, but their logic in viewing continued national and individual involvement with the trade.

Both the pathetic and logical appeals used in these publications relied on a particularly salient assumption that illustrated an important moment in the evolution of race theory. Though he rarely used the word "race," Benezet constantly referred to and attempted to debunk proslavery contentions about the inferiority of Africans. He brought up the distinctions between "Blacks" and "whites" in order to dismiss them as myth and misrepresentation. He genuinely believed "that the *Negroes* are generally sensible humane and sociable people, and that their Capacity is as good, and as capable of Improvement as that of the Whites."[30] He blamed the corrupting nature of slavery for inducing "Idleness" among Africans transported to labor in the colonies. In his *Short Account*, he used sections of travel narratives to illustrate that Africans were industrious and prosperous in their native lands.[31] The "savage character of African" did not compare with the iniquities of "white" Europeans. He even accused white slavers of instigating the cruelty

---

[30] *A Short Account* 7.

[31] Benezet published a longer account of African culture taken from travel narratives. *Some Historical Account of Guinea* (Philadelphia, 1771; reprinted London, 1772; new ed.

and oppression of African monarchs by creating a demand for labor. Benezet also argued that "Blacks" did not lack for intellect, so they were wholly capable of appreciating their natural liberties and suffered equally under oppression. "Some who have only seen Negroes in an abject state of slavery, broken-spirited and dejected, knowing nothing of their situation in their native country, may apprehend, that they are naturally unsensible [sic] of the benefits of Liberty ... but these are erroneous opinions."[32] While he acknowledged that Africans in some areas were "savage and barbarous," he contended that such people existed in all countries. However, Benezet only acknowledged that Africans were equal in capacity, not in "civilization." For example, his admiration of Guinea culture stopped short of accepting its religious practices. He believed that Africans benefited from a European, specifically Christian, education.

Benezet's commentary reveals the beginnings of an important schism between the rhetoric of antislavery and the rhetoric of proslavery. The issue of race, a subject that would be refined and developed over the course of the debates, proves central to both religious and secular antislavery arguments questioning the "right" of Europeans to enslave another people. Benezet's repeated reference to color also indicates the prevalence of this discourse in colonial American culture. These "color-coded" comments demonstrate how entrenched cultural perceptions of difference were in order to provide a pronounced distinction between the master and slave. Each of his tracts argued on behalf of the innate "humanity" of "Negroes," while at the same time pointing to their difference. Benezet not only believed that Africans could be educated; he believed that Africans *needed* to be educated. The distinction between his comments and the proslavery rationale he opposed rests in the difference between "inferiority" and "backwardness." Both terms infer a hierarchy among world cultures, but the notion of "backwardness" at least allows the hope of being able to catch up. The consequence for race theory that was emerging at the time was a separation between "natural" and "cultural." Slavery advocates believed that the "natural" state for the African was a state of slavery, whereas antislavery advocates argued that true African bondage resulted from "cultural" ignorance. Benezet was on the cusp of a crucial argument about race that would dominate the slave-trade debates in the 1790s.

The most valuable contributions of these publications were their appeal beyond the select communities in Pennsylvania in their nascent push for reform. Benezet's directed commentary and use of first-person accounts provided strategies that were copied by other writers over subsequent decades. His publications crossed the Atlantic and made a particular impression on another antislavery crusader— Granville Sharp. I must note that while Benezet ingeniously combined religious and secular arguments to denounce the trade, he was not advocating a specific legislative action like abolition. The primary thrust of his antislavery writing was

---

London, 1788) expanded on his arguments regarding the "humanity" of Africans and the value of their native cultures.

[32] *A Caution* 15.

to problematize every aspect of the slave trade, from acquisition in Africa to sale in the colonies. He believed that if he could educate his audience regarding the deleterious effects of the trade on both Africans and Europeans, they would stop purchasing slaves. Without the demand, the supply would gradually dwindle and the trade itself would become unnecessary. Benezet counted on market forces to stop slavers, a hope his successors did not share.

Slavery, Granville Sharp, and English Civil Law

Christianity provided both the initial foundation and language for sustained critiques of slavery in the early eighteenth century. While colonial and metropolitan antislavery efforts operated independently until 1770, they shared the same basic premise. Slavery was antithetical to Christianity and opposition to slavery emerged primarily from Protestant religious discourses.[33] In the American colonies, this discourse came from Quaker beliefs and was later taken up by the Methodists. In England, the antislavery argument coincided with and developed under the Evangelical movement within the Anglican Church. These writers, regardless of denomination, repudiated biblical justifications of slavery and formulated their attacks based on "the doctrine of Christ." Each of these groups believed in the corrupt and corrupting nature of slavery, which ran counter to the true Christian impulse. Critiques in England and the American colonies began with concern for the spiritual well-being of the slaves who were denied proper instruction and baptism in the "true faith." They wrote of the dangers to the character of the Christian master, which came of having absolute power over the body of the slave. One early strategy used to counter the justifications of slavery was to reframe Great Britain's involvement with African societies. Antislavery clergy believed that a Christian had a responsibility for educating the unenlightened. Using religion as a basis, these initial activists created a multi-layered critique with which they hoped gradually to erode the proslavery position. However, while the same arguments may have been used, writers in Great Britain and the northern American colonies diverged in terms of strategy.

The term "slavery" in English publication at the beginning of the century referred to multiple acts and conditions, many of which were entirely unrelated to the African trade.[34] Some publications discussed the practices of "Moors" and their

---

[33] Early writers pointed to French and Spanish practices and argued that the "Papacy" endorsed slavery. This belief, an accurate reading of papal support dating back to the era of Columbus, reinforced arguments about the degraded nature of Catholicism.

[34] Usage of the term to refer to servitude and bondage dates back to the early seventeenth century; however, the term "slave-trade" refers exclusively to African slavery and first appeared in William Snelgrave's *A New Account of some Parts of Guinea, and the Slave Trade* (London, 1734).

enslavement of hapless English travelers.[35] Europeans published accounts of their experiences with slavery in the East, like Samuel Ockley's *An account of southwest Barbary: containing what is most remarkable in the territories of the King of Fez and Morocco, written by a person who had been a slave there* (London, 1713). Another typical association was with "popery" and the heightened fear that England would be subjugated by the French. The activities of the Jacobites in Scotland inspired many pamphlets describing "English liberty," such as *The Liberties of England asserted, in opposition to popery, slavery, and modern innovation* (London, 1714).[36] The most common image of African slavery came from Aphra Behn's *Oroonoko, or The Royal Slave* (1688), which had already been published in several editions and dramatized in Thomas Southerne's *Oroonoko* in 1695. Another popular tale of European atrocity involved a shipwrecked sailor (Inkle) who was saved by an Indian maiden (Yarico) and nursed back to health. After living with her in connubial bliss for some time, Inkle was rescued by a European ship and he sold Yarico into slavery to the ship's captain.[37] However, while these authors may have moved their audiences by sympathy or perhaps titillation, antislavery clergy utilized different tactics to appeal to their audiences at this time.

Interest in the soul of the slave provided an initial ploy for attacking slavery in England and raised concerns among traders and planters. Some writers claimed that a singular benefit to slavery was the exposure (and indoctrination) of Africans to Christianity. Colonial owners had the additional task of instructing their slaves and encouraging their conversion. Antislavery clergy not only accused slaveowners of neglecting this sacred duty, but they further argued that once a slave became a "Christian," he or she could no longer be enslaved. Baptism became a symbol of freedom for the African, and some missionaries sought to instruct plantation slaves of this fact. Some writers attempted to reconcile the two conflicting responsibilities, contending that baptism did not result in manumission. For example, Anthony Hill's *Afer Baptizatus: or, the negro turn'd Christian* (London, 1702) was a two-part sermon that first established the necessity of baptism among slaves and second, refuted the "vulgar opinion" that slaves were subsequently entitled to their freedom.[38] This "vulgar opinion" proved significant enough to

---

[35] Europeans also had a thorough knowledge of the Arab/Islamic slave trade that both predated and continued after the abolition of the transatlantic slave trade.

[36] A similar set of pamphlets were published in the 1740s as fears of the second Jacobite uprising materialized.

[37] The story of Inkle and Yarico first appeared in Richard Ligon's *History of Barbados* (1675) and was later popularized in Richard Steele's *Spectator*. Yarico had multiple identities as Indian maiden and African slave, but she came to symbolize the "primitive" victim of European "civilization." See Frank Felsenstein's *English Trader, Indian Maid: Representing Gender, Race, and Slavery in the New World: An Inkle and Yarico Reader* (Baltimore: Johns Hopkins University Press, 1999).

[38] Hill printed a second, longer edition in London, 1704.

warrant an official statement regarding the status of converted slaves in England, specifically the Yorke-Talbot opinion of 1729 and Harwicke opinion of 1749. The resulting opinions, though legally questionable, solidified the proslavery position in Great Britain for most of the century.

Early antislavery efforts in Great Britain responded to and addressed the issue of slave presence solely within the mother country. While the practice of slavery in the colonies was a subject of concern, many early writers focused their efforts on critiquing slave holding in "England." This practice involved only domestic servitude and did not require the same degree of labor as the type of slavery experienced in the plantation economy. The concept of "British" slavery did not really begin to appear in antislavery writing until the 1770s. West Indian and American planters would often bring slaves with them when visiting England, and these slaves would perform the same duties as servants. Aristocratic families also began to keep slaves in their households, treating them as pets and curios to be displayed. Publications like the *London Gazette* ran runaway slave notices and advertisements for selling slaves throughout the century. Even *The Tatler* ran one notice for the sale of a slave boy in London.[39] Perhaps the visible presence of these "Negro" servants discomfited members of the clergy. I do not claim that the antislavery rhetoric arose purely from altruistic impulse. For whatever reason, a general distaste for the practice of slavery in "England" prompted antislavery agitation. Some agitators asserted that receiving the sacrament of baptism freed slaves and others added that simply coming to England resulted in freedom. These opinions combined Christian beliefs with the powerful discourse of "English liberty" that contributed greatly to antislavery efforts later in the century. Slavery supporters countered that the slave was "commercial property" and therefore did not qualify for protection under civil law. This conflict was strong enough to warrant formal statements to resolve the issue.

Two important opinions in the early century supported the claims of property over person and effectively stymied antislavery efforts for several decades. These statements issued by important men did not result from any legal case; thus, the case law regarding the status of the slave in Britain remained undecided until the Somerset case in 1772. The issue of ownership ultimately came to the question of whose "rights" took precedence in Great Britain—the master's or the slave's. Though no legal case regarding the validity of slavery in England had been presented in court, the question had legal significance. In 1729, Sir Phillip Yorke, the Attorney General, and Charles Talbot, the Solicitor General, issued a statement that supported the position of the slave holder in England and denied slaves any "right" to freedom. They stated:

---

[39] These advertisements and notices continued well into the nineteenth century, even after the Somerset decision and the abolition of the slave trade. For studies of African presence in Great Britain, see Peter Fryer's *Staying Power* and Gretchen Gerzina's *Black London*.

We are of opinion, that a Slave by coming from the West-Indies to Great-Britain, or Ireland, either with or without his master, doth not become free; and that his master's property or right in him, is not thereby determined or varied; and that baptism doth not bestow freedom on him, nor make any alteration in his temporal condition in these kingdoms: We are also of opinion, that the master may legally compel him to return again to the plantations.[40]

This decision set a precedent that firmly established the right to property in the body of the slave.[41] Sir Phillip Yorke, who had become the Lord Chancellor (and Lord Hardwicke), issued a second opinion in 1749 that upheld the original contentions. Neither of these opinions addressed the contentions of antislavery arguments about the nature of English "liberty." Instead, they dismissed the claims by affirming the master's right to property and essentially dehumanized the "Negro slave." However, these opinions began to be seriously challenged in the 1760s and could not maintain legal standing against the systematic opposition of Granville Sharp.

Sharp overcame the limitations of his childhood education and literally stumbled into his career as a reformer. He was the twelfth child of the Archdeacon of Northumberland, and his parents had no money to spare for his formal education, especially after putting his two older brothers through Cambridge. At fifteen, he was apprenticed to a Quaker linen-draper in London but left the profession soon after his period of apprenticeship ended. Having come from a long line of theologians, Sharp had a keen interest in understanding the nature of Christianity. His encounters with differing interpretations of the Bible and differing faiths encouraged his study of theology and perfected his research skills.[42] In 1758, he took a position as a clerk in the Ordinance Department in London, a job which left him time to devote to his researches. His older brother also worked in London as a physician, and Sharp often visited him at his clinic. On one such visit, he nearly tripped over the body of a badly beaten slave who had come to Dr. Sharp for medical attention. Seventeen-year-old Jonathan Strong had accompanied his master, David Lisle, from Barbados to England to serve as his personal servant. In 1765, after a series of increasingly severe beatings, Lisle had turned the lame, half-

---

[40] Granville Sharp began his *Representation of the Injustice and Dangerous Tendency of Tolerating Slavery* (1769) by quoting this opinion, which he copied from *The Gentlemen's Magazine*, vol. XI.

[41] The opinions issued by Yorke and Talbot did not have the legal precedent of case law, but they were cited by lawyers in subsequent cases. See David Brion Davis, "Antislavery and the Conflict of Laws," *The Problem of Slavery in the Age of Revolution* 469–522.

[42] In one of his debates with a Jewish man, his opponent suggested that no one could truly argue biblical interpretation without a thorough knowledge of Hebrew. Sharp accepted the challenge, studied Hebrew and Greek, and was able to overwhelm his opponent. See E. C. P. Lascelles, *Granville Sharp and the Freedom of Slaves in England* (Oxford, 1928; reprinted New York: Negro Universities Press, 1969).

blind Strong into the streets. Strong sought the services of Dr. Sharp and helped open the eyes of his brother, Granville, to the iniquities of slavery.

Sharp began his crusade against slavery in England out of sympathy for one man and outrage over the idea that humans could be legally held as property. All of his biographers agree that prior to this incident, he had little interest or understanding of the condition of slaves in England or her colonies. His conversion to Evangelism evoked a strong reformist impulse that found an ideal cause in Jonathan Strong. This arbitrary moment initiated a chain of events that culminated in the organized anti-slave-trade effort of the late 1780s and 1790s. After Strong had healed, Sharp and his brother found the young man a position working for a grocer. In 1767, Strong's master discovered his slave in good health and sought to reclaim his property to sell in Jamaica. Strong sent a frantic appeal from jail to Sharp, who immediately intervened to secure his release. However, in the ensuing lawsuit, Sharp was shocked to discover that the earlier opinions supported Lisle's claim to ownership of Strong without respect to his treatment of the man. The Yorke-Talbot and Hardwicke opinions, while regarded as setting legal precedent, did not have the backing of law, and Sharp found such utter lack of legal substance to be offensive. The case of Lisle vs. Strong precipitated an exhaustive two-year study of English civil law, which resulted in the publication of Sharp's first antislavery tract.

A Representation of the Injustice and Dangerous Tendency of Tolerating Slavery (1769) provided the first systematic challenge to the legality of slavery in Great Britain and became a foundation for antislavery critique. The primary purpose of this lengthy tract was to refute the belief that English civil law supported African slavery (see Figure 2.2). Organized in four parts, this tract proved to be the most systematic objection to proslavery justifications that relied on both the law and the Bible. Part I began with the "opinion" stated by Yorke and Talbot in 1729, and Sharp listed numerous examples from case law that set a different precedent. He correctly simplified the issue of slavery in England to a conflict between the owner's right to property and the slave's right to liberty.[43] Part II responded to proslavery claims that as English law predated the institution of African slavery, its protections did not extend to the enslaved person. In his response, Sharp pointed out that if this was the case for Africans, then all foreigners could not be held accountable for their actions on English soil. In Part III, Sharp offered a "solution" (albeit tongue-in-cheek) for colonials who would lose their "property" in the bodies of their slaves. He proposed that all slaves sign a contract to return to the colonies if brought to England, and this proposal transformed into a scathing critique of colonial law, which he treated as distinct from English law. While the colonies passed their laws on the authority of the mother country, these laws supported an institution that had no precedent in English civil law and therefore remained separate from English civil law. The tract ended with a systematic consideration of the practice

---

[43] This dichotomy was the crux of Jonathan Strong's case and would be taken up more successfully in the case of Stewart vs. Somerset in 1771.

Fig. 2.2a Granville Sharp, title page, "Extract from *A Representation of the Injustice and Dangerous Tendency of Tolerating Slavery.*" London: Printed 1769. Philadelphia: Reprinted by Joseph Crukshank, 1771. Courtesy of the Library of Congress, Rare Books Division.

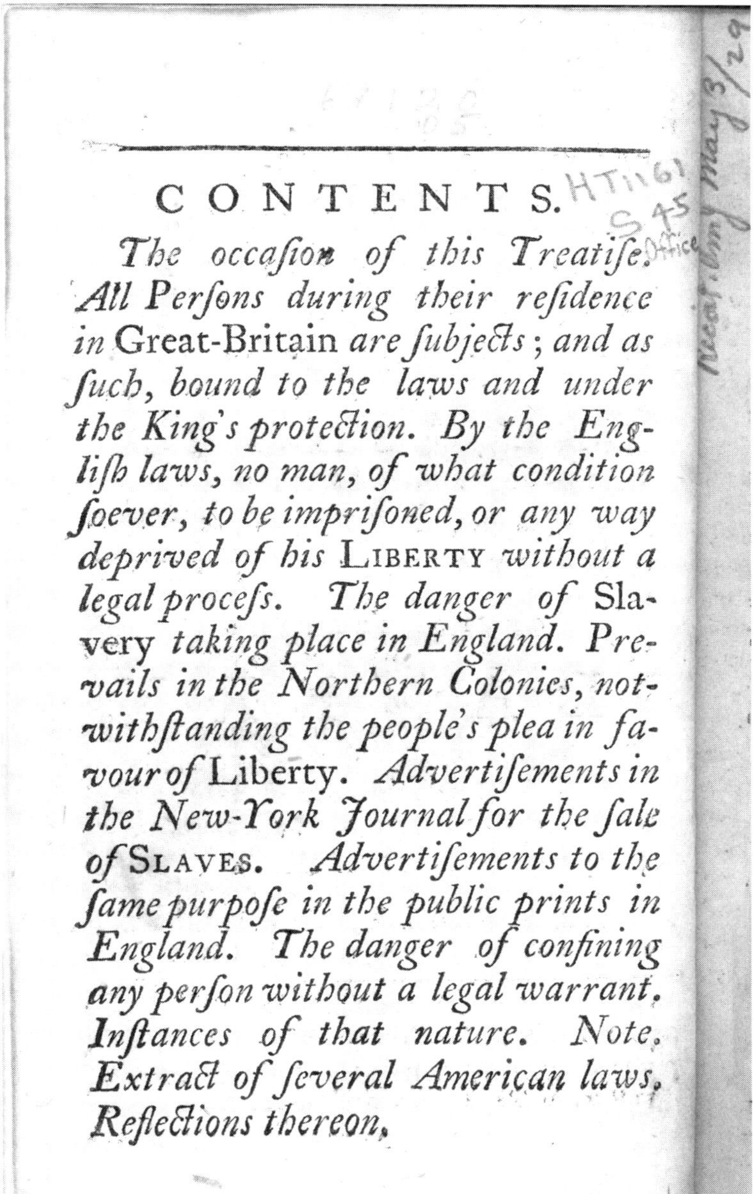

CONTENTS.

The occasion of this Treatise. All Persons during their residence in Great-Britain *are subjects; and as such, bound to the laws and under the King's protection. By the English laws, no man, of what condition soever, to be imprisoned, or any way deprived of his* LIBERTY *without a legal process. The danger of Slavery taking place in England. Prevails in the Northern Colonies, notwithstanding the people's plea in favour of* Liberty. *Advertisements in the New-York Journal for the sale of* SLAVES. *Advertisements to the same purpose in the public prints in* England. *The danger of confining any person without a legal warrant. Instances of that nature. Note. Extract of several American laws. Reflections thereon.*

Fig. 2.2b   Granville Sharp, advertisement, "Extract from *A Representation of the Injustice and Dangerous Tendency of Tolerating Slavery*." London: Printed 1769. Philadelphia: Reprinted by Joseph Crukshank, 1771. Courtesy of the Library of Congress, Rare Books Division.

of "villenage" [sic] and refuted proslavery claims that England had established and exercised a form of enslavement in its past. Sharp sought to discredit this line of defense from being used in court by owners like David Lisle to reclaim their slaves. *A Representation* had only one printing and was written primarily for an audience of lawyers. However, the sentiments expressed in this publication became popular arguments within antislavery writing in Great Britain.

The rhetorical circumference and act described in Sharp's first publication pointedly differed from the Quaker, colonial protests typified by Benezet. For Sharp, the significant changes he sought to enact (or counteract) had to do with *English* law, which applied primarily to England and barely affected the colonies. He quoted important legal decisions affecting practices like Scottish vassalage, but he left the colonial legal system as a separate entity to be amended by the colonists.[44] He clearly delineated two discrete spheres of influence in which the institution operated. The colonial sphere was beyond his research because their toleration of slavery indicated a critical distance from the precepts of English civil law. He stated that "Slavery is by no means tolerated in this island, either by the law or custom of England" (7). The laws of the periphery should not be allowed to contaminate the laws of the center, and Sharp characterized colonial slave laws as written "to the indelible disgrace of the British name" (19).[45] This distinction between mother country and colony resulted in a definition of "act" that was limited to the Great Britain. Sharp defined the "act" as the actual condition of enslavement, and in doing so, his tracts focused on the implications for the agent and the object of agency. His writing did not incorporate varying scenes or censure forms of agency as was commonly found in colonial critiques of the slave trade. Instead, he focused on complicating the legality of the act by examining the character of the agent, in this case the colonial slave holder returning to England. He also created a new space for a conflicting agent, namely the African slave, who was transformed from object to "subject" on English soil. "[F]or every Negro Slave, being undoubtedly either man, woman, or child; he or she, immediately upon their arrival in England, becomes *the King's property* in the *relative sense* ... and *cannot*, therefore, be '*out of the King's protection*'" (19).[46]

---

[44] Sharp's first tract is clearly directed at a relatively small audience in London, so his references are primarily to "English" customs. However, a transformation occurs in his own writing over the next two decades that indicates a shift in thought from "English" to "British" identity.

[45] The discussion of colonial law is the only instance in this tract that Sharp looks beyond England and uses the term "British." He states, "It is a shame to this nation, and may in time prove very dangerous to it, that the British constitution and liberties should be excluded from any part of the British dominions" (51, note).

[46] In a note, he extends this sense of subjecthood to include residents of the colonies as well, although he does not press the point in his main text. "Every inhabitant of the British colonies, black as well as white, bond as well as free, are undoubtedly *the King's subjects*, during their residence within the limits of the *King's dominions*" (72).

A Representation relied almost wholly on logical appeals to establish the "humanity of the African" and the devotion to "liberty" evinced by English civil law. The fundamental conflict, in Sharp's perception, occurred between the protection of "private property" and the rights owed to "human nature." He conceded that "the Laws of the Realm do most certainly secure to every man, without exception, his *private property*, but it must be likewise remembered, that the nature of every kind of *property* ought to be considered" (11). No one could claim the right to "*private property*" in the body of a man because all humans possessed a natural right to liberty. He questioned, "how is [the slave] to be divested of his *human nature*?" (16). Sharp utilized syllogism to prove that Africans ranked above "*things of a base nature*," such as "horses, dogs, cats, &c." Therefore, to subject a human to the same type of ownership as "beasts" was outside the purview of law. In a more radical turn, he argued that, as human beings could not be dismissed as property in England, the African slave became a subject of the King. This revolutionary inclusion of the African subject interrogated both the notion of citizenship and the "tyranny of the slave holder." Sharp set the rights and privileges of the slave above that of the slave holder, suggesting that these subjects were less entitled to the protection of the Crown. The slave-holding subject had become corrupted by the absolute power granted through the institution by claiming to supersede the rights of the lawful monarch. "Every petty planter, who avails himself of the service of the Slaves, is an arbitrary monarch, or rather a lawless Basha in his own territories" (82).[47] The most sacred premise of English civil law rested on the security and respect for human liberty. "This [English] law breathes the pure spirit of liberty, equity and social love; being calculated to maintain that consideration and mutual regard which one person ought to have for another, howsoever unequal in rank or station" (104). This "pure spirit" needed to be shielded from the taint of colonial distortion and disregard of natural rights.

Sharp also introduced a religion-based argument in order to add another dimension to his contentions about the dangers of colonial corruption. As a "God-fearing" and devout member of the Church of England, he expressed a genuine concern about the "degradation" of Christianity in the colonies. He castigated the behavior of "licentious" slaveowners and characterized them as "unChristian." In a note about the severity of colonial laws, he commented that harsh punishments meted out to Negroes who struck a white person regardless of extenuating circumstances were unjust. "No allowance is here made for any unjust provocation ... from licentious, drunken, or fraudulent white man, who may be pleased to disgrace Christianity, by calling himself *a Christian!*" (49). Sharp advanced a dual critique that simultaneously

---

[47] The use of the term "Basha" (which is actually a corrupted form of "Pasha") reflects perceptions of the East as degraded, encouraging abuses of liberty. Sharp calls upon an existing prejudice in order to emphasize how "unnatural" the institution of slavery is to England. The association of slave-holding colonials with "foreign" depredations adds another layer of distance between subjects of Great Britain and her colonies. This colonial corruption of "British" purity becomes a trope in antislavery writing in the 1780s and '90s.

questioned the "Christian" nature of the colonist and warned of the repercussions of such behavior on the mother country. He distinguished between "true" and "nominal" Christians, castigating slave holders for their "exercise of despotic power over their fellow subjects." While these "nominal christians" courted their own damnation, their actions adversely affected the welfare of Great Britain. "Oppression is a most grievous crime; and the cries of these much injured people (though they are only poor ignorant heathens) will certainly reach to Heaven!" (72).[48] Sharp would fine-tune these objections in later tracts.

The utility of *A Representation* became clear when another opportunity to destabilize the practice of slavery in Great Britain arose with the case of James Somerset. The details of the case resembled Jonathan Strong's situation and allowed Sharp the opportunity to present a more compelling defense. Somerset came to England from Virginia in 1769 as the property of and personal servant to Charles Stewart.[49] During his time in England, Somerset served his "master" faithfully until Stewart made plans to return to the Colonies and sell Somerset. Frightened by the prospect of returning to colonial slavery, Somerset left Stewart and found shelter in London with antislavery sympathizers. Stewart had booked passage on a ship captained by John Knowles, whom Stewart enlisted to recover his property. Knowles kidnapped Somerset from London and detained him on the ship. However, Somerset's friends immediately petitioned Lord Mansfield, Lord Chief Justice of the Court of King's Bench, and prevented Knowles' ship from setting sail for Jamaica. On 3 December 1771, Lord Mansfield issued a writ of habeas corpus directed to Mr. Knowles requiring that he produce the body of James Somerset in court.[50] The ensuing legal battle took several months to resolve, and Somerset's lawyers relied heavily upon Sharp's tract for their arguments. Ultimately, the question in the case came to a decision of whether or not English civil law acknowledged the practice of slavery. While Lord Mansfield respected Lord Hardwicke's opinions of 1729 and 1749, he hesitated to affirm by legal precedent the idea that English law condoned slavery. As Sergeant Davy, an officer of the court, stated, "The air in England is too

---

[48] Sharp did evidence the same optimism and willingness to acknowledge the capabilities of the African as Benezet. While he argued against slavery on the basis of their undeniable humanity, another component of his argument contended that African slave labor took away jobs from more deserving "white" subjects in Great Britain. Ironically, this argument would be advanced by slavery advocates in subsequent decades.

[49] See Steven M. Wise, *Though the Heavens May Fall* (New York: Da Capo Press, 2005) for an in-depth analysis of the legal implications of Somerset's case.

[50] The details of Somerset's situation are recounted in Francis Hargrave's *An Argument in the Case of James Sommersett A Negro, lately determined by the Court of King's Bench* (London: printed for the author, 1772). Mr. Hargrave served as one of the counsel for Mr. Somerset, and he recounted Captain Knowles' opening statement regarding Somerset's history. Also note that I have used the regularized spelling of Somerset's name in accordance with how it appears in twentieth-century historical commentaries.

pure for slaves." Like Sharp, Lord Mansfield was content to see colonial practices remain in the colonies.

During the course of the trial, Sharp published "An Appendix to *A Representation of the Injustice and Dangerous Tendency of Tolerating Slavery*" (1772) that encapsulated his arguments against slavery in Great Britain. Lord Mansfield's series of unnecessary delays in coming to a decision seemed to indicate another proslavery victory. This considerably shorter tract focused on the main points of his objections, namely the spurious claim for property rights and the anti-Christian behavior of slave holders. He argued:

> Let the Slave holder remember, also, that his being thus deprived of his imaginary Property, cannot be considered otherwise ... than merely as *a private loss*; whereas, if such an *unnatural right* be admitted without due consideration of the superior *Personal Right* of the Negro, a worse Vassalage ... would in time be introduced into this free Christian Country, by which *the Publick* would *be materially injured*, as well *in Honour*, as *in Morals*, and *National Safety*. (11)

Since the plaintiff's lawyers relied on the ancient practice of villeinage to justify slavery in England, Sharp warned that granting this concession would merely open the law to graver misconceptions. He reframed the purpose of the case as a conflict between West Indian law and English law. Allowing colonial law to triumph would "draw down upon us [by which he means Great Britain *and* her Dominions] some dreadful and speedy *national* calamity" (28). To establish the inhumanity of West Indian practices, he also quoted from Benezet's *A Short Account of that Part of Africa Inhabited by Negroes*, which he had reprinted in 1768.[51] By recounting some of the abuses of the slave trade, Sharp began to show an awareness of the greater problem of slavery in the colonies. While his focus remained on the metropole, he opened his pen (and his mind) to the idea that more important issues might exist beyond the exercise of law in England.

Sharp began a correspondence with Anthony Benezet in 1772 that helped reshape his understanding of slavery and his purpose as an antislavery activist. He established his familiarity with Benezet's writing and the Quaker resistance in *A Representation*. When Benezet became aware of the Somerset case, he printed an abridged version of Sharp's tract in Philadelphia (1772). After this printing, he wrote Sharp a letter dated 14 May 1772 and sent him copies of *Some Historical Account of Guinea* (1772), which detailed the history of "that iniquitous traffick."[52] He urged Sharp to concentrate efforts on effecting an end to the transatlantic slave

---

[51] In his tract, Sharp misquotes the title as "A Short Account of the Slave Trade," but he refers to Benezet as the author.

[52] The letters between Sharp and Benezet are found in Wilson Armistead's *Anthony Benezet*, and they have been annotated in George S. Brookes, *Friend Anthony Benezet* (Philadelphia: University of Pennsylvania Press, 1937). All page references are to Brookes's volume.

trade, stating that "[i]t is certainly incumbent on every lover of God and man to use their best endeavours to stop this unnatural and barbarous traffic" (291). In the same letter, he indicated a growing need to have the King and Parliament intercede in order to halt the slave trade to the colonies. Sharp's response dated 21 August 1772 endorsed the idea that appealing to Parliament to limit the African slave trade would be most appropriate. However, Sharp also demonstrated his sense of a separateness or division between the governance of Great Britain and her colonies. He wrote that "respect must be paid to *the rights of the Colonies*; ... because the colonies have a right *themselves* to prohibit such importation respectively in their own Assemblies, with the King's concurrence" (420).[53] His freely offered advice about the most appropriate manner to petition Parliament and the King seemed to indicate that the "problem" was a colonial issue. However, his continued communication with other colonial activists, like Benjamin Rush and Benjamin Franklin, slowly began to broaden his worldview.

The correspondence between Benezet and Sharp has several important implications for the development of national identity in the debates. The first letter exchanged immediately establishes the interconnectedness between colony and mother country through the vehicle of print. Benezet abridges and prints Sharp's tract for colonial audiences to illustrate that slavery is not supported by English law. He also sends copies of colonial pamphlets to Sharp and provides an introduction for John Wesley, another avid antislavery activist. In his response, Sharp indicates that he has distributed Benezet's tracts. He begins to contemplate the idea of demanding legislative action against the African slave trade, though he still views the issue from an English (rather than colonial) perspective. By working with colonial activists and establishing a strong connection with Benezet, he transforms the purpose of his activism from slavery in "England" to the British slave trade, which encompasses at least three continents.[54] In his letter to Benezet dated 7 July 1773, he reveals that "every opportunity that I could possibly get to myself (and Sundays in particular, after service) has been employed in reading and collecting materials to forward the undertaking which you have so much at heart" (424–425). Whereas Benezet gradually narrows his critique from the European to the British slave trade, Sharp's critique begins with British activities. The correspondence with Benezet also encourages Sharp to expand his appeals and incorporate more of a Christian perspective in his tracts. He, like Benezet,

---

[53] Sharp strongly supported the American colonists' appeals for greater representation. In 1774, he published *A Declaration of the people's natural right to a share in the legislature, which is the fundamental principle of the British constitution of state* in London. The first edition was reprinted in Boston, Philadelphia, and New York; the second edition appeared in London in 1775; and the third edition was published in Dublin in 1776.

[54] The British slave trade touched Europe, Africa, North America, South America, and Asia, but activists tended to view the trade as a triangular configuration touching Europe, Africa, and North America.

becomes increasingly concerned with the heavenly repercussions for the "nation" if slavery continues unchecked.

The favorable decision in the case of Somerset may have (supposedly) ended slavery in Great Britain, but colonial slavery was an issue that also required attention. Sharp began to take up colonial arguments and published his objections directly in the American colonies. The publication of the Reverend Thomas Thompson's *The African Trade for Negro slaves shewn to be consistent with principles of humanity and with the laws of revealed religion* (1772) prompted an immediate response that became Sharp's first engagement with biblical justifications of slavery.[55] Thompson's tract used Mosaic law to justify the keeping of slaves and to legitimize planters' assertion of property rights. Printed in Canterbury and London while the Somerset decision was still pending, the tract clearly sought to influence Mansfield's judgment in favor of the planters. Sharp's response was a short tract entitled "An Essay on Slavery" (1773), which he published in Burlington, New Jersey, after the resolution of Somerset's case. "An Essay on Slavery" refuted Thompson's contentions by contextualizing scriptural evidence, redefining the notion of "Christian," and taking up the concept of "National Sin." Thompson argued that since slavery existed among the Jews as documented by the Old Testament, "the buying and selling of slaves is not contrary to the law of nature" (15). Sharp countered the conclusion by illustrating how many Jewish practices were not consistent with the law of nature. "Many things were formerly tolerated among the Israelites, merely through the mercy and forbearance of God, in consideration of their extreme frailty and inability, at that same time, to bear a more perfect system of law" (20). In other words, society had evolved considerably from the time of the Israelites; thus, the English were able "to bear a more perfect system of law."

Sharp's rebuttal focused primarily on understanding and (re)defining the attributes of a "Christian." His text moved pointedly away from the Old Testament to the New Testament, which reinforced the outdated basis for Thompson's argument. Not only were Jewish laws inconsistent with the law of nature, but they "were certainly, annulled or rather *superseded*, as it were, by the more perfect doctrines of *universal benevolence* taught by Christ himself" (23).[56] Another quality of being a "Christian" was the way in which "the glorious system of the gospel destroys all *narrow, national partiality*; and makes *us citizens of the world*" (25).[57]

---

[55] Thomas Thompson, *The African Trade for Negro Slaves consistent with Humanity and Revealed Religion* (Canterbury: Printed and Sold by Simmons and Kirby, Sold also by Robert Baldwin, London). No publication date appears on the title page of this tract, but based on references within the text, the year of publication was probably 1772. Also published in Philadelphia, 1772.

[56] See chapter 3 of Christopher Brown's *Moral Capital* for a discussion of Sharp's odd mixture of High Church and Evangelical religious convictions.

[57] Again, Sharp's essay contains an ironic foreshadowing of proslavery arguments. The "citizen of the world" attribute becomes associated with trader and planter perceptions

In defining a "Christian" as "citizen of the world," he urged "true Christians," as opposed to "nominal christians," to alleviate the distress of "thy neighbor," even when the neighbor may be "heathen." He even opposed the practice of setting national interest before Christian principles. "[W]e must not, for the sake of *Old England*, and its *African trade*, or for the supposed advantage, or imaginary necessities of our *American* colonies, lay aside our *Christian charity*" (29). His disgust with Thompson extended to the entire nation, which he characterized as "an overgrown *society of robbers*, a *mere banditti*," for the tolerance of slavery.[58] The "more perfect" doctrines of Christ combined with the "more perfect system of law" to make the idea of perpetual service in the form of African slavery "anti-Christian." Sharp concluded his essay by returning to the concept of nationhood, but he spoke in terms of national culpability. Sharp cleverly appropriated a phrase from Thompson's tract and claimed that slavery was the "NATIONAL SIN." The sins of the colonies reflected poorly on the mother country, and he cautioned that Britons would suffer as a "nation." Sharp expanded this idea further in his next tract, *The Law of Retribution; or, A Serious warning to Great Britain and her colonies founded on unquestionable examples of God's temporal vengeance against tyrants, slave holders, and oppressors* (1776).

Sharp employed nationalist rhetoric to incite fear in his audience about the consequences of slave holding by narrowing his critique to the British slave trade. He still separated colonial and metropolitan activities, claiming that "GREAT BRITAIN, indeed, keeps *no Slaves*, but publicly encourages the *Slave-trade*" (305). He stressed that the "nation" as a whole would suffer from the illicit acts taking place in the colonies. For Sharp, the "nation" carried multiple associations that narrowed and widened depending on the nature of his critique. When denouncing colonial practices, the concept of nation narrowed to Great Britain (sometimes, England), and Sharp depicted an oppositional relationship between the "purity" of the mother country and the "corruption" of her peripheries. However, this tract also emphasized that soon Britain would suffer as a "nation" because of the sins of slavery. In this sense, he referred to Britain and her Dominions as jointly sharing in divine condemnation. "*National* Wickedness, from the beginning of the World, has generally been visited with *National* Punishments: and surely no *National* Wickedness can be more heinous in the sight of God than a public toleration of *Slavery and Oppression!*" (10–11). He indicted the "public Toleration" and "*Royal Assent*" in Great Britain that rendered them "Parties in the *Oppression*, and (it is to be feared) Partakers of the Guilt!" (17). This shared culpability broadened Sharp's sense of purpose in bringing an end to a corrupt institution. His earlier work

---

of global commerce in the 1780s and '90s.

[58] Sharp evidences no awareness that some of the settlements were in fact penal colonies populated deliberately by "robbers" and "banditti." Georgia, the state with the worst slave conditions in the American colonies, was founded as a dumping ground for Great Britain's convicts. However, no antislavery writers appeared to have made any connection between these facts.

focused only on Great Britain and believed that colonists bore the responsibility for their own change. However, in speaking of divine retribution for a "NATIONAL SIN," Sharp demanded parliamentary intervention to address this detriment to the welfare of the British nation. Even the colonies desired the end of the "*Iniquity, Inhumanity*, and *destructive Influence* of the AFRICAN SLAVE-TRADE" (306–7).

This focus on sin and retribution resulted in three more antislavery tracts that definitively countered all "Christian" justifications of slavery while censuring traders and planters. *The Just Limitation of Slavery in the Laws of God* (1776),[59] *The Law of Passive Obedience* (1776), and *The Law of Liberty, or, Royal Law* (1776) established significant counter-arguments to justifications of slavery taken from Scripture.[60] These tracts maintained that slavery was wholly incompatible with Christ's doctrine and therefore wholly incompatible with "English" ideals. *The Just Limitation of Slavery* systematically debunked proslavery interpretations of Scripture as an attempt to "subvert the express command concerning *brotherly love* due to *strangers*" (10). Once he had established the antithetical relationship between the divine and slavery, Sharp sought tentatively to extend the belief that slavery should not exist anywhere in British dominions. He wrote, "But it is not enough that the Laws of England exclude *Slavery* merely *from this island*, whilst the grand Enemy of mankind triumphs in a toleration, *throughout our Colonies*, of the most monstrous *oppression* to which human nature can be subjected!" (2). Clearly, his viewpoint has shifted from seeing the colonies as separate entities to seeing them as reflections of the "morality" of the mother country, specifically England. Sharp also began to direct a more pointed critique of the "character" of the slave holders, characterizing them as "tyrants and oppressors." He cautioned both traders and planters "let that man, who endeavours to deprive others of their just privileges as *brethren*, take heed lest he should thereby unhappily occasion his *own rejection* in the end" (66).

The Law of Passive Obedience continued his Scriptural rebuttal to and admonition of slavers who quoted St. Paul's advice to "masters" as a historical and religious justification. He censured the master who claimed "*absolute property*" in the body and service of the slave, but depicted a kind of slave nobility in submitting to the master. "The slave violates no precepts of the gospel by his abject condition, provided that the same is *involuntary* ... but how the master who enforces *that involuntary servitude*, can be said to act consistently with the Christian profession, is a question of a very different nature" (12). By questioning the motives of traders and slave holders, his tract privileged the greater spiritual

---

[59] *The Just Limitation of Slavery* was published with several appendices, including Sharp's "Essay on Slavery" that was first published in New Jersey. Another important appendix recounts "Reports of Determinations in the several COURTS OF LAW AGAINST SLAVERY, &c." in which some legal cases indicate that the Somerset Decision was taken to apply retroactively.

[60] The tracts were originally published separately in London, in 1776, and reprinted the following year bound together and sold as a book.

character of the slave through his or her "passive obedience." He further stated that the "true and proper ground for *patriotism*" came from a nation whose "rulers and magistrates" demonstrated a "true Christian" sentiment of excusing personal injury but punishing public transgressions (77). Sharp used the term "nominal Christian" in other tracts to characterize the tolerance of slavery, but in this tract he targeted traders and planters more directly. These "nominal Christians" tarnished the good name of all Britons by fostering and perpetuating an "EVIL" practice. In the *Law of Liberty*, Sharp underscored this point defining "liberty" through two fundamental precepts—"THE LOVE OF GOD, and THE LOVE OF OUR NEIGHBOR." The tolerance and practice of African slavery violated both precepts and threatened the belief in liberty. In an appeal to the entire nation, Sharp admonished "the whole Community—every Individual (without excepting even those who never had the least Concern in promoting *Slavery*) is personally interested in the Consideration of this Subject!"(46–47).

The tracts published towards the end of the 1770s demonstrated significant transformations in Sharp's circumference, audience, and perception of the problem. He began to acknowledge the connections between colony and mother country, which broadened his outlook on the "iniquities" of slavery. His initial concerns developed in response to the visible presence of poor and abused Africans in London, but they gradually expanded to include the enslaved populations in the American and West Indian plantations. As his awareness of the issue grew, he began to direct his appeals to wider audiences. Sharp understood that permanent changes could only come through legislative action, so his first tracts addressed legislators or readers familiar with English law. However, the perception of slavery as a blight on the British public (instead of confined colonial transgressors) necessitated a change in strategy. His later tracts appealed to "true Christians" and "the Subjects of the British Empire." The "problem" of slavery necessitated looking beyond the mother country and finding a more definitive solution. While Sharp only alluded to abolition at this point, his criticism of trade and ownership clearly indicated that some form of official action would be required. His writing created a basic framework for antislavery critique that proliferated the focus on the slave trade beyond the efforts of the Quaker community. He provided the foundation for arguments that would become tropes in anti-slave-trade literature produced in subsequent decades.

Beginnings of a "British" Resistance to Slavery

Neither historians nor literary scholars have adequately examined the preliminary dialogue between colonial and metropolitan antislavery activists that led to the formation of the abolitionist societies in the 1780s. Research details the changes in social, economic, and political factors that made slavery completely intolerable to a wider segment of the British population. However, arguments asserted in tracts prior to the formation of organized societies rate little discussion.[61] The general consensus holds that organized and concerted resistance did not emerge until the 1780s. The "British" abolitionist movement, influenced by multiple factors, succeeded in mobilizing public opinion in a manner that both drew upon and instigated significant changes in culture.[62] By positing an overly linear narrative for the emergence of antislavery, historians focus on the timing of sustained resistance. Colley locates the rise in interest as a response to the successful rebellion of the American colonies. David Turley identifies religion as the dominant idiom in antislavery writing and the primary impetus for critiquing slavery. Davis and Robin Blackburn relate antislavery efforts to the general climate of reform that prevailed in Great Britain at that time.[63] I acknowledge the merit of each viewpoint and agree that each one had a significant impact on the movement. However, the limitation of these arguments becomes apparent when examining the shifts in rhetoric that occurred over the 1760s and '70s. How did the separate colonial and metropolitan antislavery efforts come together in order to establish a common goal? The abolitionist movement became a "British" movement because of the conversation and exchange of ideas between these early antislavery crusaders.

Examining the arguments of writers before the campaign was organized also complicates the linearity of the abolitionist narrative. Initial antislavery efforts in Great Britain and the American colonies shifted goals between publications, and they often operated without a sense of common purpose. Activist arguments range in scope from a broad critique of the entire institution to a focused critique of one aspect (for example, the slave trade). They propose solutions that similarly vary from immediate emancipation to gradual manumission after a set term of service. Judging from the array of responses, I contend that the proposed abolition of the slave trade in the 1780s evolved from several important conversations that occurred a decade previously. The movement emerges from a series of transformations in both rhetoric and ideology of an earlier period. While religion remains the foundation of antislavery protest, secular arguments gain prominence

---

[61] Seymour Drescher does address the arguments of the "preabolitionist era" briefly, but he gives more credence to Clarkson's publications in the 1780s. See "People and Parliament: The Rhetoric of the British Slave Trade," *Journal of Interdisciplinary History*, 21:2 (Autumn, 1990): 245–260.

[62] Many studies have documented the interaction between culture and the mobilization of public opinion in the antislavery movement. See David Turley's *The Culture of English Antislavery, 1780–1860* (New York: Routledge, 1991) and J. R. Oldfield's *Popular Politics and British Anti-Slavery: The Mobilisation of Public Opinion Against the Slave Trade, 1787–1807* (Manchester: Manchester University Press, 1995).

[63] Robin Blackburn's, *The Overthrow of Colonial Slavery: 1776–1848* (London: Verso, 1988) does not focus solely on the British antislavery campaigns. His analysis examines antislavery agitation in Europe and contends that popular opinion had little to do with effecting change. The work of abolition occurred under the auspices of the European elite and shored up oligarchical power.

as writers seek to appeal to wider audiences. Activists initially appear to have had little sense of a relationship between colony and mother country in terms of slavery. However, that awareness grows out of the open dialogue between key figures in the nascent anti-slave-trade movement. The language of earlier tracts indicates a loosely constructed understanding of "empire," a concept that comes to dominate the organized effort in the 1780s and '90s.[64] I argue that the organized movement emerged as "British" precisely because of the evolution in discourse that occurred in the 1770s.

The antislavery efforts of the early eighteenth century had been confined to regional areas and reflected regional concerns. Colonial American writers confronted all facets of the institution on a daily basis, so their publications approached the "problem" from a particular perspective. Since slavery was firmly entrenched in social and economic aspects of American life, activists advocated a more gradual solution. The first step to eradicating this institution from colonial life was to stop replenishing the existing population. American writers wanted to convince their audiences that perpetual enslavement was a "sin," and that new slaves should not be supplied to an already corrupt institution. Redressing the condition of existing slaves would come after the trade had been stopped. Writers in Great Britain had a different imperative that structured the nature and content of their antislavery protest. The number of slaves in the mother country in no way equaled the number of slaves in the colonies. Since crops did not demand the kind of labor required in colonial plantations, slave holding was primarily an urban phenomenon. The slaves in domestic service worked mainly in cities like London or Bristol or Liverpool and performed the same duties as "free-born" British servants. Therefore, abolishing slavery in Great Britain was feasible.

Colonial and metropolitan activists worked independently towards differing goals and utilized particular rhetorical strategies to effect change. The northern American colonies had less need for slave labor, but the continuous influx of slaves to suit the southern colonists' demands made slaves too easily accessible to the north. As well, the active slaving ports in cities like New York kept the image of slavery constantly at the forefront of awareness. Resistance to the institution began with the slave trade and antislavery writers focused their critique on the acquisition and purchase of slaves. The pervasiveness of slavery in the colonies depended on proslavery rationalizations that stripped Africans of human sentiment and stressed their innate suitability for plantation work. Antislavery activists believed that collective action on the part of individuals could gradually erode

---

[64] David Armitage, *The Ideological Origins of the British Empire* (Cambridge: Cambridge University Press, 2000). In his study, Armitage classifies the expansion of Great Britain into the New World and the East Indies as the "second British empire." Colonial acquisition in the Atlantic World and the East made Great Britain more self-consciously "imperial" than during the first "empire" in which the boundaries of Britain remained within the confines of the islands. Armitage characterized this second empire as "Protestant, commercial, maritime, and free."

the institution to its eventual abolition. They endeavored to motivate members of their audience, who consisted primarily of northern slave holders with a relatively small number of slaves, to stop purchasing new slaves. Thus, they concentrated on the slave trade to begin their push for antislavery reform. Problematizing the slave trade necessitated the use of logical and pathetic appeals designed to humanize the Africans and their suffering. Benezet's tracts provided useful first-person accounts of misery experienced by captured Africans at every stage of the trade, from the appalling conditions of the slave forts to the horrors of the middle passage.[65] His accounts contradicted the popular contentions of West Indian and southern American slave holders and called into question all justifications for enslavement. Focusing on the African also circumvented potentially dangerous indictments of slave holders in general. Colonial writers did not wish to alienate a significant portion of their audience by attacking the character of all people who owned slaves.

Writers from the mother country were not bound by the same constraints as colonial writers and felt they could reasonably advocate for the abolition of slavery in Great Britain if not throughout her colonies. Their tracts appealed to more selective audiences of lawmakers and men in positions of power, rather than the general public. Since the majority of Britons in the mother country did not own slaves, writers did not have as strong an imperative to direct their arguments to larger audiences. Sermons preached against slavery usually occurred in areas where enslavement might be witnessed, specifically metropolitan areas like London. However, the goal of such sermons attempted to disprove biblical interpretations rather than sound a call to action. Activists demonstrated more concern with formal legislative or legal injunctions against slavery, instead of relying on the compassion of individuals to discontinue the practice. Their tracts set forth logical appeals for "preserving liberty" and the "purity" of the mother country. They problematized slavery as a "colonial disease," contagion from which Great Britain should be preserved. Sharp's language displayed no hesitation in attacking and condemning the character of the colonial slave holder. Instead, his early writing narrowly delineated a core audience of legislators and judges of *England* whom he called upon to effect an end to the institution as exercised in Great Britain.

The 1770s introduced a new purpose and direction for activists who deplored the practice of slavery. Writers in this decade experimented with different rhetorical appeals and slowly began to address wider audiences. Increased dialogue between activists in colony and metropole resulted in a gradual convergence in purpose. In terms of publication and influence, Benezet and Sharp distinguished themselves as the primary antislavery activists in North America and Great Britain. When Benezet opened a dialogue with Sharp in 1772, he introduced the idea of eliminating the

---

[65] Benezet did not gather all his testimonials personally and often relied on previously published tracts to support his own points. However, his work circulated to larger, more diverse audiences and other antislavery writers (for example, William Dillwyn, Thomas Clarkson, and John Wesley) cited and quoted the accounts reproduced in his tracts.

slave trade through legislative means.[66] This suggestion set in motion the discussion amongst antislavery writers regarding the focus and goal of their efforts. American colonial and "British" presses published and distributed tracts that crossed the Atlantic and other geographic boundaries. Before the onset of the American Revolution, Sharp had an active correspondence with several colonial antislavery writers, and he arranged for the publication of their work in Great Britain.[67] While Sharp continued to denounce slavery, he began to introduce critiques of the trade coming from the colonies into his work, which came to influence the work of other writers.[68] His writing also began to acknowledge the interconnectedness of colony and mother country in his warnings of divine retribution. Secular arguments against slavery gradually narrowed to concentrate on the "inhumanity" of the trade.

This interchange between colonial and metropolitan activists helped to produce a greater sense of combined resistance. Critique of the slave trade opened English objectors to the possibility that slavery was more than a colonial contagion. The conversation in the seventies began to reflect the emerging sense of "British identity" and "empire" as descriptions of the trade proliferated. Ships involved in the trade started their journey in "English" ports, specifically Bristol, London, and Liverpool. The sailors involved in capturing and securing Africans came from all over Great Britain, and they suffered numerous fatalities during the perilous journey from Africa to the New World. While the majority of slave holders and slaves may have resided in the colonies, slave trading involved the active participation of the mother country. In a sense, the slave trade evolved as truly a "British" practice that engaged people from all parts of the country and "her Dominions." This understanding precipitated the widening of circumference among all writers in the 1770s and 1780s and a new sense of Britain's association with her colonies. Though many continued to construct an oppositional relationship, the colonies became more visible in public discourse, which contributed to the developing sense of empire.[69]

---

[66] Sharp had made no mention of the slave trade or appealing to Parliament in his prior work. In his first letter to Sharp, Benezet urged him to consider focusing efforts on petitioning Parliament to dismantle the trade, and this letter appears to be the first time Sharp had considered the idea.

[67] In a letter to Benjamin Rush dated 21 February 1774, Sharp explains that he was unable to find a publisher for Rush's *An Address to the Inhabitants of the British Settlements in America, upon slave-keeping* because the "Sale of it would not Defray the expence." He comments that he reprinted Benezet's *Historical Account of Guinea* and he eventually gave away more copies than were sold (Brookes, 446–447).

[68] I do not mean to understate the importance of the London Quakers in spearheading the movement against the slave trade. When colonial correspondence was interrupted by the war, Sharp stayed in contact with London Quakers and worked with them extensively through the 1780s and '90s.

[69] The focus on the trade also led indirectly to a greater awareness of the East Indian "colonies" in the 1790s. The sugar boycotts of that decade advised some consumers to purchase East India sugar because it was grown without the use of slave labor.

The antislavery writing of John Wesley reflected this new synthesis of colonial and metropolitan objections by appealing to both audiences. He wrote copiously on multiple subjects that attempted to reform the less equitable aspects of British society—one of which was slavery. Wesley joined Quaker objectors in attempting to erase the practice of slavery among his congregants.[70] By the late eighteenth century, he had amassed a significant number of members who spanned Great Britain, Ireland, and the American colonies. The geographic diversity of his audience influenced the nature of his writing and he attempted to incorporate the concerns of all his congregants. His most famous tract, *Thoughts Upon Slavery* (1774), combined elements of both Benezet's and Sharp's work to make his case to both colonial and metropolitan audiences. Published first in London and reprinted the same year in Philadelphia, Wesley's tract went into five editions some of which were sold at Methodist "preaching-houses" in London.[71] He opened his comments with a brief synopsis of the origin and temperament of Africans, quoting heavily from Benezet's *Some Historical Account of Guinea*. He addressed proslavery arguments about the legality of slavery, for which he relied on Sharp's analysis of English law. While Wesley critiqued the entire institution of slavery, a considerable portion of his tract discussed the miseries of the slave trade.

Wesley's tract demonstrated the emerging sense of "Britishness" and relied on pathetic appeals to describe the "inhuman" acts of traders and masters. He combined religious and secular perspectives by appealing at once to Christian sentiment and ideas of "Justice and Injustice, Cruelty and Mercy" (30). When he criticized the trade and practices in the colonies, he used inclusive words like "us" and "our" to indicate a measure of shared culpability between slave holders and non-slave holders. In his questioning of the slave trade, Wesley demonstrated an understanding of the interconnectedness of activities taking place under British aegis. He asked, "Who can reconcile this treatment of the negroes, first and last, with either mercy or justice?" (30). His sustained critique of traders and holders offered a systematic refutation of common proslavery arguments of the time. He employed an innovative metaphor in attacking these justifications by slave holders, comparing their behavior to that of wolves. By likening their actions to those of beasts, a comparison that was normally applied to Africans, he effectively turned the table on slavery apologists. Wesley advised, "Be you a man! Not a

---

[70] Wesley founded Methodism as a set of Christian principles that still operated within the Anglican Church. While his actions did not match the radical and often sensationalist tactics of earlier Quakers, he drew his comments against slavery directly from the writings of Anthony Benezet. For a history of Wesley and the founding of the Methodist church, see Bernard Semmel, *The Methodist Revolution* (New York: Basic Books, Inc., 1973).

[71] *Thoughts Upon Slavery* went through three editions in 1774, which were printed in London by R. Hawes and sold in Philadelphia by Joseph Crukshank. H. Reynall printed a supplement to Wesley's tract in 1774. The fourth edition was printed in Dublin (for W. Whitestone) in 1775. The tract was reprinted in London in 1784, and a fifth edition appeared in London in 1792. I quote from the first edition published in London in 1774.

wolf, a devourer of the human species! Be merciful, that you may obtain mercy!" (49). While he directed his warnings towards slave holders, he hoped to incite the reform impulse in all of his followers.

The foundations of antislavery protest shaped by Benezet and Sharp allowed for the expansion of authorship and rhetorical appeals in subsequent decades. Their tracts focused not only on the ills of slavery but on the negative repercussions for the nation as well. The writers who followed took up these claims and began to define in more precise terms the anti-British nature of slavery and the slave trade. In doing so, the language of the debates gradually moved from "English" to "British" attributes. Subsequent publications involved both a refutation of the necessity of slavery and increasingly significant definitions of "national character." The coalescing of purpose that appeared through the writing of the antislavery crusaders depicted the slave trade, in particular, as a *national* problem. Each attack on the slave trade developed the idea of the nation and its place in the international arena, and the beauty of this criticism was that anyone could participate.

Problematizing slavery and the slave trade prepared the way for the expansion of arguments over the late 1770s and '80s. The work of these pioneering activists impressed upon later writers the necessity of building coalitions across regions of Great Britain. Efforts to mobilize public opinion in both urban and rural areas inspired a commensurate broadening of appeal across class, race, and gender lines. Antislavery and anti-slave-trade writers demonstrated shrewdness in capturing public interest that rapidly challenged the proslavery advantage. As the interest in the cause grew, more people sought to join the efforts in proliferating the message. The building of enthusiasm instigated a simultaneous expansion of authorship, appeal, and form of publication. I would argue that the campaign against the slave trade cohered as a *public* enterprise by encouraging the active participation of all members of British society.

Chapter 3
Proliferating Antislavery Arguments and the Creation of an Activist Community, 1772–1789

The works of Benezet and Sharp raised public consciousness about slavery to such a degree that more people felt compelled to write on the issue. The emphasis of the writing continued to focus on problematizing slavery to the general British public. However, the rhetorical strategies and forms of appeal expanded to accommodate different perspectives and to incorporate a diverse array of authors. Twentieth-century critics, like Davis, Midgley, and Turley, fail to appreciate the significant changes in antislavery arguments that occurred in the period directly preceding the formation of the first abolitionist societies. While Robin Blackburn does an admirable job of tracing the development of antislavery writing, he pays little attention to the nuances of argument focusing instead on the larger historical context of the idea.[1] Brown corrects many of these oversights in his study; however, close textual analysis is often secondary to addressing broader trends. This period before the formation of an organized abolitionist society proved to be a time of experimentation in which writers tried out a variety of appeals in the hopes of capturing the sympathies of their audiences. As the sentiment against slavery grew and the arguments began to concentrate on abolition of the slave trade, public sympathies became more responsive to the developing body of literature. Over the course of the 1770s and '80s, resistance to slavery and the slave trade in Great Britain produced a dynamic climate for literary expression. The subject matter allowed authors an astonishing degree of literary license in depicting and dramatizing the effects of slavery. Growing enthusiasm for antislavery sentiment also had a considerable impact on the developing sense of national character and attributes of the Briton. The proliferation of appeals that occurred directly contributed to the emerging discourse of national identity by challenging homogeneous constructions of British society.

Antislavery agitators evolved a strategy of argument over the 1770s and '80s that opened the movement to the larger British society. The initial exchanges between antislavery and proslavery writers occurred primarily among educated "white"

---

[1] See "The Origins of Anti-Slavery" in Robin Blackburn's *The Overthrow of Colonial Slavery* 33–66.

men, usually ministers or prominent members of various Christian communities.[2] The form of their exchanges was most often the sermon or prose essay. Benezet's use of eye-witness accounts offered some variety in print expressions of antislavery ideology, and the testimonial soon became a standard device in antislavery prose essays.[3] Both the form of writing and the nature of the writer limited the methods and tactics used to express antislavery ideas. For example, sermons focused almost exclusively on debunking biblical justifications of slavery in a purely reactive manner to the arguments of proslavery clergy. Esoteric arguments about theology were not proving to be an effective tool for motivating large segments of society to enact "positive" social change. The limited form of appeal addressed similarly limited audiences—limited by region and by interaction. Sermons and prose essays had a restricted circulation whose aim was to raise the consciousness of a circumscribed audience. Writers like Sharp concentrated on circumscribed, urban (specifically London) audiences, while clergy spoke mainly to their congregations. This piecemeal form of appeal could not effectively gather support on a larger scale to push for reform. Activists needed to expand both their audience and their membership for any real change to occur.

As the organized anti-slave-trade movement came into being, both authorship and form of writing became more diverse. The "problem" of slavery and the slave trade began to engage both the greater reading public, as well as individual writers who felt moved to contribute to the debate. Antislavery sentiment gained increasing public approval, and more writers from different backgrounds added their varying perspectives on the depth and virulence of the problem to British society. The differing perceptions of these writers influenced both the shape of national conscience and the shared cultural image of the Briton. As the audience for antislavery sentiment expanded, a rising number of writers contributed variations in ideology, social identity, and rhetorical appeals to building a case against Great Britain's involvement with the institution. For example, more women became involved in the movement and they relied heavily on pathos appeals in their poetic expressions against slavery.[4] The work of these women writers has typically fallen

---

[2] While race theories solidified over the course of the movement, early antislavery writers were very aware of their "race," that is, their "whiteness" and position as Europeans, when constructing their arguments. Arguing on behalf of African slaves, oftentimes in the absence of any sustained contact with those slaves, limited their perspective and claims.

[3] The use of testimonial in Quaker prose has a long history dating back to their own persecution in the seventeenth century. See Clement Hawes' *Mania and Literary Style: The Rhetoric of Enthusiasm from the Ranters to Christopher Smart* (Cambridge: Cambridge University Press, 1996).

[4] I use the term "pathos" in the Aristotelian sense to mean "putting the audience in a certain frame of mind" in order to effect a "stirring of the emotions." However, I also evoke the pathos inherent in Adam Smith's conception of sympathy as the ability to experience another's emotions as an "impartial spectator." Smith's concept of the "impartial spectator" is outlined in *The Theory of Moral Sentiments* (1759).

under the category of sentimental or Romantic writing. Recent work by Deirdre Coleman and Suvir Kaul situate women's abolitionist writing within literary movements, whereas I seek to read their writing as developing in accordance with larger rhetorical trends used to persuade the British public. Brycchan Carey describes the "rhetoric of sensibility" as a "practical mode of expression" (9). I argue that it also proved to be the most efficient mode of expression for widening antislavery appeals and expanding the circumference of the argument. Similarly, the genre of the slave narrative that developed in these decades as former slaves wrote of their experiences in captivity, demonstrated a deft melding of pathos and logos in their rhetorical appeals. The inclusion of these "marked" voices necessitated that writers reconceptualize and adjust, at least temporarily, the characteristics of national identity and the normative image of the Briton.

This chapter analyzes the expansion of antislavery/anti-slave-trade voices to include the seemingly disenfranchised and traces the changes in rhetorical appeal as the British public grew more interested in the cause. Scholars have already established the enormous popularity of women's writing and writing by former slaves during this time and the implications of this writing for public discourse.[5] I am more interested in how writers opened the discourse itself to make space for competing images and new appropriations of the term "Briton." Inclusion of multiple voices clamoring to express antislavery rationale results simultaneously in a reshaping of national identity. Benezet and Sharp helped focus for their audiences the primary and most immediate issues involving the institution of slavery that needed to be addressed. They provided a basic framework for antislavery arguments that relied upon a shared perception of cultural identity, and they opened avenues of publication for other writers to express their sentiments. As the "antislavery spirit" spread through British society, writers began to experiment with expressing activist sentiment through other genres.

Antislavery activists claimed the Somerset Decision as a decisive victory for their cause. By loudly claiming this victory, writers could assert that the love of liberty was the most valuable trait of the Briton, which far outweighed the benefits of a corrupt institution. More writing focused on depicting the atrocities of the middle passage, diversifying the writing across genres. The often dry recounting of first-person experiences with slave trading and slave holding did not fully engage public sympathies. Poetry provided a more effective form to depict both the horrors of slavery and the compassion of the morally upright Briton. The most powerful testimonials of antislavery writing—the slave narrative—also claimed a powerful (albeit transitive) role in defining "Briton." The tone and substance of slave narratives changed between the publication of Gronniosaw's *Narrative* in 1772 and Equiano's *Interesting Narrative* in 1789. These changes reflect the increasingly well-defined image of the British citizen and the attempt

---

[5] See Ferguson's *Subject to Others*, Fryer's *Staying Power*, and Clare Midgley's *Women Against Slavery: The British Campaigns 1780–1870* (London and New York: Routledge, 1992).

by seeming outsiders to enter into the dialogue of national identity. The greater variety of perspectives encompassed by antislavery sentiment allowed normally disenfranchised voices a position from which to speak.

Interpreting Mansfield through the Logos of Liberty

For antislavery activists, Somerset's trial provided a valuable opportunity to develop and sharpen their rationale for a systematic critique of the slave institution. At the time of the trial, no organized movement to end slavery or the slave trade existed. Authors like Benezet and Sharp had just begun to challenge public apathy, but proslavery interests still held sway in Parliament. Though Sharp distributed his antislavery pamphlets outlining the legal reasons for rejecting slavery to members of the Parliament and the judiciary, no broad-scale courting of public opinion had yet been envisioned. Somerset's trial instigated important changes in rhetoric and demonstrated a potential public interest in colonial misdeeds. This case proved pivotal in focusing the previously scattered attention of activists around a finite and achievable goal—establishing that slave holding was illegal under English law. Sharp and his colleagues very shrewdly recognized the potential of this case well before slavery supporters, and they carefully built their arguments around this understanding. They made a case for Somerset believing that the precedent set by Lord Mansfield's decision would prove central to future challenges to African slavery. By "abolishing" slavery in England, or at least claiming to have "abolished" slavery in England, writers felt confident that the decision would gradually spread to the colonies and put a stop to slave holding.[6] While they immediately began suggesting that the decision should extend to the colonies, most writers recognized that immediate and complete emancipation was improbable because proslavery interests were too firmly entrenched in Parliament. Instead, they attempted to initiate a domino effect by questioning the legality of slavery in the empire.

The arguments presented on Somerset's behalf sought to undermine colonial interests by depicting their laws and practices as counter-national. Perhaps the most lasting effect of Mansfield's decision and the subsequent antislavery interpretation was the division created between colony and mother country. Antislavery activists applauded the higher moral caliber of "English civil law" and its condemnation of slavery. A highly significant contention in Somerset's defense stated that the law abhorred slavery and could not support the corrupt institution on British soil. In their triumph, the defense lawyers extrapolated from this contention that colonial law could not legitimately recognize slavery without defying the spirit of English law. Proslavery interests argued in vain that colonial law was based on the laws of the mother country, but they could not defeat the compelling language

---

[6] In actuality, Mansfield's ruling only pertained to the right of the slave holder to remove a slave forcibly from England. Thus, Stewart's right to property in the body of his slave was merely limited and not forfeited.

of antislavery activists. Even when written in dry legalese, arguments in favor of "liberty" trumped those favoring colonial property rights. While I do not suggest that these arguments produced any immediate results in the practice of slavery, they did offer a line of argument that began to capture more public interest. These activists not only denounced colonial laws but viewed them as antithetical to the spirit of the nation. The colonies had taken advantage of the benevolence of the mother country and created a system of oppression that violated the noble character of British liberty.

The rhetoric in defense of Somerset's "liberty" transcended the facts of the case to define the "true" characteristics of the "English."[7] Proslavery interests claimed an inviolable right to property in the body of their slaves and quoted English law in support of that right. Antislavery interests counterposed the fundamentally "British" belief in liberty, which superseded any entitlement to property. Ultimately, the main point under debate revolved around the question of which concept English law valued more highly—liberty or property. Other activists recognized the importance of this distinction and the potential implications of Lord Mansfield's decision. By shifting the argument to a debate over the value of liberty, antislavery writers discovered a potent strategy in appealing to public interest. Before the conclusion of the case, *A Plan for the Abolition of Slavery in the West Indies* (1772) was anonymously published in London.[8] In the preface, the author claimed to have written the plan and initially "thrown aside" the paper but the current case had "revived the memory." He fully appreciated the greater ramifications of the case, stating that "it may be hoped, that the claim of property in the person of our fellow-creatures will, in this island at least, soon receive an effectual check" (ii). In the conclusion of his preface, he affirmed: "Every man is a *liber homo*, without distinction of *persons* or of *colour*" (iv). Those beliefs in the innate liberty of all men would be repeated and grow in strength of conviction over the course of the next two decades.[9]

Antislavery writing in the 1770s underwent significant changes because the judicial system in Great Britain finally appeared to be taking a stance against slavery.

---

[7] Colley, *Britons*, 106–117. Colley located the forging of British identity partially in the conflict between English and Scottish. As the more inclusive term "British" gradually became superimposed over "English," the primary attribute of identity that emerged was a belief in liberty. Antislavery activists utilized this belief both to shape their arguments and advance their depictions of national identity.

[8] Maurice Morgann, *A Plan for the Abolition of Slavery in the West Indies* (London: William Griffin, 1772). For an analysis of Morgann's tract as an early argument for emancipation, see Christopher L. Brown, "Empire Without Slaves: British Concepts of Emancipation in the Age of the American Revolution," in *The William and Mary Quarterly*, 56:2 (April 1999): 273–306. Brown establishes that Morgann was the author of "the first British publication to offer a concrete, if quixotic, emancipation scheme" (276).

[9] Belief in innate liberty does not presuppose equality, a clever distinction exploited by abolitionists who still believed in the innate inferiority of Africans to European society.

Prior to the Somerset decision, biblical arguments and eye-witness testimony were used to impress the inhumane nature of slavery upon the public. Writers needed to establish first that the institution of slavery was fundamentally flawed. Their intent was to call attention to a problem that existed, and the majority of an essay or sermon concentrated on defining the extent of the problem. Authors offered very few concrete proposals to ameliorate the conditions of slaves, and proposals for abolition ranged from gradual to immediate. However, the rhetoric changed noticeably after Sharp's legal victory, which critics of slavery soon utilized to the advantage of their cause. By finding for Somerset, Lord Mansfield supported the belief that English civil law did not condone African slavery and would not condone African slavery without the passage of "*positive* law."[10] Antislavery writers quickly capitalized on the opinion that was the precipitating event for organizing the anti-slave-trade movement. The sensationalist trial appealed to London audiences and encouraged other writers to disseminate their ideas more widely, and the propaganda circulated in the wake of the decision had a powerful impact on mobilizing public opinion and providing a foundation for later arguments concerning national identity.[11]

The shift in rhetoric after Somerset involved two important strategic claims made against slavery that began to transform the relation of antislavery to proslavery. First, activists claimed that Somerset's release from bondage validated the belief that "the air in England was too pure for slaves," a statement that many subsequent publications quoted frequently.[12] The "triumph of liberty" in Great Britain revealed cracks in the colonial edifice and the institution of slavery could no longer claim unequivocal support from the mother country. If slavery could not exist in the mother country, how could it exist on British soil anywhere? Based on their interpretation of this ruling, activists questioned how Britons could endorse a separate set of laws for the colonies, and proslavery interests began to fear that their own laws would soon come under siege. Second, Mansfield's ruling inaugurated an era of change that involved a legal and ideological transfer of support from

---

[10] Stewart's lawyers brought up the practice of villeinage as an appropriate precedent to African slavery, which proved to be a tactical error. Sharp's extensive research on the ancient practice enabled Somerset's lawyers completely to invalidate the use of past custom to justify current practices.

[11] Details about the number of antislavery pamphlets printed and their method of distribution are difficult to know for this early period of mobilization. However, the language of the tracts definitely indicates that the pamphlets were intended for wider circulation. See, for example, my comparison between Sharp's *A Representation of the Injustice* that was directed at lawyers and law-makers to Hargrave's summary of the Somerset trial that was frequently quoted in other publications such as *The Gentleman's Magazine* ("Developing the West Indian Proslavery Position after the Somerset Decision," *Slavery and Abolition* 24.3 [2003]: 40–60).

[12] Sergeant Davy, who attended the trial, uttered these words after Mansfield handed down his decision.

proslavery interests. Once again, this change was neither immediate nor effective at addressing the problem of slavery in the decade of the 1770s. However, the change effected in the reading public's taste for antislavery publications helped generate the momentum for abolitionist societies formed in the late 1780s and '90s. Writers proclaimed that the Somerset decision reversed the previous opinions upholding slaveowners' interests in Great Britain. They also claimed a major victory for the right to liberty over property rights, which established the innate humanity of Africans in the eyes of British law. Though Lord Mansfield affirmed none of these claims, antislavery activists hailed him as a crusader for English liberty—specifically, their version of English liberty.[13]

Interpreting Mansfield's ruling as a reversal of previous rulings enabled antislavery activists to begin aggressively campaigning for change. Publications that immediately followed the decision instructed and informed the public about the ramifications of this legal decision, including how to effect change in the institution of slavery. Within months of the court's decision, Francis Hargrave, one of the counsel for Somerset, published an edited account titled "An Argument in the Case of James Sommersett a Negro" (1772) (see Figure 3.1). Hargrave's tract served two purposes: first, to educate the public regarding the national importance of the case, and second, to provide other lawyers with a primer for defending similar cases that could arise in the future. His commentary condensed and refined Sharp's arguments from *A Representation of the Injustice and Dangerous Tendency of Tolerating Slavery* (1769) and Somerset's defense during the trial. Hargrave stressed that "The questions, arising on this case, do not merely concern the unfortunate person, who is the subject of it .... They are highly interesting to the whole community, and cannot be decided, without having the most general and important consequences" (11). He made the repercussions of this case more salient to the public by cautioning that if Mr. Stewart's right of property over Somerset prevailed then "domestick slavery, with it's [sic] horrid train of evils, may be lawfully imported into this country, at the discretion of every individual foreign and native" (11). Hargrave both expanded the "community" to whom antislavery was an issue and attempted to make the issue more applicable to the average person.

Hargrave's comments clearly established a division between colony and homeland, drawing his rhetorical circumference tightly to exclude colonial audiences. Early antislavery writers, including Sharp, distanced themselves from

---

[13] In 1786, Lord Mansfield published a statement denying that his ruling was intended to eliminate slavery in Great Britain. His comments were quoted extensively in proslavery texts, but he could not counter the abolitionist interpretation of his legal decision. See *A Letter to Philo Africanus upon Slavery in answer to his of the 22nd November, In the General Evening Post; together with the Opinions of Sir John Strange, and other eminent lawyers upon this subject, with the Sentence of Lord Mansfield, in the case of Somerset and Knowles, 1772, with his Lordship's explanation of that opinion in 1786*, signed by "Candidus" (London: Printed for W. Brown, 1788).

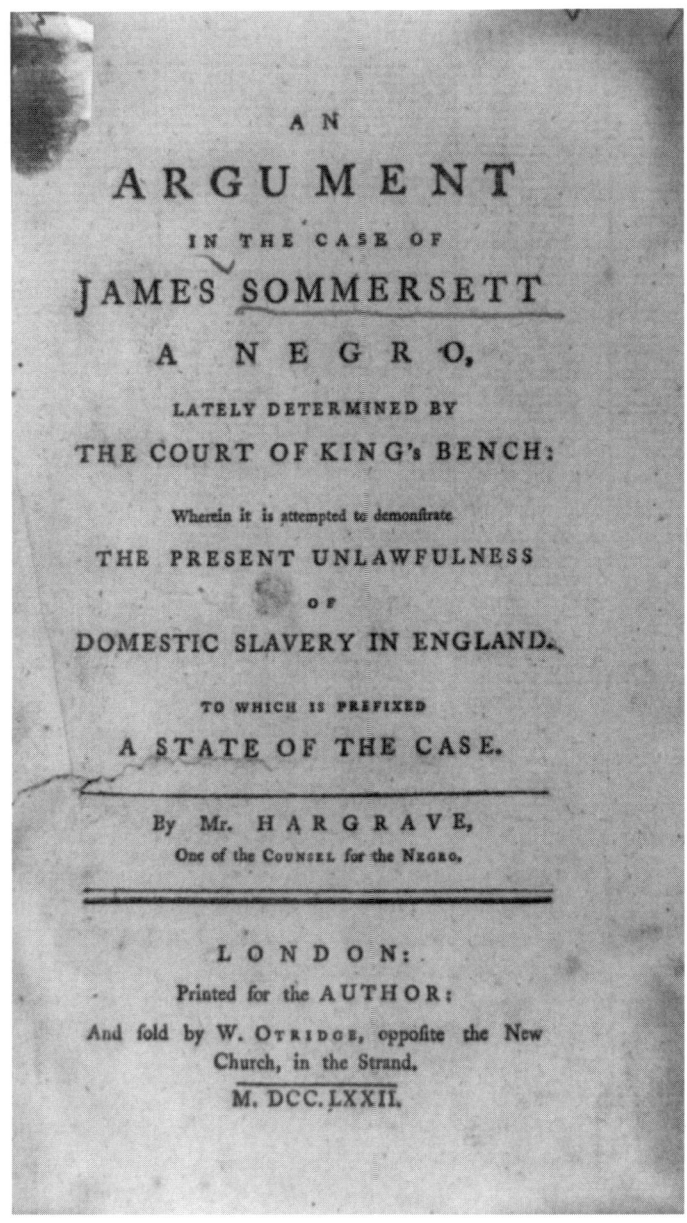

Fig. 3.1 Francis Hargrave, title page, *An Argument in the case of James Sommersett a Negro, lately determined by the court of King's Bench.* London: Printed for the author, 1772. Courtesy of the Library of Congress, LC–USZ62–90721.

the colonies in a manner that diminished the importance of the "empire." Of course, maintaining "empire" was a strong component of the proslavery argument. By treating the colonies as corrupted satellites, these authors did not initially look beyond the mother country in "solving" the "problem" of slavery. In that regard, early writers imposed artificial limits on their prose to appeal to a wholly "English" audience. Significant changes in the nature of the debate would later necessitate a reconfiguration of Great Britain and her relationship to her colonies. Hargrave also set Great Britain apart from the corruption infesting other parts of the world (for example, Spain, Turkey, the east and west coasts of Africa) but warned that this separation was under threat— "this country, so famous for public liberty, will become the chief seat of private tyranny" (8). He also considered the legality of Stewart's claim against the precedents set by English civil law. Though his study was not as exhaustive as Sharp's tracts, Hargrave reinforced Sharp's contentions about the superiority of English laws in protecting individual liberty.[14]

Lord Mansfield's ruling raised high hopes in antislavery activists in Great Britain and the American colonies who believed that the institution of slavery would come to a natural end. Antislavery activists in the colonies hoped that English precedent would extend to the colonies and Great Britain would enforce the Somerset/antislavery writer's vision of the law. Colonial writers contended that relief from the iniquities of slave-trading and slave-keeping would soon be at hand. In *An Address to the Inhabitants of the British Settlements in America upon Slave-Keeping* (1773), Benjamin Rush urged colonial readers to consider the judgment in favor of Somerset as a triumph of right over wrong.[15] First published in Philadelphia, the essay reflected both the decisions of the metropole and the concerns of the colonies. By interpreting Mansfield's ruling as valuing liberty over property, activists opened avenues of protest that questioned the legality, validity, and necessity of slavery as a colonial institution. Though complete abolition was Rush's eventual hope, he could more immediately advocate the dismantling of the slave trade. Rush urged his readers to "unite in petitioning the king and parliament to dissolve the African company" (21). He characterized these traders as an "incorporated band of robbers" and encouraged his readers "to expect

---

[14] Hargrave asserted that "the law of England never recognized any species of domestic slavery, except the *antient* one of *villenage* [sic] now expired, and has sufficiently provided against the introduction of a *new* slavery under the name of *villenage* [sic] or any other denomination whatever" (25). His arguments against villeinage closely follow Sharp's tract and demonstrate the powerful influence of Sharp on his work.

[15] This work was attributed to Rush in the *Dictionary of American Biography*, though his name does not appear on the title page. He originally published the pamphlet in Philadelphia in 1773, which was reprinted the same year in Boston and New York, and Connecticut in 1775. A pamphlet rebuttal entitled, *Slavery not forbidden by Scripture; or, A defence of the West-India planters* by a "West Indian"—Richard Nisbet—appeared soon after the original publication in 1773, and Rush printed a second edition of his pamphlet in the same year with a response to Nisbet and identifying himself as "a Pennsylvanian."

relief from this application" when "the Clamors of the whole nation are rallied against them" (21). Rush's use of the term "nation" had deeper meaning given the climate of discontent in the American colonies. He seemed caught between conflicting impulses to honor the culture in his land while capitalizing on the apparently progressive attitude of Great Britain. His tract included a call to action addressed to "Ye men of SENSE and VIRTUE—Ye ADVOCATES for American Liberty, rouse up and espouse the cause of Humanity and general Liberty" (28). Rush was among a growing list of American antislavery activists who noted the hypocrisy of revolutionary ideals.

The relationship between Britain and her colonies grew increasingly complex over this time, and antislavery publication reflected this complexity in significant and particular ways. With the perceived success of the Somerset decision, antislavery publications in the 1770s offered strategies for gradually freeing slaves and reintegrating them into the workforce on colonial lands. The plans for emancipation varied in the level of sympathy expressed for slave-holders, particularly with respect to the amount of compensation, if any, they should receive. However, the nature and tone of these publications evinced the growing schism between Great Britain, her West Indian colonies, and her American colonies. While serious antislavery efforts originated in the American colonies, revolutionary fervor trumped the cause and effectively pushed colonial antislavery protest into the background for decades. A polarization occurred between Britain and the West Indies in terms of denouncing or supporting slavery. The British antislavery movement appeared to take place exclusively in the metropole, while the proslavery response increasingly began to originate entirely from the West Indies. These colonists, unlike the "Americans," became increasingly isolated from metropolitan audiences as their self-interest in the institution of slavery revealed itself with mounting clarity. When the public began to participate more actively in the issue, proslavery writers found their position significantly weakened. Indeed, the increasing severity of invective against the trade became interchangeable with the colonies themselves. John Wesley's postscript to *A Serious Address to the People of England with regard to the State of the Nation* (1778)[16] denounced the trade and the West Indian colonies in powerful language and tied their destruction to the betterment of the nation. "The total, final destruction of this horrid Trade, would rejoice every Lover of Mankind: Yea, tho' all our Sugar-Islands (so the inhabitants escaped) were swallowed up in the depth of the sea" (28). Clearly, the West Indies had become an ideal site on which to center critiques of slavery and the slave trade.

Great Britain's increasingly untenable relationship with her North American colonies also contributed to the vilification of the West Indies. Antislavery and anti-slave-trade protests in North America had more support, primarily because not all of the colonies were based on slave economies. Also, the southern American

---

[16] Printed by R. Hawes and sold at the Foundery in Moorfields and at the Rev. Mr. Wesley's preaching houses in town and country, 1778.

colonies did not require the same number of fresh slaves since the slave population had been successfully reproducing itself for decades.[17] While an active American slave trade continued into the middle of the nineteenth century, their reliance on imported labor did not begin to match West Indian needs.[18] Island plantations required a larger numbers of slaves and were heavily reliant upon the trade to replenish their labor force. American colonial activists could advocate abolishing the trade as an initial step in dismantling the institution of slavery partially because the southern plantations were more self-reliant. Their rhetoric helped characterize West Indian slavery as crueler and more contradictory to the English nation's love of liberty. A second major factor leading to the polarization between Great Britain and the West Indies was the socio-political changes occurring in the American colonies that culminated in the American Revolution (1776–1783). The growing desire to create a separate nation, independent of the metropole, had larger repercussions on the discourse of liberty underlying the antislavery arguments. Samuel Johnson's *Taxation No Tyranny* (1775) identified the "the loudest yelps for liberty" as coming from "the drivers of negroes."[19] American antislavery activists repeatedly pointed to the hypocrisy of the revolutionary cries for liberty from citizens who profited from the labor of slaves, but they were caught up in multiple struggles that appropriated the concept of liberty to better the lives of specific groups of citizens. West Indian colonists chose to remain a part of the empire and viewed the American cause as treasonous. In England, many writers felt that the American cause strongly threatened the notion of a superior English/British sense of liberty, and when the revolution proved successful, they sought to assert their superiority by focusing on another region of the empire.

A critical shift occurred in antislavery rhetoric between the American colonies and Great Britain from the 1770s to the 1780s. The impetus for this shift came from a confluence of factors that involved changing identifications of liberty. Writers in Great Britain defined the love of liberty as a singularly English concept that the colonies had perverted by practicing slavery. Colonial antislavery writers appropriated this belief in agitating for the abolition of the slave trade and eventual dismantling of the institution. However, the love of liberty also became the rallying cry of revolutionaries who sought to separate from the mother country. They asserted that *American* liberty would triumph against the oppressive practices of

---

[17] The most thorough and detailed study of the transatlantic trade is Roger Anstey's *The Atlantic Slave Trade and British Abolition, 1760–1810* (Atlantic Highlands, NJ: Humanities Press, 1975).

[18] Though the United States outlawed the slave trade the year after Great Britain, slave ports in major cities, such as New York, continued to operate well into the 1850s. In fact, Captain Nathaniel Gordon has the dubious honor of being the only American tried and executed for his participation in the slave trade after its abolition. See James Rawley's *London, Metropolis of the Slave Trade*.

[19] Samuel Johnson, Taxation no tyranny: an answer to the resolutions and address of the American Congress (London: Printed for T. Cadell, 1775) 89.

the corrupt mother country. The movement for revolutionary reform excluded slaves from the concept of liberty, an openly hypocritical move that did not go unnoticed either in the colonies or in Great Britain. Colonists in the north benefited from southern plantation slavery, and northern slave holders had little interest in losing their property. Northern revolutionaries also could not jeopardize their relationship with Southern colonists by openly supporting antislavery petitions. Colonial antislavery reformers did not wish to separate from Great Britain and believed that parliamentary action would provide the only effective means of abolishing first the slave trade and next slavery altogether. Quakers continued to wage a pamphlet war against slave-trading without the widespread popular support that would come to characterize efforts in Great Britain. Sharp and his colleagues did not evince an awareness of colonial turmoil in their 1776–1779 antislavery publications, though Sharp was in regular correspondence with Benezet. By the time the American war registered with activists in Great Britain, they had also begun to realize that Lord Mansfield's decision was not sufficient to limit or eliminate slavery.

This historical conjunction of events affected both the tone and content of antislavery rhetoric in the 1780s, which culminated in the establishment of the London Abolitionist Society in 1787. The success of the American colonies in separating from Britain and forming an independent nation called into question the superiority of English liberty and citizenship. How could the country continue to profess higher standards when a group of its own subjects using cries of liberty had defeated British troops in battle? The loss of the American colonies proved a national embarrassment that antislavery rhetoric could partially ameliorate by rallying the public around the cause of abolition. Writers in Great Britain pointed to the duplicity of the Americans who spoke of liberty and practiced slavery. In essence, the slave trade became the issue through which British writers could reclaim the concept of liberty from the American revolutionaries.[20] Antislavery publication in Great Britain experienced a strong resurgence after 1782, and more writers from diverse backgrounds began to take part in the debate. The conversation on slavery had definitely shifted from the former American colonies to Great Britain, but not without specific changes. In the 1780s, British antislavery efforts began to coalesce into a unified movement with a clear goal—abolition of the slave trade. As argued in Chapter 2, British writers' focused on the slave trade because of a direct exchange of ideas from Quaker antislavery activists in Pennsylvania to activists in London, as evidenced in the correspondence between Benezet and Sharp. With the loss of the American colonies, writers also narrowed the location of their critique to the West Indies. Slave trading became synonymous with the West Indian islands and the debates initiated a critical transformation in language.

---

[20] Though the government of the United States abolished the slave trade the year after Britain, metropolitan writers felt they had rescued the concept of liberty from the inherently corrupt Americans. This feeling would intensify during the second abolitionist campaign in the 1820s and '30s.

One example of the growing popular success of antislavery ideas appeared in the recasting of the terms "planter" and "merchant" as deceptive euphemisms for "slave holder" and "slave trader." Authors used these descriptions as pejorative indicators of the corrupt nature of men who engaged in the acts of owning and trading in slaves. These terms became the clearest marker of the politics of any given publication. Antislavery and abolitionist writers indicted both masters and traders in their pamphlets, reproducing in vivid detail the vice inherent in each occupation.[21]

With the narrowing of their critique to the transatlantic slave trade, British anti-slave-trade writers redefined the elements of the Burkean dramatic pentad in the process of reclaiming the concept of liberty. Manipulating each element—act, scene, agent, agency, and purpose—allowed writers to develop new rhetorical strategies that had enormous public appeal. Descriptions of act and scene began to concentrate on the treacherous methods of acquiring slaves and the horrors of the middle passage. Defining the act narrowly as the trade allowed writers to incorporate multiple scenes that established the global nature of the problem. As the scene shifted from West Africa to the slave ship to the West Indies, British audiences gained a new understanding of the scope of the act. Proslavery writers justified trading as vital to the maintenance of national prosperity, so anti-slave-trade writers diminished the purpose of the act (that is, slave trading) by depicting both agent and agency as morally flawed. The proposed solution of abolition would allow for the replacement of the "fallen" agent with a "redeemed" agent. In other words, the sinful act (slave trading) perpetrated by the corrupt slave trader could be transformed into a redemptive act (abolition) by the moral Briton. The rising belief in a national conscience became a crucial mitigating factor for the evolving rhetorical strategies employed by anti-slave-trade activists.

By depicting their agency and shared humanity, writers introduced a new agent into the debate of the 1780s—the African. Pamphlets included details on how valiantly Africans fought against being enslaved. The most notable of these publications was Thomas Clarkson's *An Essay on the Slavery and Commerce of the Human Species* (1786).[22] He scathingly characterized slave merchants as "*receivers*" and dramatized the process of selling human beings. Other writings depicted Africans as "fathers," "brothers," "mothers," and "daughters," using these titles to illustrate how they existed in complex social networks before being "kidnapped" into slavery. Authors combated the simplistic and often animalistic descriptions published by proslavery writers of this supposedly savage sub-species.

---

[21] I separate the term "antislavery" from "abolitionist" in order to make a historical distinction. Though antislavery writers advocated some form of abolition prior to 1787, the London Abolitionist Society formed for the express purpose of abolishing the slave trade. Thus, I use the term "abolitionist" to describe writers who published after the formation of the society.

[22] Published in London by the Quaker abolitionist, James Phillips; published in Dublin by P. Byrne and W. Porter; revised and enlarged 2nd ed. published 1788.

The "nobility" and "eloquence" of Africans came to replace "bestial" and "savage" as descriptors, which were often used by West Indian supporters. Enslavement of "our Fellow-Creatures" left a "stain" on "National character." While antislavery and abolitionist writers varied widely in their opinions of African capabilities, they were all willing to acknowledge a basic humanity.[23] This acknowledgement definitively expanded the argument for liberty.

An effective strategy for indicting the actions of slave traders focused attention on the natural liberty of Africans. Previous appeals made by colonial and metropolitan writers portrayed slave holding and slave trading as antithetical to the English character. How could lovers of liberty limit the rights of another group of people? This "brave and most generous" people could not tolerate, let alone endorse, an institution that was no longer sanctioned by English law. When this strategy became the calling card of revolution, British writers began subtly to transfer their emphasis to the innate liberty of African people. By what right did British traders purchase the liberty of inherently free people when that liberty was never voluntarily surrendered? Clarkson's *Essay* depicted "an imaginary scene" in which an "African," demonstrating intelligence and clarity, bitterly commented upon the "*liberty*" of his "fellow-creatures." James Ramsay's *Essay on the Treatment and Conversion of African Slaves in the British Sugar Colonies* (1784) directly addressed this point. "Had nature intended negroes for slavery, she would have endowed them with many qualities which they now want. Their food would have needed no preparation, their bodies no covering; they would have been born without any sentiment for liberty" (199).[24] In other words, cognizance of liberty separates man (in this case, African) from beast.

James Ramsay's tract sparked a firestorm of controversy with proslavery writers and helped to initiate a new era of pamphlet writing. The first rebuttal to his contentions appeared only months afterward and at least four more responses appeared within two years. His *Essay* was actually quite conservative in its proposals when compared with later pamphlets. He advocated that plantation owners in the West Indies had a responsibility to the spiritual and cultural education of their slaves. Unlike other activists, Ramsay had personal experience with the trade and slave holding. He owned slaves for a period of time, and he supported his assertions with examples from his own life. Though the bulk of his

---

[23] I acknowledge that "white" writers appropriated the African "voice" to achieve their ends; however, this appropriation did instigate a systematic challenge to proslavery assumptions about African abilities (or lack thereof). I would further argue that the work of these writers created a space for "black" writers by attracting an interested audience.

[24] James Ramsay, *An Essay on the Treatment and Conversion of African Slaves in the British Sugar Colonies* (London: Printed and sold by James Phillips, 1784; Dublin, Printed for T. Walker, C. Jenkin, R. Marchbank, L. White, R. Burton, P. Byrne, 1784). Ramsay believed that the African slaves in the colonies could benefit from Christianization, if properly taught, and placed them on par with Europeans in terms of innate humanity, but not in terms of civilization.

argument concentrated on the capability and desirability of educating slaves, he castigated the transatlantic slave trade and even accused John Hawkins, the first English trader, of initiating it. The greater anathema, in Ramsay's opinion, was that "a nation most highly favoured of liberty, is viewed as taking the lead in this odious traffic" (29). The recent *Zong* incident also contributed to the strength of Ramsay's criticism.[25]

This later well-publicized case involving the insurers and owners of the slave ship *Zong* hinged on a critical distinction between humanity and property. This distinction became the crux of the proslavery argument in the 1770s and 1780s and was the basis of Stewart's claim on Somerset. Though Mansfield purportedly denied the claim to property in 1772, he had a much different opinion in 1783. The facts of the *Zong* case revealed that proslavery interests were still relatively secure in the early 1780s. While on a slaving voyage to Jamaica in 1781, Captain Collingwood of the *Zong* made the decision to throw overboard and drown 132 slaves.[26] His excuse for the atrocity was that the slaves were dying slowly on board the ship and the ship's supply of water was dwindling. Collingwood murdered these people ostensibly to protect the resources of the healthy and relieve the suffering of the sick. Upon his return to England in 1783, the ship owners filed a claim with the insurers for the value of the drowned "merchandise," but the insurers refused to pay so the case went to trial. The jury initially supported the ship owners' claims and when the insurers continued to refuse to pay, the case came before Lord Mansfield. Lawyers stressed that this case was about property, "*chattels or goods*," and the primary question was not one of humanity but of "necessity." The "necessity" of destroying property mid-voyage created a viable insurance claim. While the final outcome of the case, if any, was never publicized, the effect on antislavery mobilization was immediate.

When the details of the incident became known to the public, antislavery activists had a highly visible and incredibly powerful tool to influence public opinion of the slave trade. On 18 March 1783, an eyewitness account of the first trial appeared in *The Morning Chronicle and London Advertiser*. The writer characterized the behavior of the sailors as "flagrant acts of villainy and impunity" and cautioned that "humanity be not wounded" by these perceived "English barbarians."[27] Upon reading this account, Olaudah Equiano approached

---

[25] The awareness of the *Zong* incident created a powerful and growing feeling of discontent among the antislavery activists. Captain Collingwood's inhumane behavior horrified many readers and directly contributed to the support of anti-slave-trade arguments. For a detailed account of the incident, see F. O. Shyllon, *Black Slaves in Britain* (London: Oxford University Press, 1974) and James Walvin's *Black Ivory*.

[26] Reports of the number of slaves thrown overboard vary in newspaper accounts of the incident, often claiming as many as 150 casualties. Historians, like Davis and Walvin, have settled on 132 as the most accurate count of the atrocity.

[27] A similar trial in 1792 also incited public disgust at the atrocities committed aboard slave ships. Captain John Kimber was accused of murdering a fifteen-year-old slave girl

Granville Sharp with the information, and Sharp immediately began organizing a campaign to demand that the sailors be held responsible for their actions.[28] Some present-day historians have noted that the *Zong* incident did not have much of an impact at the time. Linda Colley states that the case "passed almost without notice" and Seymour Drescher asserts that the case became important "only in retrospect, *after* the emergence of popular abolitionism."[29] Both analyses rely on the legal implications of the case, of which there were admittedly none. However, other historians have commented on the profound impact this case had on later abolitionist work. Though the sailors were never tried for murder, antislavery writers began to push the idea of abolishing the slave trade. Ramsay published *An Inquiry into the Effects of Putting a Stop to the African Slave Trade, and of Granting LIBERTY to the SLAVES in the BRITISH SUGAR COLONIES* (1784) in London, and four other antislavery publications appeared within the year, a veritable explosion of tracts since 1776. Each tract stressed the innate humanity of African people and more progressive writers referred to the victims of the middle passage as "brethren." These tracts addressed metropolitan audiences rather than lawmakers in attempt to build a sense of public outrage.

Another trend in argument by Anglican and Dissenting clergy, who had long been active in the antislavery movement, recast the concept of liberty as a particularly Christian virtue. Sermons against slavery and the slave trade characterized both acts as more heinous when practiced by Christians.[30] "The Christian religion was designed to communicate liberty, peace, and happiness, throughout all ranks, orders, and degrees of men."[31] This view of Christianity appealed to readers who appreciated both the high moral tone and the sense of superior solidarity. Most antislavery sermons did not approach the denunciation of slavery from an exclusively sectarian, albeit predominantly Protestant, point

---

during the middle passage by hanging her upside down on deck and whipping her to death. Though Kimber was acquitted, his actions inspired Isaac Cruikshank's famous cartoon, "The Abolition of the Slave Trade" (see Figure 5.2).

[28] Granville Sharp attempted to convince the court to try the sailors for murder (the captain of the ship had died soon after his return), but there is no known record of what became of the case.

[29] Colley 352, and Drescher, *Capitalism and Antislavery: British Mobilization in Comparative Perspective* (New York: Oxford University Press, 1987) 60.

[30] The antislavery movement in Britain has traditionally focused on the work of Christian denominations like the Quakers and the Methodists. However, Anglican clergy played an important role in combating proslavery religious justifications for slavery and have long been ignored by scholars for their contributions to antislavery. For an excellent discussion of this oversight and its impact on slavery studies in Great Britain, see Nicholas Hudson, "'Britons Never Will Be Slaves': National Myth, Conservatism, and the Beginnings of British Antislavery," *Eighteenth-Century Studies*, 34.4 (2001): 559–576.

[31] Thomas Bradshaw, *The Slave Trade inconsistent with Reason and Religion*. A sermon preached in the parish-church of Tottenham Middle-Sex on Sunday, March 16, 1788 (London: Printed and Sold by W. Richardson, 1788) 6.

of view. Regardless of denomination, the (Protestant) Christian Briton could take comfort in having a clearer understanding of the value of liberty than other religions, specifically Islam and Catholicism. This argument made religious justifications of slavery particularly egregious. Proslavery sermons began to incite regular controversy and several published rebuttals. For example, the Reverend Harris's *Scriptural Researches on the Licitness of the Slave Trade, shewing its conformity with the principles of natural and revealed religion, delineated in the sacred writings of the Word of God* (1788) garnered five published responses in the same year. Sermons offering Biblical justifications could not compete with the "high moral" claims of antislavery ministers. The outpouring of compassion by these ministers made clerical support of the institution seem more sinister and a gross misinterpretation of the Bible. These clergy exposed a disjunction between agent and act in which the act proved antithetical to the nature of the agent. The proof of this incompatibility between agent and act involved first establishing what the predominant nature of the Christian was, specifically a belief in personal liberty. By tying Christianity to the concept of liberty, writers not only reinvigorated the use of religion in the debate but tied "Christian" (as opposed to "Anglican") firmly to national characteristics as well.

Antislavery ministers, regardless of denomination, conducted a highly complex rhetorical campaign that operated on two levels. First, they sought to reclaim the character of the Christian in order to invalidate particular, state-sponsored behaviors, that is, the slave trade. Second, they sought to create a national conscience, strongly dependent upon their definition of Christian morality, to which the state was accountable. "True" Christians could not countenance slavery, and as Great Britain was a Christian nation, Britons could not countenance slavery either. "The very idea of trading the persons of men should kindle detestations in the breasts of MEN—especially of BRITONS—and above all of CHRISTIANS."[32] In this sermon, the Reverend James Dore stressed humanity, nationality, and spirituality in order of increasing importance. His comment exemplified the complex construction of national identity emerging from the rhetoric of this debate. Another sermon, delivered by Thomas Burgess, expressed outrage at the support given to the trade by writers in a "free Christian country!" that was proud of "possessing more genuine liberty than any other country ever enjoyed."[33] Antislavery clergy defined liberty as a specifically Christian virtue and traced a wider circumference by stressing the necessity of Christian conversion for the unenlightened. These clergy revitalized older arguments for conversion and definitively defeated their

---

[32] James Dore, *A Sermon on the African Slave Trade, preached at Maze-Pond, Southwark, Lord's day afternoon, November 30, 1788* (Published at request. London: Printed by R. Wayland and Sold by J. Buckland, C. Dilly, M. Curney, and W. Button, 1789) 12.

[33] Thomas Burgess, *Considerations on the Abolition of Slavery and the Slave Trade upon grounds of Natural, Religious, and Political duty* (Oxford: Sold by D. Princes & J. Cooke; J. & J. Fletcher; and by Elmsly, White, Payne, Cadell. London, 1789) 81–82.

proslavery opposition. By associating a particular religious conviction with the character of the Briton, Anglican and dissenting ministers effectively silenced religious proslavery arguments. They also contributed to the growing belief in British superiority over other European nations with regard to national morality.

Over the course of the 1780s, the value of liberty developed as the foremost characteristic of the humane, moral, and Christian Briton. The entire institution of slavery threatened this conviction and degraded the virtue of Great Britain in the eyes of the civilized world. To restore the balance, British legislators needed to take steps to abolish the dreadful institution, beginning with the trade. As the activism of the decade began to narrow towards a specific goal, organizers agreed that focusing on the slave trade would be the logical first step towards eventually abolishing the institution of slavery. Anti-slave-trade writers believed that no virtuous man could participate in the trade, and no man "born free in nature" could be subjugated by it. The Quakers had already begun to agitate for the abolition of the slave trade, and they sought to effect change through legislative channels. Guided by this example in 1787, Granville Sharp, Thomas Clarkson, and others formed the Society for Effecting the Abolition of the Slave Trade.[34] Using the money from their growing list of subscribers, they financed the publication and dissemination of tens of thousands of pamphlets to restore the true meaning of liberty to Great Britain.[35] Their pamphlet campaign was so effective, one disgruntled proslavery advocate commented that the "flood" of "free publication" had "tainted" the minds of the public.

Pathos Appeal and the Politics of Oppression

A highly effective strategy for gaining public sympathy for the antislavery cause involved the use of pathos appeals. Benezet incorporated first-person accounts by sailors, slave ship physicians, and West Indian merchants in his writings.[36]

---

[34] Wylie Sypher, *Guinea's Captive Kings: British Anti-Slavery Literature of the XVIIIth Century* (New York: Octagon Books, 1969). Sypher identifies the original founders as Sharp, Clarkson, Philip Sansom, John Barton, James Philips, William Dillwyn, Samuel Hoare, George Harrison, Joseph Woods, Richard Phillips, Joseph Hooper, John Lloyd, and Josiah Wedgewood. These men proliferated antislavery tracts that varied in form over the next four years and made significant contributions to the cause (19).

[35] Minutes of the committee meeting published in London on 12 August 1788 (not all minutes were available) include a detailed accounting of the amount collected from subscriptions and their allocations. They published 17 different tracts, a total of 79,734 copies, for £1,106 19d. 9s. The largest print runs of anti-slave-trade tracts were 11,500 copies of the Account of the Debates in Parliament, 14,000 copies of the Dean of Middleham's Letter, and 6,025 copies of Alexander Falconbridge's *Account of the Slave Trade on the Coast of Africa* (London, 1788).

[36] Benezet did selectively edit these testimonials in order to express more of an antislavery sentiment than the original authors may have intended. For a discussion

In addition to establishing his own credibility as an antislavery advocate, the testimonials also served to illustrate the inhumane practices of traders, planters, and overseers. Other prominent antislavery writers, like John Wesley, reproduced Benezet's accounts in their own tracts because they recognized the persuasive strength of personal recounting. The majority of people involved in the institution of slavery either supported the practice or were reluctant to speak against it. Antislavery advocates did not have an inexhaustible supply of tales to reproduce, but, by fictionalizing stories of oppression, they could produce sensationalized images to evoke public sympathy.

The use of emotional appeals in antislavery writing expanded the forms of protest to include fiction, poetry, and artwork, and each new medium offered the opportunity to present arguments more creatively to wider audiences. I deliberately avoid using the terms "sensibility" or "sentimental" because I am less concerned with the "literariness" of the appeals than I am with their role in cultural construction. The more prosaic and didactic essays seemed directed at a more formal audiences of judges, lawmakers, parliamentarians. For example, Clarkson's *An Essay on the Impolicy of the African Slave Trade* (1788) presented logical arguments that touched on the suffering inflicted by the slave trade without overtly appealing to sentiment. He and other essayists included numbers and percentages of casualties, both European and African, to persuade their audience of legislators of the need for abolition. However, logic did little to evoke the sympathies of the general reading public. A poem like Thomas Day and John Bicknell's *The Dying Negro* (1773) illustrated individual suffering and personalized the argument for readers to understand the effects of enslavement on specific people.[37] In this poem, which was supposedly based on a true story, a negro man chooses death over re-enslavement by his former master and writes to his white fiancée of his decision. "Fool that I was! enur'd so long to pain, / To trust to hope, or dream of joy again." The hopelessness of his situation simultaneously humanizes the slave and illustrates the inhumanity of bondage. Another critical point was the authors' choice to illustrate a "factual event" occurring between a black man and white woman. Unions between white females and black males were anathema to the West Indian colonists who enacted laws to prevent such an occurrence.[38]

---

of Benezet's use of travel narratives, see Srividhya Swaminathan, "'That Creature of Propaganda': Anthony Benezet's Depictions of African Oppression," *British Journal of Eighteenth Century Studies*, 29 (2006): 115–130.

[37] This poem, while admittedly problematic, represents one of the first in a long tradition of abolitionist verse to use the "rhetoric of sensibility." See Carey's *British Abolitionism and the Rhetoric of Sensibility* for a complete analysis of *The Dying Negro*. The poem was printed in three editions in 1773, 1774, and 1775; and reprinted separately in 1787, 1793, and as late as 1814. I deal with the first edition of the poem as appended to Sharp's *A Representation of the Injustice*.

[38] The most virulent condemnation of these unions came from Edward Long, who charged white women in the West Indies to keep white men from straying to black women.

The language of the poetry dramatized the atrocity of slave-holding in manner that more realistic accounts could not. As Hannah More put it, "Rhetoric or verse may point the feeling line, / They do not whet sensation, but define."[39] Defining sensation is clearly a more powerful position both from a persuasive and an argumentative standpoint.

The enlargement of antislavery appeals coincided very fortuitously with major developments in literary trends of the late eighteenth century, specifically the expansion of the novel. The emergence of the sentimental novel, as Markman Ellis's study shows, attracted an "unprecedented audience" that crossed gender and class boundaries.[40] This fiction developed with an eye towards reform, without focusing on any single issue. The link between sentiment and slavery is well established in numerous works of secondary criticism, and critics focus their studies on tracing influences. Some privilege the issue of slavery as directly contributing to the development of the sentimental novel, while others argue the opposite. Also well studied is the level of insincere and contrived sentiment in depictions of slavery. Brycchan Carey comments that "works of sentimental fiction containing an antislavery message tended to crowd the antislavery sentiment into a few pages interpolated into the main narrative" (64). How this linkage between sentiment and slavery allowed for a broadening of antislavery appeals has not been discussed. The sentimental novel offered rich literary territory for the (re)construction of the images of slavery to gain public sympathy for an "oppressed" people.

One of the most commented upon examples of this expression of sentiment by an "oppressed" African occurs in a short passage of Laurence Sterne's *Tristram Shandy* (1760–67). In this scene, a young negro girl uses feathers tied to a cane as a fan to flap away the flies rather than killing them. Uncle Toby remarks, "She had suffered persecution, Trim, and had learnt mercy." Presumably, the "mercy" of the girl has no apparent parallel in the "mercy" of the slaver. During his correspondence with Ignatius Sancho, Sterne made his antislavery sentiments quite plain by stating, "I never look *Westward* (when I am in a pensive mood at least) but I think of the burdens which our Brothers and Sisters are *there* carrying—& could I ease their shoulders from one ounce of 'em, I declare I would set out this hour upon a pilgrimage to Mecca for their sakes."[41] A number of observations can be made

---

See Roxann Wheeler's *The Complexion of Race* (Philadelphia: University of Pennsylvania Press, 2000).

[39] Hannah More, *Slavery, A Poem* (London: Printed for T. Cadell, 1788). The London Abolitionist Society commissioned More to write this poem in 1788 as the Parliamentary hearings to abolish the slave trade were in full swing.

[40] For a discussion of the role of the sentimental novel in popular politics of eighteenth-century Britain, see Markman Ellis, *The Politics of Sensibility*.

[41] In his first letter to Sancho (24 July 1766), *The Letters of Laurence Sterne*, ed. Lewis Perry Curtis (Oxford: Clarendon Press, 1935) 285–286. For a discussion of the relationship between Sterne, Sancho, and the issue of slavery, see Ellis's "'The house of bondage': sentimentalism and the problem of slavery" in *The Politics of Sensibility*.

about the nature of Sterne's antislavery belief. The parenthetical qualification of "pensive mood" and the comment about Mecca, particularly since British traders drew from West African nations that were not predominantly Muslim, reveals only a casual understanding of the issue. However, Sterne still feels a need to write his sentimental scene with the African. Regardless of motive, the image produced had wide public appeal and helped to ingrain specific views on the sensibility of Africans that directly contradicted proslavery claims about their nature.

Antislavery literature has a complex relationship to the movement because not all authors were actively involved in abolition. In fact, many authors created and used antislavery tropes mainly as a means of artistic expression, rather than a radical statement of protest. One can almost separate the two groups of writers into the dedicated and the dilettantes. Scholarship on antislavery fiction and poetry has focused critique mainly on the depiction of Africans and the quality of the writing. Wylie Sypher's *Guinea's Captive Kings* (1969) posits an antislavery literature that "wilfully [sic] ignores fact" to create literary tropes like the "noble Negro." He characterizes the "mass propaganda" of literature produced with antislavery themes as an "extension of the Enlightenment." Later critics, like Srinivas Aravamudan, identify orientalist elements in the fiction and poetry that serve the form more than the cause.[42] Alan Richardson describes the verse as rife with "vapid sentiment, stock description, stereotyped characters and situations, and patently false portrayals of Africa and of Afro-Caribbean slaves."[43] While the literary value may be questionable, the eighteenth-century reader found something compelling, and definitely titillating, in these descriptions, and the later abolitionist societies capitalized on this interest.

What purpose, then, does a rhetorical analysis of antislavery literature serve? Judging the value of each author's contribution to furthering the discourse of abolition seems both time-consuming and ultimately fruitless. Canonical works of fiction and poetry did not emerge solely from antislavery thought; however, the presence of antislavery thought in these canonical works does attest to the popularity of the topic. Authors such as Henry Mackenzie and William Blake, who were only indirectly involved in antislavery work, still felt compelled to write (and illustrate) against the institution of slavery. Instead of evaluating the quality of the work, we should frame the questions differently. Fictional and poetic expression, as opposed to non-fictional essays and factual accounts, offered new avenues of protest that contributed greatly to the mass mobilization of public opinion. These new forms of antislavery/anti-slave-trade expression included a more diverse body of writers who were able to incorporate their particular perspectives into strategies of protest.

---

[42] See, for example, Aravamudan's *Tropicopolitans*.

[43] Alan Richardson, Introduction, *Slavery, Abolition and Emancipation: Writings in the British Romantic Period*, gen. eds. P.J. Kitson and D. Lee, Vol. 4 *Verse*, ed. Alan Richardson (London: Pickering and Chatto, 1999) x. All references to abolitionist poetry are taken from this volume unless otherwise indicated. See also Suvir Kaul's *Poems of Nation, Anthems of Empire*.

Literary expressions of antislavery sentiment revealed genuine anxieties about a degraded British national character—anxieties of liberty, religion, and race.

Though the writers of these works may have been initially conflicted about the appropriate solution to slavery, they were very clear about the repercussions to the British nation. Fictional and poetic representations of slavery spoke as volubly about the writer as they did about the "oppressed people" who often became the objects in their work. In the dedication to the 1775 edition of *The Dying Negro*, Day cautioned readers to "remember, there is a people who share the government and name of Britons; among whom the cruelty of Sparta is renewed without its virtue" (viii). His comparison to the ancients indicated the conflicted belief in British superiority. Spartans, renowned for their valor and martial strength, also possessed a cruel nature, and Day warns Britons against emulating only the harsher aspects of Spartan society. Of course, inherent in this comparison is the superiority of British culture that makes possible the similarity to Sparta. To ameliorate the situation, Day and other writers urged their audience to restore the image of the "true" Briton. This image emerged from poetry and prose as white, Christian, and "Freedom-loving." The masculine, "martial" aspect to national identity was reframed over the course of the 1770s and '80s as white women's participation in the movement grew.[44] Writers depicted the suffering of Negroes to raise compassion in the citizenry and to combat "Britain's foulest stain." They repeatedly implored "Christians" to consider the repercussions of their actions because "national sins" had "national judgments." Participation in the "man-degrading mart" would not be tolerated by the true Briton, who, unlike the slave holder and slave trader, had not been corrupted by the practice of slavery.[45]

Poetry of the late 1780s defined the nature of the Briton and began to ask serious questions about the nature of empire. Yearsley's *A Poem on the Inhumanity of the Slave Trade* compared Muslim and Spanish slave-holding practices to the British and asked, "Briton, dost thou / Act up to this?" Poets called the nation to account for practices that ran counter to principle. "Britannia," by her very nature should triumph over tyranny and oppression; however, as Hannah More succinctly stated in *Slavery, A Poem* (1788), "Conquest is pillage with a nobler name." More's conservative beliefs did not keep her from seriously probing the nature of empire. In her poem, she also asked, "Does thirst of empire, does desire of fame, / (For those are specious crimes) our rage inflame?" Apparently, an empire based on

---

[44] See Clare Midgley's *Women Against Slavery*. She notes the early involvement of Quaker women in the fight against the slave trade and slavery, but the initial anti-slave-trade societies consisted mainly of men. British women became involved at the local level by crafting petitions, soliciting signatures, and writing verse (20). Women did appear on the rolls of local societies as early as 1788; however, they were more actively involved in the second abolitionist campaign beginning in the 1820s. For an analysis of women's literary contribution to antislavery, see Moira Ferguson's *Subject to Others*.

[45] See David Dabydeen's *The Black Presence in English Literature* (Manchester: Manchester University Press, 1985).

tyranny and oppression did not have any real value. However, these women were not wholly opposed to the notion of an empire; rather, they advised caution against an immoral empire. Antislavery poets sought to "return" Great Britain and her empire to a position of global exemplar. To do this, poets and novelists isolated the elements of national character for critique and advocated abolition of the slave trade as the means for restoring the balance.

One method of drawing a distinction between the "true" Briton and the corrupt slave holder or trader revolved around the African's innate sense of liberty. Antislavery writers stressed the similarity between Africans and Europeans in that regard. "*These*, who in regions far remov'd from this, / Think, like ourselves, that liberty is bliss."[46] The slave's value of liberty over the value of his own life became a common theme for antislavery writers who sought to gain the sympathy of the audience. "When could I better die, / than thus for friendship, love, and liberty?"[47] Several poems included stories of slaves who chose to die when their liberty was threatened. Bryan Edwards, a prominent *proslavery* advocate, acknowledged the bravery of these slaves in "The Negro's Dying Speech on his being executed for Rebellion in the Island of Jamaica" (1777). The moving speech begins with the invocation "In Freedom's cause I bar'd my breast,— / In Freedom's cause I die."[48] Both poets and novelists depicted slave tortures and punishments in minute detail furthering the trope of the "noble African."

Two common tropes developed around the depiction of the African slave— the noble being who resisted the constraint of his natural liberty and the poor creature who bowed down under the weight of enslavement. Authors expressed genuine admiration for slaves who chose "liberty" over "life in vain." Ann Yearsley related the story of a man who deliberately bled to death after his leg had been amputated, a common punishment for runaways. Rather than attribute this incident to the "Negro's stubbornness," she used a "more *glorious* epithet, and that is *fortitude*" to describe his character.[49] The descriptions reduced to simple binaries: "Liberty or Bondage, Life or Death." The second trope, the "Sons of Mis'ry," implored compassionate Britons to release them from their enslavement.

---

[46]   Edward Rushton, "West-Indian Eclogues: Eclogue the First" (London, 1787).

[47]   Hugh Mulligan, "The Lovers, an African Eclogue," *Gentleman's Magazine* (March 1784).

[48]   Bryan Edwards, "The Negro's Dying Speech on his being executed for Rebellion in the Island of Jamaica," *The Universal Magazine* (November 1777). The image of the noble African who dies fighting for freedom dates back to Aphra Behn's *Oroonoko* (1688).

[49]   Ann Yearsley, *A Poem on the Inhumanity of the Slave Trade* (London, Printed for G. G. J. and J. Robinson, 1788). The note follows the line "What crime / Merits so dire a death?" The story she retells involves a "Coromantin slave in Jamaica." The "Coromantin" slaves were renowned for their fierceness and bravery, so they often appear in antislavery writings. Also, Jamaica had a large community of escaped slaves (Maroons) living in the hills. The Coromantins and the Jamaican Maroons were commonly featured in the trope of the "noble" African warrior.

Writers appropriated the voice of the slave to lend authenticity to their work. While this appropriation has led critics to question their motives as proto-racist and patronizing, I would argue for a different reading that is much more subversive. Sentimental literature incorporated character variety and interiority to give the reader a better understanding of the character's thoughts. By including the "thoughts" of the African slave, writers directly and viciously attacked proslavery advocates and the apathetic public. As members of the dominant group, white writers could use harsher language and critique British behavior more candidly than any "African" voice.

Both noble and pathetic characterizations (or caricatures) of slaves allowed antislavery activists to hold up a "mirror" to the public. Most of their discourse focused on the negative impression that slaves had of their British "captors." In the words of the Negro, "What are England's rights, I ask."[50] Questioning the "WHITE SAVAGE" with regard to his behavior—white women's role in slavery was virtually invisible—involved establishing standards of British civilization and character. If the beleaguered African's "sighs" served only to "excite the Briton's drunken joy," then how could the nation be accounted "first of EUROPE's polish'd lands"? Hannah More denounced slavery as "the luxury of British pride," referring to the alcohol traded to African princes for slaves as "pleasing poison." Though the African kings' complicity with the trade was also critiqued, the Europeans still bore the brunt of responsibility. The institution of slavery represented a double failing with respect to national character: one, that the country "where the soul of freedom reign'd" would tolerate such an affront to freedom; and two, that the nation would model such uncivilized behavior before less advanced societies. Antislavery literature, particularly writing published between 1787 and 1789, indicated a sincere distress that Britons' participation in trading and owning slaves raised doubts about religion and race.

British national identity revolved around a belief in benevolent Christianity that the corrupt practices encouraged by slavery seriously threatened. The distinction between "nominal" and "real" Christians became increasingly vital to the rhetoric of national identity and the rhetoric of antislavery.[51] Writers pointed out that the "*unjust, cruel,* and *oppressive*" practices of traders and masters were "directly *contrary* to the doctrines of *Christ*." In many texts, "Christian" and "Briton" were used interchangeably to elicit an emotional response from the audience and

---

[50] William Cowper, "The Negro's Complaint" (London, 1788). Cowper's poems remain the finest examples of antislavery verse

[51] While Jonathan Swift used the term "nominal Christian" in his *An Argument against the Abolishing of Christianity in England* (1711), Granville Sharp introduced the term with respect to antislavery in *A Representation of the Injustice and Dangerous Tendency of Tolerating Slavery* (1769), where he explained at length the differences between the character of the "nominal" and the "real" Christian. His work was highly influential on subsequent writers' attempt to understand the relationship between Christianity and African slavery. For a more detailed discussion, see Chapter 2.

reinforce the link between nation and religion. Poets were especially harsh in their condemnation of slavery spuriously sanctioned by religion. The "Christian Tyrant" whose "faithless," "selfish," and "renegade" ways invited "God's wrath" defiled the true nature of the benevolent Briton. "Christian oppression" was intolerable; any attempts to reconcile it with doctrine proved sacrilegious; and slavery threatened not only the spirit of Christianity but its image in the eyes of the unenlightened as well. The oppressive customs of traders, masters, and overseers supposedly gave slaves a genuine contempt for Christianity. Authors lamented again at the poor example set by the behavior of their countrymen. Bryan Edwards' Negro derided his audience by challenging, "Now Christian, glut thy ravish'd eye." This hypocrisy of the oppressor also held significant ramifications for the solidifying concept of race.

The concept of race became increasingly pertinent to the antislavery argument in depicting both the situation of Africans and the behavior of Europeans. Outlining the nature of color distinctions became a crucial piece of the race argument and each camp used "colour" to advance their agendas.[52] Though Roxann Wheeler argues that "Christianity, civility, and rank were *more explicitly* important to Briton's assessment of themselves," she does not examine how "white" became a constructed color category in abolitionist discourse (7). Thus, color in the anti-slave-trade debates did have an impact on the construction of race beyond the other factors Wheeler identifies. The anxiety between the attributes of "whiteness" and "blackness" manifested itself in the character portrayals of traders and Africans. Though more critical attention has been given to the image of the African slave in prose and poetry, antislavery sentiment demonstrated an equal concern with the "white" slave holder and trader. Like Christianity, writers associated "whiteness" with purity and beauty, a natural opposite to Edmund Burke's sublime. However, the behavior of whites involved with slavery seriously threatened that association, particularly the idea that "[t]he white man's pleasure is the Negroes pain."[53]

Poetry and fiction of the late 1780s also made more references to the abuse of African women than other publications. Women poets, like Hannah More, Ann Yearsley, and Helen Maria Williams included several lines about the abuse and desperation of slave women on the ships and plantations. In "A Poem on the Bill Lately Passed for Regulating the Slave Trade" (1788), Williams depicted the despair of a mother on a slave ship who ultimately commits infanticide rather than allow her infant to be enslaved:

> No more, in desperation wild,
> Shall madly strain her gasping child;
> With all the mother in her soul,
> With eyes where tears have ceas'd to roll,

---

[52] The use and enforcement of color distinctions by proslavery writers will be discussed in detail in Chapter 4.

[53] Rushton, "Eclogue the First."

> Shall catch the livid infant's breath,
> Then sink in agonizing death![54]

The graphic description is also noteworthy in that the "mother" is not coded as African or black. Williams plays upon the universality of a mother's love that establishes a common bond with the British mother.

The novels approached the issue of the white male's complicity with slavery from two different perspectives, demonstrating the dual anxieties of self-policing and outsiders' perception.[55] First, writers characterized the direct participants in slavery and the slave trade (ships' captains, sailors, planters, overseers, and so on) as being corrupted by the practice. For example, in Henry Mackenzie's *Julia de Roubigné* (1777), Savillon comments to his friend Beauvaris in letter 28 about life in the colonies: "To a man not callous from habit, the treatment of the negroes, in the plantations here, is shocking."[56] Mackenzie's character reiterated a common charge leveled against planters and traders for decades—slavery corrupted the master as much as the slave. Novelists detailed the cruelty of slave holders to illustrate the inhumane and "unChristian" manner in which they treated their slaves. In Dorothy Kilner's *The Rotchfords* (1786), a rescued slave boy dispassionately recounts the brutality of his master:

> [M]y master sell me to my new master *Chromis*; he very cruel, and make me carry *great big* load upon my back, much bigger than me could. So me tumble down, and then my master whip me, and call me lazy *black* dog, and give me no bit to eat, for one, two days, because he say me lazy. Indeed, master, me not *help* it; me not strong enough. But master *Chromis* said he *make* me strong, so he *was* whip me sadly, and shut me in the cold, with the coals, because me *black* they not dirt me.[57]

---

[54] Helen Maria Williams, "A Poem on the Bill Lately Passed for Regulating the Slave Trade" (London, 1788) lines 25–29. This poem lauds the passage of a bill to regulate the carrying size of British slaving ships. Many activists believed the bill to be a harbinger of abolition rather than the stalling tactic that it actually was. For a discussion of Williams' poetry, see Deborah Kennedy's *Helen Maria Williams and the Age of Revolution* (Lewisburg, PA: Bucknell University Press, 2002).

[55] The image of the cruel white mistress did not become common until the nineteenth century. The involvement of Creole women in plantation slavery became a much more serious issue during the second abolitionist campaign and many writers during the first campaign chose not to address the cruelty of "white" West Indian women towards "black" (female) slaves.

[56] All references to fictional work will be quoted from *Slavery, Abolition and Emancipation: Writings in the British Romantic Period*, gen. eds. P.J. Kitson and D. Lee (London: Pickering and Chatto, 1999), Vol. 6: *Fiction*, ed. Srinivas Aravamudan. The editors of the series provide facsimile reprints of the original works. Mackenzie 13.

[57] Dorothy Kilner, *The Rotchford's; or the Friendly Counsellor* (London: Printed and Sold by John Marshall, 1786) 77.

Kilner's novel demonstrated the conflicted beliefs of many antislavery/anti-slave-trade activists of her time. While she detailed the atrocities committed against the slave, she used a pidgin dialect that gave the character an air of stupidity. She made particular note of the master's use of color distinction to justify his cruelty. Kilner's tale does reinforce the image of the corrupt planter who takes advantage of his absolute power over his slave.

The most satirical illustration of this corruption appeared in an anonymous novel titled *Adventures of Jonathan Corncob, Loyal American Refugee, Written by Himself* (1787). The author spends part of his time in Barbados, and he immediately notices the differences in color from "the sable African" to the "pale Quadroon." In one scene, Jonathan visits a plantation in which the owner provides a "beauty of a somewhat lighter hue" to be his servant, after Jonathan expresses his dissatisfaction with the darker-skinned slaves. He mistakenly believes that she is meant to serve him sexually, though it "shocked the morality of my ideas." Initially pleased with Barbadian hospitality, Jonathan comments, "What a pity that Barbadoes [*sic*] should be so subject to hurricanes!" [58] His tongue-in-cheek comment refers to the charge by antislavery activists that the frequent hurricanes and tornadoes in the West Indies are examples of God's wrath. Chapter XIII begins with a reference to "The West-Indian way of white-washing, or rather the true way of washing the blackmoor white." In a truly troubling scene, the author relates the systematic rape of generations of female slaves by white masters to produce increasingly fair-skinned offspring who are the product of incest. The final testament to the corruption of whiteness occurs when a planter, who has survived a hurricane with his wife and plantation intact, bemoans the loss of "twenty negroes … and six of them were she's … and big with young, oh, oh!" (145) The white slaveholder's comment underlines the treatment of human beings as livestock. In a pointed reversal, Jonathan also comes to view the hurricanes as examples of divine retribution for the atrocities committed by slave holders.

The second perspective often used in fiction and poetry dramatized the African's view of the white man. White writers frequently appropriated the African voice as a self-reflexive critique conveying negative "black" opinions of the "whites." Dorothy Kilner's *The Rotchfords* was a conduct book for children intended to teach "virtue" and included a strong statement against racial prejudice. When the Rotchfords rescued the young slave boy, Pompey, who had been abandoned by his owner, they questioned him about his experiences. Pompey (a generic slave name) responded to their kindness with an emotional expression of his gratitude. "Me tank you mistress, … me will love you for be so kind, as much as if you black; but me do not love all white people! White people very bad! very cross! very cruel! Me no love white people." (88) The simplicity of the boy's sentiment is intended to evoke shame in the white reader. Also important is the immediate and favorable

---

[58] 117. In Cowper's "The Negro's Complaint," the slave questions God about the tortures he has endured. "Hark! He answers!—Wild tornadoes / Strewing yonder sea with wrecks, / Wasting towns, plantations, meadows, / Are the voice with which he speaks."

reception to any expression of kindness that reveals the ability to lead by kindness rather than cruelty.

The anxiety over being judged and found wanting by black people consistently appeared in antislavery poetry, particularly in the late 1780s. Poems included invectives by captive and tortured slaves who cried "May ev'ry curse attend this pallid race!" Slaves propitiated God and asked Him to "hurl destruction on each cruel White." The often violent and bitter denunciation of whites aimed to represent the anger of the Negroes.[59] Some writers stressed that common blood flowed through common veins. The Rotchfords' children were surprised to find that Pompey's blood was just as red as their own. Cowper's character stated, "Skins may differ, but affection / Dwells in white and black the same," while William Blake's "The Little Black Boy" (1789) proclaimed, "And I am black, but O! my soul is white."[60] In 1788, Josiah Wedgwood distributed the best-known image of antislavery—that of the kneeling slave who questioned "Am I not a Man and a Brother?" I do not contend that every antislavery writer believed in full equality between blacks and whites—quite the opposite. Though activists varied in the extent of their belief regarding the African's competence, almost every writer believed in the inherent superiority of whites. Thus, the actual failing and source of anxiety stemmed from lack of a proper model of white "civility" that black people could emulate. Wheeler traces this notion of civility to early exchanges between Africans and Europeans documented in early eighteenth-century travel narratives (102). However, the definition of civility changed in the work of abolitionists who read "white" as more of a character than a color. This "white" nation became problematized by the publication of work by authors who viewed themselves as black and British.

Claiming a (Protestant) Christian Ethos: Black Voices and British Identity

The recovery of "authentic" African voices from the eighteenth century has invigorated historical and literary scholarship for the last thirty years. Historians sought to reconstruct the history of black people in Great Britain, a history that predated enslavement and colonial expansion into the West Indies. Landmark studies by Folarin Shyllon and Peter Fryer cited historical documents that placed the arrival of the first Africans in the British Isles as early as the sixteenth

---

[59] This strategy became highly problematic after the Haitian Revolution in 1791. Even these dramatized and hypothetical scenarios proved too disconcerting for the British legislators. Quotes taken from Rushton, "Eclogue the First."

[60] Blake's poem is a fairly controversial statement of antislavery ideology and some critics argue that it did not have an abolitionist slant. His illustrations for John Gabriel Stedman's *Narrative of a Five Years' Expedition against the Revolted Negroes of Surinam*, 2 vols. (London: Printed by J. Johnson and J. Edwards, 1796) portrayed the slave's situation with more overt sympathy.

century.[61] Though the black population in Britain would never rival the population in the colonies, the metropolitan public was quite familiar with their presence, particularly in London.[62] By the end of the eighteenth century, black writers had also made their presence known in multiple forms of publications that spanned a variety of genres.[63] Literary critics have analyzed this body of literature in terms of race relations, perceptions of slavery, and contributions to the abolitionist cause.[64] Most studies have focused on the process of identity formation revealed by the poetry, slave narratives, and abolitionist prose generated by the few published black writers of the time. Scholars have acknowledged the importance of black writers to the abolitionist cause and their contribution to the cultural milieu of the time. I seek to add to this existing body of scholarship by examining the impact of Afro-British writing on the formation of British national identity.

Black writers occupied a highly complex rhetorical position vis-à-vis their predominantly European audiences, the timing of their publications, and their personal identities. Most writers shied away from describing the more horrific aspects of slavery, though slave tortures became a common feature in white authors' writings on slavery. Afro-British (or African-American as in the case of Phillis Wheatley) authors demonstrated a greater awareness of the fact that most of their audience benefited in some way from slavery, either by the use of slave-grown goods or the wealth of the colonies. This awareness led to a certain amount of circumspection in their writing, even when addressed to sympathetic audiences, as in the case of Ignatius Sancho. As the abolitionist movement grew in strength and popular support, black authors could express their sentiments with greater clarity and honesty. For example, Phillis Wheatley's *Poems on Various*

---

[61] The first recorded instance of Africans setting foot on British soil occurred in 1555. See F. O. Shyllon, *Black Slaves in Britain* and *Black People in Britain, 1555–1833* (London: Oxford University Press, 1977); Peter Fryer, *Staying Power*; and Jagdish S. Gundara and Ian Duffield, eds., *Essays on the History of Blacks in Britain* (Brookfield, VT: Ashgate, 1992).

[62] The practice of keeping black servants was quite popular among the upper class in London, and the aristocracy were known to keep African children as "pets." Bristol, Liverpool, London, and Manchester were major port cities from which slave ships sailed and to which they returned from the colonies bringing West Indian plantation owners and their slaves. Major metropolitan newspapers carried advertisements for slave auctions and runaway slave notices until the abolition of slavery in 1834.

[63] For collected examples of African writing in English, see Paul Edwards and David Dabydeen, *Black Writers in Britain, 1760–1890* (Edinburgh: Edinburgh University Press, 1991) and Vincent Carretta, ed., *Unchained Voices: An Anthology of Black Authors in the English-Speaking World of the 18th Century* (Lexington: The University Press of Kentucky, 1996).

[64] See Gretchen Gerzina, *Black London*; Keith A. Sandiford, *Measuring the Moment: Strategies of Protest in Eighteenth-Century Afro-English Writing* (Selinsgrove, PA: Susquehanna University Press, 1988); and Helena Woodard, *African-British Writings in the Eighteenth Century: The Politics of Race and Reason* (Westport, CT: Greenwood Press, 1993).

Subjects (1773)[65] expressed none of the accusatory rage of Cugoano's *Thoughts and Sentiments on the Evil of Slavery* (1787). The language and tone of these publications shifted significantly in response to the authors' desire to define their racial and cultural identities.[66] Africans in Great Britain and the American colonies found themselves in complicated situations that required a reworking of societal perceptions and their position in the British context.

Publication by black authors in the 1770s and '80s served a dual purpose of developing an Afro-British identity and establishing a political stance against slavery. By telling their tales in poetry and prose, these writers sought to reclaim, or more appropriately to invent, a national and cultural identity that had been stolen from them through the institution of slavery. The writers of this time negotiated the complex process of identity formation and effected changes in cultural perceptions of Africans and the slave-trade debates. By participating in nationalist discourse, they problematized the image of the Briton as racially homogeneous. With the exception of Phillis Wheatley, all major Afro-British writers saw themselves as members of British society and evinced a desire to restore that society to its proper greatness.[67] They echoed many of the sentiments of their English and Scottish counterparts, but their work demonstrated an additional awareness of a racialized and subordinated self.

Literary theory provides useful terms and concepts that can be used to examine the complex process of Afro-British identity formation. W. E. B Dubois coined the term "double consciousness" to describe the black person's negotiation between European and African identities. The term is useful when applied to the earlier time period that is the subject of this study. Paul Gilroy offers a more nuanced notion of "double consciousness" with respect to the Afro-British identity construction. He opposes the concept of "cultural insiderism" that seeks to "construct the nation as an ethnically homogenous object" against the space from which black writers

---

[65] See Phillis Wheatley, *Complete Writings*, ed. Vincent Carretta (New York: Penguin Books, 2001).

[66] Only one West Indian writer of note published in London during the time of the first abolitionist movement—Francis Williams. The third son of free blacks in Jamaica, Williams became the subject of an "experiment" conducted by the Duke of Montagu "to discover, whether, by proper cultivation, and a regular course of tuition at school and the university, a Negroe might not be found as capable of literature as a white person" (Edward Long's *History of Jamaica*, 1774). Williams studied at Cambridge and returned to Jamaica after completing his degree. He wrote his poetry in Latin, which was translated and published by the highly biased and most vehement advocate of the racial inferiority of Africans, Edward Long. See Vincent Carretta's *Unchained Voices* 72–76.

[67] Wheatley's poetry reveals a greater complexity given her divided loyalties between Great Britain and America. Though she was first published in London, Wheatley cultivated an African-American identity that was fraught with contradictions. Her contribution to British national identity will be explored later in this section.

challenge this cultural absolutism.[68] In the language of the slave-trade debates, this "cultural insiderism" manifests itself as a promulgation of English identity into a broader British identity. The African Briton, who has no claim to either English or any other regional identity (that is,, Scottish, Welsh, or even Irish), destabilizes cultural homogeneity by the very act of writing.[69] The subject position of such writers occupies a noticeable gap in the construction of British identity by acknowledging the connection between the African and the Briton. Other than Granville Sharp, no antislavery writer addressed the notion of Afro-British citizenship or subjecthood. Instead, writers like Ottobah Cugoano and Olaudah Equiano, John Stuart and Gustavus Vassa respectively, claimed the "right" to represent themselves.

The "hybrid" Afro-British identity produced politically significant rhetoric that interrogated and then re-envisioned the primary attributes of the Briton.[70] Texts spoke on multiple levels to address simultaneously the author's message, the current political climate, and the audience's assumptions about the author's capabilities. The layered consciousness inherent in each text created a tension for both writer and audience that forced a certain re-evaluation of British culture. Afro-British writers used language in a highly sophisticated manner designed to appeal to British audiences and to critique British culture. Most writers chided their audience for not actualizing the most laudable attributes of British character. They appropriated the language of religion, which they had been taught for the ostensible purpose of "civilizing" them, to advance their antislavery views and criticize aspects of British character. Christianity provided a fruitful avenue of entry into the discourse of identity. Each writer examined in this section grounded his or her comments in Christian belief, possibly because they viewed Christianity as a leveler of difference. Ukawsaw Gronniosaw, Phillis Wheatley, Ignatius Sancho, Ottobah Cugoano, and Olaudah Equiano utilized Christian doctrine eloquently and shrewdly to critique their subject positions within British society.[71]

[68] Paul Gilroy, *The Black Atlantic: Modernity and Double Consciousness* (Cambridge: Harvard University Press, 1993).

[69] Gilroy states, "The most heroic, subaltern English nationalisms and countercultural patriotisms are perhaps better understood as having been generated in a complex pattern of antagonistic relationships with the supra-national and imperial world for which the ideas of 'race,' nationality, and national culture provide the primary (though not the only) indices" (11).

[70] The concept of "hybridity" has multiple meanings ranging from biological to linguistic. All definitions challenge "sameness" with "difference" to effect a transformation that contests the status quo. "Hybridity" caused a "transmutation of British culture into a compounded, composite mode" (Young 23). For an excellent discussion of this concept and its implications for the African diaspora, see Robert C. Young, *Colonial Desire: Hybridity in Theory, Culture and Race* (London: Routledge, 1995).

[71] I have chosen to focus my analysis on these five writers because they reflect both the culture and times in which they wrote and are very familiar to the British public of their time. For other writings by authors of African descent, see Vincent Carretta's *Unchained Voices*.

James Albert Ukawsaw Gronniosaw related the story of his enslavement in the form of spiritual autobiography, framing his entire life as a quest for Christ. Published first in Bath in 1770, *A Narrative of the Most Remarkable Particulars in the Life of James Albert Ukawsaw Gronniosaw, An African Prince, as Related by Himself* was intended to bring the author and his family out of poverty.[72] The preface recommended the tract to the "Notice and Attention of every Christian reader" as a testament that Christ's doctrine was accessible to people even in "Regions of the grossest Darkness and Ignorance." Unlike publications by subsequent authors, Gronniosaw's text was initially filtered through the English consciousness during the process of writing. According to the preface, his amanuensis, "a young LADY from the town of LEOMINSTER," originally recorded the story "for her own private Satisfaction." In a sense, his narrative was co-opted from the beginning by his patrons. Regardless, the text performed a highly subversive function simply by relating the details of his life. His narrative challenged stereotypes of African capabilities and slave holders' claims that Christianity would not benefit slaves.

Gronniosaw's conversion narrative corrected erroneous impressions of African life and initiated a tradition of revolutionary teaching. His story begins in Bornou, Nigeria where he was a favored son in a large and close-knit family. The depiction of his family life belied proslavery claims about the animal nature of Africans and contradicted spurious contentions about the lack of familial sentiment within African societies. Furthermore, Gronniosaw's questioning of his native religion indicated an innate intelligence that exceeded "bestial" capabilities. His charming expression of faith disarms the reader and creates a deceptive sense of submission to the European Christians with whom he came in contact. I suggest an alternate reading that investigates the disjunction between race and culture in this admittedly mediated narrative. Though Gronniosaw never directly indicted the white race, he seemed to imbibe their prejudices against "blackness" in the course of his religious education. However, he reinterpreted "blackness" in the Christian context and made the concept independent of skin color. A pivotal scene in his narrative occurs after his enslavement and arrival in New York. He was cautioned against cursing by an old slave who warned him of "a wicked man call'd the Devil, that liv'd in hell, and would take all that said these words, and put them in the fire and burn them" (11). When he repeated this caution to his mistress, the "wicked man" became the "black man" indicating Gronniosaw's awareness of color prejudice. Whether this textual difference occurred as a result of the speaker or the writer does not matter. The more important fact came from the African's desire to instruct.

This text took on the subversive function of teaching Christian readers the true meaning of faith that was accessible to non-European people. The belief in God, whom Gronniosaw referred to as "Father and BEST Friend," functioned as a

---

[72] Gronniosaw's text went through four editions that same year and was reprinted in Newport in 1774. The narrative was also published in Leeds, Wales (in translation), and Ireland, but never in London. Gronniosaw's narrative was republished in 1809 in the United States and Great Britain, with new editions appearing until 1814.

great leveler of difference. His inherently "corrupt nature" invoked the beliefs of other British Christian writers, and he understood that the only path to spiritual enlightenment was through Christ—a belief he shared with *every Briton*. The title page of the text began with a biblical epigraph promising to bring the "Blind" to the "Light."[73] When filtered through Gronniosaw's "diasporic identity," this epigraph gained a greater significance.[74] Not only did he presume to teach Christians, perhaps even upbraiding them for unChristian behavior, he located this critique in England. His disillusionment on reaching a land where he "expected to find nothing but goodness, gentleness and meekness" functioned as a powerful criticism aimed at supposedly "civilized" people. He further stated, "all that grieved me was, that I had been disappointed in finding some Christian friends, with whom I hoped to enjoy a little sweet and comfortable society" (25). Though he eventually found pious friends, his "disappointment" with English Christians served as a subtle yet pointed critique of English character. His concluding comment reiterated this criticism: "As Pilgrims, and very poor Pilgrims, we are traveling through many difficulties towards our HEAVENLY HOME, ... when the LORD shall deliver us out of the evils of this present world" (39). He claimed an equal status with white Britons by using the common term "Pilgrims," and he encompassed Great Britain in his characterization of the "evils of the present world."

Phillis Wheatley utilized a similar language of high Christian ideals to express her antislavery sentiments covertly. Wheatley's situation was complex, monitored, and mediated much like Gronniosaw's narrative positioning. While I would not classify her as necessarily Afro-British, her poetry demonstrated the negotiation involved in forming a hybrid identity.[75] Though she had few memories of her African heritage, she had a more extensive education that allowed her a greater capacity for self-expression. Her hybridity was further complicated by her additional connection to a burgeoning American consciousness. Wheatley's poetry issued from the nexus of competing subjectivities and nationalities. Perhaps the most eloquent demonstration of these multiple subjectivities surfaced in her letter

---

[73] "I will bring the Blind by a Way that they know not, I will lead them in Paths that they have not known: I will make Darkness light before them and crooked Things straight. These Things will I do unto them and not forsake them." Isaiah 42:16.

[74] Helen Thomas, *Romanticism and Slave Narratives: Transatlantic Testimonies* (Cambridge: Cambridge University Press, 2000). This excellent study places writings by former slaves in a larger literary tradition. Thomas describes the process of identity formation present within the narratives as a "diasporic identity" characterized by a fluid interpretation of self. "As a site of constant transformation, the diasporic identity's entry into the western symbolic order effected a confirmation and simultaneous disruption of that established order in terms of its subjection to and destabilization of manifestations of colonial power" (159).

[75] See David Grimsted's "Anglo-American Racism and Phillis Wheatley's 'Sable Veil,' 'Length'ned Chain,' and 'Knitted Heart,'" *Women in the Age of the American Revolution*, ed. Ronald Hoffman and Peter J. Albert (Charlottesville: University Press of Virginia, 1989). 338–444.

to the Reverend Samson Occom, the Native American convert who actively spoke out against slavery. The *Connecticut Gazette; and the Universal Intelligencer* published a fragment of the original letter on 11 March 1774. Wheatley expressed her antislavery sentiments with a candor that was not present in her poetry: "Those that invade [the natural rights of Africans] cannot be insensible that the divine Light is chasing away the thick Darkness which broods over the Land of Africa." While she identified herself as "African," she also characterized Africa as a land of "thick Darkness," thereby demonstrating her European perspective. As Christianity spread through Africa, Wheatley believed that the "glorious Dispensation of civil and religious Liberty" would follow.

Poems on Various Subjects, Religious and Moral (1773) had a profound impact on British society for many years after its publication in London.[76] Wheatley's poetry inspired abolitionist writers in both Great Britain and America to challenge the racist theories of slavery advocates. Before her poems could be published, several white men had to attest to their authenticity—even the preface referred to the "Author" in the third person. However, Wheatley asserted her own voice in her poetry through form and language. She composed in the classical tradition, demonstrating her keen intelligence, her ability to master complex forms, and the breadth of her learning. Her position within John Wheatley's household infused her work with a secondary layer of meaning. Though she was highly educated, even beyond the standards of the average Englishman, she composed her poetry while she was still a slave. This fact constrained her work from being overtly abolitionist and forced her to find creative and indirect ways to express her true feelings.

Wheatley's poetry focused on various forms of "liberation" that she addressed through the theme of death and the Christian faith. Eleven of her poems addressed a death of someone in her personal sphere, attesting to her wide circle of friends. While each poem lamented the loss of loved ones, Wheatley stressed a common theme of release to greater rewards. "On the Death of a young Lady of Five Years of Age" began with a caution to the girl's parents not to mourn unduly: "On the kind bosom of eternal love, / She finds unknown beatitude above." Wheatley reproduced Christian belief in a heavenly reward, but her subject position as a slave added another nuance to her belief. Not only has the child ascended to a better place, "She feels the iron hand of pain no more." Wheatley could just as easily have been referring to her own condition of enslavement from which the promise of heaven offered a release from the pain of perpetual servitude. In another poem, "To a LADY and her Children, on the Death of her Son and their Brother," she defined the act of dying as having "left mortality's sad scenes behind / For joys to this terrestrial state unknown." Wheatley's equal access to the "joys"

---

[76] Later in her life Wheatley published individual poems to which the British public may or may not have had access. Most of these were printed in American periodicals, so I cannot be sure that metropolitan British readers ever read them. I will therefore consider only Wheatley's London publication for my analysis.

of heaven complicated the justifications of her subjection on earth. In comforting her friends on their loss, she also comforted herself that the suffering she endured would eventually come to an end.

Her more overt antislavery sentiments emerged in seemingly innocuous poems that covertly asserted her hybrid identity and demonstrated her awareness of the world. She defined her position as "Afric's muse," in several poems, a persistent reminder to the reader of her hybrid identity. She used the term "race" in a non-specific manner that encompassed all humans, rather than just Africans. Wheatley stressed the fundamental equality of man in the eyes of Christ, while continuing to assert her position as "vent'rous *Afric*." In her most famous poem, "On Being Brought from Africa to America," she stated, "Remember, *Christians*, *Negros*, black as *Cain*, / May be refin'd, and join th' angelic train." The positioning of the second comma possibly served as a subversive indicator of a common heritage—even white Christians could be "black as *Cain*." Again, Christianity served as a mode of forming a hybrid identity and restored a measure of agency to the oppressed subject. Wheatley chastised her readers not to sin: "Ye blooming plants of human race divine, / An *Ethiop* tells you 'tis your greatest foe."[77] Her critiques of her own failings also carried the subtle undertones of instruction on character in society:

> But how is *Mneme* dreaded by the race,
> Who scorn her warnings, and despise her grace?
> By her unveil'd each horrid crime appears,
> Her awful hand a cup of wormwood bears.
> Days, years misspent, O what a hell of woe!
> Hers the worst tortures that our souls can know."[78]

Though she styled the dread of "Recollection" on her own behavior, the words served to chastise British and American participants in a practice that "dar'd the vengeance of the skies." Wheatley ultimately chose to define herself as "American," but her negotiation of the interstices between Europe and Africa contested the homogeneous cultural construction of British as white, male, and Christian.

A second, more serious challenge to "cultural insiderism" arose with the posthumous publication of the letters of Ignatius Sancho in 1782.[79] Among Afro-British writers, Sancho held a position of singular privilege in the "protection of the great, and the friendship of the literary." He was the first black man to warrant an entry in the *Dictionary of National Biography*, and his letters revealed close

---

[77] "To the University of CAMBRIDGE in NEW-ENGLAND."

[78] "On Recollection."

[79] All references to Sancho's work relate to Ignatius Sancho, *Letters of the Late Ignatius Sancho, An African*, ed. Vincent Carretta (New York: Penguin Books, 1998). During his lifetime, he published several musical compositions, *Theory of Music* (now lost), two plays (also lost), and numerous newspaper essays (xiii).

friendships with literary and theatrical luminaries such as Laurence Sterne and David Garrick. Sancho had already achieved recognition for his letters during his lifetime when one appeared in Sterne's posthumously published *Letters* (1775) and the January 1776 edition of *The Gentleman's Magazine*.[80] Perhaps the most radical element to his letters surfaced in his belief that he *had* a position within society. In the preface to his *Letters*, his editor described his writings as illustrations of "epistolary talent, of rapid and just conception, of wild patriotism, and of universal philanthropy" (8). Sancho displayed an active civic responsibility and felt confident in sending suggestions for improvements to *The General Advertiser*.[81] While he clearly considered Great Britain to be his home, Sancho was always aware of his reduced status attributable to his African descent. His letters abound with references to himself as "dark-faced friend," "Black-a-moor," and the slightly sarcastic "poor, thick-lipped son of Afric."

Sancho appeared to enjoy reproducing in a mocking manner public assumptions about the nature of the African. The level of familiarity displayed in his letters, particularly those to Mr. Meheux, revealed a certain understanding of the ridiculousness of racial stereotypes. His pet name for Mr. Meheux was "monkey," a fascinating revision of beliefs regarding African descent and proximity to the apes. Many of his comments about his "black brethren" referred to their capabilities in an ironic manner. For example, in letter XII of volume I written to Mr. Browne, Sancho addressed his reader as "my child," yet he included the following commentary:

> I thank you for your kindness to my poor black brethren—I flatter myself you will find them not ungrateful—they act commonly from their feelings:—I have a dog will love those who use him kindly—and surely, if so, negroes—in their state of ignorance and bondage will not act less generously, if I may judge them by myself—I should suppose kindness would do any thing with them;—my soul melts at kindness—but the contrary—I own with shame—makes me almost a savage. (45)

Sancho "represented" his entire race in this passage, and he both reproduced and exploded stereotypes of African sensibility. His statement about cruelty turning him "savage" could only be read as irony, a fact reinforced by his utterly mundane request for "half a dozen cocoa nuts" that followed. He clearly viewed the

---

[80] In his introduction, Carretta documents that Sancho was a sufficiently recognized public figure during his lifetime that he may have anticipated the publication of his letters after his death. His work was published by subscription and did so well that his widow realized over £500 from more than 1,200 subscribers for the first edition (xv).

[81] Sancho's *Letters* included three schemes for the improvement of the country: regulating the number of sailors on ships, and two probably comical plans to reduce the national debt by selling the gold plate of the aristocracy, and a plan to put hairdressers to work as soldiers.

"African temperament" as capable of refinement rather than an innate component of his or any other black person's nature. In recommending a young black man for employment, Sancho described his personality as "the sulky gloom of Africa dispelled by Gallic vivacity—and that softened again with English sedateness."[82] Whether or not Sancho actually believed any of the cultural stereotypes about Africans, he seemed to reproduce many of them with a tongue-in-cheek brand of humor. He definitely evinced an appreciation for English society.

The historical period of Sancho's writings reflected the generalizing of "Englishness" to "Britishness" and the patriotism engendered by outside challenges to national character. Several of his letters dealt with the sense of betrayal felt in the wake of the American uprising. He demonstrated the English/British disdain for Ireland and advocated punishing Irish temerity by stopping the exportation of potatoes.[83] In the same letter, he lamented over the country "ruined by the choicest blessings ... —ruined by victories—arts—arms—and unbounded commerce." His "love of country" manifested itself in numerous letters and constituted a disruptive act in the public consciousness. As a result of publication, Sancho's letters inserted a different image of the African into the discourse of national identity.[84] He clearly shared a common feeling of citizenship with his friends, albeit one that was tempered by his race and Great Britain's participation in slavery. He anticipated antislavery arguments about the benefits to the British empire that would come from abolition. Sancho hoped "that this cursed carnage of the human species may end—commerce revive—sweet social peace be extended throughout the globe—and the British empire be strongly knit in the never-ending bands of sacred friendship and brotherly love!"[85]

Phillis Wheatley's and Ignatius Sancho's writings negated the vicious stereotypes of Africans as savage and uneducable in proslavery tracts. Though their antislavery sentiments were couched in careful and subtle language, especially in Wheatley's case, they opened avenues for serious protest by both white and black abolitionists. Their writing proved that slaves could not be dismissed as uncivilized, less intelligent, or less human than any other British citizen. By the end of the 1780s, the British public proved more accepting of the harsh criticism directed at slave holders and slave traders. The final two narratives, to be discussed in this section, were both written by Afro-British writers who benefited from the work of their predecessors that prepared the British public for their harsh invectives.

---

[82] Volume I, Letter XXIV, addressed to Mr. Browne, 12 August 1775, 60.

[83] Volume II, Letter XLIV, addressed to Mr. Rush, 20 October 1779, 185.

[84] Though Sancho demonstrated his political consciousness repeatedly, a very telling example of his configuration of self as citizen occurred in a letter addressed to Mr. Stevenson 17 January 1780. "I do request you to thank Mr. W— for me, and tell him he has the prayers—not of a raving mad whig—nor fawning deceitful tory—but of a coal-black, jolly African, who wishes health and peace to every religion and country throughout the ample range of God's creation!" Volume II, Letter LXII, 210.

[85] Volume I, Letter LIV, addressed to Mrs. Cocksedge, 5 November 1777, 106.

Ottobah Cugoano and Olaudah Equiano openly and unapologetically critiqued the institution of slavery and British complicity with the agents of enslavement. Their hybrid identities did not subsume the African to the European as did Gronniosaw, Wheatley and Sancho. Instead, they confronted the claims of British superiority and insisted that the public adhere to these standards. During a time when the belief in African racial inferiority solidified, Cugoano and Equiano's narratives performed a genuinely subversive act of questioning British character and self-perceptions.

Cugoano's *Thoughts and Sentiments on the Evil of Slavery* (1787) directly attacked European racism and British hypocrisy in sanctioning slavery.[86] Unlike previous publications by Afro-British authors, his publication was not revised, edited, compiled, or transcribed by a white intermediary.[87] His project in this essay involved castigating European, specifically British, participants in the enslavement of Africans from the subject position of an equal, perhaps even a better. Like Gronniosaw and Wheatley, Cugoano negotiated his hybridity through religion, and Christianity became his primary argument against enslavement. His text interrogated "apostate Christians" and racial categorization based on color, adding another dimension to the construction of national character.

Cugoano's project in *Thoughts and Sentiments* revolved less around the creation of Afro-British identity and more around holding Britons accountable for their actions. He repeatedly aligned himself with the maligned Africans, his "countrymen in complexion," but his strong faith in Christianity separated him from his native land. He obviously wrote for a white, Christian, and British audience, and he defined their national character even while self-identifying as African. In his text, he called upon "noble Britons" to honor their purported virtues, characterizing Great Britain as the "Queen of Nations." However, he warned that even a great nation invited divine wrath when harboring "apostate Christians." The "depredators, robbers, and ensnarers of men can never be Christian," and by this pronouncement, Cugoano damned "slave procurers" as wholly unfit for any contact with Africa (25). He advocated mass conversions of Africans to Christianity, which he defined as "the system of benignity and love, and all its votaries are devoted to honesty, justice, humanity, meekness, peace, and good-will to all men" (66). Based on this definition, Cugoano attributed greater piety to the converted African, a direct snub to the image of the white and morally superior Briton. Once again, Christianity became the great leveler of difference in both racial and national contexts.

The most radical claim advanced by *Thoughts and Sentiments* stemmed from a re-visioning of color and race distinctions. Working within a Christian framework, he associated blackness, not with complexion, but with character. "A good man will neither speak nor do as a bad man will; but if a man is bad, it makes no difference

---

[86] All references to Cugoano's text come from Quobna Ottobah Cugoano, *Thoughts and Sentiments on the Evil of Slavery*, ed. Vincent Carretta (New York: Penguin Books, 1999).

[87] In fact, Carretta has found evidence to suggest that Olaudah Equiano edited and perhaps wrote sections of Cugoano's polemic.

whether he be a black or a white devil" (12). He dismissed racial hierarchy by describing variations in color as "incidental," and he labeled those who believed in race differences as "ignorant" and "insolent." Cugoano complicated the association of "race" with religious practices, as proslavery writers tended to conflate "white" and "Christian." He problematized this correlation by essentially creating the category of "apostate Christian," which significantly contributed to nationalist discourse. In white antislavery writing, authors urged their audience to restore national honor by abolishing the slave trade. Traders and planters were seen as violators of "true" British identity. In Cugoano's view, traders and planters were not British at all. His repetitive indictments of participants in the institution of slavery involved a complete disenfranchisement from nationality and from religion. His text, more so than other antislavery texts, drew a sharp distinction regarding the attributes of British national character and the conduct of slave traders and slave holders. "But surely law and liberty, justice and equity, which are the proper foundations of the British government, and humanity the most amiable characteristic of the people, must be entirely fled from their land, ... for supporting and carrying on such enormous wickedness" (76). All the characteristics prized by the Briton demanded immediate and complete abolition of slavery, not just the slave trade.

The most strident assertion of Afro-British identity emerged in the writings of Olaudah Equiano, or Gustavus Vassa as he was also known. The clearest evidence of his hybrid identity came from his use of these two names interchangeably in his autobiography. More than any other writer, Equiano actively sought to combine the African and British cultural ancestry to which he felt he belonged.[88] He aggressively campaigned for the abolition of the slave trade, publishing frequently in *The Public Advertiser* and refuting proslavery arguments.[89] He identified fluidly as "one of the oppressed natives of Africa" and as a "Briton." In a letter to Raymund Harris, whose *Scriptural Researches on the Licitness of the Slave Trade* (1788) had outraged a significant number of antislavery activists, Equiano characterized the trade as a "national sin" that would have dreaded consequences. "May God give us grace to repent of this abominable crime before it be too late!"[90]

---

[88] The most controversial claim made against Equiano's narrative came from proslavery writers who claimed that he was actually born in the United States. While Equiano vehemently denied the accusation, it cast doubt on the authenticity of his narrative. Vincent Carretta has found evidence which shows that Equiano might in fact have been born in South Carolina. See his "Olaudah Equiano or Gustavus Vassa? New Light on an Eighteenth-Century Question of Identity," *Slavery and Abolition*, 20.3 (December 1999): 96–105.

[89] Carretta refers to Equiano's support of abolition as a "secular conversion" influenced by his interaction with key figures like Granville Sharp. See Vincent Carretta, "Turning Against the Slave Trade" in *Equiano the African* (Athens: University of Georgia Press, 2005).

[90] *The Public Advertiser*, 28 April 1788. All references to Equiano's work come from Olaudah Equiano, *The Interesting Narrative and Other Writings*, ed. Vincent Carretta (New

He signed the letter "Gustavus Vassa, The African," a decisive marker of his hybrid identity. Equiano maintained this sense of hybridity even in the face of proslavery denials of his African birth. While scholars grapple over the implications (and veracity) of this claim, I contend that Equiano's desire to establish a connection to his African heritage had a significant impact on the development of his identity.[91] Whether colonial or Africa-born, Equiano self-consciously styled himself as Afro-British. His writings also revealed that negotiating these often contradictory loyalties involved complex slippages between "us" and "them." Examples of these slippages abound in Equiano's most substantial work, *The Interesting Narrative of the Life of Olaudah Equiano, or Gustavus Vassa, The African* (1789).[92]

Equiano's narrative echoed many of the sentimental arguments of white antislavery writers with added glosses of personal experiences. His seemingly unassailable credibility prompted proslavery writers to publish claims that he had falsified his experiences in Africa.[93] *The Interesting Narrative* went through nine editions from 1789 to 1794 and was published throughout England as well as Edinburgh and Dublin. The list of subscribers for the first edition included several prominent abolitionists, including Granville Sharp and Thomas Clarkson.[94] Equiano drew upon the sentimental tradition and made liberal use of pathetic appeal in describing his experiences with enslavement. His retelling of life in Africa stressed the innate love of liberty within Africans and the strong family connections that he had. He also reiterated in three separate instances the antislavery trope of the heroic African choosing death over enslavement.[95] Unlike Cugoano, he recounted in great detail the several instances of cruelty he witnessed during his travels through the West Indies and the southern American colonies. In these

---

York: Penguin Books, 1995). See also James Walvin's *An African's Life: The Life and Times of Olaudah Equiano, 1745–1797* (London: Cassell, 1998).

[91] S. E. Ogude traces Equiano's debt to travel narratives in his long descriptions of his childhood in Africa. See *Genius in Bondage: A Study of the Origins of African Literature in English* (Ife-Ife, Nigeria: University of Ife Press, 1983). For perspectives on how to teach the *Narrative*, see "Forum: Teaching Equiano's *Interesting Narrative*" in *Eighteenth-Century Studies* 34 (Summer 2001): 601–624.

[92] See also "Equiano and the Politics of Literacy" in Arvamudan's *Tropicopolitans* for longer discussion of Equiano's construction of "narrative self" and British nationalism.

[93] Equiano denounced these claims both in person and in print, accusing his attackers of falsifying evidence in order to support a corrupt institution. However, in light of Vincent Carretta's discovery, the proslavery writers may have been correct.

[94] For a thorough analysis of Equiano's publishing history and his connections to the abolitionist community, see Vincent Carretta's introduction.

[95] Equiano complicated this trope by distinguishing his experience of slavery from that of other Africans. He noted at several points the generosity of his master, and he was afforded the opportunity to make enough money to buy his freedom. When his master treated him "waspishly," "I used plainly to tell him my mind, and that I would die before I would be imposed upon as other negroes were" (120). Clearly, he depicted his experiences as markedly different from that of the average West Indian slave.

descriptions, his tone vacillated between identifying with the "oppressed" and speaking on their behalf. He even wrote of his participation in the slave trade as a sailor on merchant vessels, but he qualified his behavior toward "the live cargo" as more "humane" and "just." This admission, stated matter-of-factly and with little remorse, indicated his ability to straddle the distinction between oppressor and oppressed. He made a point to stress his kind treatment of the slaves, but he also included that part of his life for specific ends. I argue that Equiano's enslavement more than his contested African childhood provided a link to his "African" identity, and his participation in the slave trade furnished one link to his "British" identity. Equiano's perspective as both victim of and participant in the institution of slavery resulted in a complicated understanding of national identity.

In his text, Equiano rejected measures of "Britishness" based on race and proposed a national identity that stemmed from religion and civilization. He drew a clear distinction between the "true" Britons and the corrupt traders of the West Indies. In many instances, he used the term "white" to describe the dishonest men who participated in the slave trade. Early in the narrative, "whiteness" became associated with "savagery" in a neat reversal of prejudice. His depiction of the traders who stole him from his native land turned the trope of the degraded African against the supposedly civilized Briton. "[T]he white people looked and acted, as I thought, in so savage a manner; for I had never seen among any people such instances of brutal cruelty; and this not only shewn [*sic*] towards us blacks, but also to some of the whites themselves" (57). Equiano also contradicted the notion that "whiteness" was synonymous with "European civilization." He cautioned, "Let the polished and haughty European recollect that *his* ancestors were once, like the Africans, uncivilized, and even barbarous" (45). The rhetorical positioning within this statement demonstrated the duality that Equiano embodied. He acknowledged and reinforced European perceptions of an "uncivilized Africa," but he clearly saw himself as a beneficiary of European, particularly British, civilization. His narrative also appealed to the "British" and the "Briton," as opposed to the "English," indicating the partial solidification of a unified national identity. He recast the mission of the Briton by charging him or her with the task of civilizing and Christianizing the untutored, but not uneducable, African.

Like his predecessors, Equiano believed that the Christian religion was a key component of British identity and had been bastardized by the institution of slavery. His full and complete conversion served to separate him from his African ancestry. "I viewed the unconverted people of the world in a very awful state, being without God and without hope" (191). Equiano's location when he had his conversion experience proved highly significant and deeply symbolic. He signed on to a trading voyage that ran from London to Cadiz, Spain, so he was surrounded by white, "British" sailors, who constantly blasphemed. In the face of their disbelief over his religious awakening, he commented, "I became a barbarian to them in talking of the love of Christ" (191). The juxtaposition of "barbarian" and "Christian" must have been a deliberate choice because Equiano was well aware of scriptural justifications of slavery. In this scene, he problematized two major proslavery arguments regarding African inferiority and the efficacy of Christian conversion. Equiano set himself above these sailors in his true devotion to Christ, and he vilified slave traders as having even less of a claim to the divine. He separated himself from the "nominal Christians" and "Christian depredators" whose livelihood directly contradicted biblical teachings. He used the term "*Christian master*" in an ironic, if not oxymoronic, fashion to point out the antithetical nature of slavery to Christianity. In a sense, his conversion to true Christianity justified his participation in British culture and politics over that of the slave trader and slave holder. His narrative concluded with an appeal to "British senators" for a speedy restoration of Britain's honor. "I hope to have the satisfaction of seeing the renovation of liberty and justice, resting on the British government, to vindicate the honour of *our* common nature" (232, italics mine).

Contributions by Afro-British writers added yet another layer of perspective on the institution of slavery. As antislavery appeals to the public grew in popularity, more writers entered the debate. Thus, the antislavery platform incorporated more voices—a greater variety of opinions—that significantly influenced national characteristics. The multiplicity of subject positions added dimensions to the composition of a "British" conscience that moved beyond simplistic constructions of race, gender, and class. In this manner, the antislavery position represented a greater cross-section of the British public. The proslavery argument, by contrast, represented a very small but very influential sector of the British population.

Efforts to mobilize public opinion in Britain expanded the nature of the debates into new ideological territory over the course of the 1770s and '80s. While standard religious arguments remained an important aspect of antislavery and proslavery dialogue, the antislavery camp realized the necessity of broadening their appeals. The message that slavery was a national problem required different strategies that moved beyond local and regional pleas. Writers needed to capture the interest of the nation, by whatever means, in order to effect significant change. In capturing this interest, the nature of antislavery activism opened up to include more voices and perspectives. No longer was the protest only coming from clergy and directed at specific congregations. By appealing to the "Briton," writers from diverse gender, race, and class backgrounds could construct an image of national identity that included them. While I would not argue that all antislavery writers believed in the most inclusive form of this identity, they did share a common goal of proliferating their message across the mother country. To that end, activists incorporated and accepted a more expansive definition of the Briton. The proslavery response contested, redefined, and limited this identity in innovative ways.

The dynamic climate of reform did not go completely unchallenged by the status quo, and proslavery writers responded to the shifts in antislavery rhetoric with their own set of reforms. While no unified "proslavery" strategy existed prior to the 1780s, the escalating list of sins attributed to slave traders and slave holders necessitated an appropriate response. The gathering of public support shook many planters and merchants out of their complacency and the belief that the institution was safely established in British commerce. When the traditional arguments in support of slavery ceased to address antislavery concerns in an adequate fashion, slavery supporters had to devise new strategies to defend their livelihoods. The attack on the slave trade threatened both the livelihood of planters and merchants and their legitimacy in the newly configured "moral" nation. Proslavery writers had to propose a different version of national identity that validated the practice of slavery and reaffirmed their own place within the British nation.

Chapter 4

The Proslavery Rebuttal: Developing New Strategies of Defense, 1770–1789

Until the 1770s, writers in Great Britain and her colonies had no need to organize a systematic defense of the institution of slavery. The general public appeared largely apathetic about the concerns of early antislavery activists who questioned the morality of slave holding and slave trading. This public apathy stemmed from a number of different sources. Great Britain's entry into slave trading and the establishment of colonies was comparatively later than that of other prominent European nations, specifically Spain, Holland, and Portugal. Early debates about the morality of slavery addressed the more circumscribed audience of the aristocracy, Parliamentarians, and the clergy. The middle and working classes had little understanding of how the slave colonies functioned, let alone the plight of the slaves. By the time the general public became aware of slavery, it was a fait accompli, a necessary evil to be tolerated in order to maintain commerce and "national prosperity."

Many colonials believed that the consumer demand for New World merchandise also established a continual need for slave labor in the production of commodities like sugar, tobacco, and cotton. The mercantilist economy in Great Britain emphasized the importance of trade for maintaining the welfare and prosperity of the British citizenry. Colonial goods were largely luxury items that had initially been limited to upper-class and wealthy consumers, but they were now increasingly available to the middle and working classes. The wealth generated by colonial settlements, the value of continued trade with these settlements, and the British public's consumption of slave-produced wares seemed to guarantee unqualified support for colonial slavery. However, the successful anti-slave-trade campaign forced advocates of slavery to develop a new and more sophisticated rationale for the institution.

While no one would contend that slavery went unopposed prior to this organized effort, the institution was part of the status quo and viewed as integral to the continued economic prosperity of Great Britain. The only consistent opposition to slavery in the seventeenth and early eighteenth century came from the pulpit. Antislavery clergy waged a largely reactive campaign against proslavery clergy who mined the Old Testament for proof that the Bible supported African slavery. These early exchanges did little to educate the public about the evils of slavery, nor did they pose a significant threat to colonial slave trading or slave holding.

As a result, no clearly defined proslavery argument materialized to counter early antislavery claims of unChristian and immoral behavior fostered by the institution of slavery. However, important transformations in the public perception of slavery and the developing British "national character" helped to shift the balance of power from the proslavery to the abolitionist camp. This process instigated a significant rethinking of the arguments in favor of slavery as writers were called upon increasingly to justify the West Indian way of life. The most dynamic period for these new arguments emerged in the last two decades of the eighteenth century, during the most active time of abolitionist publication. The advent of compelling abolitionist writers and an influential court decision revealed cracks in the status quo.

Most scholarship on the first abolitionist campaign focuses exclusively on the activities of the antislavery societies and often relegates proslavery writing to the background. Older analyses, such as Eugene Genovese's *The World the Slaveholders Made* (1969) credit the antebellum South with the clearest articulation of the proslavery position. Studies like Paul Finkelman's *Proslavery Thought, Ideology, and Politics* (1989) and Larry Tise's *Proslavery: A History of the Defense of Slavery in America, 1701–1840* (1987) offer excellent and comprehensive analyses of the various arguments in proslavery thought. More recent works like David F. Ericson's *The Debate over Slavery* (2000) attempt to examine the interaction of proslavery and antislavery, specifically in the context of antebellum United States. While later works have acknowledged the proslavery discourse of the West Indies, few critics have closely examined the interaction between proslavery and antislavery ideologies. In spite of studies like Tise's *Proslavery*, historians continue to locate the solidification of the proslavery position in the nineteenth century, specifically the American South.[1] While this period presents ample evidence for examination, almost exclusive focus on the antebellum South devalues the contributions of West Indian planters to the definition of proslavery arguments. I contend that the proslavery position solidified during the slave-trade debates and incorporated a specific set of assertions intended to justify the existence and rehabilitate the image of plantation societies. Proslavery writers challenged abolitionist charges and developed sophisticated rhetorical strategies to defend the institution to the eighteenth-century British audience.

This chapter traces the evolution of the major proslavery arguments that developed from 1770 to 1792 and analyzes their implications for the formation of British national identity. These rebuttals offered a different construction of national identity that emphasized commerce and trade as the primary elements

---

[1] Tise mentions the major arguments generated by West Indian writers during the first and second abolitionist campaign, although he does not go into a great deal of depth regarding the nuances of their tracts. His primary purpose is to establish that many of these arguments did not originate in the "American South" as older historians would claim. See "Proslavery Heritage of Britain and the West Indies, 1770–1833," in *Proslavery: A History of the Defense of Slavery in America, 1701–1840* (Athens, GA: The University of Georgia Press, 1987).

of the nation. The impetus for these writings came primarily from the threat that merchants and planters rightly perceived as resulting from the Somerset decision and from the growing support for the antislavery cause. The rhetorical framing of proslavery arguments shifted in response to Lord Mansfield's ruling along with the proliferation of these arguments. Proslavery writers responded to the antislavery attacks following the decision by using increasingly sophisticated rhetorical strategies that demonstrated an awareness of crucial changes in public sympathies. The tone and content of these publications set up the extent to which advocates of slavery felt threatened by Somerset's manumission.[2] Proslavery writers attempted to establish a superior ethos as compared to antislavery writers in order to reclaim representations of slavery. For example, one strategy employed by most authors involved identifying themselves by occupational titles, such as "West India planter" or "A Merchant," in an attempt to underscore the validity of their text. Unlike claims made by antislavery writers who had never visited the West Indies, these writers maintained that direct experience with slavery afforded them a clearer, less biased perspective. The most notable difference in language between proslavery and antislavery tracts appeared in the terms used to describe those who were involved with the institution. In keeping with proslavery conventions, I have shifted from using the terms "traders and owners" to the more innocuous terms of "merchants and planters." Proslavery pamphlets and tracts offered an opposing image of national identity—of the commercially savvy, "white" Briton poised to outstrip other European powers in trade. Authors constructed a self-consciously "white" identity and utilized race discourse to underscore their superiority over their slaves. Proslavery writers responded to the threat of abolition by creating a dynamic set of arguments that proved highly sensitive to the shifts in antislavery rhetoric and the discourse of national identity.

Invalidating Antislavery Interpretations of the "Mansfield decision"

The Somerset decision and subsequent antislavery interpretations of the ruling shattered the complacency of the merchants and planters who relied on slave labor for their livelihoods. The immediate significance of this case was the destruction of precedent. Lord Mansfield's ruling essentially reversed two prior opinions regarding the legality of slavery in England and threatened the validity of colonial laws respecting slavery. Though the decision had little impact on the actual practice of slavery in Great Britain or her colonies, the antislavery interpretation of the decision questioned slave traders' and slave holders' ability to reconcile the practice with the ideals of the Briton. The larger issue that grew out of this decision involved the definition of national character and who qualified under that definition. Activists turned the tables on traders and planters by casting doubt on

---

[2] A portion of this chapter was published as "Developing the West Indian Proslavery Position after the Somerset Decision," *Slavery and Abolition* 24.3 (2003): 40–60.

the humanity of those who claimed "property rights" in human beings. By issuing a writ of habeas corpus for James Somerset, Granville Sharp and his colleagues forced the court to recognize the humanity of the slave. Charles Stewart, Somerset's master, claimed that a slave was first and foremost property and therefore subject to the will of his owner. When Mansfield refused to acknowledge the validity of this claim, he left the institution of slavery vulnerable to attack. A unified proslavery position began to coalesce in response to this prominent legal decision against an institution that most planters regarded as the status quo.

Prior to the 1770s, no standard or unified proslavery "position" existed in Great Britain or her colonies. Defenders of slavery, comfortable in their belief that the status quo would be maintained, produced reactive rather than proactive arguments in response to antislavery accusations. Most tracts and sermons written to justify the institution directly addressed charges made by a specific tract or sermon written against the institution. The audience for these publications tended to be limited to the specific city or colony (by which I mean Pennsylvania, New Jersey, Barbados) in which the tract was printed. Oftentimes, the rebuttals appeared only once and rarely warranted a second printing or subsequent editions.[3] These printings generally tended to be limited (often by the funds of the author) and distributed personally rather than sold. I do not contend that writers were unaware of the rhetoric being produced by their compatriots in other parts of Great Britain and her colonies; however, they did not perceive a need to build a transatlantic defense of slavery.

Writers in Great Britain, the West Indies, and the American colonies each preferred an ad hoc strategy of argumentation and type of publication based on the nature of the resistance faced. In Great Britain, this resistance primarily took the form of sermons, so most early proslavery publications also took the form of sermons asserting biblical justifications of slavery. By contrast, the West Indies produced very few direct justifications for slavery because planters and merchants encountered almost no opposition on the islands. Instead, writers documented "histories" and "journals" of colonization that included primarily commerce-based, biblical, and to a lesser extent "positive good" arguments legitimating slavery.[4] Limited cross-Atlantic dialogue took place between proponents of slavery, who had no real need to create a collective defense against the sporadic publications criticizing the institution. Planters and merchants wrote from a position of security and viewed antislavery moralizers as more of an annoyance than a significant threat.

---

[3] Some tracts were reprinted much later in the 1780s and '90s in order to combat the growing popularity of the anti-slave-trade movement.

[4] The "positive good theory" of slavery surfaced in Southern American proslavery thought by the 1820s according to Civil War historians in the US. The theory, which appeared earlier in West Indian and metropolitan publications, asserted that Africans were better off as slaves of the British than they were in their native countries. Larry Tise's *Proslavery* illustrates how writers from each region made use of this argument long before the nineteenth century.

A unified proslavery position was not entirely feasible prior to the formation of abolitionist societies because the practice of slavery varied greatly amongst the different colonies. In rhetorical terms, the scene–act ratio had a more critical effect on proslavery writing since the scene delineated the act more definitively than in antislavery writing. Regional differences between writers determined the author's direct experience with slavery, and most proslavery writers wrote from an "eye-witness" position of authority. Slave laws and conditions of enslavement differed across the American and West Indian colonies, so writers had a more nuanced understanding of the act of "slavery." Cotton, tobacco, and sugar were all labor-intensive crops, but the slave experiences on each type of plantation differed in important ways. Slaves also worked as domestic help and on small farms, adding another scenic dimension to the shifting definition of the act. The scene defined the nature and severity of the act in ways that would direct the development of a unified proslavery argument in the face of organized resistance. American colonials witnessed a greater variety in the practice of slavery, whereas the people residing in Great Britain and the West Indies had a narrower image. Both northern and southern American colonists held slaves, but the primarily domestic slavery of the north differed from the plantation slavery of the south, offering several interpretations of the act of slavery.[5] Within Great Britain, only the residents of major cities (for example, London, Bristol, Edinburgh) saw African slaves, and their duties as domestics may not have differed too greatly from the duties of white, "British" servants.[6] As seen in Chapter 3, an Afro-British identity emerged later in the century, so I mark the term "British" as being contextually specific to the proslavery argument. Residents of the West Indies saw the majority of slaves confined to sugar plantation work, which was the antithesis of domestic servitude. Thus colonial planters, colonial merchants, and slave holders in the mother country did not necessarily share a common perception of slavery. To assume all proslavery writers shared a single vision of the institution would result in an anachronistic and misleading reading of documents before the Somerset decision, when, I would argue, a unified proslavery "movement" began to form. The nature of the proslavery writer and his audience transformed significantly over the period of the debates as antislavery writers began to focus almost exclusively on West Indian plantation slavery and vilify planters.[7]

---

[5] By domestic slavery, I refer to householders who did not own plantations but kept a small number of slaves as servants in their homes. Plantation slavery refers to the large number of slaves who were put to work on the cotton, tobacco, and sugar plantations in the West Indies and the Americas. Though plantation owners also used slaves as domestic help, I simplify the distinction for the sake of my argument.

[6] Race discourse also solidified during the debates and the proslavery position maintained the important distinction between "British" and "African."

[7] We have very little evidence of women's proslavery writing from this time period. While proslavery sentiments did appear in travel narratives like Janet Schaw's *A Journal of a Lady of Quality* (1774–1776), published pamphlets were authored almost exclusively by

Both the purpose of proslavery publication and the characteristics of proslavery authorship addressed an elite audience prior to 1772. Most writers did participate actively in a reform discourse that involved making the institution of slavery, specifically the slave trade, more efficient. Ironically, these reformists targeted the slave trade for its abuses of commerce long before antislavery writers focused their attentions on abolishing the trade. Colonial planters and traders felt so confident that the institution of slavery was integral to the well-being of Great Britain that they sought to improve the efficiency of the trade by regulating the Royal African Company. Of course, the purpose of these reforms had little to do with ameliorating the condition of the slave and everything to do with increasing the profits of the merchant and the planter. Slave traders to the West Indies and the Americas wrote bitter diatribes against the abuses of the Company and the unfairness of the monopoly granted by the Crown. They directed their tracts to parliamentarians in the hopes of breaking the monopoly and opening the trade to more independent traders. Early publications were often printed for the author who would distribute them personally to select legislators in the House of Commons or House of Lords. Since reform could only be effected through legislation, writers primarily concerned themselves with addressing political figures. The general public had no place in this agitation for reform, since slavery was considered a public benefit rather than a public issue. Most advocates probably never considered addressing their concerns to the general public until the rise of antislavery sentiment made that neglect dangerous. Instead, these writers cited numerous abuses by agents of the Royal African Company that led to unfair prices for slaves and misrepresented the British in Africa.[8] Such tracts were published in London from the 1740s onward and appeared until the abolition of the slave trade. In fact, this reform discourse later proved very valuable in arguing that abolition of the slave trade would be unnecessary given the proper regulations.[9]

Before 1770, the majority of proslavery rebuttals issued from the American colonies, particularly the northern colonies, where radical antislavery sentiment

---

men. Even Schaw's narrative was circulated only in manuscript form and was not published until 1921.

[8] One example of this type of publication is *Considerations and Remarks on the Present state of the Trade to Africa; with Some Account of the British Settlements in that Country, and the Intrigues of the Natives since the Peace; candidly stated and considered. In a Letter Addressed to the People in Power more particularly the Nation in general.* By a Gentleman, who resided upwards of Fifteen Years in that Country (Lonnon [*sic*]: Printed for and Sold by Mess. Robinson and Roberts, 1771). The author's comments presage many of the rhetorical strategies that are used after the Mansfield decision.

[9] The use of proslavery reform rhetoric had certain drawbacks after the publication of Adam Smith's paean to free labor. While West Indians expressed the need for a continuous supply of slaves from Africa, free labor advocates pointed out that the enormous and tragic turnover on plantations could be avoided if laborers worked voluntarily.

gained momentum before crossing the Atlantic.[10] Quaker activists in Pennsylvania and other writers in Massachusetts and Connecticut challenged many proslavery writers to defend the institution with a regularity not required of West Indian and English proponents. The Quakers had a long history of antislavery agitation and had managed to eradicate slavery almost completely from their own community. Also, antislavery publications in the American colonies were more numerous, possibly because the authors were better able to identify and attack specific examples of brutality that more of their audience was likely to have witnessed. Writers from both the northern and southern American colonies defended the institution of slavery on moral and religious grounds. They utilized many of the arguments that eventually came to be part of the proslavery position, namely biblical, racial, and economic justifications for the institution. Proslavery writing in the American colonies also demonstrated a confidence that the institution of slavery would never be dismantled. These writers viewed slave trading and slave holding as intrinsic to the fabric of colonial society, and Great Britain's desire for the well-being of her colonies would not allow some radical fringe elements to endanger this system. However, Lord Mansfield's decision in the case of James Somerset shook proslavery complacency in a manner that resounded throughout the "British empire."[11]

In the immediate aftermath of Lord Mansfield's decision, several proslavery writers published responses to antislavery activists who called for an end to slavery. Most writers did not have access to the courtroom in which the case was tried. However, within months of the decision, Francis Hargrave published *An Argument in the Case of James Sommersett* (1772) in which he detailed the primary arguments against slave holding in England. The main point that excited proslavery rebuttals was the idea that accepting African slavery would allow the (re)introduction of domestic slavery into England.[12] Antislavery activists asserted that the prized attribute of "liberty" would be violated and, if unchecked, planters would continue to bring African slaves into England who would directly compete with English servants for positions. This fear seemed to have been the cause of Lord Mansfield's ruling and the overturning of precedent. Proslavery writers pointed out the illogic of the decision by claiming that African slaves would actively seek to

---

[10] For a thorough discussion of the American proslavery movement see Tise's *Proslavery*. He identifies about a dozen proslavery tracts produced before the American Revolution which responded to approximately the same number of antislavery tracts.

[11] I use the term "British empire" because several colonial tracts dealing with trade and commerce refer to their position within the empire. Colonial writers of the late eighteenth century clearly viewed themselves as part of an imperial project extending from the East Indies to the West.

[12] Hargrave's tract analyzed the ancient practice of villeinage which some proslavery writers cited as a precedent for slavery in England. However, the practice did not grant "masters" absolute dominion in the same manner; thus, Hargrave argued that villeinage did not establish a basis for African slavery.

come to England, thereby flooding the job market with unwanted and illegitimate labor. Later in the debates, they would push this claim further by contending that "black" domestics would deprive jobs from "native whites." Authors also felt that the decision violated their rights as British subjects, and the judgment ignored the needs of the colonies. They even referred to the ruling as the "Mansfield decision" in their publications, a neat rhetorical move that effectively erased Somerset as an active participant in the case.[13] Planters expressed outrage that the ruling favored "Africans" over the "true" citizens of the empire. This perceived threat to their lives and livelihoods impelled planters to publish their interpretation of English law, which did not support Mansfield's erroneous decision.

The initial rebuttals to antislavery interpretations of Mansfield signaled a critical shift in authorship that transformed the nature of proslavery publication. Most of the authors were residents or former residents of the West Indies, and all of the tracts were published in Great Britain. While the number of vocal slavery advocates in the West Indies grew, American colonials seemed to lose interest in defending the institution—at least to "British" audiences. The discourse of liberty in the 1770s with respect to African slaves emphasized a clear divide between the interests of the mother country and the interests of her colonies. Though American antislavery writers acknowledged the hypocrisy of American cries for liberty, the momentum of independence soon subsumed other concerns. Slavery advocates in these colonies no longer felt pressured to defend their way of life to their own countrymen, while they were embroiled in an increasingly violent struggle over much larger issues.[14] Of course, in the aftermath of the revolution, representatives from slave states ensured the continuation of the institution and had several concessions, such as the 3/5 Compromise,[15] written into the Constitution. Non-slave-holding revolutionaries could not afford to alienate a significant contingent of their supporters by pressing the issue of abolition. The American Revolution

---

[13] I have found no evidence that other scholars have noted this verbal slippage in identification. All contemporary analyses refer to the ruling as the "Somerset decision," attesting to the effectiveness of antislavery propaganda.

[14] A few of the tracts printed by West Indians mentioned the relevance of the Mansfield decision to the American colonies. Estwick's response even "answers individually for every American subject of the king" when defending the validity of slavery and colonial law. However, American writers seemed hardly aware of Mansfield's decision—or pretended to be unaware of the decision. For example, Richard Nisbet, a prominent proslavery writer in Philadelphia, published *Slavery Not Forbidden by Scripture, or a Defence of the West-India Planters* (1773) as a response to Benjamin Rush who clearly mentioned the ruling in favor of Somerset in his own publication. Nisbet does not touch on the Somerset case, even peripherally, in his defense of the planters, nor does he relate his argument to the practice of slavery in the American colonies.

[15] According to the 3/5 Compromise, an African slave counted as three-fifths of a person; by this means Southern states could inflate their population figures to obtain greater representation.

successfully derailed the budding antislavery movement in those colonies, and held abolitionists in abeyance for several decades to follow.

In direct contrast, the West Indies considered itself an integral part of the empire and had a vested interest in thwarting abolitionist propaganda aimed, in their view, at destabilizing that empire. The growing agitation in the American colonies diminished the impact of the Mansfield decision there; however, residents of the West Indies continued to feel close ties to Great Britain and relied on trade with the mother country. They fully appreciated the threat posed by the Mansfield decision and hastened to carry out damage control. Most of the direct responses to post-Somerset, antislavery propaganda originated from West Indian planters and merchants who published primarily in London. Though presses existed in Jamaica and Barbados, those in London reached wider audiences who were comprised both of the elites and the everyday folk. Of course, the large population of absentee landowners living in London off the profits from the Caribbean also utilized London presses as the primary site of the proslavery rebuttal. After the ruling became publicized, West Indian writers began to publish numerous tracts and pamphlets and eventually came to dominate the proslavery response to the antislavery/abolitionist movement.

The catalyst for organizing a proslavery response that actively began to refute antislavery rhetoric occurred with a legal ruling in 1772.[16] Though attacks on slavery seemed to find an increasingly receptive audience in the general public, Parliament and the courts had consistently upheld planter and merchant claims.[17] The belief that the legal system fully supported and encouraged slavery created a sense of security that was seriously threatened by the antislavery interpretations of the Somerset decision. Though Mansfield protested the extent to which his ruling applied to the status of slaves in England, the perceived granting of liberty began a dialogue on the relationship between natural rights and this unnatural practice. The Mansfield decision destabilized the institution in three critical ways: first, by reversing previous opinions that favored planters and merchants; second, by questioning the status of Africans within the British empire, and third, by threatening the legality of slavery in the colonies. These fissures opening in the institution of slavery forced writers to change their tactics by appealing to wider audiences and establishing a counter-discourse of national identity.

Until the Somerset case, all challenges to planters' rights in England had been answered by affirming the owners' entitlement to the bodies and the labor of their slaves. As Stewart's lawyers argued, the writ of habeas corpus could not

---

[16] For a description of the Somerset case and Mansfield's ruling, see Chapter 2. The case was briefly reported in the London papers, but most of the details we know about the incident come from Francis Hargrave's *An Argument in the Case of James Sommersett*. Though the source is highly biased, proslavery advocates referred to Hargrave's publication when crafting their rebuttals to the decision of the court.

[17] The blatantly unjust ruling in the Jonathan Strong case (1769) provided the impetus for Sharp's exhaustive study of English civil law.

be applied to an individual's property. Habeas corpus requires that the body of the person specified in the writ be brought before the judge or court.[18] The slave did not possess the autonomous and independent "body" acknowledged by English law, so the entire case had an invalid premise. James Somerset had been purchased legally from English slave traders in the West Indies, and he therefore did not have any claim to personhood in the eyes of the law.[19] The previous opinions of Yorke-Talbot (1729) and Hardwicke (1749) reaffirmed this lack of personhood by denying the slave any right to manumission based on his or her own actions. Conversion to Christianity, baptism, or the act of traveling to England had no effect on the legal standing of a slave as property.[20] The ability to recognize the personhood of a slave, in the form of manumission, rested solely within the rights of the owner. Until the master willingly released his right to property in the "body" of his slave, the slave in question had no legal recourse in the colonies or in the mother country. This insistence upon absolute dominion over the body of another human being contributed greatly to the moral arguments being used on behalf of Somerset. Owners' rights in England suffered a severe setback when Somerset's lawyers convincingly argued against the right to property in the "body" of the slave.[21]

The legal arguments in Charles Stewart vs. James Somerset pitted the right to property against the right to liberty which initiated a discussion on the personhood of slaves from a legal perspective. As publications prior to this case attested, "Negroes" or "slaves" were often listed as commodities in the rosters of English trading vessels and descriptions of English commerce.[22] The right to property was so ingrained in the colonial argument that "A West Indian" wrote a tract to help

---

[18] The prerogative writ is *habeas corpus ad subjiciendum* which specifies that the body of a person "restrained of liberty" be brought before the court in order to determine whether he or she has been restrained lawfully (*Oxford English Dictionary*, 2nd ed., 1989).

[19] The term "personhood" is mine and does not appear in the legal documents of the period. I prefer this term to "humanity" because the latter term has many implications beyond the legal fact of existing as a human being in the eyes of the law.

[20] The full text of these opinions can be found in Volume 18 of Thomas Bayley Howell, *A Complete collection of state trials and proceedings for high treason and other crimes and misdemeanors from the earliest period to the year 1783* (London: Printed by T. C. Hansard for Longman, Hurst, Rees, Orme, and Browne, 1816–26).

[21] A similar case tried in Scotland in 1774 took four years to yield a verdict. Joseph Knight sued for freedom from his owner John Wedderburn and the court found that no precedent for slavery existed in Scottish common law.

[22] One of many examples occurs in *A Treatise upon the Trade from Great-Britain to Africa; Humbly recommended to the Attention of the Government*, By An African Merchant (London: Printed for R. Baldwin, 1772). He discusses the importance of the trade to Africa and lists the imports or "returns" of the trade as "gold, ivory, wax, dyeing woods and negroes." The placement in the list, even the use of the lower-case letter, indicates the commodification and dehumanization African slaves endured in slavery.

Mansfield come to the proper decision.[23] He proposed to "drop the term slavery," blaming the term for supporting the lawsuit "with the fuel of heated passions and imaginations," and use instead the term "*Property*."[24] The resolution of the case in favor of Somerset represented a real betrayal of the colonial plantocracy that had come to rely on the security of their property rights. Lord Mansfield ignored the weight of precedent that upheld Charles Stewart's claim on his slave, ruling that "Immemorial usage preserves the memory of *positive law*, long after all traces of the occasion, reason, authority and time of its introduction are lost." No "positive law" had been passed to affirm planters' property rights and resultant commodification of human beings. For that matter, no law had ever been passed legalizing slavery in Great Britain or her colonies. This pronouncement incited an uproar among proslavery writers in defense of planters' rights, and the most famous of these writers, Edward Long, immediately issued a response to Mansfield's ruling in which he skillfully identified the hypocrisy of the demand for "positive law" to establish planters' property rights.[25] Long argued, "As our trade esteemed Negroe labourers merely a commodity, … so the parliament of Great Britain has uniformly adhered to the same idea … and hence the planters … deemed their Negroes to be fit objects of purchase and sale, transferable like any other goods or chattels" (4). His response underscored both planter outrage and the major argument slavery advocates used to justify their actions—commerce.

A notable divergence between the focus of antislavery attacks and the proslavery rebuttal occurred as a result of this concentration on commerce. The antislavery writing immediately following the Mansfield decision highlighted how the ruling outlawed the existence of slavery in England. The group whose "rights" were directly negated were the planters, or slave holders in antislavery parlance. Early writers concentrated on disseminating the idea that this initial blow to slavery would eventually destroy the entire institution. Not until the end of 1780s with the formation of the Society for the Abolition of the Slave Trade did writers begin to focus on dismantling the trade between Africa and the colonies. By contrast, proslavery

---

[23] Samuel Estwick, *Considerations on the Negroe Cause commonly so called, addressed to the Right Honourable Lord Mansfield, Lord Chief Justice of the Court of King's Bench, &c., by a West Indian* (London: Printed for J. Dodsley, 1772). Though the tract was written before Lord Mansfield made his ruling, a postscript to the first printing indicates that the author published his work after the case had been decided.

[24] Estwick goes so far as to disclaim the existence of slavery altogether with his verbal slippage between "slave" and "property." In no law, except criminal law, are Negroes referred to as "slaves"; rather, they are "goods and chattel," which are much more benign terms. Estwick rationalizes that criminal law must use the term "slave" because "property" cannot be punished. He never addresses the inherent contradiction in his analysis.

[25] Edward Long, *Candid Reflections upon the Judgment lately award by The Court of King's Bench* (London: Printed for T. Lowndes, 1722). While it is difficult to know how many copies each author had printed, each of these tracts excoriating the Mansfield's decision only went through one printing—a marked contrast to many abolitionist pieces.

writers seemed to identify the threat to the slave trade (and trade in other African goods) immediately. Both planters *and* merchants emphasized the importance of the trade, which was, as one writer put it, "absolutely and essentially necessary" to the welfare of the British state. In *A Treatise upon the Trade from Great-Britain to Africa* (1772), "An African Merchant" stressed that "[t]he very land of England depends upon the sea; to commerce we owe the encrease [*sic*] of our national treasure, the breed and excellency and plentiful supply of seamen ... in short, every advantage which can excite a spirit of industry to acquire the comforts of life" (3–4).[26] Edward Long warned that "[a] nation supported wholly by its trade, cannot long continue to flourish if the laws of her commerce are set at variance with her municipal laws" (3). Planters and merchants demonstrated a fuller realization of the interconnectedness of trade and slave societies. While the language of antislavery activists betrayed a certain naiveté about economic interdependence, proslavery counter-arguments evinced a shrewd understanding of the immediate danger, not to slave holding, but to slave trading.

The most significant threat to both commerce and the institution of slavery came with the idea that no nation could deprive a human being of his or her "personhood." A key component in Charles Stewart's claim involved Somerset's status as property under English law. Stewart's lawyers endeavored throughout the whole trial to make his case based on property, arguing that Somerset's personhood was not relevant. However, as Granville Sharp argued in *A Representation of the Injustice and Dangerous Tendency of Tolerating Slavery* (1769), slaves coming from Africa could not be divested of their *"natural rights"* by an act of English law. He wrote, "because he was not born in slavery (as are many unhappy persons in the English plantations) but was *free* born; of human, not base, parents; parents who had as much right to their *natural liberty*, as the wild animals," the slaves brought to the colonies were subjects of the King (10). Proslavery writers found this assertion of the slave subject to be anathema, and they countered it with an opposing vision of the Briton. They responded by distinguishing between "the free-born Briton," who was the "natural-born subject" or "native Briton," and the "foreign" African slave. As Long stated in *Candid Reflections*, "this class of people were neither meant, nor intended, in any of the general laws of the realm, made for the benefit of its genuine and natural-born subjects" (13). Proslavery writers, specifically Edward Long, hastened to deny that any "Negro" either "born in the realm" or "out of the realm" could become a *"natural-born subject."* Regardless of place of birth, all "Africans" remained foreigners under the jurisdiction of

---

[26] An African Merchant, *A Treatise upon the Trade from Great-Britain to Africa; Humbly recommended to the Attention of the Government* (London: Printed for R. Baldwin, 1772). There is a certain irony contained in these remarks as the injurious effects of the slave trade on British seaman became a major point of argument between proslavery and antislavery writers. The proslavery position will be discussed at length in the following sections of this chapter.

the King, without the protections of the King.[27] "An alien, in the construction of our English law, is not properly under the King's protection, ... until he is enfranchised by act of Parliament" (Long 35). The Mansfield decision constituted neither an act of Parliament nor the enfranchisement of African slaves. Estwick carried this argument further by citing the charter for the Royal African Company as a definitive legal document or "positive law" in favor of slavery and the right to property in a slave. The charter granted the Company rights to trade in "land, forts, castles, slaves, military stores, and other effects," thereby defining African slaves as property by an act of Parliament.

Some writers turned the discourse of the slave as subject against the interests of other, more legitimate subjects of the realm, who functioned under comparable forms of domination. West Indian writers used this tactic more than others to defend their rights as masters and to argue on behalf of "rightful citizens." As "free-born Britons," the planters and merchants who brought their property to Great Britain had a greater right to the protection of English law. By what rationale could any legal system justify superseding the rights of natives in favor of foreigners? Planters and merchants argued that their right to the labor of a legally purchased slave should be respected anywhere in the world and *especially* in Great Britain. Writers also characterized the Mansfield decision as favoring African slaves over the English working classes. They set up an oppositional relationship between African slaves and the English lower classes that questioned the validity of granting the slave rights denied to "lawful" subjects. If a servant in Great Britain refused to perform the duties for which he or she was hired then that servant was punishable under English law. The planter questioned in defense, "but my slave must be *discharged*, and gain his *liberty* at the expence [*sic*] and by the loss of my *property*" (13).[28] Planters and merchants asserted that the labors of a slave did not exceed the labors of other types of servitude practiced both in Great Britain and her colonies. "Shall we retain an indentured servant, who is one of our brethren in hard and disagreeable service; and yet under a vain pretence of liberty, set an alien free at once, whose *whole* time we have purchased?" (5).[29]

---

[27] This statement directly contradicts Granville Sharp who in his *Representation* argued that "All persons during their residence in Great-Britain are subjects; and as such, bound to the laws and under the King's protection." See Figure 2.2(b).

[28] *A Treatise upon the Trade from Great-Britain to Africa* includes several appendices in which the author quotes other writers who support his contentions. Appendix B contains excerpts from three "treatises" published by "Mercator," who is thought to be Sir John Gladstone, in June and July of 1772. As I cannot find the first printing of these tracts, I cite them by the page on which they appear in the appendix.

[29] The conditions of indentured servitude were very harsh in the colonies, particularly the West Indies, so the comparison is apt. However, as antislavery writers quickly pointed out, the period of indenture was finite, but the slave lost his or her liberty in perpetuity. For patterns of emigration, see Henry A. Gemery, "Markets for Migrants: English Indentured Servitude and Emigration in Seventeenth and Eighteenth Centuries," in *Colonialism and*

The fear of slaves being considered subjects of the realm also intensified the concern that the Mansfield decision would destabilize colonial law. Antislavery writers seized the opportunity to extend the arguments against Stewart's claims on Somerset to slavery in the colonies. If such an institution could not be tolerated in the mother country, how could her colonies justifiably practice such an atrocity that had now been formally condemned by English law? Mercator speculated hysterically about the implications of freeing slaves in the West Indies and the specter of slave rebellions that would follow. "Conquest would make them our masters ... to the utter stagnation of trade, the destruction of commerce, and the infinite loss of the West-India proprietors, merchants, and others connected with them" (10) (see Figure 4.3). Though this response represented an extreme form of the early reactions to Mansfield, colonial planters had a legitimate concern about the danger to their property. They emphasized the enormous cost to the realm should the highly profitable West India colonies be beggared by fleeing or rebelling slaves.[30] Reformists were quick to propose changes in colonial law in an attempt to satisfy critics who denounced the immorality of slavery. However, proposing those changes was another strategy to reinforce the legality and the validity of colonial law. Amending the law was quite different from dismissing it. Slavery advocates agreed that this "national breach of faith" represented a "repugnancy" to "commerce" and would result in serious damage to "national prosperity."

Antislavery writers effectively transformed one legal decision into a question of national character. They lauded the efforts made on behalf of one slave and generalized his ruling to all of England. The rhetoric used to claim this enormous victory for righteousness emphasized the compassion and respect for liberty inherent in *all* Britons. Thus, their arguments claimed to invalidate the practice of slavery not only in England, but in her colonies as well. More important, they cast doubt on the character of merchants and planters, going so far as to question their identities as "true Britons." Antislavery writers based their appeals on mobilizing the public, so they chose to create and define elements of a national character that separated the legitimate from the illegitimate subjects of the Crown. Proslavery writers perceived their livelihood, their way of life, their very place in the nation to be under threat. Having chosen this terrain, antislavery writers pushed slavery advocates to justify not only slavery but their identity as Britons.

Migration; Indentured Labour before and after Slavery, ed. P. C. Emmer (Dordrecht, The Netherlands: Martinus Nijhoff Publishers, 1986).

[30] West Indian colonials had been dealing with periodic slave rebellions, particularly in Jamaica, almost from their founding. Thomas Holt's *The Problem of Freedom: Race, Labor, and Politics in Jamaica and Britain* (Baltimore: Johns Hopkins University Press, 1992) explains the powerful influence of slave rebellions on Jamaican planters and the effect of these rebellions on the calls for abolition. Though the revolution in St. Domingue is cited as postponing abolition of the slave trade for another decade, slave rebellions were a very real threat to West Indian planters, who felt that their fears had been vindicated by the horrifying events in the French colony.

Colonial writers responded to this challenge by creating another image of the Briton as cosmopolitan businessman. When arguing for the supremacy of property rights, planters often invoked competition with other nations as an inducement to maintaining the slave trade and acknowledging slavery in the colonies. The "kingdom of commerce" could not function if crippled by laws that gave other nations, specifically France and Spain, the advantage in trade. The colonies depended on the labor and trade with Africa for their functioning, and denying slavery in England unfairly privileged foreign traders over the legitimate citizens of the colonies. Estwick recommended that Mansfield propose a law forbidding the transportation of Negroes into England rather than declaring them free once they reached the country. "[B]y this act you will preserve the race of Britons from stain and contamination; and you will rightly confine a property to those countries, upon whose prosperity and welfare the independent being of this country rests" (44).

The dire implications of Mansfield's ruling, as promised by antislavery activists, did not come to pass and planters continued to bring their slaves to England without too much fear of manumission. However, the ideological shift that occurred instigated significant alterations in the status quo and signaled changes in the balance of power. The number of antislavery publications grew steadily during the course of the 1780s, culminating in the formation of the Society for the Abolition of the Slave Trade in London and other cities across Great Britain. A major strategy used to elicit public sympathy depicted the harsh conditions of West Indian slavery and the atrocities committed by corrupt slave holders. Proslavery interests realized they could no longer rely on a sympathetic legal system and Parliament to look after their interests. They were also aware of the growing need to counteract the negative representations of slavery rapidly disseminating throughout country.[31] The next phase of the proslavery rebuttal involved contesting the validity, accuracy, and veracity of antislavery depictions of the slave trade and life on the West Indian plantations.

Developing Counter-Arguments and Rhetorical Strategies

As the feeling against slavery began to draw more support from multiple strata of society, proslavery writers experienced the first threat to their previously secure way of life. Antislavery writing developed particular rhetorical strategies to capture the public's interest and titillate their imagination in the two decades following Mansfield's decision. Authors employed pathetic appeals in more of their essays and pamphlets in order to increase awareness of the problem and advocate for solutions. The most common form of this appeal involved illustrations

---

[31] A simple check of print records listed in the English Short Title Catalogue shows that antislavery publications were distributed in London, Bristol, Edinburgh, Dublin, Manchester, and Liverpool. The period between 1787 and 1793 experienced the greatest number and diversity of publications that spanned the whole of Britain.

of the middle passage and plantation life. Portraits of the abject African pervaded literature and became a commonplace in other types of publications. Even writers without overt abolitionist intentions utilized tropes of slave oppressions. How did proslavery writers respond to these negative depictions of slavery? The detailed recounting of slave tortures and "despotic" colonial laws proved very compelling to metropolitan audiences. Proslavery writers had to develop strategies designed to counter and neutralize these highly titillating portraits.

The proliferation of antislavery depictions of slave trading and holding necessitated a more considered proslavery response. Regardless of the narrow legal implications of Mansfield, the perceived effects seriously disrupted the status quo in Great Britain. Planters and merchants regarded the gradual shift in the balance of power with alarm and began to oppose antislavery claims with more seriousness. The most disruptive outcome of antislavery interpretations of Mansfield, from the perspective of slave holders, involved the new adversarial relationship between Britain and her colonies. Mansfield's decision called into question the validity of colonial laws that slave holders, particularly in the West Indies, believed had royal and parliamentary sanction. Antislavery writers depicted the horrors of slavery to distinguish further the difference in morality between the colonies and the mother country. They used graphic descriptions to drive a strategic wedge between the commercial and moral interests of the nation. However, most antislavery writers had a major weakness in their use of second-hand testimony—a lack of personal experience.[32] Proslavery strategists quickly exploited this weakness by discrediting pathetic appeals of antislavery texts with their own, more valid descriptions.

The critical shifts in the relationship between Great Britain and her colonies over the 1770s and '80s significantly influenced proslavery strategies over time. Since antislavery activists proclaimed that the "natural right" to liberty trumped property rights by English law, proslavery strategists were forced to reformulate their arguments regarding the validity of slavery. They continued to rely on biblical justifications that argued British practices were consistent with Old Testament and New Testament doctrines. However, antislavery claims clearly presented new challenges even to these time-tested validations of slavery. The charges of "inhumanity" leveled at planters and merchants demanded a more detailed rationale than the Bible could supply. Thomas Thompson's *The African Trade for Negro Slaves, consistent with Humanity and Revealed Religion* (1772) included an additional validation of colonial slavery by examining the "humanity" inherent within the practice. Thompson distinguished British colonial slavery from the "merciless system of the church of *Rome*" and declared that the more humane practices did "honour to the subjects of the *British* crown" (7). Unlike previous religious publications, this author focused more on the treatment of slaves in the colonies most likely with the intent to counter antislavery accusations. He argued

---

[32] The three major exceptions to this lack of personal experience were the tracts produced by Alexander Falconbridge, John Newton, and James Ramsay; Ramsay proved to be both more prolific and more controversial in his writings against slavery and the slave trade.

that the slave trade was "as vindicable as any species of trade whatever" and that "slavery then had its origin from a principle of humanity, and averseness to shedding blood" (21). However, charges of "inhumanity" could not be sufficiently addressed through scriptural refutation. Writers like Anthony Benezet and Granville Sharp had introduced a new strategy of critique that forced slavery advocates to rethink their tactics.

Antislavery writers proved very adept at manipulating public sympathies, so proslavery writers had to find and exploit the weaknesses in their arguments. Since most antislavery images of the middle passage and plantation life came from secondhand accounts, the most glaring weakness stemmed from the limited credibility of the authors. Benezet's work relied heavily on secondhand testimonials of merchant and planter cruelty, some of which he had copied from an earlier, anonymously printed antislavery tract. Many prominent writers after Benezet lifted their descriptions from his work, the most famous example being John Wesley's *Thoughts Upon Slavery* (1774). Benezet attributed his testimonials to particular men who had served on slave ships and plantations in order to establish his ethos. Other writers, like Sharp, were not nearly as diligent. As the "oppressed African" became a trope in literary forms, authors did not bother to claim a source for their depictions. Thus, proslavery writers had a powerful rhetorical strategy that could be used to combat the negative portrayals of the institution of slavery—an ethical appeal based on personal experience.

To attack antislavery ethos effectively, most writers had to take into account the impact of negative slave depictions on the public. Antislavery writers had persuaded the general public to accept their depictions of enslavement as the "true condition" of Africans in the colonies. They created the scenes, defined the agents, and vilified the act. By successfully claiming this rhetorical power, writers effectively challenged the status quo and placed slavery advocates increasingly on the defensive. The relationship between colony and mother country underwent several changes and redefinitions, specifically with respect to the slave-trade debates. Subjects in the mother country began to understand that slave practices differed according to region and conditions of each colony, albeit with a bias towards the antislavery depictions of these differences. The public's image of the colonial slave holder sharpened as a result of negative antislavery portrayals. All of these factors combined to necessitate two different appeals to ethos in proslavery rebuttals—local authenticity and eye-witness testimony. Writers sought to discredit antislavery tracts while highlighting their own, more accurate portrayals of slave conditions. Over the course of the 1770s and '80s, authorship, scene, and agency underwent multiple transformations in proslavery writing, which attempted to reclaim representations of slave trading and slave holding.

Since these activities were largely supported by Parliament and the Crown, the proslavery campaign emerged as a primarily defensive response to antislavery claims. This defensiveness took on new significance as government support began to weaken in the wake of public outrage. Also, antislavery writers changed their strategies to include serious and inflammatory attacks against the character of merchants and planters. As their claims began to broaden in scope, the proslavery responses needed to move beyond traditional justifications that had sufficed in earlier decades. They had to counter personal charges of "inhumanity," "dishonour," and "despotism." Antislavery writers claimed a "superior sense of liberty" and argued for the "natural rights" of Africans. They charged the institution with corrupting slave holders because of the "absolute power" exercised by the master over the lives of his slaves. Proslavery writers needed to defend their practices *and* their characters, which instigated a critical shift in authorship by the 1770s. No longer could sympathetic clergy counter critiques of slavery without addressing the realities of trading and plantation life. Additionally, the revolutionary fight for independence in the American colonies de-emphasized the antislavery resistance and limited the need for proslavery response. Rebuttals came with increasing frequency, and almost wholly, from West Indian planters and merchants.

Though American slavery was condemned, the most virulent criticism by activists focused on the West Indies. In the early 1770s, American antislavery writers hesitated to castigate fully their own colonial practices and often concentrated their attention on West Indian practices. For example, Benjamin Rush's *An Address to the Inhabitants of the British Settlements in America upon Slave-Keeping* (1773) vilified West Indian planters and advocated the abolition of the slave trade. As the American slave colonies no longer relied solely on the trade to supply their plantations, the proposed abolition would primarily affect the West Indian planters. Rush's commentary evoked an almost immediate response and Richard Nisbet's *Slavery Not Forbidden by Scripture, or a Defence of the West-India Planters* appeared in the same year.[33] Published in Philadelphia, a city known for its antislavery leanings, Nisbet's tract was among the first to question seriously and systematically the credibility of writers like Rush who had little or no direct experience of slavery. Other authors had questioned the ethos of antislavery publications in the past, but their defense of slavery did not focus on discrediting the writers themselves, merely their logic. In his preface, Nisbet referred to the "malevolent slander" that had been "exaggerated beyond the most distant bounds of probability." He characterized Rush's tract as "abuse levelled at an entire body of people," and the overgeneralized portrait of West India planters could be "refuted by every school boy." Not only were Rush's comments deemed petty, but his logic was also subject to extended critique.

West India planters were clearly put on the defensive by the portrayal of slavery in the islands. The emerging sense of both colonial and metropolitan audiences centered on the detrimental effects of plantation slavery as epitomized by the West

---

[33] Richard Nisbet, *Slavery Not Forbidden by Scripture or a Defence of the West-India Planters, From the Aspersions thrown out against them, by the author of a pamphlet, entitled, "An Address to the inhabitants of the British settlements in America, upon Slave-Keeping,"* By a West Indian (Philadelphia, 1773). In the epigraph to his essay, Nisbet quotes Shakespeare: "But he that filches from me my good Name, / Robs me of that, which not enriches him, / And makes me poor indeed" (*Othello* iii.2).

Indies. The number of critiques of the southern American colonies steadily fell over the course of the 1770s, and the American slave holder was not vilified to the same extent as the West Indian planter. One possible reason for this milder criticism stemmed from the differences in slavery among the various colonies. Sugar proved to be a more labor-intensive crop than tobacco or cotton. Since the main product of the West Indian colonies was sugar, the conditions of slavery were more grueling than in the southern American colonies.[34] The scene of critique underwent a major transformation and became localized in the sugar plantation colonies of the West Indies. As these colonies also supported the bulk of the slave trade, they presented antislavery writers with a compact target on which to focus. Antislavery writers rarely distinguished in their accounts if and how practices varied across individual islands, with the exception of analyses of specific laws. Rather, they tended to address the West Indies as a whole, giving credence to planter critiques of their lack of familiarity with the sugar colonies. Another factor influencing the change of circumference was the American Revolution. The turbulence and demands for liberty coming from those colonies stifled the local antislavery activists and redirected the attention of British activism. Writers in Great Britain did point out the hypocrisy of American claims, but they were eventually forced to acknowledge that they could not effect positive change in that environment. By the mid-1780s, most writers were aware of the American rebellion and the failure of the British army to quell it. The West Indies, however, were too reliant on the metropole even to contemplate revolution.

The rhetorical struggle to control public perceptions of the "agent" of slavery added another dimension to the proslavery rebuttal. Antislavery writers defined this agent as colonial planter or trader. Proslavery writers, in critiquing this argument for reform, recast the "agent" as a loyal citizen of the empire and interrogated the motives of activists. Advocates for slavery characterized their opposition as overly idealistic and unrealistic in their proposed reforms. Nisbet and many of the writers who would follow capitalized on the reform impulse that was gaining momentum in Great Britain to propose greater regulations for the institution of slavery. The major flaw of antislavery writing, according to Nisbet, was the failure to suggest feasible solutions to the problem. Of course, that criticism also involved a skillful redefinition of the "problem." Advocates viewed slavery as a firmly entrenched institution of both empire and commerce, albeit with "its particular abuses"; however, that was not "sufficient" to "condemn" the institution "totally." They

---

[34] I do not mean to imply that conditions in southern American colonies were easy, but the mortality rate tended to be lower in those colonies and the slave population did reproduce itself in some of them. Of course, variations do exist but antislavery had as little interest in such nuances in the southern colonies as they did in the West Indies. Many antislavery writers produced statistics, with varying degrees of accuracy, to attest to the fact that the American South still had the advantage and used these statistics to vilify further the conditions of the West Indies. The most comprehensive study of these statistics is Roger Anstey's *The Atlantic Slave Trade and British Abolition, 1760–1810* (1975).

were prepared to concede that the institution suffered from poor management and improper regulation, all of which could be rectified by appropriate legislation. Nisbet criticized Rush and his compatriots on the grounds that "[i]nstead of advising some wholsome [*sic*] regulations and improvements, they spend their time in fruitless reproaches, and afterwards declare that slavery ought to be utterly abolished, as if their dictates were to be implicitly followed" (1). The answer, according Nisbet and his successors, was better management and reform.

Proslavery writers cleverly co-opted the rhetoric of reform to counter antislavery arguments and to accommodate the demands of the public. To be sure, suggestions for reform had been proposed by slavery advocates in the past, before the start of the abolitionist campaign. These reforms, however, focused on the monopoly of the Royal African Company, the condition of the forts along the West African coast, and trading practices in Africa. Their stated purpose was to encourage trade and increase prosperity, both their own and the nation's. In other words, they concentrated solely on commerce-based arguments designed to appeal to a wealthy and powerful legislative audience. However, these commerce-based arguments could not adequately combat the rising belief in humanitarian social reform. Writers like Nisbet, Long, Estwick, Tobin, and others managed to fulfill two goals with the same strategy. By proposing their own reforms of colonial law and slaving activities in Africa, they discredited the "naive" and "irresponsible" schemes of antislavery activists and illustrated their willingness to make positive change. However, proslavery writers had a much more serious problem in trying to redeem their own image in the eyes of the public.

The negative images of the merchant and the planter found a highly receptive audience in the British public and proved particularly difficult to counter. Antislavery writers relegated the slave merchant to a particular species of evil in that his actions affected many lives across Africa. They accused merchants of inciting wars among tribes in order to increase the supply of slaves. Writers recounted the horrors of the middle passage in lurid detail and focused on the particular victimization of African women. Perhaps the most vivid description of the sailors' predation upon African women occurred in John Newton's *Thoughts Upon the African Slave Trade* (1788). "When the Women and Girls are taken on board a ship, naked, trembling, terrified ... they are often exposed to the wanton rudeness of white Savages" (96). Newton even referred to the women as "prey" and commented further "[w]here resistance, or refusal, would be utterly in vain, even the sollicitation [*sic*] of consent is seldom thought of" (96). The details rarely differed and the effectiveness of the antislavery strategy often lay in the repetition of stories between texts. For example, Thomas Cooper's *Letters on the Slave Trade* (1787)[35] quotes Clarkson's *Essay on Slavery* to comment on the "unrestrained commerce of sailors with female slaves" (13). A certain prurient fascination

---

[35] Thomas Cooper, *Letters on the slave trade, First published in* Wheeler's Manchester Chronicle; *and since reprinted with additions and alterations, by Thomas Cooper, Esq.* (Manchester: Printed by C. Wheeler, 1787).

with the macabre emerged from these detailed accounts of the slave trade that seemed to titillate as much as to appall. Activists added another dimension to their negative portrayal by expanding critiques into other media such as cartoons and illustrations. Negative depictions of the slave merchant had not proliferated nearly to the extent of illustrations regarding the evils of plantation life.

By the late 1780s, the depiction of planters became a common element of antislavery writing, and planters, themselves, found these depictions to be both politically and psychologically disturbing. Even after the campaign focused primarily on the slave trade, West Indian planters continued to author the majority of publications in an attempt to reconstruct their deeply maligned characters. A distinct split in characterization emerged in indictments of slavery, which can best be described through perceptions of agent and act. Descriptions of the slave trade tended to involve an act–agent ratio in which the act induced the cruelty of the agent. Plantation life, however, revolved around the agent–act ratio, where the agent inspired the cruelty of the act. In other words, the colonial planter suffered from more virulent indictments of his character while the slave merchant was less frequently the subject of such attacks. James Tobin, a staunch defender of slavery, wrote "it seems to be the universal aim of every author who has occasion to mention a West India planter, to render that name synonymous with a cruel and relentless task master" (26).[36] Planters were further stigmatized as "wicked," "inhuman," and "advocates of oppression." The West Indian "nabob" represented a threat to the British concept of liberty and violated the "natural rights" of men by employing slave labor.[37] Antislavery writers envisioned the plantations as petty dictatorships, each controlled by an "absolute" ruler. The colonial plantocracy felt persecuted by these depictions and bitterly resented the presumption of antislavery writers. Their strategy to combat these negative portrayals once again relied on questioning the ethos of the writers.

Before proslavery writers could reclaim the portrayals of plantation life and slave trading, they had to discredit the antislavery assessment of their actions. They launched a two-fold attack that questioned the credentials and the motives of antislavery writers. First, they denounced the damaging portrayals of "typical" conditions on slave ships and plantations. These depictions were "ill-founded,

---

[36] James Tobin, *A Short Rejoinder to the Reverend Mr. Ramsay's reply: with a word or two on some other publications of the same tendency* (Salisbury: printed for G. and T. Wilkie, London: by E. Easton, Salisbury, and J. B. Becket, Bristol, 1787). Tobin's essay was part of a publication war that ensued in the mid-1780s over James Ramsay's antislavery tracts.

[37] The term "nabob" is a corruption of the Urdu word "nawab"(meaning petty prince or chieftan) and was originally applied to East India merchants who had made their fortunes overseas and returned to England. The term came to represent colonial wealth and was applied, albeit less frequently, to West Indian planters and merchants. The trial of Warren Hastings in the later century revived the use of the term with all its contemptible implications of oppression.

partial, and unjust," disseminated by "specious pretenders" to humanity. Some writers dismissed the authors and their accusations as "unreasonable." "There are no *arguments* in *abuse*; and as I address myself only to persons of enlarged and liberal minds, I have nothing of that sort to apprehend."[38] John Matthews stated that his essay addressed the "assertions" made by abolitionists "as my *own knowledge and information* may suggest" (163, emphasis mine). Others used a more subtle approach and requested that antislavery writers "endeavour" to be better informed in terms of "real existence" of facts. The standard for acquiring better information clearly came out of firsthand accounts and personal experience on the island. Many proslavery writers signed their rebuttals by their occupations, such as "A Planter," "An African Merchant," "A West India Planter." Since most of the authors of these pseudonymous tracts later identified themselves, I would argue that the pseudonym was intended to establish the credentials of the author. In some cases, as in the debate between James Ramsay and James Tobin, the proslavery writer was challenged to claim his tract. Antislavery writers interpreted the use of the pseudonym as a way of launching anonymous attacks against their pamphlets. Therefore, the authenticity of "A Planter" required no further proof, and though antislavery writers cited sources who carried similar credentials, they did not merit consideration as theirs were "exaggerated tales" by "mariners" whose opinions made them less than "competent judges." In other words, the stories of malcontents provided little credible support for criticism of an institution so important to the British empire.

The best example proving proslavery reliance on ethical appeals occurred in the furious publication war over James Ramsay's antislavery tracts.[39] In 1784, Ramsay published two tracts, *An Essay on the Treatment and Conversion of African Slaves in the British Sugar Colonies* (see Figure 4.1) and *An Inquiry into the Effects of putting a stop to the African Slave Trade, and of granting Liberty to the slaves in the British Sugar Colonies*, both of which strongly denounced the practice of slavery in the colonies and proposed a plan to replace slave labor gradually with free labor from Great Britain.[40] Though Ramsay's pamphlets were neither the most

---

[38] John Matthews, *A Voyage to the River Sierra-Leone on the Coast of Africa with an additional letter on the subject of the African Slave Trade* (London: Printed for B. White and Son, 1788), 162.

[39] Ramsay has been largely forgotten in historical scholarship on slavery and the slave trade. However, his impact on proslavery rhetoric earns him a critical place in the abolitionist movement. For a brief biography of Ramsay, see Folarin Shyllon, *James Ramsay: The Unknown Abolitionist* (Edinburgh: Canongate, 1977). And for a discussion of Ramsey's multiple writing styles in his *Essay*, see also "'Read this, and Blush'": The Pamphlet War of the 1780s," chapter 4 in Brycchan Carey's *British Abolitionism and the Rhetoric of Sensibility*

[40] *An Essay on the Treatment* and *An Inquiry into the Effects* (London: Printed and Sold by James Phillips, 1784). Ramsay claimed that both tracts had been written during his tenure in the West Indies and had been reviewed by several West Indians before publication.

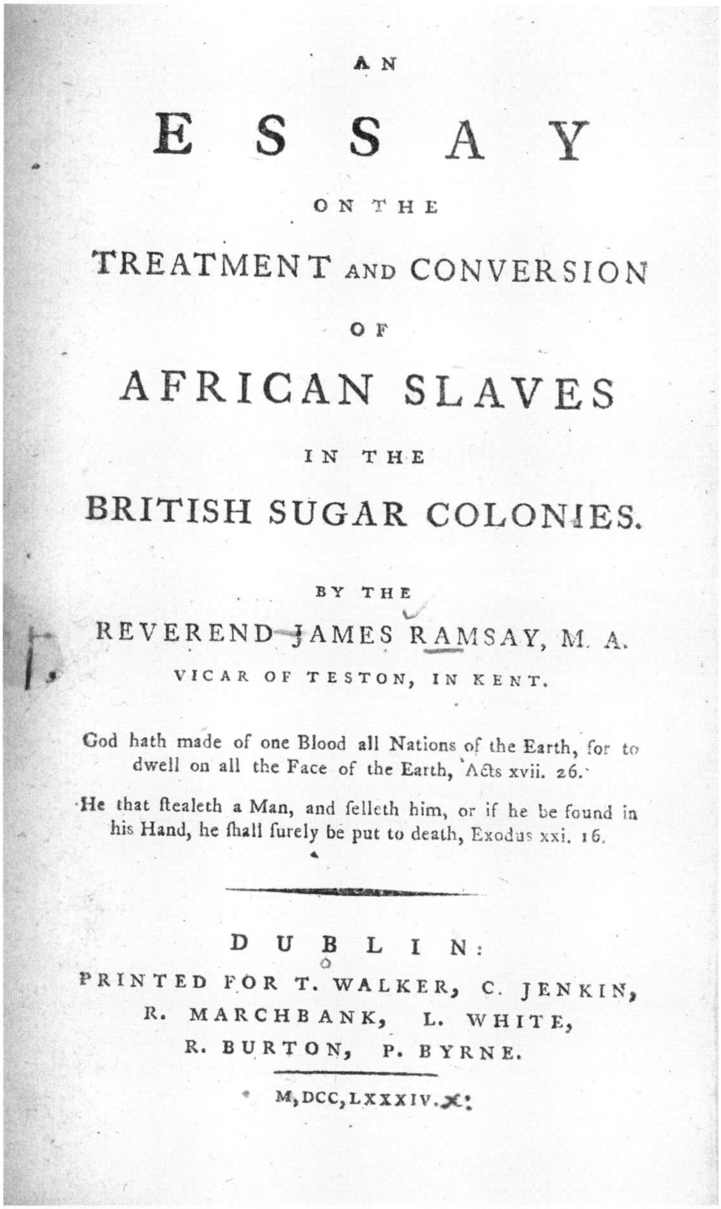

AN

ESSAY

ON THE

TREATMENT AND CONVERSION

OF

AFRICAN SLAVES

IN THE

BRITISH SUGAR COLONIES.

BY THE

REVEREND JAMES RAMSAY, M. A.

VICAR OF TESTON, IN KENT.

God hath made of one Blood all Nations of the Earth, for to dwell on all the Face of the Earth, Acts xvii. 26.

He that stealeth a Man, and selleth him, or if he be found in his Hand, he shall surely be put to death, Exodus xxi. 16.

DUBLIN:
PRINTED FOR T. WALKER, C. JENKIN,
R. MARCHBANK, L. WHITE,
R. BURTON, P. BYRNE.

M,DCC,LXXXIV.

Fig. 4.1 James Ramsay, title page, *An Essay on the Treatment and Conversion of African slaves in the British Sugar Colonies*. Dublin: Printed for T. Walker, C. Jenkin, R. Marchbank, L. White, R. Burton, P. Byrne, 1784. Courtesy of the Library of Congress, Rare Books Division.

radical nor the most incendiary of antislavery publications at that time, his work received immediate attention from proslavery writers. His contentions extended beyond the accusations made by other antislavery writers and challenged the West Indian way of life on a more fundamental level. Ramsay's solid credibility to make first-hand, personal observations about trading and ownership made him a far greater threat to the validity of proslavery rebuttals. In his preface to *An Essay on the Treatment and Conversion of African Slaves*, Ramsay stated that "the reader has here the remarks of about twenty years experience in the West-Indies, and above fourteen years particular application to the subject" (vii). His remarks could not be so confidently dismissed as naive or misinformed by proslavery writers.

Ramsay described the failure of colonial laws in protecting slaves and critiqued the behavior of slave holders. He used specific examples of laws in Nevis, Jamaica, Grenada, and St. Christopher that denied slaves "humane treatment." He compared "English" slave laws unfavorably to the French "Code Noir" and claimed: "The English have not paid the least attention to enforce by a law, either humanity or justice, as these may respect their slaves" (62). As for the nature of slave masters, he lamented "Our countrymen are left, each to be guided by his own changeable temper, and to be influenced by a semblance of self-interest; nor have they any tie on them, in their behaviour to the wretches under them" (64). Ramsay discredited planter claims that self-interest alone would prevent the abuse of slaves, and strongly critiqued the negative effects of practitioners who exerted absolute control. John Newton, who also wrote from the perspective of having participated in the trade, did not elicit nearly the same level of response from proslavery writers. One possible reason for this oversight might have been the humility of Newton's tone in seeking to point out that not all traders and slave owners behaved so badly, while Ramsay used language that was much more accusatory and libelous. However, although Ramsay commented harshly on the "capricious cruelty" of some masters, he also acknowledged the existence of masters who did treat their slaves with care. In his rebuttal to critics in *An Inquiry into the effects of putting a stop to the African slave trade*, he explained:

> Indiscriminate blame was never intended. Planters are like, are not worse than, the common run of men; many would not lose by comparison with the better sort of people in Britain. It is their situation, it is the very nature of slavery, that leads to all that inconsiderate oppression and suffering which take place in the relation of master and slave (5–6).

Rather than blaming slave holders directly for their "inhuman" behavior, he indicted the corrupting nature of the institution. He placed more emphasis on scene and act in influencing the nature of the agent. As conciliatory as Ramsay attempted to be in his writing, his remarks incited the anger of many proslavery writers who promptly sought to reclaim for themselves the representation of their laws and practices.

The almost immediate rebuttals to Ramsay's tracts sought to reclaim the representation of the West Indian lifestyle and establish the necessity of slavery. The first response came from "Some Gentlemen of St. Christopher" who denounced Ramsay as "publishing erroneous and ungenerous charges."[41] They noted, "The general desire of the island to have this Answer published, has fully appeared from the number of Subscribers, above one hundred and fifty copies have been engaged before the work was half printed off" (ii). Ramsay had "dipped his pen in gall," but those who wrote in response, "as men of humanity," equitably addressed his remarks, particularly his "impracticable scheme" for abolition. The tract mixed detractions of Ramsay with attempts to redeem the image of planters in St. Christopher. They included letters attesting to Ramsay's poor performance as minister on the island; the fact that he had once owned slaves; and that instead of freeing his slaves, he had sold them. After attacking Ramsay's character, they recounted the history of the island and detailed instances of sanctioned slave holding in English and Scottish histories. The tract concluded by drawing several "conclusions," the three most significant being that

> purchasing slaves is not only allowed, but expressly commanded in holy writ— That they are happier as slaves, and in a more civilized state, than they would be as freemen—That our kind and proper treatment of them is the duty enjoined by divine laws and ought to be confirmed (where it is not already) by those of the mother country and colonies (99).

These conclusions formed the crux of the proslavery rebuttal in the 1780s. Though this response was not published in Great Britain, subsequent responses to Ramsay's publications indicate that London proslavery writers were aware of these claims.

The most active exchange of accusations and explanations occurred between James Ramsay and James Tobin, "late of His Majesty's Council in the Island of Nevis." Tobin published *Cursory Remarks upon the Reverend Mr. Ramsay's Essay* (1785) under the pseudonym a "friend to the West India colonies, and their inhabitants." Like the "Gentlemen of St. Christopher," Tobin proposed "to remove a train of very unjust and ill-founded notions, which have been long encouraged, by the productions of uninformed writers, to the prejudice of as worthy, as useful, as loyal, but as *misrepresented*, a set of subjects as any in the dominions of Great Britain" (iii).[42] He echoed indictments of Ramsay's motives as stemming from "pique and resentment" or "the ardent desire of popularity." Tobin conducted an extensive critique of the allegations made by Ramsay's *Essay* and sought to

---

[41] *An Answer to the Reverend James Ramsay's Essay, on The Treatement and Conversion of Slaves, in the British Sugar Colonies, By some Gentlemen of St. Christopher* (Basseterre in St. Christopher: Printed by Edward L. Low, 1784).

[42] James Tobin, *Cursory Remarks upon the Reverend Mr. Ramsay's Essay on the Treatment and Conversion of African Slaves in the Sugar Colonies* (London: Printed for G. and T. Wilkie, London; E. Easton, Salisbury, and J.B. Becket, Bristol, 1785).

correct the depictions of harsh colonial laws and the mistreatment of slaves. He cast doubt on Ramsay's loyalty to Great Britain by focusing on Ramsay's glowing descriptions of the French "Code Noir." To honor the policies of a competing nation and set them as an exemplar for Britons was anathema. He also claimed that the conditions for the laboring poor in England, Scotland, and Ireland were much harsher than the condition of plantation slaves. Tobin's publications demonstrated precisely the threat posed by *An Essay* in depicting the cruelty of planters and the degraded West Indian lifestyle.

The battle for representing West Indian planters and merchants continued over the next two years with several exchanges between Ramsay and his detractors. In 1785, Ramsay published *A Reply to the personal invectives and objections contained in two answers, published by certain anonymous persons* in which he derisively commented upon the use of pseudonyms by his detractors.[43] He challenged particularly the author of *Cursory Remarks*, whom he characterized as "an anonymous libeller [*sic*]," to support his refutations with credentials. Ramsay denounced the comments as coming from a "snide and pernicious man," a charge which Tobin hastened to negate. In *A Short Rejoinder to the Reverend Mr. Ramsay's reply* (1787), he commented on Ramsay's hostility to his original remarks and angrily protested against the dehumanization of the West Indian planter in antislavery polemic. He derided the latter's suggestion "that the descendents of British parents have souls differently formed from those of their honest ancestors; and that every man's ideas of truth, justice, and humanity, are immediately obliterated as soon as he unfortunately ventures to pass the tropics" (112). Tobin supported Great Britain's participation in the slave trade and stated "the *English* are now become the *honourable slave-carriers* for other nations, as Mr. Ramsay chooses sneeringly to term them, [which] every candid *Briton* must readily ascribe to the *commercial*, rather than to the *unfeeling*, spirit of his countrymen" (37). Tobin noticeably regarded the privileges of commerce as an appropriate rejoinder to the accusations of "inhumanity." He stressed the intrepid and entrepreneurial spirit of the merchants and planters, describing them as "noble" as opposed to rapacious. He also recognized the agitation of other antislavery activists, namely Sharp and Benezet, but did not afford their writing the same detailed analysis as Ramsay warranted.[44]

---

[43] James Ramsay, *A Reply to the Personal Invectives and Objections contained in two answers, published by certain anonymous persons, to An Essay. By James Ramsay, MA Vicar of Teston* (London: Printed and Sold by James Phillips, 1785). In this rebuttal, Ramsay also mentions an ongoing newspaper critique of his work in the *Monthly Review*.

[44] One more printed exchange occurred between Ramsay and Tobin that essentially quibbled over the minute details of each other's contentions. Ramsay published *A Letter to James Tobin, Esq. Late member of His Majesty's Council in the Island of Nevis. From James Ramsay, AM, Vicar of Teston* (London: Printed and Sold by James Phillips, 1787) in which he doubted that Tobin had actually authored *Cursory Remarks*. Tobin's final response, *A Farewell Address to the Rev. Mr. James Ramsay; from James Tobin, Esq. To*

The controversy stirred by Ramsay's publications clearly arose more from his credentials than his statements. The proslavery contingent had a formidable enemy in their midst whose comments could not be dismissed as "ignorant," "uneducated," "naïve," or from an outsider's perspective. In the following years, Ramsay would take on scriptural justifications for slavery and colonial representations of slavery, condemning both as patently "false." He used his "insider" knowledge of the institution and colonial life to support his contentions. While other antislavery writers regularly denounced the behavior of masters without necessarily offering examples, Ramsay could recount specific instances of "barbarity" that he had witnessed. His experiences enabled him to refute planter assertions about the state of West Indian slavery. Since they could not discredit his experiences, most writers countered his remarks by insisting that their slaves were better off on the islands than in Africa. They contended that only a small fraction of masters treated their slaves in an inhuman or cruel manner. That small fraction should not be used to chastise the whole planter population across all of the islands. Since those few who delighted in abuse could be effectively regulated by changes in colonial law, writers began to speculate on the deeper motives of Ramsay's critique. They claimed that jealousy and a less-than-genuine interest in slave welfare spurred his writing, claims that would extend to other antislavery writers.

Planters and merchants questioned the motives behind the graphic and "biased" descriptions of slave trading and slave holding. The inflammatory descriptions had the potential to do more harm beyond the naive push for abolition. These unfavorable, often destructive portraits directed undue attention at lawful subjects and "laboured to inflame the Passions, and prejudice the Minds of the Community, by various publications, intending Mistatements of Facts, and Misrepresentations of character."[45] Some authors speculated that antislavery writers took pleasure in maligning honest businessmen with their unfounded accusations, instead of focusing on more important issues. The reform impulse of antislavery writers could be better utilized in trying to ameliorate the conditions of the legitimate subjects of the crown. Slavery advocates turned the demand for "humanity" around and held antislavery writers to their own standards. In *An Apology for Negro Slavery*, Gordon Turnbull proclaimed, "Humanity has no need to visit distant regions, or to explore other climates, to search for objects of distress in another race of men! Here, at her very door there are enough" (63).[46] Turnbull cited the poor conditions

---

which is added a letter from the Society for Propagating the Gospel, to Mr. Anthony Benezet of Philadelphia (G. and T. Wilkie, London; E. Easton, Salisbury; and J. B. Becket, Bristol, 1788), refuted Ramsay's claims once again.

[45] Robert Norris, *A Short Account of the African Slave Trade collected from local knowledge from evidence given at the bar of both houses of Parliament, and, from tracts written upon that subject* (Liverpool: printed at Ann Smith's Navigation Shop, 1788) 14.

[46] Gordon Turnbull, *An Apology for Negro Slavery: or, The West-India Planters Vindicated from the charge of inhumanity. By the author of Letters to a Young Planter* (London: Printed by J. Stevenson, for J. Strachan, T. Faulder, and W. Richardson, 1786).

under which miners labored and the number of people imprisoned for debt as more appropriate beneficiaries of reform. Thomas Maxwell Adams asked his readers to

> suffer your minds to contemplate coolly the number of *vagabonds* you have throughout the Kingdom; contemplate also the multitudes of unfortunate men released from time to time out of prisons by acts of grace, which set them at liberty, 'tis true; but at the same time, leaves them at little better more than *the liberty of starving*.[47]

Slavery advocates categorized the motives of antislavery writers as "misguided" and "misplaced" given the multitude of other problems in the metropole.[48] They sought to take the focus of their audience away from the colonies and back to the mother country.

The gradual shift in the balance of power that prompted stronger rebuttals by advocates involved more than the threat to slavery and the slave trade. Planters began to understand the larger implications of antislavery contentions as a danger to their autonomy. Prior to this period, Great Britain had a laissez-faire attitude towards her West Indian colonies, doing little by way of regulation. The relationship of the West Indies to the mother country was very different from the relationship between Great Britain and American colonies.[49] As antislavery writers frequently pointed out, the colonies had a legislative and legal system independent of, though based on, metropolitan institutions. The colonies were functionally self-governing, albeit with very strong ties to the mother country. For example, the absenteeism of planters that Long commented so disapprovingly upon in his *History of Jamaica* indicated a preference for living in Great Britain over the colonies. When activists in Great Britain felt justified in critiquing the

---

Turnbull's tract had at least two recorded print runs in 1786 which was unusual for proslavery publications. Most had only one print run most probably financed by subscribers.

[47] Thomas Maxwell Adams, *A Cool Address to the People of England on the Slave Trade* (London: R. Faulder & J. Stockdale, 1788) 18. These comments had a great deal of validity and accurately described the condition of many underprivileged people in the mother country. See Nicholas Rogers' "Vagrancy, Impressment and the Regulation of Labour in Eighteenth-Century Britain," in *Unfree Labour in the Development of the Atlantic World*, Ed. Paul Lovejoy and Nicholas Rogers (Portland: Frank Cass & Co. Ltd., 1994) 102–113.

[48] For an analysis of the relationship between the antislavery movement and the working classes in Great Britain, see Betty Fladeland, *Abolitionists and Working-Class Problems in the Age of Industrialization* (Baton Rouge: Louisiana State University Press, 1984). David Brion Davis also discusses this topic in *The Problem of Slavery in the Age of Revolution*.

[49] For an excellent summary of the differences between colonies see Michael Craton, "Reluctant Creoles: The Planters' World in the British West Indies," 314–362, in *Strangers within the Realm: Cultural Margins of the first British Empire*, ed. Bernard Bailyn and Philip D. Morgan (Chapel Hill: University of North Carolina Press, 1991).

wisdom of this self-governance through the vehicle of antislavery, both planters and merchants feared the consequences both to the institution and to their way of life. The strategy to question the true intentions of activists, who seemed content to ignore the greater problems at their door while castigating their neighbors, was a highly sophisticated move.

Questioning antislavery motives offered proslavery writers an opportunity to take control of rhetorical terrain and present their own image of national identity. One writer went so far as to publish his tract "for the benefit of the starving Tin-Miners in Cornwall" (see Figure 4.2).[50] Antislavery writers created and nurtured the divide between Great Britain and the West Indies. Their polemic categorized the distinctions between the moral center (Great Britain) and her degenerate peripheries (the West Indies). Based on this distinction, they built an image of the Briton diametrically opposed to the slave holders' or slave traders' way of life. However, this rhetoric could be utilized in favor of the planter or merchant after systematically discrediting antislavery claims. The success of antislavery vilification made reconstructing the image of the Briton to account for colonial lifestyles an absolute imperative. Planters and merchants also had a better sense of empire and the necessity of maintaining the competitiveness of British trade. Reformers could claim the betterment of society, but colonials established their interest in the prosperity of the nation. Admonishing reformists to concentrate on legitimate subjects of the empire allowed writers to argue effectively for their continued autonomy and their version of national identity. The proslavery rebuttal moved from offering merely defensive arguments to constructing a counter-image of the Briton that focused on commerce- and race-based characteristics.

Counter-Images of Identity: The Slave-Holding Briton

Both West Indian planters and slave merchants felt the antislavery attack on their characters to be unfair, but the general public seemed highly receptive to these negative portrayals. Early petitions against slavery cited West Indian planter and merchant cruelty as cause for the abolition of the slave trade. This apparent popularity of antislavery depictions proved more menacing as the number of antislavery publications increased. Their construction of slave holder and slave merchant as possessing qualities exactly opposite to British morals and character presented a serious threat that had to be addressed. If the "normal" Briton could not tolerate slavery than how could the slaver holder or slave merchant be a Briton? The emerging discourse of national identity offered a compelling vehicle for reform that antislavery activists exploited quite ingeniously. However, the

---

[50] James M. Adair, *Unanswerable Arguments against the Abolition of the Slave Trade with a Defence of the Proprietors of the British Sugar Colonies, Against certain malignant Charges contained in Letters published by a Sailor, and by Luffman, Newton, &c.* (London: Sold by J. P. Bateman, 1790).

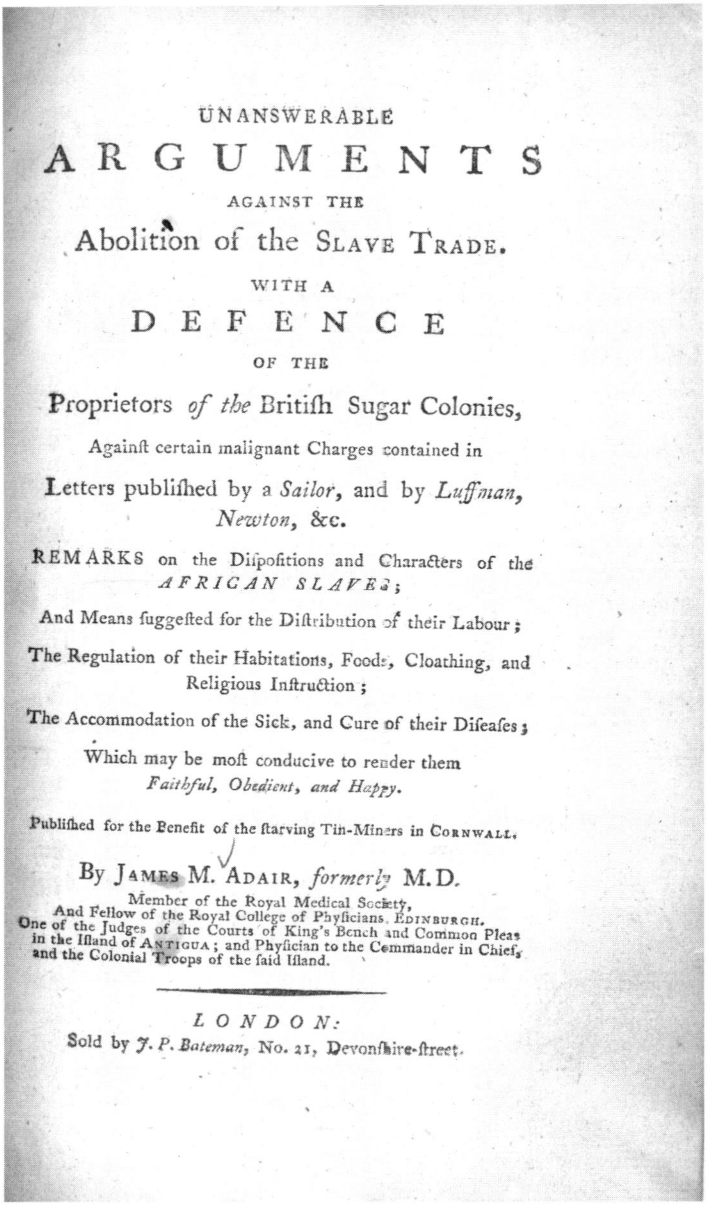

UNANSWERABLE
ARGUMENTS
AGAINST THE

Abolition of the SLAVE TRADE.

WITH A

DEFENCE

OF THE

Proprietors *of the* British Sugar Colonies,

Against certain malignant Charges contained in

Letters published by a *Sailor*, and by *Luffman*, *Newton*, &c.

REMARKS on the Dispositions and Characters of the *AFRICAN SLAVES*;

And Means suggested for the Distribution of their Labour;

The Regulation of their Habitations, Foods, Cloathing, and Religious Instruction;

The Accommodation of the Sick, and Cure of their Diseases;

Which may be most conducive to render them *Faithful, Obedient, and Happy.*

Published for the Benefit of the starving Tin-Miners in CORNWALL.

By JAMES M. ADAIR, *formerly* M.D.
Member of the Royal Medical Society,
And Fellow of the Royal College of Physicians, EDINBURGH.
One of the Judges of the Courts of King's Bench and Common Pleas in the Island of ANTIGUA; and Physician to the Commander in Chief, and the Colonial Troops of the said Island.

LONDON:
Sold by *J. P. Bateman*, No. 21, Devonshire-street.

Fig. 4.2 James M. Adair, title page, *Unanswerable Arguments against the Abolition of the Slave Trade with a Defence of the Proprietors of the British Sugar Colonies.* London: J. P. Bateman, 1790. Courtesy of the Library of Congress, Rare Books Division.

proslavery response from the West Indies proved equally adept and sophisticated in appropriating this discourse for their own ends. The rhetorical terrain of national identity became a critical issue in the dialogue between camps, and proslavery constructions eventually pushed antislavery/anti-slave-trade activists to refine their own image of the Briton. In defining national identity, West Indian writers far outdistanced their American counterparts in argumentation and strategy.

The counter-discourse of national identity had to address the image of the Briton constructed and widely distributed by antislavery activists. Their notion of national identity focused on particular attributes that were antithetical to the practice of slavery. Writers like Ramsay and Clarkson explicated biblical passages to prove that tolerating slavery was anti-Christian. They characterized the institution as a blight on Christian charity and a betrayal of missionary obligations. Activists extolled the superior conception of liberty that Britons valued and respected more than other "civilized" nations, and they believed all human beings deserved equal access to personal liberty. They viewed African slaves who had been captured and transported from their native land as "oppressed" and "deprived" of their "natural rights." I do not mean to suggest that antislavery activists were free of racial bias. Though the degree of "racism" differed among activists, most antislavery writing agreed that Africans were less civilized than Europeans. The most vehement opposition posed by activists involved the reduction of slaves to "property." In arguing for the innate humanity of all slaves, antislavery writers discounted the commercial argument on which most proslavery responses had been based.[51]

Planters and merchants had to formulate a rebuttal that valued their contribution to the nation and reintegrated the concept of slavery into the public consciousness in a positive way. These writers had to reframe their ethical appeals to establish their credibility as "true Britons." They had to attack three key points in antislavery rhetoric that denied them full participation in the emerging national consciousness. First, they had to underscore the contribution of commerce, specifically mercantilism, to the prosperity of Great Britain. Second, they had to find an entry into humanitarian discourse and its powerful claims for "rights" and "liberty." While historians continue to debate the effects that an emerging capitalist system had on abolition, proslavery writers demonstrated a definite "self-interest" in guarding the mercantilist venture.[52] The same writers who advocated "free trade" and the lifting of the Royal African Company's monopoly on slaving, denounced Adam Smith's economic theories as "idealistic" and "impractical"

---

[51] When the focus of the campaign narrowed to the slave trade, activists had to address the commercial benefits of trade and commerce. They used Adam Smith's theories of "free labor" to counter proslavery arguments for the economic necessity of slave labor.

[52] Though Eric Williams' thesis in *Capitalism and Slavery* (1944) remains controversial, many scholars continue to find validity in some of his arguments. For an analysis of Williams' thesis in relation to more recent scholarship, see Barbara L. Solow and Stanley Engerman, eds, *British Capitalism and Caribbean Slavery* (Cambridge: Cambridge University Press, 1987).

for the colonies.⁵³ Third, planters and merchants had to create a clear and rigid distinction between themselves and their slaves. This distinction materialized with increasing clarity in the discussion of "race."⁵⁴ The late eighteenth-century planter discourse increasingly associated "race" with "colour" in a manner that laid the foundation for the race theories of the nineteenth century. Ultimately in these writings, the recasting of the agent of slavery expanded into the creation of the agent of empire.

A major difference between antislavery and proslavery perspectives involved an understanding of Great Britain's relationship to her colonies and to other parts of the world. The proslavery worldview was a good deal more global and interconnected than antislavery writers understood at this time.⁵⁵ While antislavery activists wanted to polarize national identity by region, planters and merchants advocated a more inclusive sense of nation. For example, antislavery texts persisted in diminishing the West Indies as "colonies" or "dominions," whereas West Indians viewed their islands as important parts of the "British empire." The vehement condemnation of the West Indies drew distinct geographical boundaries around the mother country and her peripheries and limited access to "true" attributes of national character. The harsher critiques of the 1780s portrayed West Indians as somehow separate and excluded from the values of Great Britain. Antislavery focus on a superior sense of "liberty" clearly implied that the West Indies could not fully realize this belief because of the corrupt institution on which the colonies were built. Proslavery writers desired to mend the ideological schism between colonies and mother country that was described in antislavery tracts. Planters and merchants viewed the world from a trade-based and commercial perspective, which dictated that they have a sense of the interconnectedness of nations. They viewed the West Indies as an integral appendage of the mother country, so the concept of Great Britain encompassed their colonial holdings as well as the British Isles. Some writers, particularly Edward Long, placed colonial practices above

---

⁵³ Holt summarizes the threat of humanitarian economic arguments as follows: "The system stymied the progressive transformation of human feeling and was contrary to God's immanent historical design. Thus stripped of both its economic and its religious defenses, slavery became just another pecuniary interest vulnerable to competing interests" (*The Problem of Freedom* 24).

⁵⁴ See Benjamin Braude's "The Sons of Noah and the Construction of Ethnic and Geographical Identities in the Medieval and Early Modern Periods," *William and Mary Quarterly* 54 (1997): 103–142. While twentieth-century scholars have commonly accepted the "curse of Ham" thesis of African oppression, Braude illustrates that the history of this thesis is a good deal more complex and a function of seventeenth-century biblical exegesis.

⁵⁵ See Emma Rothschild, "Globalization and the Return to History," *Foreign Policy* 115 (1999): 106–116.

that of the mother country in terms of superior sense and wisdom.[56] Proslavery writers also believed in the value of trade as another time-honored quality of the *English* that should become a defining characteristic of the *Briton*.

Writers promoted the idea of Great Britain's superior sense of commerce and strength in naval trade by playing on national pride. They repeatedly underscored the importance of colonial trade goods to the prosperity of the nation and lauded the "*commercial* spirit" of their fellow countrymen. In recounting the history of various colonial enterprises, these writers stressed how British settlements outstripped other European colonies in terms of wealth and prosperity. Writers appropriated antislavery rhetoric about "humanity" and declared British trade to be more "humane" than the trade practiced by other European countries. The most telling examples of national pride surfaced in responses to Ramsay's claims about the superiority of the French "Code Noir." One indignant writer complained, "To the English, a people fam'd for humanity, the settlements of other nations are held up as patterns of clemency."[57] They accused antislavery writers of attempting to "prepossess the nation" by negatively portraying the West Indian colonies and their contribution to the wealth of the nation. They stressed both the commercial and the experiential value of this trade to all British subjects. A major argument that emerged from this claim characterized the slave trade as a "nursery for British seamen." Writers claimed that the slave trade provided "British" seamen an opportunity to learn valuable and marketable skills during the voyage.[58]

Proslavery writers demonstrated the potential danger to the nation inherent in arguments for abolition as a way of discrediting antislavery arguments based on "humanity." Any attempts to dismantle the institution of slavery, either partially or wholly, would have disastrous repercussions for the "rightful" subjects of the Crown. Emancipation of any sort was "impracticable" both for reasons relating to "national finances" as well as "political motives." Writers described the slave trade as the crucial "Link" in the "chain" on "which our Manufactures so immediately depend." The dire consequences of destroying this "Link" would halt "every

---

[56] Craton's "Reluctant Creoles" provides an excellent discussion of Long's *History of Jamaica* with respect to his beliefs about the superiority of Jamaican society. See also Elizabeth Bohls, "The gentleman planter and the metropole: Long's *History of Jamaica* (1774)" in *The Country and the City Revisited: England and the Politics of Culture, 1550–1850*, ed. Gerald Maclean, Donna Landry, and Joseph P. Ward (Cambridge: Cambridge University Press, 1999).

[57] *Remarks on a Pamphlet written by the Reverend James Ramsay under the title of Thoughts on the Slavery of Negroes in the American colonies* (London: Printed for and Sold by J. P. Batemen, 1784). This writer misattributed the pamphlet to Ramsay when it was actually written by Joseph Wood. However, Ramsay did hold up the French colonies as an example to the British West Indies, so the author's comment still applies.

[58] This argument was swiftly discredited by Clarkson and other writers, who used statistics to show that the mortality rate on slave ships was higher than ships engaged in other forms of trade.

Improvement" of the West Indies, thereby causing a "Diminution" of the "Produce of the Lands." They criticized fellow citizens who would advocate for the welfare of "strangers" at the expense of their "brethren." Since the colonies were established in good faith and at the behest of Crown and Parliament, how could anyone justify contributing to their "total Destruction"? The defense of the slave trade increased as antislavery writers began to focus their efforts on abolishing it. In appeals to the public, advocates stressed "YOUR OWN *individual and national benefits and advantages* derived from *that trade*" (Adams 21). They shifted the focus from their own interests in order to stress the point that abolition went against *national* interests. The trade was not merely a two-way conduit between Africa and the West Indies. Thus, the "irresponsible" proposals for abolition became a "national" detriment.

Writers appropriated powerful antislavery ideas to show the "inhumanity" of abolition because it would curtail the "rights" and "liberty" of the planters. They made these claims by stressing the importance of an institution that actually supported a variety of people, both in the colonies and the mother country. While the consumer public might merely have been denied products, colonial subjects, including but not limited to planters and merchants, would have been denied their livelihood. Some authors criticized antislavery activists as "unfeeling" and "cruel" towards their own countrymen, many of whom would be impoverished by the dissolution of the slave trade and slavery. Writers commented that "innocent" families would experience "total ruin" in order to reinforce the idea that antislavery writers were disloyal to their "white" brethren. Indeed, the motives of antislavery writers were suspect because they directly violated the "rights" of colonial society.[59] In *A Short Account of the African Slave Trade* (1788), Norris pointed out:

> though the Liberty of Negroes seems now to be the favourite idea, the Liberty of Britons to pursue their lawful Occupations should not be forgotten ... the Right which every Man in it possesses, to carry on his own Business, in the way most advantageous to himself ...; and the *Consciousness* which he has, of the steady Protection of the Laws, in the Prosecution of it" (13).

Calls for abolition impinged upon planters' rights, not only to property but also to pursue their occupations unmolested. Merchants and planters underscored the fact that their occupations had received "national sanction" by "acts of Parliament." Slavery advocates pointed to the hypocrisy of antislavery activists, whom they accused of selectively applying "natural rights" and thoroughly ignoring their own. Norris marveled that "the mistaken zeal of *a few* could instigate the Legislative so grossly to invade the Rights of Individuals" (21).

---

[59] Of course, writers only intended for this claim to apply to "white" members of colonial society and had no interest in arguing on the behalf of mixed blood or freed men and women.

Graphic portrayals of this unnatural reversion of loyalty played on numerous planter fears revealing a fundamental "race" conflict. William Dent's 1789 cartoon titled "Abolition of the Slave Trade, or The Man The Master" lays out in detail the potentially disastrous consequences of abolition (see Figure 4.3).[60] Published in London at the peak of the abolitionist movement, this political cartoon richly presents the worst case scenario in which the idea of payback figures prominently in the planter imaginary. The central image of violence shows a black man wearing European garb beating a white man (presumably the planter) who is dressed rather primitively. The white man's kneeling position is reminiscent of the popular Wedgwood antislavery medallion,[61] and in the background the reversal continues with former slaves celebrating on the right while whites in loincloths labor on the left. Interestingly, the alternative title of "The Man The Master" implies a curious interchangeability that acknowledges humanity but questions the fitness of Africans to perform in leadership roles. As this is a proslavery cartoon, the author does not seem to be aware of the irony in his depiction of white servitude, which seems to imply a similar cruelty when the roles are reversed. However, the idea of equal status is quickly dispelled by the pidgin English in which the former slaver (and new "Master") exclaims, "Wow Massa, me lick a you and make you worky while me be gentleman—curse a heart—." The caption seems to point to the slave's simplistic understanding of plantation economy, as evidenced by the stockpile of "PRODUCE." The cartoonist also states planters' fears overtly since the caption under the celebrating black men reads "RETALIATION for having been held in captivity."

The commercial implications of abolition are made very clear by the foreground and background of the cartoon. On the left, barrels of "PRODUCE" lie unsold because they are "waiting for a purchaser owing to the enhanced price." Two figureheads at the base of the central image tout the labels of "ABOLITION" and "REGULATION"—the foolscap on the head of the figure of abolition reads "FOLLY" giving little doubt as to the opinion of the artist. Regulation, on the other hand, is touted as "WISDOM"—a proslavery strategy that becomes the strongest counterpoint to abolitionist claims. It is much easier to acknowledge that a system needs improvement to temper the utter rejection of the system itself. In the background, two other aspects of commerce are highlighted that also follow closely the tropes of proslavery rhetoric. On the right side, foreign traders (possibly French) with visible accents negotiate sales with an African slave merchant. The competition from other nations who would not be hobbled by abolition was a genuine concern to British merchants.

---

[60] Though no author for this print is listed by the Library of Congress, Professor Jeremy Black identifies that author as William Dent and the publication date as 26 May 1789.

[61] Possibly the most popular image of the abolitionist movement, the Wedgwood medallion appeared in numerous forms as a way of advertising allegiance to the cause. For a discussion of the creation, reproduction, and dissemination of the medallion, see Oldfield's *Popular Politics*, 155–160.

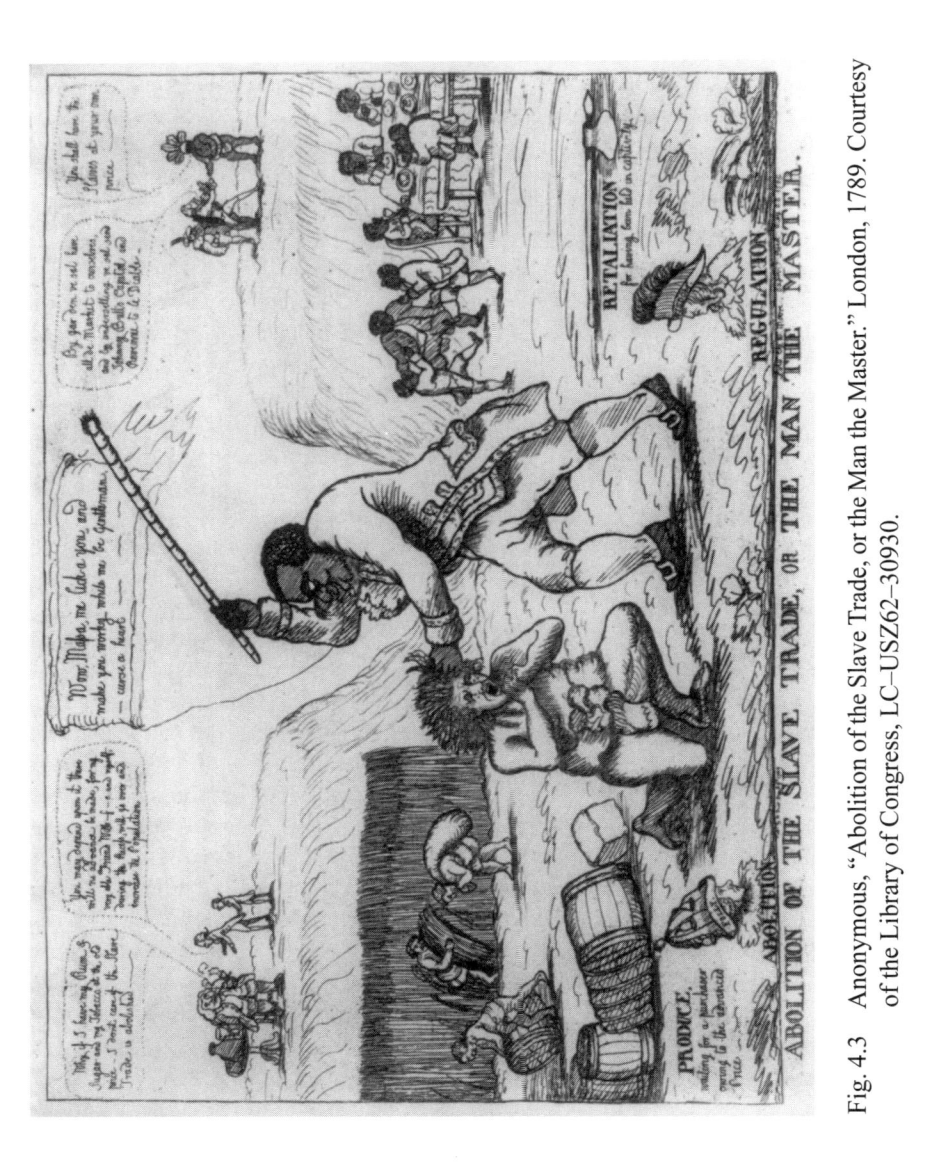

Fig. 4.3 Anonymous, "Abolition of the Slave Trade, or the Man the Master." London, 1789. Courtesy of the Library of Congress, LC–USZ62–30930.

Perhaps the most interesting exchange takes place on the left side and illustrates the proslavery bitterness about the privileging of metropolitan activism over the interests of the empire. The plump figure of John Bull stands next to his table, smoking his pipe, and exclaiming, "Why if I have my Rum & Sugar and my Tobacco at the old price—I don't care if the Slave Trade is abolished—." The disaffected and persecuted planter stands to lose everything when faced with an unsympathetic consumer. The response from abolitionists seems clearly dishonest in this context. One figure states, "You may depend upon it there will no advance be made, for my very olde Friend Wilbe-f-ce and myself during the Recess, will go over and increase the Population—." The statement seems especially ludicrous in the context of increasing the population of whites to labor on the plantations. Perhaps this exchange hearkens back to Ramsay's scheme to replace "unfree labour" with white indentured servants—a plan that slavery advocates regarded as foolhardy and utterly impractical. Moreover, the play on "no advance" suggests both the false assurance that no change in production or price will result and a certain hobbling of commerce. This statement suggests the ways in which slavery advocates utilized the progress narrative in a commercial context to argue for regulation over abolition—a topic that will be discussed further in Chapter 5.

The greatest source of planter and merchant outrage stemmed from antislavery valuations of Africans over "native" Britons. The willingness to curb planter rights for the benefit of a group whose "natural condition" was a "state of barbarity" baffled even the most reform-oriented proslavery writer. They needed to show why African slaves could not be properly considered under British definitions of "natural rights" and "liberty." One strategy, as discussed earlier, involved reclaiming depictions of slavery to assert that the English laborer was in a more precarious position than the colonial slave. A second, more significant, strategy relied on defining slaves in terms of racial characteristics that made them "naturally" resistant to understanding ideas of British "liberty" and "civilization." Some writers further contended that slavery was a "natural condition" in Africa, a land where the "sacred plant" of liberty had never been known. Planters sought to establish that slaves did not require antislavery efforts and actually had a better life in the colonies. To do this, they developed an ideology of race that would provide an integral component to the definition of national identity.

Much has been written about the genealogy and transformations in race theories of the Western world. Twentieth-century scholarship has been devoted to understanding the origin and evolution of what might be the most powerful cultural construct of the modern world. Scholars like Ivan Hannaford have traced the use of "race" arguments, albeit with different constructions, back to ancient times by studying the various reasons for stratification within Greco-Roman society.[62] The "modern" concept of race differs greatly from the ancient concept,

---

[62] Ivan Hannaford, *Race: The History of an Idea in the West* (Baltimore: The Johns Hopkins University Press, 1996). Hannaford's work was ground-breaking in scope and depth of analysis. While subsequent scholarly publications take issue with and expand

and Hannaford contends that the "first stage" in the development of a conscious idea of race occurred primarily in the eighteenth century. He examined the work of several prominent philosophers, particularly Montesquieu, Hume, Blumenbach, and Kant, who inflected race theory with a new dimension that accounted for the emerging belief in "natural rights." Hannaford wrote, "a new relationship had to be established among body structure, bodily endowment, and mind, and here the argument was advanced that all three had a bearing on something new called "national character" (189). In the connection between race and nation, he theorized the development of a new form of state. "Some writers promoted a natural and physiological state, others a state in which the conduct of life would be governed entirely by the economic, administrative and moral criteria" (214). These conflicting attitudes of what, rather than who, constituted the state formed the crux of the proslavery "race" argument.

Another distinction created in the explication of race theory involved the function of discourse in elucidating various meanings of race. David Theo Goldberg's work demarcates very subtle differences in the discourse of race that inflects the concept both historically and culturally. He distinguishes between race, racist, and racialized as coming from different sites grounded in culture and discourse.[63] In *Racist Culture*, Goldberg identifies the combination of aesthetics and "natural qualities" that defined the emerging "race discourse" of the eighteenth century. He argues, "Aesthetic value solidified into natural law, which in the eighteenth century was considered as compelling as the laws of nature, economics, and morality precisely because they were all deemed to derive from the same rational basis" (30). Aesthetic valuation alone was insufficient to explain racial categorization, even among contemporary eighteenth-century philosophers; however, the relation of the physical to the mental—outward appearance to inner civility—persisted as a critical component of late eighteenth-century race theory.

Slavery advocates defined "race" as an integral component of national identity, but their definition emerged from abolitionist pressures. While most theorists agree in locating the formation of modern race theory in the late eighteenth century, few examine the nature of proslavery racial distinctions outside of the need to justify the institution. I argue that the pseudo-scientific "race theory" of the nineteenth century emerged from a more complicated version of "race" forged in proslavery arguments. Constructions of Africans as "cursed" or "barbaric," which were based in religion rather than science, appear

---

aspects of Hannaford's analysis, his discussion of "race" as a Western concept provides a useful base on which to begin deconstructing proslavery rhetoric.

[63] David Theo Goldberg, *Racist Culture: Philosophy and the Politics of Meaning* (Cambridge, MA: Blackwell Publishers, 1993). This highly theorized explication of race explores the discursive intersections between race, modernity, and subjectivity. See also, David Theo Goldberg, ed., *Anatomy of Racism* (Minneapolis: University of Minnesota Press, 1990).

to have remained constant among generations of planters and merchants. By viewing African enslavement as sanctioned by religion (and government), both groups could salve their consciences, and this race discourse changed little as slavery became the foundation of the West Indian colonies in particular. In this estimation, twentieth-century critics are guilty of the same over-generalization about West Indian beliefs as eighteenth-century abolitionists because, prior to the abolitionist campaigns, proslavery theories of race were not nearly so rigid. Long's claims about the similarity of "Negroes" to "*orangutans*," which were much more akin to the "scientific" theories of later centuries, were both far-fetched and extremist during his time. Planters disproved these beliefs on a daily basis, particularly given the attempts to "breed whiteness" into their mixed-blood offspring. Over the course of the slave-trade debates, proslavery race theory also became a more unified position and came to reflect more extremist views. As abolitionists used rhetoric to construct a national identity that effectively privileged the slave over the master, the master felt compelled to reclaim his rights as a true subject of the nation. Abolitionist pressure shaped the nature of proslavery race theory by compelling "white" planters and merchants to create an identity in direct opposition to the African slave.

Proslavery writers defined and utilized a discourse of race that relied on aesthetic distinctions in order to elucidate a "racialized national character." The earliest accounts of interactions with Africans established their "uncivilized," "savage," and "barbaric" existence. Under pressure from early slavery protesters, clergy developed scriptural justifications for the institution that deemed Africans to be "a cursed race." The sins of Ham damned the people of Africa, who wore the mark of damnation on their "dark skins." As pressure from antislavery activists continued to mount, proslavery writers took greater care in establishing a link between the supposedly unattractive physical qualities of slaves and their "debased" natures. The "flat nose" and "wooly hair" became inflected with greater meaning than mere adaptations to climate. These traits proved less desirable than the "patrician" features of the European precisely because they became associated with "barbarism." A hierarchy of world societies emerged that marked nations by their level of civilization. Africans represented the lowest rung in the ladder of civilization and Europeans, specifically the British, represented the highest rung. The marker of level increasingly came to be associated with physical appearance, namely color. While proslavery writers were not the only ones to rely on the terms "white" and "black" to make distinctions, they standardized the attributes relating to each color and standardized the interaction of race and national identity. The color-coding of West Indian society was "necessary" to maintain order and civilization in the colonies.

The most extreme example of "racialized discourse" occurred in Edward Long's *History of Jamaica*. His extensive discussion "of Negroes" (in Volume 2, third book) revealed a deep-seated disdain for the "darker races" who were "naturally inferior to whites." Long commented admiringly on the work of David Hume, whose disapproval of slavery notwithstanding, could find no redeeming feature of "African society."⁶⁴ Long's pseudo-empirical commentary on the various "classes" of Africans in Jamaica demonstrated the utter impossibility of "blacks" ever attaining the intelligence and civilization of "Whites." Long went further and classified all Africans as an entirely different species, inhabiting a kind of halfway space between man and ape. Though he acknowledged with considerable distaste the unions between blacks and whites in the West Indies, he was quick to deny that any great elevation of intellect occurred. Long was most famous for his remarks about the inability of "mulattos" to reproduce and African women's sexual congress with "orangutans"— radical sentiments even among proslavery writers. He did comment on the extraordinary case of Francis Williams, a free black man who was educated extensively in England and published poetry in Greek and Latin. However, Long dismissed Williams as an anomaly whose advanced education separated him from his black brethren. He also commented derisively on how Williams shunned the company of his kind after returning from England to Jamaica. This snobbery seemed to confirm his beliefs about the strict divisions of colonial society.

Most proslavery writers attempted to establish a definitive portrait of "natural" African characteristics that made colonial slavery more a blessing than a curse. Since biblical justifications were no longer as convincing or seemed to suffice, racial traits served to validate the "humanity" of slave trading. The Negro, by his or her nature, existed in a state of savagery that prompted him to "harass his Neighbor" well before the advent of European traders. In fact, Europeans had brought an unprecedented level of civilization to the land of "cannibals." Planters and merchants strongly refuted antislavery depictions of the idyllic African existence. As one writer described it:

> The whole race, existing in a state of anarchy, endeavour to engross an arbitrary sway. Almost perpetually contentious, they seem to scorn the leagues of amity, and seldom remain at perfect peace, either with their immediate neighbours, or with the bordering nations. Mutual oppression is their established system, and none who have obtained the power of committing injuries will ever own that they deserve reproach.⁶⁵

This description reinforced not only the innate barbarity of Africans, but their difference from Europeans. Again, proslavery writers characterized the differences in extreme terms in order to validate their own behavior as Christians and as Britons. Writers reinforced beliefs in these "racial characteristics" to justify

---

⁶⁴ David Hume's essay "Of National Characters" (1742) with its famous footnote that "all races" were "inferior to whites" was a great favorite of proslavery writers. His justification for this belief came from the observation that no African society had produced anything of note in the fields of arts or sciences.

⁶⁵ Rowland Cotton, *Extracts from an account of the state of British forts, on the Gold Coast of Africa, taken by Capt. Cotton in 1777* (London: Printed for J. Bew, 1778) 17.

colonial slavery and the slave trade and to displace the image of the "pathetic" slave. They reproduced the *topos* of "lazy" and "indolent" slaves who benefited from the industry of plantation life. Adams' *A Cool Address* contended that "A man who is neither *by nature nor industry* prepared for a right way of living, should, upon account of his own weakness and incapacity, be under the controul [*sic*] of others" (30).

The lesser nature of the Africans that made them so ideal for plantation life also excluded them from full integration into British society. The "negroes" may have been fine workers, under the frequent application of the lash, but they were not "equals" even to the lowliest white colonist:

> Those, who are acquainted with the African genius and temper, must know, that negroes are so intolerably ignorant and inconsiderate, that they, at present, do no more work, in general, than they are compelled to do by the terrors of punishment.[66]

This statement contrasts African indolence with British industry and also takes a sly dig at abolitionists who lacked first-hand knowledge of slaves. Turnbull's *An Apology for Negro Slavery* strongly denounced the idea that Negroes could be placed on the same plane as whites, even if they possessed the "natural rights" accessible to all. "But allowing that they *are born equal* with white men, yet, a minute of observation, or thorough knowledge of their character and disposition, seems to evince that they are not at all fitted to fill the superior stations or more elevated ranks in civil society" (34). However, the virtue of colonial enslavement rested primarily on the opportunity to civilize and Christianize blacks outside of the deleterious atmosphere of their homeland. Norris's *A Short Account of the African Slave Trade* claimed that "the House of Bondage, strictly speaking, may be called a Land of Freedom to them" because of the comfortable circumstances in which the slaves existed on the plantations (9). He also stated that planters prevented their slaves from "exercising Cruelty on others" and were "always protected themselves" (9).

While the motives for defining racial characteristics may seem fairly transparent, writers added another dimension to this discourse by defining "whiteness." Most race studies focus exclusively on analyzing the dominant culture's subordination of the ethnic minority through the rhetoric of race. Even Roxann Wheeler, in arguing against the importance of phenotypic representations of race in the eighteenth century, does not view "white" as a construct, only a marker of complexion. Certainly, the negative portrait of slaves emerged from a strong belief in the inherent "inferiority" of the "colored" races.[67] All tracts authored by proslavery

---

[66] *Consideration on the Emancipation of Negroes and on the Abolition of the Slave-Trade. A West-India Planter* (London: Printed for J. Johnson and J. Debrett, 1788) 9.

[67] Both Hannaford and Goldberg note that physical anthropologists, naturalists, and philosophers made similar statements about Native Americans, "Orientals," and Indians,

writers made some reference to the "necessary evil" of slavery attendant upon an already degraded race. However, an equally compelling argument began to emerge regarding white labor. Antislavery writers, like James Ramsay, proposed that the "unfree labour" of Africans should be replaced by indentured servants. The limited tenure of servitude would enable colonists gradually to replace "unfree labour" with "free labour." Planters and merchants found this argument to be especially troubling. Their response was to produce histories of the islands that recounted the high rate of "white" mortality. Norris established that "the labour of African slaves has been found indispensably necessary for the cultivation of the West India Islands and the American Plantations, from the utter impossibility of white people being able to undergo that Fatigue" (10). Writers turned this sympathy for "white brethren" against antislavery activists who agitated on behalf of "foreigners." Why suggest "that our white fellow subjects should toil in these sultry climates, that the Africans might indulge their natural laziness in their own country"? (10). The debate between both camps over the use of "free labour" had a significant effect on racializing labor. "Free" became associated with "white" as most writers in either camp did not express a willingness to bring African "free" labor to the West Indies.

A more insidious consequence of bringing greater numbers of "free" (read "white") labor to the West Indies surfaced out of the fear of slave insurrection. The highly imbalanced ratio of "whites" to "Negroes" in the colonies fostered a perpetual dread of slave revolts. Several unsuccessful revolts had been quelled over the course of colonization. Jamaica supported a "Cimarron" or "Maroon" community of runaway slaves who were the source of continual planter anxiety. The argument for increasing the number of "white" indentured servants might logically have a welcoming audience in the planters. However, they strongly resisted the notion of "white labour." Part of this resistance came from the unsuccessful integration of indentured labor in earlier colonial periods that resulted in disastrous mortality rates. The labor-intensive sugar crops of the West Indies relied completely on a steady and hardy source of labor. Another reservation came from the idealistic portrait of conditions of indenture written by antislavery activists. Slavery advocates viewed indentured servitude as a form of "white slavery" that was cruelly overlooked by the self-proclaimed champions of humanity. Proslavery writers added another dimension to the unsuitability of "white labour" for the West Indies—role reversal. Planters feared that if Negro slaves saw "white slaves" working beside them in the fields then the respect for white authority would be lost. Many writers envisioned scenarios in which the slave was able to turn the table on his master. Tobin warned in *Cursory Remarks* "that an African negro will enjoy the heartfelt triumph, of seeing half a score *white slaves* crouching abjectly at his feet, and trembling at his very nod" (22). His caution sought to mediate the sympathies of metropolitan audiences by offering an opposing portrait of the vindictive rather than grateful African. This potent

---

whose level of civilization could not hope to compete with European/British attainments.

image played on assumptions of racial superiority by attempting to elicit disgust for African dominance in the "white" or "native" British public.

The distinct portrait of the Briton that materialized in proslavery rhetoric incorporated both colonial concerns and antislavery ideals. Writers emphasized the importance of trade to the well-being of the colonies and the mother country. They put forth a more global (and imperial) vision of "nation" that included the colonies and depicted them as a critical mainstay of "British" commerce. When antislavery writers advocated on behalf of the historical and moral significance of "liberty" to British character, proslavery writers reminded the public of the singularly "British" valuation of property. Appropriating the discourse of "natural rights" allowed planters to argue that their "right to property" had been ignored, a right affirmed by so historic a document as the Magna Carta. After rebutting the charges of "inhumanity," planters described the slave trade as a kind of liberation from "tyrannic" and "savage" African societies. They juxtaposed the paternal treatment of plantation slaves to the uncertain futures of "white labourers." More important, they constructed "whiteness" as a site of natural privilege endowed by superior intellect and more advanced government. The proslavery Briton emerged as more globally focused, trade savvy, "free-born," and *white*.

The debates over the slave trade intensified over the next two decades as slavery advocates witnessed a gradual shift in the balance of power. They continued to form primarily reactive arguments against antislavery assertions; however, these arguments were more sophisticated and rhetorically complex than anything published prior to the most active period of the debates. They subverted many pathetic appeals by broadening the scope of analysis to encompass the British poor and laboring classes. The increasing success of reform rhetoric compelled authors to propose regulations intended to ameliorate the conditions of enslavement in the colonies. Regardless, they could not match the creativity and persistence of antislavery writers who incorporated new strategies to argue for abolition in the 1790s. The proslavery argument continued to rely on ethical and commercial appeals to combat parliamentary bills to abolish the slave trade. On the surface, their cause appeared to result in total failure as abolitionists finally succeeded in passing their bill in 1807.

The proslavery "campaign" emerged from a defensive position maintaining the status quo to propose fresh arguments for its continued existence. The inexorable shift in the balance of power in the late 1780s and '90s seemed to reframe most proslavery arguments into stalling tactics rather than feasible solutions. Their publications and rhetorical tactics could not stave off the growth of antislavery support. As the movement took shape and began to propose a well-defined solution to the problem of the slave trade, slavery advocates were forced to intensify their efforts to sway public opinion. While the campaign may not have appealed to the larger British public, it did succeed in pushing abolitionists into a defensive position. Activists in the 1790s took proslavery accusations seriously and attempted to reconcile their seemingly hypocritical behavior. The slave-trade debates became a dynamic dialogue as each side honed its arguments and evoked responses from each other. If success were measured only by the passing of the abolitionist bill, then proslavery writing would fade into obscurity. However, given the form of national identity that emerged from the debates, one can see that proslavery writers made an integral and important contribution to the image of the Briton. National identity in the 1780s and '90s was forged through opposition, and each side contributed to the attributes of national character so clearly defined at the turn of the century.

Chapter 5
Whose Victory? Abolition and the Construction of British Identity, 1788–1807

The rich and evocative dialogue between proslavery and antislavery camps helped transform the nature of British culture and national character. As the movement solidified and focused on immediate abolition as the most appropriate solution, each side perfected rhetorical strategies to interrogate the conflicting viewpoints and perceptions of the nation. Advocates for the slave trade and abolitionists both demonstrated a keen awareness of the subtle shifts in the opposition's contentions, and each responded to the other with considered rebuttals. While the abolitionists had more success at mobilizing public opinion in favor of their cause, proslavery writers also amassed a small but influential group of sympathizers. By the beginning of the 1790s, neither side felt assured of victory and this doubt motivated writers to sharpen and hone their arguments. Each group developed its vision of the Briton to further political, social, and certainly economic agendas. In the later stages of the debates, the rhetorical terrain of national identity became the most common backdrop for abolitionist and proslavery opinions. The most dynamic phase of the slave-trade debates actually lasted only four years; however, the changes in argument over those years shaped national identity in significant ways.

While the abolitionist movement has received a great deal of scholarly attention, it has rarely been studied in the context of the interaction with the proslavery campaign.[1] Most critics treat this social movement as somehow separate from the opposition that had, as I contend, a significant role in the development of strategies and tactics. Academic debates tend to focus on determining how much of an impact the movement actually had on bringing about the end of the slave trade, and the enormous success of abolitionist societies in amassing support from virtually every level of British society. Petitions, for example, reflected an impressive degree of support from working- and middle-class Britons in cities across the mother country. Organizers in major centres such as London, Bristol, Edinburgh, and Dublin coordinated successive petition campaigns from 1788 to 1792, gathering more signatures with each year. The campaign to abolish the slave

---

[1] Brycchan Carey's *British Abolitionism and the Rhetoric of Sensibility* does discuss proslavery writing in the use of "sentimental" arguments; however, his analysis examines the incidence of sentimental rhetoric rather than the reaction to or interaction with antislavery appeals.

trade mobilized public support in an effective and efficient manner, far outstripping the opposition in its number of supporters. J. R. Oldfield's *Popular Politics and British Anti-Slavery* traces the changes in demographics and organizing strategies to which rural and urban "publics" responded so favorably.[2] Other studies analyze the manner in which abolitionist societies allowed previously disenfranchised populations a voice in effecting positive change.[3] All such analyses assume a particular teleology, themselves based on a certain unfolding of national history, and focus too narrowly on the goals of the abolitionist campaign.[4]

Most scholars of this period are inclined to divide the proponents of abolition and regulation into separate and discrete groups, each with a wholly oppositional agenda. Once the bill for abolition was signed into law, the putative victors of the debates were the anti-slave-trade activists. Historians concede that the slave trade continued for a number of years afterward, but ultimately the movement was a success.[5] To what degree abolition owes its success to the actual movement is a very different question among slavery historians. The secondary literature examines this moment in history by focusing on the copious output of writers and activists in order to assess the social, philosophical, and literary contributions of the abolitionist movement. The individual nuances of the debates and interactions between the different camps have not been examined in a full-length study. In order truly to understand the rhetorical implications of debates and their effect on British culture, both sides need to be studied together. In other words, scholars have been

---

[2] J. R. Oldfield, *Popular Politics and British Anti-Slavery*. Oldfield's study focuses primarily on the petition campaigns and their organization. In 1788, activists presented 100 petitions against the slave trade gathered countrywide from both cities and rural townships. By 1792, the number of petitions had soared to 519.

[3] The majority of work has been done on gender and the role of women in the antislavery movement. See Clare Midgley's *Women Against Slavery*, Moira Ferguson's *Subject to Others*, and Charlotte Sussman's *Consuming Anxieties: Consumer Protest, Gender, and British Slavery, 1713–1833* (Stanford: Stanford University Press, 2000). For other analyses of the role of rural and working class members of abolitionist societies, see Robin Blackburn's *The Overthrow of Colonial Slavery*, and Betty Fladeland's *Abolitionists and Working-Class Problems*.

[4] Indeed, many historians ignore the proslavery contribution or mention their arguments with little analysis. Davis addresses the proslavery argument in his compendious 1973 study, *The Problem of Slavery in Western Culture,* more so from the American response, and historians of American slavery have detailed analyses of American proslavery. With respect to the first abolitionist campaign, most critics do not even credit the activities of proslavery writers as forming a counter-campaign against abolition.

[5] Marika Sherwood in *After Abolition: Britain and the Slave Trade Since 1807* (London and New York: I.B. Tauris and Co., 2007) strongly objects to the perceived success of abolition by producing many examples of the continuing trade well after the passage of the bill. While Sherwood makes an excellent point, I do think the cultural implications of success, perceived or otherwise, during that time were quite strong and definitively shaped British national identity.

telling the story piecemeal. By the end of the eighteenth century, abolitionists and proslavery writers had shaped and informed each others' argument in significant ways. Thus, the image of the "Briton" that emerged from the debates contained attributes lauded by both sides.

While debating the feasibility of abolition, writers from each camp continued to battle over the predominant characteristics of the Briton. The audience for their arguments converged as each side attempted to influence both legislators and the general reading public. Shifts in debate necessitated that writers imagine their audience as a cohesive public body who shared important characteristics.[6] The publications of antislavery writers from 1767 to 1788 concentrated on constructing an image of the institution of slavery for colonial and metropolitan audiences. The purpose of this construction lay primarily in getting these audiences to acknowledge that a problem existed with respect to Great Britain's engagement in slavery and the slave trade. Once the institution had been sufficiently problematized, the purpose of antislavery writing transformed and writers sought to focus on providing solutions. Their strategy involved a narrowing of critique to the slave trade and proposing that the trade be completely dismantled. During this process, proslavery writers also engaged in a parallel campaign that attempted first to discredit then to question the motives of antislavery/abolitionist activists. In the face of growing public disapproval, they proposed several measures designed to regulate the trade and make it more "humane." While their purpose may have initially been to preserve the status quo (albeit with a few minor reforms), they were soon hard-pressed to justify their way of life. Each camp posed a vision for the course of the nation that pushed its particular political end. Thus, the organized resistance to the slave trade from 1788 to its abolition in 1807 furthered the debate over national character and framed an updated, sanitized, and alternative construction of British imperial identity.[7]

This chapter maps the changes in antislavery and proslavery rhetoric after the formation of the abolitionist societies in order to understand how the slave-trade debates constructed national identity. Both sides offered their visions of the Briton in an attempt to speak to particular audiences. While proslavery writers supported the losing side from current perspectives, aspects of their vision appealed to significant segments of the population during the time of the debates. From the introduction of the bill to abolish the slave trade in 1788 to the formal abolition of the slave trade in 1807, British readers demonstrated an awareness and deep

---

[6] Andrew McCann, *Cultural Politics in the 1790s: Literature, Radicalism and the Public Sphere* (New York: St. Martin's Press, 1999). His analysis applies Habermas's concept of the "literary public sphere" to the political climate in 1790s Britain. McCann delineates the conjunction of politics and aesthetics that defines the public sphere.

[7] Armitage argues, in *The Ideological Origins of the British Empire*, that people had more of a sense of imperialism in this second British empire, and the activities of the nineteenth century grew from this foundation. I offer the slave trade debate as a specific test case to support this point.

regard for the issue. Anti-slave-trade rhetoric reflected the growing public support and writers honed strategies tested in earlier exchanges. William Wilberforce's skillful speeches in Parliament proved critical to making the case for abolition.[8] Organizers of the movement broadened their appeals and used visual media, such as cartoons, paintings, and consumer items like medallions, buttons, and cameos to rally support for their cause. These new forms of address modeled for the public more specifically and more forcefully the integral components of (inter)national "Britishness." More importantly, an active dialogue emerged between abolitionists and the response from primarily West Indian advocates for the slave trade. Proslavery writers' awareness of the necessity of commerce for the well-being of the empire prompted them to propose regulating the trade rather than abolishing it. They vilified the "radical" element in abolition and used politically threatening events like the French Revolution and, more specifically, the Haitian Revolution to their advantage. Finally, I consider the last years of the debate and the vision of national identity that cohered in the early nineteenth century. The successful abolition of the slave trade did not mean an utter rejection of the proslavery Briton. Instead, a fusion of characteristics occurred that incorporated elements of the commercial and the moral character of British subjects. The identity that emerged from the rhetoric of the debates, as a tracking of rhetorical circumference demonstrates, situated the Briton in both the national and international context.

Proliferation of Abolitionist Rhetoric, 1785–1796

Each decade of the organized opposition against slavery necessitated changes in strategy for both sides. The balance of power shifted over the 1770s, '80s, and '90s until the proslavery position no longer benefited from the status quo. In fact, towards the end of the century, the status quo shifted significantly enough that slavery advocates no longer recognized their own legitimate form of trade in the attacks that captured the public imagination. The early work of antislavery crusaders convinced multiple audiences—both in the American colonies and the mother country—that the institution of slavery was corrupting and inherently diseased. Legal decisions in England and Scotland affirmed that slavery was a colonial taint from which the mother country must be protected. In the 1780s, antislavery writers intensified their critique in order to capitalize on increased public awareness of the institution. Slavery and—by the end of the decade—the slave trade became an important issue of "national" significance. Antislavery literature proliferated throughout the major cities (London, Edinburgh, and Dublin), slave ports (Bristol, Manchester, and Liverpool), and the countryside, appealing in truth

---

[8] Wilberforce used several dramatic examples of the cruelty of white slaveholders, one of which resulted in the trial of Captain John Kimber. See Carey, *British Abolitionism* 179–181.

to the "British" nation.⁹ With the formation of abolitionist societies across Great Britain, committee members planned a campaign to mobilize the public through print sources. These writers and activists organized against a particular aspect of the institution and focused their efforts on proposing a concrete solution—immediate abolition. In a strong counter-move, slavery supporters conceded that the system was imperfect and proposed a series of regulations as a solution. As the focus of the debates remained on abolition rather than regulation, each camp had to reframe its arguments and continuously update its rebuttals.

When activists focused their critiques on the transatlantic slave trade, a series of transformations occurred in the debates that produced a new discourse of identity. Both antislavery and proslavery writers utilized language that appealed to and defined their audience. In making their respective cases, they created a sense of nationalism that either denounced or incorporated the institution of slavery. However, their appeals differed in terms of rhetorical circumference. Antislavery publication centered on audiences within Great Britain and sought to distance the morality and character of the motherland from her corrupt colonies. Proslavery writers, who were primarily colonials, assumed a broader view of the British nation and incorporated the lifestyle and mores of the colonies into their construction of the Briton. They identified the threat to the slave trade well before antislavery activists focused their critiques on the abuses of the middle passage and the need for abolition of the slave trade. Two significant transformations in the debates emerged from the organized push for abolition: (1.) By focusing on the slave trade, the differing circumferences of each camp merged, and (2.) the debate became an issue of both national and international importance. The emerging sense of national identity, which both camps manipulated to meet their ends, began to take on imperial overtones.

Antislavery writers succeeded in focusing attention on the institution of slavery, but their own understanding of the problem had to change before feasible solutions could be proposed. Not all critiques of slavery even proposed solutions, and those which did outlined solutions that ran the gamut from immediate abolition of the entire institution to gradual manumission with the integration of freed blacks into colonial society. The focus of most antislavery publications in the 1770s and early '80s was establishing awareness, primarily in metropolitan audiences, that slavery damaged the character and reputation of the British nation. Antislavery publications encompassed multiple circumferences that shifted depending on geographic regions. Sharp and other writers in the mother country concentrated their appeals by writing to metropolitan audiences, mainly Londoners. References

---

⁹ After abolitionist societies formed in London between 1785 and 1788, similar societies began to form in other major cities. They used subscription fees to reprint major abolitionist works, such as Clarkson's tracts, Equiano's narrative, and Wilberforce's speeches. Also, the Quaker press in London distributed abolitionist literature to other cities. For a detailed survey of the Quaker role in printing, see Judith Jennings, *The Business of Abolishing the Slave Trade, 1783–1807* (London: Frank Cass, 1997).

to *England* in early work effectively excluded other parts of Great Britain and characterized the colonies as transgressive territories. Though later writers began to refer increasingly to Great Britain, they maintained the division between colony and metropole. Anthony Benezet and American colonial writers sought to rally support in the American colonies and so to bridge the gap between mother country and colony.[10]

Changes in circumference brought forth the organized abolitionist movement, and these changes occurred because of the interchange between colonial and metropolitan antislavery writers. Quaker activists, particularly Benezet, had a broader outlook on the institution of slavery, having witnessed the practices in Philadelphia, and they recognized the slave trade as a critical component on which to focus their critiques. Benezet shared the worldview of proslavery writers in realizing that abolishing the slave trade would severely destabilize British slavery. He communicated this goal to the British Quakers who took up the cause of abolition in Great Britain—an interchange that historian David Brion Davis refers to in *The Problem of Slavery in the Age of Revolution* as the "Quaker antislavery international." Guided by Benezet, the London Quakers focused on the slave trade as the first step in dismantling the entire institution, a threat that proslavery writers had perceived earlier. Though American activists became too involved with the revolution in their homeland to participate further in the debates, they provided the focus and goal for the British anti-slave-trade campaign. The efforts to abolish the slave trade began in earnest and Quaker abolitionists effectively communicated their goals to activists outside of their religion. Once Granville Sharp and Thomas Clarkson joined in the newly focused struggle, the organized abolitionist society formed with clear ideas of the problem and the proposed solution. Proslavery writers responded swiftly to this new challenge and concentrated their rhetoric more on justifications for the slave trade.

The convergence of rhetorical circumference between abolitionist and proslavery writers transformed the definition of the act.[11] Antislavery writers tended to define the act of slavery in the worst terms possible, without regard to

---

[10] The West Indies occupied an odd position with respect to antislavery literature. While former residents like Ramsay published critiques of colonial practices, no antislavery writing was published within the West Indies. Planters were aware of antislavery arguments coming from North America and Great Britain, but I have found no record of colonial presses in Barbados, Jamaica, Antigua, St. Christopher (St. Kitts)/Nevis reprinting any of these documents. The reason for this absence is quite clearly the result of both smaller white populations on the islands and the persistent fear of slave revolts that exposure to abolitionist tracts might have prompted.

[11] I do not make the same distinction between pro-slave-trade and proslavery. The opposition to abolition had to defend both the trade and the practices of West Indian plantation slavery. Most critiques of anti-slave-trade publications included passages describing idyllic conditions of slavery in the colonies, so the term "proslavery" accurately describes the writing of anti-abolitionist authors.

the differences in labor conditions across the colonies or even among plantations.[12] Their use of pathetic appeals dictated the form for most depictions of slavery, which concentrated on describing the oppression inherent in the institution. Proslavery writers had a more nuanced understanding of slavery as involving multiple acts whose form differed by region, crop, and climate. When abolitionists chose to concentrate on the slave trade, they delineated the act with more specificity and forced proslavery writers to change accordingly. The careful demarcation of act in the slave-trade debates influenced the type of solution proposed by each camp. For anti-slave-trade writers, abolition became the most feasible solution to correct the "problem," which had been reframed as the abuses of slave acquisition and the middle passage. For proslavery writers, the concentrated attack provided a more finite "problem" that could be successfully countered with the judicious use of regulations. No need to abandon a financially sound trade when the legislature could easily regulate operations. These "regulationists"—a term I coin to characterize the opposition more precisely—believed that the discontent with the status quo could be remedied without significantly impinging on their way of life. By the 1790s, even the most ardent supporters of slavery acknowledged that the institution suffered from some fundamental flaws. They advocated stricter regulation of the trade as the most equitable solution, a successful tactic in 1788 that possibly delayed abolition by almost twenty years.[13]

The nature of the trade necessitated a re-visioning of the problem of slavery as one that extended beyond the boundaries of Great Britain and her colonies. The merging of circumferences and act by both sides of the debates influenced the type of arguments that were used and transformed contemporary understandings of the slave trade. When anti-slave-trade writers began to detail the horrors of the middle passage, readers could no longer tie specific abuses with particular locations. In other words, the corruption of the trade was not tidily confined between the West Indies and Africa. Writers had to challenge the neat moral separation of mother country and colonies regarding the toleration of slavery in order to advocate for broader reform. They began to highlight the sense of mutual culpability that implicated subjects of the mother country in transgressions, although not to the same extent as colonials. Anti-slave-trade writers broadened their analyses to discuss the interconnectedness of African nations, British traders, *and* the colonies. Great Britain, they argued, harmed not only her own character but contributed to the degeneration of the supposedly less civil character of the African.[14] Proslavery

---

[12] When the Society for the Propagation of the Gospel in Foreign Parts gained the Codrington plantation in Barbados early in the century, they viewed it as an opportunity to showcase kind and benevolent governance of slaves.

[13] Of course, not all regulations supported the proslavery argument. The passage of Lord Dolben's bill to regulate the number of slaves on ships in 1788 was heralded as an *abolitionist* victory.

[14] Abolitionist tracts varied greatly in their perceptions of the level of African "civilization." Equiano, for example, had a much more favorable opinion of African society,

rebuttals pointed out that other European nations would gladly take up the slave trade if the British ceased to operate their own. These writers had always framed their arguments in a global and international context, and now their responses could directly counter the global, international context of slave-trade critique. As the debates escalated over the 1790s, writers from each camp acknowledged both the national and international significance of this act. Arguments regarding abolition contested not only the primary attributes of British character but also the place of Great Britain among other nations of the world.

During the 1780s, each side of the slave-trade debate honed its arguments and became more formally organized. The first abolitionist society organized informally in 1783 and consisted of Quakers in London who had been pressed by their American counterparts to begin agitating against the slave trade.[15] The original 23-member committee structured its campaign around the effort to raise public awareness, which members attempted to do by publishing articles in newspapers and magazines around the country.[16] They relied heavily on the financial support of their fellow Quakers to fund independent printings, which were intended primarily for their own community. One of the founding committee members, James Phillips, was a prominent Quaker bookseller who printed a series of abolitionist tracts and pamphlets that he distributed to Quaker and other communities. Though he printed mainly for the London market, abolitionist societies distributed much of his output into other counties in Great Britain. These politically savvy men (women did not join the rolls of abolitionist societies until 1788) understood that abolition could only be accomplished through legislative action.[17] After unsuccessfully petitioning Parliament in 1785, the Quaker abolitionist committee recognized the need for a stronger voice to advocate from within government. The supporter who combined oratorical skills with missionary zeal was William Wilberforce.

Wilberforce's biographers credit his religious conversion with prompting his interest in the slave trade and his zeal for abolition.[18] His compelling speaking

---

albeit with religious misgivings. However, most writers conceded that the British set a very poor example by their behavior, regardless of the conditions of the indigenous society. The emphasis of their arguments fell on the conduct of the British rather than the Africans.

[15] For a detailed analysis of the first abolitionist societies and their connections to the British Quaker community, see Jennings, *The Business of Abolishing the Slave Trade, 1783–1807*.

[16] Judith Jennings documents the publications in which anti-slave-trade Quakers directed their attacks: Norwich *Mercury*, Bath *Chronicle*, papers in York and Liverpool, London *Lloyd's Evening Post*, and papers in Bristol, Cork, Dublin, Kent, Sherborne, and Newcastle (24–25).

[17] The direct involvement of women in the antislavery movement is detailed in Clare Midgley's *Women against Slavery*. She documents that women participated in the movement as subscribers, and the Abolitionist Society in 1788 included 206 women (about 10 percent of the subscribers) who contributed £363.3s.6d (17).

[18] His first biographers were his sons, Robert I. and Samuel Wilberforce, *Life of William Wilberforce* (London: J. Murray, 1838; Philadelphia: Henry Perkins 1839). Several

style and affable personality quickly made him a favorite in his community. At twenty-five, he took his seat in the House of Commons as the representative from Yorkshire. Before his thirtieth birthday (about 1785), he became an Evangelical and took a keen interest in reforming society. His approach to politics applied a strong Christian morality to critical issues that addressed the improvement of lower-class social conditions. While he was aware of the agitation involving the slave trade, he was not an active supporter of abolition. In 1785, members of the Quaker committee urged Wilberforce to consider taking up the anti-slave-trade cause, and after reading Thomas Clarkson's *An Essay on the Slavery and Commerce of the Human Species* (1786), he became involved.[19] The Society for Effecting the Abolition of the Slave Trade formed in 1787, and though Wilberforce was not a member, he declared his intent to introduce the abolition bill into the House on behalf of the Society. From 1788 to 1792, the House of Commons heard testimony from shipowners, sailors, physicians, and other men directly involved with the slave trade. Abolitionists regularly printed accounts of these testimonies and spotlighted Wilberforce's eloquence in denouncing the "immoral" and "impolitick" trade. Anti-slave-trade publications cleverly used the testimony of "credible" witnesses to establish their argument that the trade was wholly antithetical to British character. Wilberforce provided an excellent model for the "true" virtues of the conscientious Briton.

When Wilberforce addressed the House in May of 1789, he had clearly studied the arguments made by both sides of the debate before crafting his appeal. He instructed the audience that he wished to consider the question of abolition with "cool and impartial reason."[20] This comment directly addressed proslavery depictions of abolitionists as "irrational" with "misguided passions." Wilberforce claimed to represent the cause "of justice, of humanity, and of freedom," all of which were concerns that transcended individual interests, such as those embodied by West India planters and merchants. From the outset, he argued for "total Abolition" of the slave trade because no "regulations" or "palliatives" could "overcome these enormities." He humorously discredited the ethos of all the traders who argued on behalf of their livelihood, dismissing their statements as *"mere opinions."*

---

studies have been published since, the most recent being Murray Pura, *Am I not a man and a brother?: The Life and Spirituality of William Wilberforce* (Toronto: Clements Press, 2002).

[19] Since most abolitionist societies had formed by the late 1780s and set their goal of abolishing the slave trade, I will no longer use the term "antislavery" to describe their publications. The term "anti-slave-trade" is both more specific and more historically accurate as a separate "antislavery" movement arose in the 1820s.

[20] William Wilberforce, *The Speech of William Wilberforce, Esq. Representative for the County of York, on Wednesday the 13th of May, 1789, on the question of the ABOLITION OF THE SLAVE TRADE. To which are added the RESOLUTIONS THEN MOVED, and a short sketch of the SPEECHES OF OTHER MEMBERS* (London: Printed at the Logographic Press, and Sold by J. Walter, C. Stalker, and W. Richardson, 1789).

He stated, "In truth, an enquiry from the African Committee whether any foul play prevails in Africa, is somewhat like an application to the Custom-house officers, to know whether any smuggling is going on" (11). By pointing out the self-interest inherent in the testimony of proslavery witnesses, he questioned the validity of their accounts and cast doubt on their motives. The utter lack of self-interest on the part of abolitionists, he argued, remained a clear indicator to the righteousness of their cause (and the "impartiality" of their testimony). His appeal spoke very strongly to the idea of the "moral" Briton whose interest in humanity superseded self-interest.

Wilberforce's argument demonstrated an awareness of the significance of abolition beyond the immediate repercussions to the British empire. He characterized abolition as "a subject, in which the interests, not of this country, nor of Europe alone, but of the whole world, and of posterity, are involved" (3). Though his description can be seen as somewhat grandiose, his portrayal of the issue gestures toward an increasingly powerful construction of national character. Proslavery writers argued that Great Britain would sustain considerable losses from immediate abolition, primarily to their perpetual enemy—France. Abolition would only empower their competitors to take a bigger share of the trade, defeating the high moral intentions of anti-slave-trade agitators. However, morality once again trumped self-interest as France's gain was "clearly no argument whatever against the *wickedness* of the trade." Wilberforce further discounted the loss of profit by declaring that "France is too enlightened a nation, to begin pushing a scandalous as well as ruinous traffic, at the very time when England sees her folly, and resolves to give it up" (44). This comment played in interesting ways on the conceit of the French as well as the British. He alludes to a kind of awakening in which Britons are the first to see the error of their ways and bear the responsibility of guiding the rest of the world to a similar enlightenment. In a portentous statement, Wilberforce proposed: "Wherever the sun shines, let us go round the world with him diffusing our beneficence" (49). His comments presaged the nineteenth-century imperial mission by illustrating the rationale used to translate empire-building into British "beneficence."

Abolitionist rhetoric incorporated a charismatic appeal to singular characteristics that Britons had perfected above all other civilized nations. Belief in *English* superiority definitely predated the sentiments I have identified as originating in abolitionist rhetoric. Subjects of England had long considered themselves superior to the French, the Dutch, and the Spanish as well as to the Scots, the Welsh, and the Irish. However, anti-slave-trade activists wrote to audiences across Great Britain, so the rhetoric appealed specifically to Britons and their "national" characteristics. The changes wrought by the abolitionist movement coincided with a number of other cultural changes occurring in the latter half of the century.[21] These debates participated in and drew from broader cultural transformations regarding the

---

[21] Linda Colley's *Britons* does a good job of providing broad overviews of the various strains of political and social thought that contributed to the formation of national identity. However, by treating the abolition as a foregone conclusion, she underestimates the importance of the movement for identity construction and nineteenth-century imperialism.

formation of British national identity. Their distinctive contribution lay in what I call the commitment to world leadership. As the concept of the "Briton" in abolitionist writings grew to incorporate varying social classes, races, and regional origins, more subjects felt included in what became a national project with a global scope. These writers seemed to engage in simultaneous goals forging a national character from internal and external stimuli. While the slave trade was an internal problem for the British people, its exercise affected other European and African nations. Delineating national character became imperative to the immediate goal of abolition and the larger sense of international obligation. After all, Britons needed to set a good example for the rest of the world. Wilberforce was not the only writer (or speaker) to recognize the international implications of abolition and Great Britain's emerging role on the world stage.

Abolitionist writers proved highly enthusiastic about their duty to precipitate great moral change both at home and abroad. The Parliamentary inquiry into the abuses of the slave trade began in 1788, and some writers prematurely predicted victory for their cause. Helen Maria Williams' "On the Bill Which Was Passed in England for Regulating the Slave-Trade; A Short Time before its Abolition" (1788) revealed her optimism and sense of impending triumph for the cause. Her poem addressed Lord Dolben's bill regulating the carrying capacity of British slave ships, but she clearly believed that its passage was a harbinger of more definitive action. She exclaimed, "BRITAIN! The noble, blest decree / That soothes despair, is fram'd by thee! / Thy powerful arm has interpos'd." Admittedly, her sentiments can be described as poetic hyperbole, but Williams illustrates the growing sense of pride in British morality, which was superior to the morality of other civilized nations. She further distinguished the significance of this bill by declaring, "O, first of Europe's polish'd lands / To ease the captive's iron bands; / Long, as thy glorious annals shine, / This proud distinction shall be thine!" This conviction of being first among European nations to take positive action against slavery figured prominently in abolitionist rhetoric.

The conflict over the primary attributes of the "Christian" in the latter stages of the debate also shaped the development of national character. Both sides claimed a "Christian" identity by approaching their understanding of the term from totally conflicting perspectives. From the outset of Britain's involvement with the trade, .biblical justifications for slavery supported the institution and the "natural" subjugation of Africans The traditional Anglican clergy shored up the questionable moral position of plantation slavery by quoting Old Testament examples and St. Paul's doctrine pertaining to bonded labor. Resistance to the institution came primarily from dissenting sects of Christianity, (for example, the Quakers), and dissenters within Anglicanism (for example, the Methodists), which had limited influence in the mother country.[22] However, the rise of the Evangelical fervor in

---

[22] The interaction of Protestant sects in eighteenth-century Britain is very complex and highly influential in the formation of national identity. Linda Colley's analysis thoroughly accounts for the importance of religion without examining the interaction between

Anglicanism radically changed the "Christian" position on slavery within the Church of England. Now members of the established church—like Beilby Porteus, who later became Bishop of London, and William Wilberforce—completely rejected biblical justifications for slavery and the slave trade. Proslavery Church of England ministers could dismiss the writings of Quakers and Methodists as sentiments of radicals. However, they could not so easily ignore the resistance to slavery coming from within their own church. Anglicans who resisted proslavery interpretations sought to reclaim Christianity for the righteous and correct the misinterpretations of biblical slavery propagated by their fellow clergymen.

The clash between abolitionist and proslavery authors over the definition of Christianity produced an active discourse about British characteristics. Both camps agreed that Christianity and religious principles were a mainstay of national character; however, religion had served the contradictory purpose of validating and repudiating the institution of slavery. Many proslavery writers continued to assert that the African slave was better off serving a Christian master rather than a heathen prince. Granville Sharp, a dedicated member of the established Church, began to discredit standard biblical interpretations with his publications in the 1770s. Proslavery clergy were more strongly challenged to defend their views and show the consistency of their practices with the higher tenets of Christianity. In 1788, Raymund Harris published *Scriptural Researches on the Licitness of the Slave Trade* in which he proposed to show the "conformity with the principles of the Law of Nature delineated in the Sacred Writings" with slavery.[23] This tract became the last gasp of proslavery justifications based on the Old Testament. Harris used many of the arguments from previous publications, citing Mosaic law and Abraham's practice of keeping bond slaves as support for the slave trade. His comments attacked Granville Sharp's tracts most directly, and he dismissed the possibility of divine retribution when the Bible did not account slave trading and slave holding to be sins. Harris also responded to the discourse about "natural rights" that anti-slave-trade writers used to invalidate the institution. He described how Mosaic law was modeled after the Law of Nature and therefore consistent with the current practices of slave traders. His arguments illustrated the extent to which proslavery clergy were forced to engage abolitionist claims about the antithetical nature of Christianity and slavery.

The struggle over defining the attributes of the Christian played a crucial role in the debates and influenced the emergence of competing versions of national

---

Christianity and abolition. My study builds upon Colley's examination in order to isolate the contributions of the abolitionist movement in shaping the Christian Briton.

[23] Raymund Harris, *Scriptural Researches on the Licitness of the Slave Trade, shewing its conformity with the principles of natural and revealed religion, delineated in the sacred writings of the Word of God. Reverend R. Harris* (London: John Stockdale, 1788). A second edition of the tract was published in Liverpool by H. Hodgson in 1788 and reprinted in Maryland by John Winter in 1790. Interestingly enough, Harris did not use the standard arguments from Paul, which made his tract especially vulnerable to criticism.

character.[24] Harris's comments elicited immediate and furious denunciations from anti-slave-trade activists who repudiated the proslavery version of Christianity. They countered the arcane priestly laws of the Old Testament with Christ's doctrine and claimed a more legitimate or "truer" understanding of the religion. Though ancients may have practiced slavery, the more enlightened and advanced British society should condemn such practices. A subtle shift in argument transformed the anti-slave-trade responses from merely reacting to proslavery justifications to contributing evidence of fresh interpretation. Three refutations appeared in the same year as Harris's tract and all three proposed a different perspective on Christian doctrine.[25] The common element for all tracts was the belief that the institution could not receive any religious sanction. Instead of relying wholly on biblical verses that contradicted the practice, writers began to claim that compassionate Christians should be intolerant of slavery. The emphasis on Christian benevolence created a figurative split in the Church that was rhetorically inflected as well. The slave-holding Christian became a throwback to an earlier and less enlightened time. In *Scripture, the Friend of Freedom* (1789), its author used the arguments in *Scriptural Researches* to create a divide in practices of Christianity and to isolate the proslavery clergy: "While Mr. H. glories in having proved that enslaving a fellow-creature is no act of injustice, I shall rather glory in being a member of a church whose ministers could not hold forth such arguments, without departing from its doctrines, and contradicting those *benevolent principles*, which *Protestants* in general, of *every denomination*, esteem inseparable from the *Christian Religion*" (79). Anti-slave-trade activists represented themselves as having a broader and more progressive view of Christianity (that is, Protestantism).[26]

The negotiation of Christian identity had powerful implications for the development of theories of race at this time. While anti-slave-trade writers

---

[24] I would note that the term "Christian" in these tracts is used specifically to mean Protestantism. Catholicism was viewed as a separate and degraded religion both for its corrupt church and its continued support of slavery. Interestingly enough, Raymund Harris was later discovered to be Don Raymondo Hormaza, a Spanish expatriate and ex-Jesuit priest (Tise 79).

[25] William Hughes, *An Answer to the Reverend Mr. Harris's "Scriptural Researches on the Licitness of the Slave Trade" By W. Hughes* (London: Printed for T. Cadell, 1788); William Roscoe, *A scriptural refutation of a pamphlet, lately published by the Rev. Raymund Harris, intitled, "Scriptural Researches on the licitness of the slave trade" In four letters from the author to a friend* (London: Printed for J. Phillips, 1788; Printed for B. Law, 1788); Henry Dannett, *A Particular examination of Mr. Harris's Scriptural researches on the licitness of the slave trade* (London: Printed and Sold by T. Payne; Oxford: D. Prince and Cooke, 1788).

[26] David Spadafora's *The Idea of Progress* illustrates the manner in which the emerging progress narrative in the eighteenth century reinvigorated Christianity and gave the religion a new sense of purpose. Abolitionists propagated this narrative by tying intolerance to the slave trade with "progressive" thought and damning the opposition as backward and archaic.

opposed the use of scripture to justify enslavement, they also advocated a higher purpose in British dealings with Africa—missionary work. A critical characteristic in abolitionist definitions of religious identity in Britain was the desire to "raise the lustre of the Christian name," a purpose particularly stressed by the Evangelical supporters. Writers frequently pointed out that no African could possibly wish to convert to the religion of the "oppressor." They denounced the "ruthless avarice" of Christians and chastised the slave traders in Africa for setting such a poor example. The natives had "learn'd to dread the Christian's trust" and abolitionists strongly condemned the "toils spread by a Christian hand."[27] Some writers warned of God's displeasure for treating "fellow-creatures" with such disrespect. The more radical authors characterized slaves as "brethren," a term that raised the ire of many slavery advocates. The idea of "national recrimination" became a compelling claim for the Anglican anti-slave-trade activists. The West Indies were already experiencing the effects of their ill-gotten gains, so the mother country would have to face the repercussions of condoning such actions in the near future. As Cowper recounted in "The Negro's Complaint," "Wild tornadoes / Strewing yonder sea with wrecks, / Wasting towns, plantations, meadows, / Are the voice with which he speaks." Most abolitionist writers discounted Old Testament slavery as symptomatic of an older, less civilized time. The advances of society, particularly in recent memory, dictated that such archaic institutions were out of place in progressive eighteenth-century society. Abolitionists developed a hierarchy of cultures that did not regard Africans as a sub-species (or separate species as Long's extremist views claimed). Instead, they ascribed to an ideology of "racial historicism" that viewed African societies as less developed.[28] "Injur'd Afric" could benefit in multiple ways from Christian benevolence—first, by ending the traffic in human beings and second, by bringing the civilizing influence of Christianity to heathen cultures.

    The abolitionist delineation of race differed considerably from proslavery writings and became a powerful tool in denouncing the opposition. By examining the rhetoric of both camps, I illustrate how each group claimed for itself a clearer understanding of the primary attributes of national character. Abolitionist rhetoric stressed the high moral character of Britons and reframed previous practices of slavery as lapses in judgment. In asserting a superior morality, anti-slave-trade

---

    [27] Quotes taken from responses to Harris' tract and *An Address to the Right Reverend The Prelates of England and Wales, on the Subject of the Slave Trade*, attributed to George Harrison (London: Printed and Sold by J. Parsons, 1792).

    [28] David Theo Goldberg, *The Racial State* (Malden, MA: Blackwell Publishers, 2002). Goldberg's extensive examination of the history and implications of race identify two strains of race theory that developed during the eighteenth century. "Racial naturalism" theorized that other races were not of the same species as the European races—the argument used by slavery advocates. "Racial historicism" gave differing races full status in terms of humanity but believed the societies to be in a lower stage of development. While both forms artificially hierarchized world cultures (with European culture standing "naturally" at the top), "racial historicism" held out the hope of eventually reaching the top.

writers endeavored to and arguably succeeded in dehumanizing the "white Savage" who engaged in the slave trade. Abolitionists made finer distinctions among the "races" that transcended simple categories like color. Discussions of the emergence of racial categories in the eighteenth century often miss the subtle nuances of the abolitionist viewpoint. Goldberg's concept of "racial historicism," which shifts the origin of African inferiority from their biology to their societies, interprets this theory as deceptively benign or kinder than proslavery constructions. He maintains that abolitionists were able to salve their consciences and perpetuate a less overt form of discrimination by claiming the desire to ameliorate the African condition and bring their civilizations up to European standards. I contend that Goldberg's distinction in racial theories of the eighteenth century allows for an examination of how a preliminary sense of "whiteness" became reconstructed during the slave-trade debates. The vilification of the West Indies and the slave-supported economy took on racial undertones in abolitionist literature. By creating a division between the high moral fiber of Great Britain and the degraded morality of the West Indies, abolitionists turned the tables on proslavery constructions of race and granted Africans greater human sensibilities than their "oppressors."

Since proslavery constructions relied heavily on color distinctions, abolitionists reframed the concept of "whiteness" to further the division between colony and mother country. In the publications of the 1790s, anti-slave-trade writers increased their use of pathetic appeal by depicting the persecution of slaves by unscrupulous and "degraded" white slave merchants and planters. Many writers shifted the focus of their descriptions from the tortures of slaves to the perpetrators of the torture. Changing the object of critique necessitated modifying certain assumptions about color. The first task involved discrediting proslavery assertions regarding the Africans' biological insensitivity to the hardships of slavery that had become entwined with assumptions about skin color. Black people experienced the pain and misery of enslavement to the same degree as white people. As Mary Birkett's *A Poem on the African Slave Trade* (1792) declared, "Let sordid traders call it what they will, / Men must be men, possess with feelings still; / And little boots a white or sable skin, / To prove a fair inhabitant within." The change in term from "black" to "sable" illustrates the abolitionist reworking of color categories. The term "sable" does not have the extreme negative connotations of "black"; indeed, "sable" refers to objects described as beautiful. Hannah More similarly denounced proslavery claims in *Slavery, A Poem* (1788): "Perish the proud philosophy, which sought / To rob them of the pow'rs of equal thought." Abolitionists compared the nature of the white trader or master unfavorably with the stoic nobility of the captured slave. "The African merchants and West India planters, are a numerous body of men; they have been accused of crimes at which human nature shudders; of rapine, torture, murder, in the most varied and horrid forms."[29] That "white" men could be

---

[29] Thomas Cooper, *Considerations on the Slave Trade; and the Consumption of West Indian Produce* (London: Printed and Sold by Darton and Harvey, J. Carter, and J. Parsons, 1791) 5.

guilty of such sins necessitated an investigation into the category of "whiteness." Clearly, the "Pale tyrant" did not merit the same degree of consideration or respect as the "true Briton."

Viewing Africans as a less advanced civilization allowed abolitionists to maintain racial superiority in a manner that did not question the inherent humanity of the African.[30] This hierarchical understanding of civilizations enabled writers to present a vision of the degraded colonial civilization that began from European advancement but collapsed through the corrupting influence of slavery. Hannah More characterized traders as "barbarians," a term that proslavery writers used freely to describe Africans. In a sense, the abolitionist characterization of the West Indies paralleled British Orientalist descriptions of the East Indies as a once great but now fallen civilization.[31] In Anna Leticia Barbauld's poem "Epistle to William Wilberforce" (1791), she cautioned "By foreign wealth are British morals chang'd." Barbauld damned the West Indies as "foreign" and believed that the produce of those colonies had a deleterious effect on "British morals." Ann Yearsley's "A Poem on the Inhumanity of the Slave-Trade" (1788) challenged the slave merchant to sell members of his own family rather than offending "*Nature*" whose "rights are violated." In her depiction, the slave owner possessed a "cruel soul" that "Unnat'ral, ever feeds, with gross delight, / Upon his [slaves'] suff'rings." The corrupting influence of slavery had degraded colonial "civilization" to such a degree that only abolition could bring about redemption.

The racialized dichotomy between the "white Savage" and the "oppressed" slave became a frequent theme of visual representation. Abolitionist rhetoric grew to encompass visual media and effectively expanded their use of pathetic appeals. Perhaps the most popular example of this new form of appeal was the seal of the London Abolitionist Society (1788). This depicted the figure of a kneeling African man in chains with his hand raised in supplication. Created as a woodcut and distributed by Josiah Wedgwood, the image proliferated throughout British society and became a widely recognized symbol of the movement, being reproduced by the society at the head of anti-slave-trade publications, on stationery, in books, in prints, on newspaper headings, and—perhaps the most famous form—as the Wedgwood medallion.[32] The text above the kneeling figure questioned "Am I not a Man and Brother?" a highly provocative query that interrogated the race categories created

---

[30] Many abolitionist poets wrote anti-slave-trade poems from the perspective of the African in order to make slave misery more vivid and visible to the reading public. They often reproduced the pidgin language of slaves, ostensibly to represent the experience with "authenticity." However, by portraying African speech in this manner, abolitionists could subtly assert European superiority over the "socially backward" African.

[31] See Thomas Trautmann's *Aryans in British India* for a comprehensive analysis of the Orientalist discourse on early Indian colonization.

[32] For a comprehensive study of the role of visual representations in abolitionist literature see Marcus Wood, *Blind Memory: Visual Representations of Slavery in England and America, 1780–1805* (New York: Routledge, 2000).

by the proslavery camp. The symbolism of the abolitionist seal encompasses more serious meanings than the diminution of proslavery race theory; however, for the purposes of my analysis, I have chosen to focus on a particular interpretation. Most abolitionists did not believe that blacks were capable and deserving of full access to British identity. Only the more radical writers such as Granville Sharp and William Fox referred to black slaves as "fellow subjects." As scholars like Marcus Wood have pointed out, the image of the kneeling black man was non-threatening to white superiority and served as "cultural absentee" or "a blank page" on which whites could inscribe their meaning (*Blind Memory* 23). I extend this reading to an illustration of the construction of national character because only the compassionate and "moral" Briton would find the image disturbing. The seal entered popular culture in the 1790s and was reproduced in brooches, hairpins, even the lids of snuff boxes. Abolition in this form became fashionable, and the implications of the kneeling black man who questioned proslavery constructions of race became an explicit part of the public consciousness.

The second powerful visual that anti-slave-trade publications reproduced in order to illustrate the cruelty of the slave trade was the plan of the slave ship. Proposed in 1788 by the abolitionist society in Plymouth, the drawing and description of the ship was based on an actual vessel, the *Brookes*. The London society took the drawing and after making a few modifications published it in 1789. The illustration depicted each level of the slave ship and explained how the "cargo" was "stored" by drawing the figures of the slaves as lying on their backs in rows (see Figure 5.1). Though Parliament had just passed a bill to regulate the carrying capacity of slave ships, the societies continued to distribute this graphic depiction of the cruel, overcrowded conditions.[33] Copies of the illustration were published in some abolitionist tracts again as a tactic for establishing the inhumanity of the trade. The stick figure representations of African bodies became an eloquent visual representation of the absolute dehumanization that occurred. The description of slave ship had the additional rhetorical function of dispelling proslavery contentions that the middle passage was comfortable and easy for the slaves. No one could dismiss the visual of human beings packed together below deck with not enough room to sit up. Proslavery writers depicted Africans as singing and playing instruments during the crossing, a feat that was obviously impossible given the close conditions. The illustration of the slave ship became an effective tool for mobilizing public sympathies against the abuses of the trade.

Another innovative strategy initiated by abolitionists during the early 1790s advocated using the market and the power of the consumer to penalize West Indian commerce. Some writers believed that abolition was in the hands of the consumer and could be effected by an organized boycott of West Indian goods, specifically

---

[33] Since some abolitionists regarded the bill as the first step towards abolition, they must have felt the need to press the issue when no further action against the slave trade was forthcoming. In *Blind Memory*, Marcus Wood has traced the evolution of this illustration and demonstrated the inaccuracies in representing conditions on the actual ship.

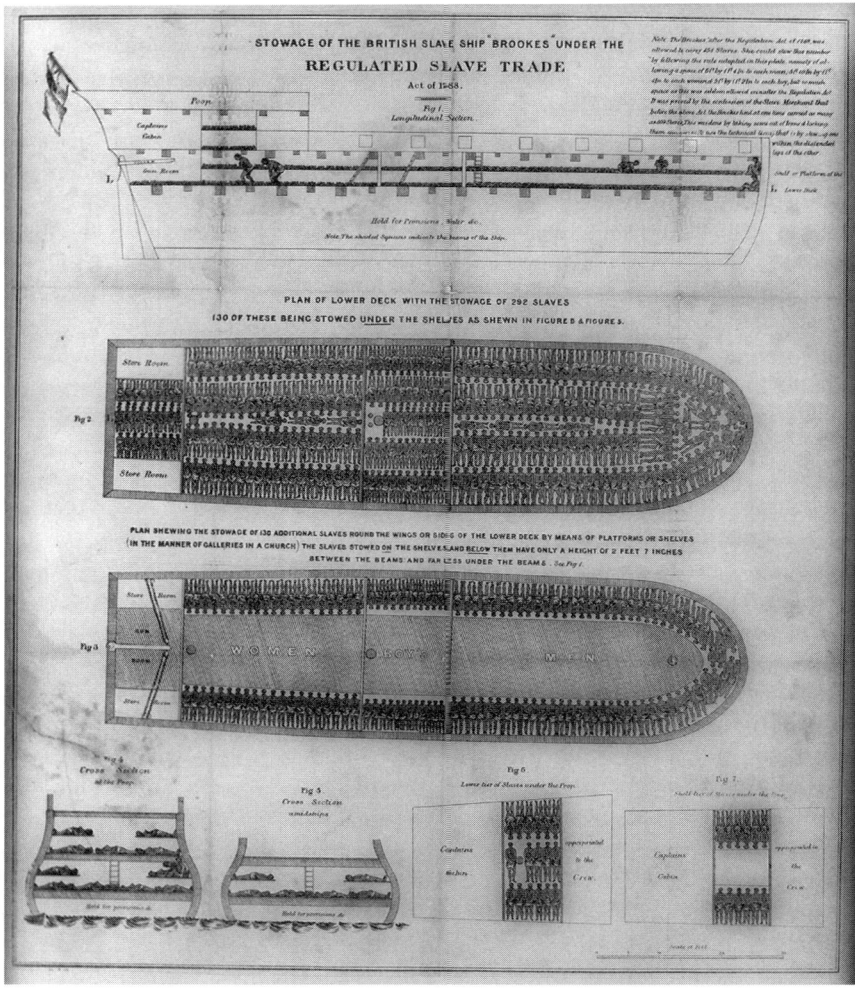

Fig. 5.1 Anonymous, "Stowage of the British slave ship 'Brookes' under the regulated slave trade." Created for Thomas Clarkson, 1788. Courtesy of the Library of Congress, LC–USZ62–44000.

sugar. While historians have debated the actual effectiveness of the sugar boycotts in prompting abolition, the language used to motivate and mobilize the public warrants separate scrutiny.[34] Perhaps the most famous publication was William

---

[34] Key historical studies on sugar and its role in abolition are Sidney W. Mintz's *Sweetness and Power* and Richard B. Sheridan's *Sugar and Slavery*.

Fox's *An Address to the People of Great Britain, on the Propriety of Abstaining from West India Sugar and Rum* (1791), which mobilized up to 300,000 families in Great Britain. He appealed directly to national pride in "claiming for ourselves the most perfect freedom" and "enjoying a degree of felicity unequalled in any age or country" (1). However, the "enlightened age" in which Britons currently lived had "greatly surpassed" the "most ignorant and barbarous ages" in terms of "injustice" and "unprecedented cruelty." He denounced trader and holder as "virulent agents of the consumer" and called upon the consumer "to redress evils."[35] While Fox's tract addressed all British subjects, subsequent calls for boycotts began to focus on a particular audience—women. The plea to reject West India sugar primarily targeted female consumers, who were asked to cease putting sugar in their tea. One writer published an anonymous tract, *An Address to Her Royal Highness the Duchess of York, against the use of sugar* (London, 1792), in which gender was directly identified. The author, who could have been either a man or a woman, stated "I cannot suppose there exists a female, possessing a heart of sensibility, who can consider at length the details of the facts which I have now hinted at, without many a deep sigh, without many an earnest wish, the world may be fairly rid of a traffic which involves in it such complicated villany" (10). The comment reproduces both assumptions about female nature and beliefs in their greater sensitivity to the issue.[36]

Targeting women as a consumer group opened an additional space for women writers in abolitionist rhetoric and made their presence visible in the depiction of national identity. The interaction of gender and abolition has been studied thoroughly for its particular ideological contribution to British society, but critics have rarely noted the contribution of women's writing to the development of national identity. While contemporary critics have illuminated the contribution of women to abolition, they have focused on the more practical contributions and inflected the ideological contributions with a feminist intent. Both Clare Midgley and Moira Ferguson focus their studies of women in abolition on reconstructing women's contributions and establishing the connection to nineteenth-century

---

[35] Fox's tract went through approximately 25 print runs between 1791 and 1800 and was distributed throughout the major cities of Great Britain and Ireland. One edition printed in Scotland claimed on the title page "Such has been the extraordinary demand for this pamphlet, that 70,000 copies have been printed off in the course of four months; and, by late accounts from England, with such success, that already upwards of 25,000 people there, have given up the use of rum and sugar" (Dundee: Printed and Sold by G. Milln and E. Leslie, 1792).

[36] Deirdre Coleman notes a more insidious aspect to the inclusion of "female sensibility" in the abolitionist campaigns. Her article examines the negative associations of women and slavery, particularly in the context of lower-class female liaisons with black men and the reports of cruelty perpetrated by Creole women in the West Indies. See "Conspicuous Consumption: White Abolitionism and English Women's Protest Writing in the 1790s," *ELH* 61:2 (1994): 341–362.

feminist organizations. The relationship between (white) women's empowerment and the later abolitionist movement has been well documented. Both critics credit the second abolitionist campaign with having a significant impact on women's roles in Great Britain. In terms of fostering a desire for female independence, the focus on the antislavery movement makes perfect sense. These analyses are accurate and insightful in their observations about the contribution of women to abolition and the shaping of feminism by abolition. However, they oversimplify the involvement and contribution of women in the first abolitionist campaign. What had emerged as a debate solely among men began actively to seek out the support and contributions of women—as consumers, as writers, as *Britons*.

The systematic targeting of women in the organization of boycotts greatly expanded the sense of national character and allowed women writers more involvement with the abolitionist campaign.[37] Most publications contained an implicit gender reference when discussing the attributes of the "humane Briton." The Wedgwood medallion provides the clearest example of abolitionist tendencies to code slavery and abolition as masculine enterprises. However, the introduction of strategies to boycott West Indian goods served to expand the perception of a male-dominated movement. The qualities of national character that made slavery such an anathema, namely "compassion," became associated with "female sensibility" when advocating the rejection of such products. This association allowed even more women to participate in the movement and publish their own beliefs about abolition. Hannah More, Mary Birkett, and others promoted boycotts in strong prose and poetry. In fact, on the title page of Birkett's *A Poem on the African Slave Trade*, she stated that the work was "addressed to her own sex." However, the poem contained powerful arguments clearly aimed at men, a fact that seems to indicate women were able successfully to integrate their voices into the male-dominated abolitionist campaigns.[38] The link between abolitionist boycotts and the proliferation of women's voices was very evident in Mary Wollstonecraft's *A Vindication of the Rights of Woman* (1792). She questioned, "Is sugar always to be produced by vital blood? Is one half of the human species, like the poor African slaves, to be subject to prejudices that brutalize them, when principles would be a surer guard, only to sweeten the cup of men?"[39] National character

---

[37] In *Women Against Slavery*, Midgley recounts that women did receive recognition for their participation in boycotts; however, the recognition was not always positive. Proslavery rebuttals to the boycotts cast women as gullible victims of scheming men, both discrediting their power as consumers and their role in the organized abolitionist movement (39–40).

[38] Moira Ferguson argues in *Subject to Others* that the boycotts allowed British women a voice in the public debates that allowed many women to publish their sentiments regarding slavery.

[39] Mary Wollstonecraft, *A Vindication of the Rights of Woman*, ed. Miriam Brody (London: Penguin Classics, 1992) 144–145. See Ferguson's *Subject to Others* for a more comprehensive discussion of Wollstonecraft's connections to the abolitionist movement and

began to incorporate an element of "femaleness," and the gendered notion of female compassion opened up a certain space, albeit subordinate, for women in the concept of the Briton.[40]

The abolitionist campaign of the 1790s allowed for multiple expansions and transformations in argument that appealed to wider audiences across Great Britain. Abolitionist sentiments proliferated into all types of publications, including cartoons and illustrations that were printed in popular magazines and books. Writers and illustrators strategically used pathetic appeals to create their image of the "true Briton." Proslavery writers had an increasingly difficult task in trying to negate the charges of abolitionists while defending an institution on which they depended. The opposition to the anti-slave-trade campaign sought to discredit abolitionist depictions of the middle passage and enslavement in the colonies. They built upon the ethical appeals, which had been used in the 1780s, to criticize both abolitionist descriptions and abolitionist goals. The naive and "irresponsible" anti-slave-trade writer sought to undermine the prosperity of the nation with a clearly unattainable objective. Proslavery writers were forced to expand their arguments in order to combat the growing popularity of the abolitionist rhetoric.

Recasting Humanity in the Planter/Merchant Image, 1788–1793

Abolitionist zeal necessitated changes in proslavery rhetoric as the debates intensified, and writers scrambled to respond to the growing support from the public for the anti-slave-trade agenda. Perhaps the most important challenge for writers was the need to regain control over representations of slavery. The organized efforts of the abolitionists in the 1790s succeeded in transforming public apathy into public agitation and destabilizing acceptance of the West Indian way of life. Abolitionist depictions made life in the West Indies and on board a slave ship transparent for many readers. The vivid recounting of atrocities committed against slaves by their masters, either on ship or on land, stimulated more than just prurient fascination in the public. Such descriptions allowed them to understand, albeit from a sensational and voyeuristic perspective, what life in these exotic locales entailed. These compelling depictions forced proslavery writers to intensify their campaign against negative portrayals and present the "true" picture of slavery.

Their publications responded to increasingly serious allegations by the anti-slave-trade camp regarding their trading practices. Indeed, by 1788 these

---

her subsequent publications. Deirdre Coleman in "Conspicuous Consumption" virtually dismisses Wollstonecraft's remarks as a veiled dig against Edmund Burke, a reading that underestimates both her commitment to social causes and her genuine empathy with slaves.

[40] This argument had more impact in the first abolitionist campaign because the second campaign incorporated more descriptions of the cruelty of Creole women, specifically toward female slaves.

allegations had succeeded in instituting an inquiry into the trade by the Privy Council. While this inquiry focused more on abuses committed in Africa during procurement and during the middle passage, the atrocities committed by slave masters also came under intense scrutiny.[41] After the Council heard evidence for and against the trade, William Wilberforce and Charles Fox sponsored a bill for immediate abolition in the House of Commons. They asked the House to find the African Slave Trade "contrary to the principles of justice, humanity, and sound policy." Since abolitionists received such strong support from within the legislature, regulationists had to increase the frequency and sophistication of their rebuttals. From 1788 to 1792, Great Britain experienced a boom in publications supporting slavery and the trade. Such publications were no longer directed primarily at upper-class readers, nor were they solely reactive documents that only rebutted antislavery arguments without posing their own questions. Often these writers defended their livelihood and the legitimacy of their way of life. They had to weaken the high moral position adopted by anti-slave-trade activists in order to argue convincingly for reform over abolition. By instigating the full investigation of British practices in Africa and the West Indies, abolitionists demonstrated to proslavery writers that the status quo was changing (see Figure 5.2). Merchants and planters could no longer rely on the unconditional support of Parliament and Crown, especially since their opposition had the backing of powerful legislators like William Wilberforce, Charles Fox, and William Pitt, the Younger.

The number and diversity of publications arguing on behalf of the slave trade did not match abolitionist publications; however, proslavery writing did increase significantly. Organized societies for abolition did an excellent job of printing and distributing their tracts to audiences throughout the British Isles. With the aid of Quaker publishers like James Phillips, they covered London with their cheap or free tracts proclaiming the evils of the slave trade. In *A Letter to the Members of Parliament* (1792), the "West India Merchant" complained bitterly about the "Wilberforcean zealots" who had littered the country and duped the public with their cheap tracts. While slavery advocates did organize small-scale societies, they did not devote the same time or resources to their campaign. Proslavery responses were not as copious and did not cover the same broad geographical area as their opposition. The majority of their publications were printed by J. Debrett or John Stockdale; however, these printers do not appear to have used their own funds for publication. Many authors funded their own publications, so the print runs were also smaller than abolitionist tracts. The ratio of literature published was

---

[41] The evidence presented before the council and later the House of Commons was the first instance of metropolitan subjects hearing of the atrocities committed by Creole women in the West Indies. The abuse mostly centered on punishing female slaves who had been taken as mistresses by their masters. As sensational as these facts were, they never really entered the abolitionist discourse against the slave trade.

Fig. 5.2 Isaac Cruikshank, "The Abolition of the Slave Trade." London: S.W. Fores, 1792. Courtesy of the Library of Congress, LC–USZC4–6204.

approximately two anti-slave-trade publications for every one proslavery.[42] Most writers published letters in the newspapers for broader coverage, but the majority of independent proslavery tracts were published in England, London in particular. For whatever reason, be it financial, social, or political, proslavery writers did not publish to the same extent as abolitionist writers. However, regulationist publications did make an impact on the legislators responsible for the deciding the question of abolition. These writers managed to delay abolition for at least a decade and their comments about empire contributed to the emergence of an imperial identity in the nineteenth century.

The organized opposition pushed proslavery writers to change their standard, commerce-based defense of slavery and to include stronger rebuttals to abolitionist charges. Though their publications continued to react to accusations made in individual abolitionist tracts, these writers had to come up with a counter-proposal to abolition. By the 1790s, no one in Great Britain was unaware of the abuses of the slave trade. The highly publicized *Zong* incident in 1783 and the publication of slave ship schematics, illustrating the inhumane overcrowded conditions in 1788 (see Figure 5.1), definitely shocked the reading public into acknowledging that a problem existed. The finality and deceptive simplicity of the anti-slave-trade solution forced slavery supporters to be more imaginative and no longer merely reactive in their rebuttals. They acknowledged a need to expand their appeals to broader audiences because they could no longer be assured of unconditional support from the legislature.[43] The most significant concession proslavery writers made during the debates was to acknowledge that the institution of slavery was flawed. While many writers had criticized the Royal African Company's monopoly on the trade, they believed strongly in the necessity and efficacy of the institution for mercantilist ends. They grudgingly conceded that the anti-monopolist critique of the Company did not address the problems of overcrowding on the slave ships. However, proslavery writers argued that abolition was too drastic a solution to a problem that would be better rectified through a series of stricter regulations. As William Knox cautioned:

---

[42] Between 1788 and 1799, abolitionists published approximately 83 tracts that were a combination of sermons, letters, poems, and long non-fiction discourses. Regulationists published approximately 39 works that were primarily rebuttals to abolition and histories of the slave trade. During this time, a robust discussion also appeared in newspapers across the British Isles, though I have not made a systematic study of the number of publications.

[43] While writers continued to publish under pseudonyms like "West India Merchant" and "Sugar Planter," more authors used their names in publication. The best known proslavery writers of the time were Gilbert Francklyn, a prominent Jamaican planter; Robert Norris, whose romantic description of the middle passage raised an uproar amongst abolitionists; Bryan Edwards, whose history of the British settlements in the West Indies rivaled Long's work; and the Earl of Sheffield, whose extensive collection of tracts pertaining to the debates constitutes one of the finest records available to twenty-first-century scholars.

the nation is roused, and will not be quieted without a reform in our conduct towards [slaves]: but have a care that your zeal does not outrun discretion, for more mischief has been done to the best cause by the interference of zealots, than by the indolence of supine governors.[44]

Supporters of slavery had to temper their defense with the understanding that Parliamentary action was unavoidable; however, abolition was an extreme and unnecessary solution to the problem. An "Old Member of Parliament" remarked:

> I wish to see the Slave Trade put under humane and effectual regulations; but cannot agree to overturn, at once, a system of commerce which has been constantly increasing for a great number of years to the apparent improvement of our revenue and marine, without having first tried many methods of remedying the exceptionable parts and preserving the rest.[45]

They argued that Parliament, having sanctioned the trade, should make every effort to regulate rather than abolish.

As the public evidenced growing sympathy for the "oppressed" slave, proslavery writers had to focus more efforts on resuscitating their image as "humane" traders and planters. The abolitionists effectively challenged their "humanity" by recounting the "punishments" or "tortures" inflicted upon slaves during the middle passage and on the plantations. These writers cited grossly inequitable slave laws from Barbados, Jamaica, Antigua, and other islands as proof that African slaves were treated "worse than Beasts." Political satirists, who lampooned both sides in the slave-trade debates, depicted slave captains, overseers, and slave owners as boorish, cruel, and sadistic.[46] The rhetoric of text and visual conveyed the message that pure self-interest dictated the actions of merchant and planter. This self-interest compared unfavorably to the supposed "altruism" of abolition, an impression compounded by testimony given in Parliament. Abolitionist presses published several selectively edited versions of the testimony, ostensibly to "educate" the public about West Indian practices. Proslavery writers sought to intervene with alternative interpretations of the evidence presented in Parliament against the slave trade. The purpose of proslavery publication in the most active stage of the slave-trade debates was, first, to combat the negative and

---

[44] William Knox, *A Letter from W. K., Esq. To William Wilberforce, Esq.* (London: Printed for J. Debrett, 1790) 17.

[45] *Doubts on the Abolition of the Slave Trade, By an Old Member of Parliament* (London: Printed for John Stockdale, 1790) 116.

[46] Marcus Wood's *Blind Memory* discusses the rich tradition of political satire that focused on the cause célèbre of the 1790s—abolition of the slave trade. His study of political cartoons of the period reveals that both abolitionists and regulationists were lampooned. While the abolitionists were mocked for their excessive sentiments (the "anti-saccharites"), the depictions of slave traders and West Indian planters were consistently vicious (see Figure 5.2).

increasingly stereotypical images of the trader and planter in their practices; and second, to advocate on behalf of regulation of the slave trade instead of abolition.

The regulationist campaign operated under a series of particular constraints that forced its proponents to be more creative in their attacks against abolitionists. Writers continued to rely heavily on ethical appeals to challenge the validity of abolitionist depictions of slavery, but the character of the abolitionists could not be questioned in the same manner as traders and planters. The desire for universal freedom and liberty advocated by abolitionists made them difficult targets for demonization, whereas the traders and plantation owners could be stigmatized by lurid portraits of slave tortures. Supporters of the slave trade found themselves in a very awkward position, rhetorically speaking, in their ability to critique the opposition. Though some characterized the motives of abolitionists as stemming from "prejudice and malignity," these accusations did not compare to the more serious charges of "inhumanity" leveled against slave traders and planters.[47] Since most anti-slave-trade authors also professed a superior understanding of morality, both personally and on behalf of the nation, proslavery authors could hardly attack their views without derogating national character. To diminish the perception of British superiority in the enjoyment of liberty and freedom would have been counter-productive; instead they sought to temper this perception with a more "realistic" viewpoint. The "humanity" claimed by abolitionists was both fanatical and unbalanced without a care for the repercussions on private citizens. Regulationists pointed out the inequities supported by British society in terms of social class and the abuses tolerated within particular occupations. They also depicted an image of stability for the plantation slave that both countermanded abolitionist accusations of abuse and exceeded the benefits of "freedom" supposedly enjoyed by the British lower classes.

Regulationists needed to construct a vision of "humanity" that incorporated and supported the practice of slavery. Lord Sheffield called himself a "friend of humanity; but of humanity regulated by reason, justice, and a sincere desire to promote the public good."[48] By emphasizing "justice" and the "public good," writers could defend the West Indian way of life and the necessity for its continuance. Parliament, in encouraging the settlement of the West Indies, had formed a compact with those planters and merchants who had succeeded in carving out their livelihood in life-threatening circumstances. How could "justice" be served if these colonials were "robbed" of their property? Authors cautioned the "votaries of humanity" not to be

---

[47] Very few regulationist writers cited "self-interest" as the motive of abolitionists. However, Wood's *Blind Memory* discusses the work of Richard Newton, a political cartoonist who began publishing his cartoons at the age of 11. Newton's first printed etching, *The Slave Trade* (1788), critiqued abolition as a political ploy engineered by Pitt and Dundas to curry favor with the king. See chapter 4 of *Blind Memory* for a complete discussion.

[48] Lord Sheffield, *Observations on the Project for Abolishing the Slave Trade, and on the reasonableness of attempting some practicable mode of relieving the Negroes* (2nd ed. with additions, London: Printed by J. Cooper for J. Debrett, 1791) 72.

"violators of justice." They also emphasized the healthy contribution that slavery made to the British economy, by which everyone benefited. In his speech during the Parliamentary hearings, Sir William Young warned that "the genuine motives of Humanity require discrimination of circumstances, of objects, and of effects." In other words, "humanity" would not suffice as a good reason to privilege one group at the expense of another. The merchants who would be deprived of their livelihood warranted equal consideration and sympathy from their own people. In spite of these cautions, the abolitionist descriptions of cruelty and sadism had an alarming effect on the public's perception of those who traded and owned slaves. Clearly, the regulationist camp had to take more active measures in order to redeem its image in the eyes of the reading public.

Proslavery writers expanded their use of ethical appeals to attack not only the credibility of abolitionist accounts of slavery but also the ideology of "natural rights." Their publications continued to refute the depictions of West Indian cruelty as "*unjust and calumnious.*" Adair's *Unanswerable Arguments against the Abolition of the Slave Trade* (1790) described the plantation as "one great family" governed by a "PATRIARCHAL" structure that saw to the well-being of all the slaves. He further contended that:

> planters are much more kind and indulgent to them than the *British, Irish,* and *North American* proprietors and managers, (*Adair is a Briton*) who sometimes afford lamentable proofs of their departure from the principles of Liberty, and the dictates of Humanity. (129)[49]

Adair and other writers questioned the veracity of abolitionist accounts by asking why a master would abuse a worker for whose nursing he would then be responsible. In other words, torturing slaves was counter-productive and resulted in greater problems for the planter. The same arguments applied to the merchants who transported their "precious cargo" across the Atlantic. Surely maintaining the health and contentment of slaves during the crossing would be in the captain and crew's best interests. While the more idyllic accounts of the voyage were dismissed, advocates argued that the horrendous conditions described in anti-slave-trade publications were similarly exaggerated.

Proslavery writers also became more aggressive in their questioning of the intent behind the purported altruism of abolitionists. "A Country Gentleman," in his explanation of why he voted against abolition, questioned how effective abolishing the slave trade would be in bettering the lives of those currently enslaved in the West Indies.[50] He referred to the limited extent of the abolitionist sympathy as an

---

[49] What is more interesting about this quotation is the fact that Adair feels the need to assert parenthetically his national identity.

[50] *A Country Gentleman's Reasons for voting against Mr. Wilberforce's motion for a bill to prohibit the importation of African Negroes into the Colonies* (London: Printed for J. Debrett, 1791).

abandonment of those already enslaved. Another strong accusation compared the activities of abolitionists with the revolutionaries in France. Since the movement encompassed both radical and conservative supporters, slavery apologists could point to radical writing in support of the French Revolution as a harbinger of things to come in Great Britain. In a scathing letter to Wilberforce, "Philo-Africanus" mockingly congratulated him for his ability "to abstract [his] attention from the paltry revolutions of Europe." Another anonymous writer characterized Wilberforce and his supporters as the "JACOBINS OF ENGLAND."[51] Gilbert Francklyn asked the provocative question, "What would the people of England think of men, who, under the familiar pretext of zeal for the rights of humanity . . . endeavour . . . to stir up the soldier, the sailor, the artisan, and the peasant, to assert their rights to an equal portion of liberty with those who now lord it over them?"[52] The critique of abolitionists in the 1790s combined the fear of anarchy with suspicions of misguided idealism. While no one argued against the importance of "liberty," writers believed that the concept could not be applied equally to all nations or to all segments of British society.

The clearest example of this strategy appeared in print soon after Wilberforce introduced the motion to abolish the slave trade. Many writers found him to be a perfect target and directed their most scathing comments against his proposal. They characterized him as "prejudiced" and "biased" against a trade that had been endorsed by the British legislature since the seventeenth century. Some writers even accused Wilberforce of attempting to subvert the "natural" order of society. The author of *A Letter to William Wilberforce, Esq.* (1790) wrote sarcastically of the unrealistic vision of "liberty" that abolitionists espoused.[53] Taking the persona of the West India planter, he applied the arguments for liberty to a wholly British context—the army. His letter represents the most imaginative proslavery rebuttal:

> Suppose you should address to the English army a letter couched in these terms—
> My friends, I have been studying the principles of liberty, and find that you are

---

[51] *A very New Pamphlet indeed! Being the truth: addressed to the people at large containing some Strictures on the English Jacobins, and the Evidence of Lord McCartney, and others, Before the House of Lords, respecting the Slave Trade* (London, 1792).

[52] Gilbert Francklyn, *Observations, occasioned by the attempts made in England to effect the abolition of the Slave Trade; shewing the manner in which Negroes are treated in the British colonies in the West-Indies: and also, some particular remarks addressed to the Treasurer of the Society for effecting such abolition from the Reverend Robert Boucher Nicolls* (London: Sold by J. Waster, C. Stalker, and W. Richardson, 1789) xvii.

[53] *A Letter to William Wilberforce, Esq. By Philo-Africanus* (London: Printed for J. Debrett, 1790). Two copies of the tract are found in the Sheffield collection, and one copy has a handwritten attribution to George Ellis. The pseudonym is somewhat tongue-in-cheek because the author contends that Wilberforce and his colleagues are helping those who do not wish to be helped. Thus, in arguing against abolition, he is a greater friend to the African.

all slaves. You are subject to laws which are not recognized by your fellow citizens; you are liable to be beaten for getting drunk, which is a pleasant action, and not naturally criminal; or for neglecting to hold up your heads, or to walk in a particular direction; neither of which things are naturally virtuous. If you think fit to change your profession, you will be whipped, or, perhaps, shot, although every man has a natural right to quit one profession for another. I think your pay very insufficient, and am convinced that you must be extremely miserable, because you will naturally make the same reflection as I have done. Perhaps some deceit has been employed in order to trepan you into the service; but even if you have voluntarily enlisted, the compact is void, because no man has a right to part with his liberty. Such a letter, Sir, would probably be considered as a proof of indiscretions rather than of humanity ... (19–20).

Philo-Africanus brilliantly demonstrated how the patriotic appeals to superior English liberty completely collapsed when applied to a different context. The critique derided abolitionist cries for "humanity" and pointed out that similar charges could be made at home. In fact, he went on to say that plantation slaves enjoyed more "liberty" than members of the army or the navy, and the punishments they received for bad behavior were no more severe than those meted out in British service. Not only were Wilberforce's petitions for liberty misplaced, they also ignored the very real problems in Great Britain. The comparison was intended to cast doubt on abolition and make a case for regulation as the best solution to fixing systemic problems.

The new regulationist strategy in the 1790s redirected, or at least attempted to redirect, the public's attention away from the sorrows of slavery to the suffering of the British poor. As compelling as the images of slavery proved to be to British readers, the conditions of poverty within the country also deserved attention. Regulationists began to question more rigorously the "misplaced sympathies" of abolitionists and their genuine commitment to bettering the lives of *all* Britons. I do not contend that proslavery writers sought to reform the class structure of British society. Their purpose was not to improve the lives of the lower classes in the mother country but to highlight the unrealistic arguments advanced by those who claimed to speak for "humanity." Clearly, one motive for this increased sensitivity to the plight of the underclasses was to discredit abolitionist appeals. Regulationists maintained that, instead of arguing for "foreigners," these "humanitarians" should focus on the downtrodden within Great Britain. Adair noted that "the British day-labourer labours much more than any town slaves, without being so well fed; that the latter, when confined to a sick bed, experience more attention, care, and comfort that the parish poor in England" (178). These contentions served a dual purpose of questioning abolitionist motives and underscoring the favorable living conditions on the plantation. A second motive for redirecting attention to the "poor *Whites*" introduced racial distinctions in the construction of the nation. Whites were the true "sons of Briton" and the efforts of Parliament were better spent protecting legitimate citizens who did not have the benefits of plantation culture. Many authors compared the life of the "starving peasant" very unfavorably to the "contented negro laborer" who could rely on his master to provide him with food, clothing, and shelter.

The sympathetic representations of slavery corresponded with an increasingly virulent delineation of race in regulationist discourse. While biblical justifications of slavery waned after the publication of Harris's *Scriptural Researches* (1788), belief that Africans were "naturally suited for these labours" persisted. Proslavery writers became more aggressive in their defense of slavery by underscoring the racial inferiority of Africans and portraying the middle passage and plantation life in idyllic terms. Writers insisted that life in the West Indies was vastly preferable to the "heathen" conditions of African societies. Africans were less than men, "*little more* than incarnate devils," according to one particularly harsh description.[54] The logical appeals of the racial defense, as I would call it, followed a hypothetical syllogism predicated on the belief that Africans were more animal than human in nature. God invested the care of animals to humans; Africans were more like animals in their behavior; therefore, Europeans had a responsibility for their care. Since African societies and people were by nature less advanced than Europeans then the enslavement of Africans in the West Indies and elsewhere conformed to the responsibilities of stewardship. Abolitionists established that African society needed to be civilized to the level of Europeans, so regulationists countered, "if we can devise no means of mending their condition in their own country, we are bound as men and Christians to assist them in removing out of it into one where their present and future happiness will be better provided for."[55] The hard work and care provided by planters in the West Indies would control the baser impulses of the African while uplifting his or her soul.

Slavery apologists expanded their arguments regarding the beneficial effects of enslavement on the character of Africans to include a more thorough justification for the slave trade. Most writers repeated the standard (or what had become standard by the 1790s) claims that Africans were "indolent" and "lazy" in their own country, that their culture lacked any discernible attributes of civilization, and that they were "inferior to Whites." As Jesse Foot concluded, "The fact is, that it is the libidinous practices of the negro which want reform."[56] The argument that Africans descended from Ham and were therefore meant to be slaves also continued to be used as a common justification. Another popular version of this contention stated that Africans were more used to slavery than "liberty" and could not appreciate the efforts being made on their behalf. The British would be highly conscious of the loss of liberty, "but an African cannot feel this strong abhorrence

---

[54] Alexander Geddes, *An Apology for Slavery; or, six cogent arguments against the immediate abolition of the slave-trade* (London: Printed for J. Johnson and R. Faulder, 1792).

[55] *A Letter from W.K.* 18.

[56] Jesse Foot, *A Defence of the Planters in the West-Indies; composed in four arguments on comparative humanity, on comparative slavery, on the African Slave Trade, and on the condition of the Negroes in the West-Indies* (London: Printed for J. Debrett, 1792) 101.

from a state which has always been present to his eyes and familiar to his mind."[57] The same writer also stated that slave laws in the West Indies were positively "benevolent" when compared against the laws in Africa. Regulationist strategy focused on depicting Africa as a thoroughly degraded continent whose cruelty to her own people established a necessity for the slave trade. Life in the West Indies, by contrast, was much more civilized and Africans could be trained to transcend their base natures. One writer even claimed, "It is a very common thing indeed, for a Negro who might be free in England, to prefer returning to slavery in the West Indies."[58] Establishing the better conditions for slaves in the West Indies over Africa had a deeper purpose for regulationist writers. They used these representations to re-establish planter and merchant "humanity" and counter the potent accusations of abolitionists.

Once regulationist writers established the humane qualities of planters and merchants, they attacked the "righteousness" of the anti-slave-trade argument. Characterizing the trade as wholly "corrupt" provided the justification for "decisive" action in the form of abolition. The torments and agonies of the "Negroes" during the crossing from Africa and the "seasoning" period in the West Indies "stained" British character with "the blood of innocents." However, proslavery writers rightfully questioned readers about the "innocents" in Great Britain who would be affected by the dismantling of the slave trade.

> Thousands of industrious Men in London, Birmingham, Sheffield, &c. &c. are employed, and give Bread to all the tender Dependencies of Wife and Children, sheltering the former from those painful Situations too often attendant on Want and Indolence, and training up the latter to the Principles of laborious Industry ... (2–3)[59]

These writers sought to educate their audiences on the greater implications of abolition for all sectors in British society. By stressing the loss of livelihood for ship-builders in the major cities, they illustrated how the slave trade was not just an issue for the residents of the West Indies. While other writers also pointed out that numerous families in the islands would be beggared if their labor source dried

---

[57] An Old Member of Parliament, *Doubts on the Abolition of the Slave Trade* 21.

[58] *A Very New Pamphlet indeed! Being the truth: addressed to the people at large containing some Strictures on the English Jacobins, and the Evidence of Lord McCartney, and others, Before the House of Lords, respecting the Slave Trade* (London, 1792) 15. Though this statement may seem absurd from the twenty-first-century perspective, there was a growing population of black poor in London who were starving. Granville Sharp's Sierra Leone project in 1788 was not terribly successful, so some blacks may have sold themselves back into slavery to avoid starvation in Great Britain.

[59] *Commercial Reasons for the Non-Abolition of the Slave Trade, in the West-India Islands, by a Planter, and Merchant of many Years Residence in the West-Indies* (London: Printed for W. Lane, 1789).

up, emphasizing the effect on metropolitan lives seemed to be a more sophisticated strategy.[60] Writers could underscore the contention that *all* subjects of Great Britain would be affected by this "rash and puerile" proposal, not just as consumers but as workers too.

This critique of abolition prompted proslavery writers to propose regulating the trade as the more "humane" solution. The number of dependents warranted that all efforts should be expended to find a more satisfactory solution to the difficulties of procuring and selling slaves. While commerce had always been integral to the justifications for slavery, the abolitionist emphasis on the lack of humanity in the trader pushed writers to reframe the traditional argument. Anti-slave-trade activists contended that the middle passage was deadly both for Africans and for the sailors. Clarkson, after extensive research, published an alarming account of the number of slaves and sailors who died in the dangerous and squalid conditions upon the slave ship.[61] Rather than a "nursery for British seaman," the middle passage proved to be a veritable "graveyard" for the British sailor. Aside from claiming that the numbers were exaggerated, most proslavery writers did not quibble too much about the actual numbers. Instead, they made a case for regulation as the more equitable and reasonable alternative to the "flaws" of the trade. They countered negative depictions of the atrocities committed on slave ships with outright denials and "true" accounts of the middle passage that portrayed the voyage in idyllic terms. Rather than focus attention on actual practices during the middle passage, most writers turned the critique back on the anti-slave-trade activists. They criticized abolition as a "vain and empty" as well as "impracticable" solution, particularly given the boost to the competition that would surely occur if the slave trade were dismantled.

Perhaps the strongest accusation regulationist writers directed at the movement centered on the disastrous implications of abolition for commerce and the "British empire." Once again, proslavery writers demonstrated a greater sense of the interconnectedness of world trade when stressing the importance of slave trading to British commerce. They defined the strength of the empire by the control of commerce—commerce that was wholly dependent upon the sea. Thomas Irving, the Inspector General of Imports and Exports for Great Britain, was called to testify before Parliament on the question of the slave trade. In his statement he warned, "The British empire is a vast body composed of a multitude of fragments, of which our marine is the general cement. Destroy this cement, the empire is destroyed;

---

[60] Abolitionists succeeded in neatly defusing this strategy by enlisting the aid of shipbuilders in major cities like Liverpool and Manchester to speak against the slave trade. They circulated petitions in the area that many builders signed, proving the effectiveness of abolitionist rhetoric, which convinced these men to go against their self-interest. As Midgley has shown in *Women Against Slavery*, women played an important part in canvassing metropolitan areas and soliciting signatures for these petitions.

[61] See Thomas Clarkson, *An Essay on the Impolicy of the African Slave Trade in Two Parts* (London: J. Phillips, 1788).

and its last citadel, namely, this island itself, is no longer safe."[62] Other writers shared his opinion and urged Parliament not to make any laws that would foster "the greatest *political* evil" or "a decay of national strength." The emphasis on martial prowess also heightened awareness of West Indian fears of slave rebellions on the islands. The explosion on St. Domingue played directly into hysterical fears of revolution and "A West India Merchant" speculated, "[s]ome convulsion in Jamaica, similar to that in Saint Domingo, may decide the fate of the West India islands, and ultimately perhaps involve that of the British Empire"[63]

The most ludicrous claim rebutted by the regulationists was the idea that other European countries would leave off their trade once Great Britain dismantled her own. This "wild, ephemeral theory" was a clear indication of abolitionist "Fanaticism," and "False Philosophy," which had effectively "obscured their reason." By ending the trade in slaves with Africa, Great Britain would only destabilize her own hard-won monopoly and help her competitors. Regulationists defined the attributes of "national character" through martial strength involving control and power over trade. The abolitionist cause, with its threat to both trading monopoly and status in the European world, represented a serious danger to more than the West Indian way of life. Slavery, as a mainstay of the British empire, could not be easily dismissed when the effects on the "legitimate" citizens would be disastrous. At the height of the slave-trade debates, both sides argued not just the question of abolition, but the state of the British empire.

Abolishing the Slave Trade and Building an Empire, 1795–1807

Over the course of the 1790s and the first decade of the 1800s, the bill for abolition underwent many changes and additions. The House of Commons did not support the bill for immediate abolition in 1792. Henry Dundas succeeded in inserting the term "gradual" as a qualifier of abolition and the bill passed by a small majority. This version stated that the slave trade would be abolished completely by 1 January 1796, and the House of Commons forwarded this resolution to the House of Lords where it languished for several years. The delaying tactics also appeared to have an effect on the enthusiasm of anti-slave-trade activists. When the bill for "gradual abolition" passed in 1792, activists considered the decision a defeat. Thomas Gisborne characterized the watered-down version of the bill as "humiliating to the character of the British Nation."[64] Proslavery forces had gained a major victory

---

[62] *Remarks upon the evidence given by Thomas Irving, Esq., Inspector General of the Exports and Imports of Great Britain, before the Select Committee appointed to take the examination of witnesses on the slave-trade* (London, Printed in the year 1791) 11.

[63] *A Letter to the Members of Parliament who have presented petitions to the honourable House of Commons for the Abolition of the Slave Trade* (London, 1792) 40.

[64] Thomas Gisborne, *Remarks on the Late Decision of The House of Commons respecting the abolition of the slave trade* (London: Printed for B. White and Sons, 1792).

because delaying abolition would only allow "the spirit of humanity and justice, now at work in Great Britain, to evaporate" (30). Fortunately, this prediction did not prove to be correct. While "gradual abolition" was a failure that preceded a lull in the debates, Wilberforce continued to renew his appeals to the House and eventually gained the necessary majority to pass a bill for immediate abolition. On 25 March 1807, the bill to abolish the slave trade was passed by Parliament and the slave-trade debates came to an end—at least on paper and in the public imaginary.[65] Clearly, the rhetoric of both camps made a lasting impression on the British public.

The rate of publication fluctuated for both camps over the final years of the debate. Though abolitionists perceived the 1792 resolution to be a defeat, they held the conviction that the battle was not over. The uprising in St. Domingue and the turmoil in France seemed to work on behalf of the regulationists; however, those events only postponed what had become inevitable by the turn of the century. From 1793 to 1797, abolitionists continued to publish, but only at half the rate of their heyday from 1788 to 1792. Women writers produced poems and short stories, and presses reprinted significant tracts, such as those written by Clarkson, Ramsay, and Newton. Regulationists confined their arguments primarily to newspapers and magazines. Between 1798 and 1804, a lull occurred in publication and the country was consumed by other matters. Still, the bill for abolition continued to be proposed in the House of Commons. At this time, regulationists published new tracts asserting the "inhumanity" of abolishing a legitimate enterprise without appropriate compensation for the owners.[66] These tracts seemed to be a last minute effort to reclaim even a small measure of the support they had once enjoyed, but the balance of power had definitively shifted to favor abolitionist goals. The slave-trade debates came to an end shortly thereafter, and abolitionist sentiments petered off for almost twenty years before the formation of the second "abolitionist" society.

British involvement with the slave trade came to be inextricably associated with the demands of empire. Both abolitionists and regulationists interpreted the impact of abolition in terms of its effects on the greater British public. While they framed their interpretations in very different ways, the ideology that they shaped involved characterizing a "Nation" and defining the "Briton." By the end of the eighteenth century, both sides could agree on certain basic tenets shaping their worldview and the place within it occupied by "Britannia." Writers from both camps exhibited great pride in the nation and had a strong sense of the British holding a singular position within the world. So unified were both camps in this sentiment that it became difficult to identify which position was being argued. "Britain, excelling

---

[65] The first campaign seemed to introduce the possibility of emancipation for existing slaves, and after the bill passed, Earl Percy immediately proposed a motion for gradual emancipation, which was quickly defeated.

[66] Though no compensation was given for abolishing the slave trade, planters did receive some remuneration for their slaves with the success of the second antislavery campaign.

in the highest qualities of the head and of the heart, has made signal progress in every pursuit which required united vigour of genius, skill, application, enterprise, courage, and magnanimity."[67] Interestingly, this author supported a proslavery position. Abolitionists and regulationists shared an understanding of Britain's "empire," though the primary function of that "empire" differed. From these similar foundations, the writers from each side of the debate evinced a different future for the British nation and different attributes of the character of her subjects.

Analysis of abolitionist and regulationist rhetoric has typically organized the arguments into neatly dichotomous points. The paucity of criticism on the proslavery campaign stems perhaps from the idea that their tracts were purely reactive. These writers are hardly credited with making sophisticated arguments that incorporated antislavery strategies by transforming their terms. For example, scholars have paid little attention to the concerted efforts to propose "regulation" as the natural opposition to "abolition." Abolitionist rhetoric has been similarly viewed as a conglomeration of Enlightenment philosophies emerging at this time. Historians such as Davis and Walvin have done excellent work tracing the genealogy of abolitionist sentiment through the philosophies of "natural rights" and humanitarianism. However, no scholars have looked to proslavery rhetoric as influencing the nature of the abolitionist argument. Just as proslavery has been viewed as purely reactive, antislavery has been viewed as purely proactive. After all, proslavery sought to maintain the status quo while antislavery sought to overturn it. However, the decade-by-decade mapping of changes in each group's arguments demonstrates that much cross-talk occurred. This cross-talk generated a more sophisticated sense of national identity and character than many researchers have heretofore understood.

Scholars of nation-building and empire do credit abolition as one defining moment in the formation of the British nation. Colley states in *Britons*, "Successful abolitionism became one of the vital underpinnings of British supremacy in the Victorian era, offering—as it seemed to do—irrefutable proof that British power was founded on religion, on freedom and on moral caliber, not just on a superior stock of armaments and capital" (359). However, the cohesive sense of "British power" that Colley acknowledges underwent substantial transformations just over the course of the anti-slave trade campaign. Her neat summary elides the negotiation and the input from multiple sources that the slave-trade debates alone contributed to nation formation. Even David Brion Davis's compendious studies[68] do not address the mutual influence of abolitionists and regulationists on each group's rhetoric and on the reading public. The foremost characteristic of the slave-trade debates was their very public nature. Every speech in Parliament,

---

[67] Dr. Bissett, *Essays on the Slave Trade* (London: W. McDowall, 1805). This short tract had no title page and was preserved in Lord Sheffield's collection with a handwritten attribution and publication date. The authors were arguing from a proslavery perspective.

[68] Specifically, *The Problem of Slavery in Western Culture* and *The Problem of slavery in the Age of Revolution*.

complex analyses of the minutes, and detailed statistics presented for and against the trade were made available to British subjects throughout the country. The active participation of writers and petitioners and the detailed accounts in major newspapers made the issue "of great national importance." While each camp had contrasting visions for the nation, tracing the changes in their arguments reveals the complexity and interconnectedness of perceptions of national character and culture.

The challenge to status quo prompted proslavery writers to defend their function within the British empire and clearly define their understanding of national identity. Prior to the 1770s, colonists felt secure in their livelihood and their necessity to British commerce. The systematic challenge of antislavery writers seriously troubled the complacency with which American and West Indian planters and merchants viewed their way of life. Their defense of procuring and utilizing slave labor transformed over the course of three decades in response to an increasingly sophisticated opposition. Proslavery interests had serious concerns about the end of the slave trade, which they perceived to be imperiled at least a decade before the first abolitionist society formed. The strong foundation in commerce that they had taken for granted now seemed to be open for critique. Indeed, the systematic criticism of mercantilism, independent of the slave-trade debates, contributed to making the plantation system obsolete. When abolitionists dismissed the products of the colonies as "luxury items," colonial writers responded with alacrity. Their perception of Great Britain encompassed and relied upon the commercial importance of the West Indies and trade with Africa. Some writers cautioned that dismantling the slave trade would damage all trade with African societies and other commodities like gold and ivory would become more difficult to procure. Regulationist writers *had* to make a case for a British national identity that was defined through the greater sense of empire.

Proslavery rebuttals concentrated on qualifying many of the claims that antislavery and abolitionist writers asserted. The initial fervor for "liberty" inspired the definition of "primitive" African societies that could not appreciate European constructs. They countered the contention that slavery had no precedent in English law with the value of "property rights." Those "property rights" extended to significant distinctions within the concept of British subjecthood. Colonials argued both for their own legitimate place as subjects of the British crown and the ridiculousness of viewing slaves as subjects. When antislavery activists called out for "freedom" and an end to "oppression," proslavery writers pointed out the "oppression" experienced by poor Britons. They highlighted the hypocrisy of organizations that lobbied on behalf of foreigners when their own people needed aid. In arguing for the "natural rights" of slaves, abolitionists trampled upon the rights of merchants and planters to conduct legitimate business endorsed by the British Parliament. After all, "one moral virtue is not to be trampled upon that another may be exalted; and that those who pretend to be the votaries of humanity must not be the violators of justice"[69] Finally, the "humanity" claimed by abolitionists could not be realistically sustained by the British government—altruism could not feed the belly. By amending the terms and accusations put forth in antislavery rhetoric, these writers demonstrated a more sophisticated understanding of the world.

Proslavery rhetoric developed arguments based on race and commerce as methods of justifying imperial expansion. The slave-trade debates occurred during a time of colonial expansion with new islands being acquired in the West Indies and the East India Company expanding its holdings in the east. Proslavery writers had good reason to rely on the primacy of trade and commerce in protecting their interests overseas. However, the formation of abolitionist societies challenged these groups to come up with more convincing reasons why certain kinds of "ownership" should be tolerated.[70] Thus, writers began to phrase their arguments in terms of "national prosperity" and "public good," a process which involved defining the "nation" and the "public." The very nature of New World slavery ingrained an imperial ideology within colonials that long predated the Victorian era. Colonial society formed on the belief in Great Britain's "right" to expand her rule over particular areas of the globe. The threat of abolition destabilized the foundations of this empire "for, our colonies, our commerce, our revenues, and our very existence as an independent nation, are involved in the consequences of this measure" (Mercator 19). The proslavery position established a "natural" hierarchy among nations and among humans (or the sub-species of humans) for "Inequality" was the "grand law of Nature." The "national character" that emerged from proslavery writing was "white," "marine," "martial," and dominant.

The development of the abolitionist position involved expanding and broadening the concept of the Briton to include other segments of the population. Though initial activists did not set out with this goal in mind, the opening of movement that gave a voice to disenfranchised groups resulted in a broadening of scope. The diversity of authors who wrote on behalf of abolition strengthened the primary appeal on which the campaign came to rely. The anti-slave-trade position defined "national character" based on a concept of "humanity" that on the surface appeared to transcend divisions of class, race, and gender. The "cause of Humanity" that had been "trampled upon and outraged" by the abuses of the slave trade indicted the West Indian merchant and planter. "One would almost think that the vilest reprobate in England, who has not been hardened by custom, or blinded by interest, on hearing of their cruelties, would sink into the dust with shame and mortification, when he considers himself a being of the same species with a West-

---

[69] Mercator, *Letters Concerning the Abolition of the Slave-Trade and other West-India Affairs* (London: Printed by C. & W. Galabin, 1807) 4.

[70] I put ownership in quotation marks because some regulationists questioned the often unlimited power granted to managers and factory owners within Great Britain. They were compared unfavorably to the plantation owner who had more interest in preserving the well-being of his slave.

India slave-dealer!"[71] Writers drew a definitive line of demarcation between those who acknowledged the horrors of slavery and those who were complicit in those horrors. This tactic was so successful that most regulationist writers commented bitterly on the systematic defamation of West Indian Britons. However, with the focus of critique falling on a discrete body of men (women were mentioned rarely and then only as tools of the dissipated slave master), activists could construct their notion of "humanity" in opposition to the "inhumanity" of slavers. Thus, while the slave trade was a "national sin," the majority of the British population could be redeemed.

The strategies used by abolitionists changed significantly through the process of responding to and countering charges made by proslavery writers. While humanity and morality were noble causes, they needed more substance to persuade an entire population to go against their "self-interest." In an epigraph from *Cobbett's Weekly Register*, which printed mainly slavery defenses, one writer dramatically quoted, "I say, Perish all (this) commerce, just as I would say, Take from me your infamy and your gold, and give me back my honour and my rags."[72] However, the sentiment that characterized "commerce" connected to the enslavement of Africans as wicked and unworthy of Great Britain's continued support grew out of opposition to the proslavery position. Thoughts of humanity alone did not push the rhetoric from concern with a distinct goal to the development of an imperial ideology. Initially, antislavery activists focused only on the mother country in terms of attacking slavery. These writers seemed to lack the sense of a greater British empire and distanced themselves from the colonies. Early antislavery rhetoric configured the "nation" as confined to the British Isles. Shifts in the debate forced these writers to develop a different understanding of the nation, one which coincided more clearly with the proslavery vision of "nation" as "empire." Writers had to counter, either explicitly or implicitly, the strong critiques about the collapse of trade as a result of abolition. The proslavery focus on commerce and the interconnectedness of world trade could not be dismissed by antislavery writers.

When abolitionists organized to begin the campaign against the slave trade, they had to broaden their perspective. Proslavery writers argued convincingly that West Indian commerce provided many useful and valued products to the mother country. Dismantling the slave trade would cripple the West Indies and permanently damage British prosperity. Abolitionists engaged this line of argument in a manner that demonstrated their growing awareness of empire. Immediate evidence of this awareness emerged in the newfound concern with Africa and African society in the writing of anti-slave-trade activists. They accused slave merchants of inciting wars in order to gain more slaves for trade and challenged

---

[71] Samuel Bradburn, *An Address to the People called Methodists; concerning the evil of encouraging the Slave Trade* (Manchester: Printed by J. Harper, 1792) 3.

[72] Thomas Clarke, A.M, *A Letter to Mr. Cobbett on His Opinions Respecting the Slave-Trade* (London: Printed for J. Hatchard, 1806). Quotation taken from *Cobbett's Weekly Register*, vol. viii, 182.

the idea that most slaves were criminals who faced harsher sentences in their native land than laboring in the colonies. They indicted the agents of the Royal African Company for their "uncivilized" conduct in their dealings with the natives. While abolitionists continued to vilify colonial planters, they also acknowledged that the colonies were an extension of the mother country. Rather than dividing colonial behavior from metropolitan morality, activists sought to extend the "civilization" that characterized Great Britain to her colonies. In a sense, they attempted to re-colonize the colonies.

Another tactic abolitionist writers developed in response to proslavery rebuttals gave Africans a "voice" in British culture. Granted, this "voice" was largely mediated through the work of white writers, but these depictions opened a new space in the conception of British identity. Depicting slaves in poetry and fiction fostered an interest in the reading public to hear the "real" stories of these "oppressed" peoples. Black writers, like Wheatley, Sancho, and Equiano, could "represent" their own experiences with Christianity, with British society, and with slavery. The number of white female writers increased in their attempts to "represent" the "sorrows of slavery." Abolitionist writers also made African women visible in new and startling ways. While I do not contend that the depictions of these women were anything other than voyeuristic, they did begin to challenge the trope of the oversexed African woman. The representation of African female lasciviousness had a long history and was often used as an excuse to disguise white male sexual transgressions. Anti-slave-trade writers challenged these beliefs by recasting the female slave as sexual prey for the depraved traders and planters. Another dimension added to the image of African femininity was the depiction of motherhood. Mary Robinson's "The Negro Girl" (1800) spoke of being "[t]orn from [her] Mother's aching breast" and sold into slavery. Hannah More and Eaglesfield Smith's *The Sorrows of Yamba; or, The Negro Woman's Lamentation* (1795) depicted a woman "[w]ith a baby at my breast" who was kidnapped from her village and sold into slavery. Poets and other fiction writers used these "pathetic" descriptions of wronged African womanhood as a means of conveying the "inhumanity" of slavery. The women served as tools for abolitionist ends, but the descriptions did create new images of the loving African wife and mother who was capable of the same degree of sentiment as her British counterpart. By establishing the humanity of both sexes, abolitionists were able to reframe the purpose of British colonial enterprise and commercial ventures.

The case for abolition incorporated an imperial ideology through both religious and secular arguments. Emphasis on "Christian" doctrine in relieving the plight of the slaves opened a discourse of missionary imperatives. Not only were Britons setting a poor example for African societies, they were denying "brethren" of Christ's mercy. Those unfortunates who had already been enslaved could at least reap some benefit through conversion. "Now I'll bless my capture, / (Hence I've known a Savior's name) / Till my grief is turn'd to rapture, / And I half forget the blame."[73] The desire to spread "true" Christianity throughout Africa and the West Indies became one purpose for the British empire. Another purpose was to set an example for the world—an example of "civilization" for Africans and an example of "humanity" for Europeans. Abolitionists insisted that once Great Britain had dismantled her trade, other European nations would soon follow. Regulationist writers characterized this argument as a "wild, ephemeral theory." However, by 1800 many anti-slave-trade activists began to assert more strongly that not only was abolition in Great Britain an inevitability, but European abolition could be as well. The selfish fears of West Indian writers should not serve as a deterrent to "moral good." In his essay "On the Slave Trade" (1796), Coleridge commented ironically, "As Society is constituted, there will be always highway robberies: it is useless therefore to prevent any *one* man from committing them. Fortunately for Travellers this logic will not hold good in law."[74] He urged "Somebody must *begin*." This belief in setting an example for the world shifted the perceived focus of the empire from self-interest to a nationally motivated mission, in both a religious and secular sense.

The issue of abolition also allowed writers to express their opinions on more substantial topics than slavery. Great Britain in the 1790s was at a crossroads of understanding itself as a cohesive nation and its place in the world. The slave-trade debates developed in scope from local disturbances to world-wide implications over the course of only four decades. This issue, admittedly one among many, produced significant and dynamic arguments that defined the nature and character of the Briton. The process involved a constant negotiation of both external and internal influences on the primary sites of contest and the gradual emergence of a unified position. Neither proslavery nor antislavery began as an organized effort with a clearly delineated purpose. Writers often responded to divisions within their own camps as well as the opposition. The development of identity followed neither a linear progression nor a clear-cut distinction between regulationist and abolitionist constructions. Ultimately, no one portrait of national identity triumphed in the public imagination. The abolitionist position was highly influenced by regulationist arguments and vice versa. The sense of empire that materialized from these debates came out of a complex negotiation of rhetorical terrain that valued the contributions of both camps in the slave-trade debates. British identity came into being through an unintentional amalgamation of the abolitionist and regulationist positions and the Briton who emerged was well-suited for imperial ends.

---

[73] Hannah More and Eaglesfield Smith, *The Sorrows of Yamba* (London, 1795).

[74] Samuel Taylor Coleridge, "On the Slave Trade," *The Watchman* no. IV, 25 March 1796. This essay was based on a lecture given in Bristol on 16 June 1795.

Epilogue
Towards an Imperial Briton

> "Thy chains are broken, Africa, be free!"
> Thus saith the island-empress of the sea;
> Thus saith Britannia.
>
> James Montgomery

The opening lines of James Montgomery's "The West Indies" (1809) illustrate several interesting assumptions made in the aftermath of abolition about the newfound relationship between Africa and Great Britain.[1] Africa was somehow freed of the burden of enslavement and its denizens could rest peacefully knowing that Parliament held the "evil trader in man flesh" at bay. Great Britain had selflessly granted this freedom to the African nations. Most important, this "island-empress" possessed the power to dismantle the trade completely. After the bill to abolish the slave trade became law, the celebration that ensued involved a genuine outpouring of feeling—not towards the African, but towards the Briton. Thomas Clarkson intoned, "for while we rejoice to think that the sufferings of our fellow-creatures have been thus, in any instance, relieved, we must rejoice equally to think that our own moral condition must have been necessarily improved by the change."[2] Suddenly, the British Parliament, which had so actively resisted this reform only a decade earlier, became a potent symbol of liberty and compassion for humankind. Great Britain had redeemed itself and "the wrongs of Africa / Cry out no more to draw a curse from Heaven / On England!"[3] The nation and its character had been vindicated, and empire had a new, moral, "Christian" basis.

These assumptions had solidified even before the bill had officially passed both houses because the British public proved so responsive to the discourse of morality and humanity. By 1805, planters and merchants involved in the trade

---

[1] *Poems on the abolition of the slave trade; written by James Montgomery, James Grahame, and E. Benger. Embellished with Engravings from pictures painted by R. Smirke, Esq. R. A.* (London: Printed for R. Bowyer, 1809). Montgomery was commissioned to write his work to be included in a collection with engravings regarding the aftermath of abolition.

[2] Thomas Clarkson, *The History of the Rise, Progress and Accomplishment of the Abolition of the African Slave-Trade by the British Parliament*, Vol. 1 (London: Printed by R. Taylor and Co. For Longman, Hurst, Rees, and Orme, 1808) 1–2.

[3] Robert Southey, "Verses spoken in the theatre at Oxford, upon the installation of Lord Grenville" (1810). Lord Grenville was credited with moving the bill for abolition through the House of Lords.

viewed abolition with a sense of impending doom. The nature of their arguments shifted from defending the trade to claiming some kind of recompense from the government when the trade was abolished. After all, their livelihoods would be severely destabilized without the regular infusion of new "labor" to the colonies.[4] Another critical component of these last-ditch efforts was an acknowledgement of what I call the "new ethics of empire" that abolitionist rhetoric had propagated freely throughout the mother country. What Boswell had so scathingly referred to as "The Universal Empire of Love" proved to be a more compelling construction than the empire of "unlawful dominion."[5] The "British Legislature," to which Clarkson dedicated his *History*, had encouraged and supported these profitable trade ventures for two centuries. The concentrated work of activists transformed parliamentary opinion drastically in only forty years. However, the failure of the proslavery argument was not in the inadequate justification of the slave trade, but in the unsuccessful (re)framing of empire.

While scholars continue to debate the proper application of the term "empire," the activities of Great Britain in the eighteenth century definitely qualify as "empire-building." Traditional studies identify the mid-eighteenth century (that is, the 1730s, '40s, and '50s) as experiencing transformative moments in the formation of the "first" British empire.[6] The primary attribute of this empire was commerce, and, as David Armitage shows, the "imperial project existed to maximize trade and national power" (8). Kathleen Wilson describes the relationship of colony to mother country as "crucial to the 'empire of the seas' that contemporaries believed Britain had, or should have, dominion over" (157). She argues further that this conception of empire was "self-serving" by "mystifying or obscuring the brutal, exploitative and violent processes of 'trade' and colonizing" (157). Linda Colley incorporates the public awareness of empire as a contributing factor in the formation of British identity. I think both studies stop short of identifying another critical shift in the formation of identity and empire that resulted from the abolition of the slave trade. The rhetoric

---

[4] Holt in *The Problem of Freedom* documents a 9.4 percent drop in the slave population of Jamaica over 14 years following abolition. While British sugar continued to be highly in demand, the production also dropped by about 9 percent, causing the slave holders to make up the difference, as one special magistrate put it, "out of the very hearts' gore" of their slaves (118–119).

[5] James Boswell, *No Abolition of Slavery; or the Universal Empire of Love: A Poem* (London: Printed for R. Faulder, 1791). Boswell's lampoon of the abolitionist cause is an exposition of the idealism displayed by abolitionist writers who claimed that once Great Britain dismantled her trade then other European countries would "naturally" follow.

[6] David Armitage argues convincingly in *The Ideological Origins of Empire* that the first empire formed in the sixteenth century with a more limited conception of territory. The "internal colonisation" of Scotland, Wales, and Ireland characterized this first empire, whereas the "external imperialism" of commerce that impelled a more "exotic" colonization characterized the second empire.

of the debates represented a clear attempt to bring out and address precisely these "dirty secrets" of empire-building in Wilson's commentary. However, once those secrets are revealed, an ideological shift occurs that significantly influences the discourse of identity and the nature of the imperial project in the nineteenth century.

David Armitage identifies the bastions of the "pan-Atlantic British empire" as "Protestantism, oceanic commerce and mastery of the seas" (8). The successful resolution of the Seven Years' War and resulting colonial expansion underscored this ideology of empire. At the height of the slave trade in the late eighteenth century, Great Britain dominated the seas and commerce was the foundation of slavery and the colonies. The importance of the "New World" colonies to British commerce and trade was undisputed. However, Armitage argues that "[t]he ideological definition of the British state, ... was a shared conception of the British Empire [between the colonies and the metropole] that could describe a community and provide a distinguishable character for it" (9). In other words, the empire existed as an ideology before it became an identity. The slave-trade debates provided a powerful discourse that reframed the "pan-Atlantic empire," British identity, and imperial ideology. However, if the peripheries helped to shape the metropole's construction of identity, what reasoning allowed the peripheries to be so wholly disenfranchised? How did abolitionists convince people from all levels of British society purportedly to unravel its empire?

Citing transformations in culture, political climate, and public consciousness can only begin to address the significance of this act. The institution of slavery was an integral component of the Atlantic world and the definition of the British realm in the eighteenth century. The establishment of colonies abroad served the dual purpose of increasing the prosperity of the mother country and competing with other European colonizing nations. The slave trade functioned as an excellent tool of the British Empire and was popularly viewed as a necessity to colonial and metropolitan prosperity. However, Great Britain dismantled this profitable trade, albeit unevenly and in a fraught manner, seemingly for the benefit of principle. The question of abolitionist success has been addressed in multiple fashions, mostly by social and economic historians. The climate of reform, the changes in economic structure, and the turbulent revolutions in other parts of the world all provide plausible explanations. A more interesting implication of this success lies in the emerging imperial identity that would dictate the actions of Great Britain over the course of the nineteenth century. The discourse of imperial identity shaped by the slave-trade debates offered a different ideology for a benign, perhaps beneficent, form of colonization. Since the post-abolition Briton remained committed to expanding commerce and trade, he or she discovered a new purpose for these acts that was founded on morality and "Christianity" rather than bondage and despair. The "pan-Atlantic" concept of the British empire was in the process of transforming into a global empire that practiced a more "ethical" form of trade.[7]

In this context, the social movement of the later century pursued a new purpose in the first decade of the 1800s. The bill to abolish the slave trade passed through the House of Commons and the House of Lords with comparatively little notice. In fact, its passing in the House of Lords was marked by only a few lines in *The Gentleman's Magazine* of April, 1807. Records also indicate that the actual enforcement of the new law was slow, and trade continued for several more years. These circumstances aside, I contend that the early nineteenth-century conception of the imperial Briton owes an important ideological debt to the slave-trade debates. Extending Armitage's formulation, the "pan-Atlantic British empire" collapsed, at least partially, when confronted with the disjuncture between freedom and bondage, liberty and slavery. The conception of Great Britain as a maritime and commercial power was not sufficient to carry over into the new, imperial or "moral" empire of the early nineteenth century. Abolition provided one avenue of expanding the self-perception of (inter)national dominance without the burden of guilt.

Proof of this belief can be found in the publications following the success of this first campaign. Since the bill passed with such limited fanfare, writers continued to print poems, tracts, and histories that translated the implications of this law to the general reading public. Inherent in these "translations" was the foundation of nineteenth-century colonization. A growing discourse of inevitability structured the new writings and became the prevailing characteristic of the new law. Abolition succeeded not just through efforts of the extraordinary but because of the "true nature" of the Briton. As James Montgomery put it in his poem "The West Indies," "the brave, the free, / the matchless race of Albion and the sea" proved to be the "natural" leaders of change among European nations.[8] This message was particularly salient given Great Britain's war with Napoleon (1799–1815). British subjects were well-positioned to imbibe the post-abolitionist message of the "favored" nation whose superior sense of liberty prevailed against self-interest. The first and arguably most important publication advancing this theme

---

[7] The concept of "ethical" trade had also been reinforced in Britain's eastern empire through the trial of Warren Hastings. By holding this "nabob" accountable for his abuse of "natives," Edmund Burke and his supporters contributed to the fashioning of the "moral Briton."

[8] In 1792, the ruler of Denmark issued a royal ordinance that slave trading to Danish colonies would cease by 1803. However, since the Danish colonies only imported a small percentage of slaves as compared with the Spanish, Portuguese, French, Dutch, and British, this decree did not make much of an impact on the transatlantic trade. The United States prohibited its citizens from engaging in the trade with Africa in 1808, and the French abolished its trade in 1815. For a complete list see "A Calendar of Events" in Davis' *Problem of Slavery in the Age of Revolution*.

was Thomas Clarkson's *The History of the Rise, Progress and Accomplishment of the Abolition of the African Slave-Trade by the British Parliament* (1808).[9]

Clarkson's history established the teleological view of abolition as the "natural" result of British morality and Christianity. His study traced the development of abolitionist sentiment through the work of "Saints" and their influence on the British legislature. Clarkson's impressive "diagram" of the principal abolitionists creates a visual of disparate roots branching towards a common and uplifting goal. Almost all of the various "branches," on which Clarkson identifies men like Granville Sharp, Anthony Benezet, Adam Smith, William Wilberforce, and of course himself, point upward in a visual confirmation of the high moral ideals of abolition. His "mapping" of the movement establishes and in essence reclaims the efforts on behalf of a highly elitist group of activists. He does not appreciate or acknowledge the efforts of Afro-British writers, working-class petitioners, or any women (with the exception of Queen Elizabeth) in his history. The omission of Equiano's narrative and campaigning efforts is particularly egregious. These omissions (re)construct an image of the abolitionist as white and male.

Race becomes an integral component of British national identity as constructed by the dialogue between slavery advocates and abolitionists. The lack of discussion about "race" or "whiteness" represents a significant gap in Colley's thesis about the primary influences on the formation of national identity. Great Britain at the close of the eighteenth century was a self-consciously "white" nation. While understanding of whiteness would be continuously reworked, the slave-trade debates succeeded in introducing the concept throughout the empire. In his two volumes of prose, Clarkson neglects to mention the efforts of the Afro-British on behalf of abolition, yet his earlier works credit Africans with the intellectual capacity to understand their condition and speak against it. He clearly viewed the most serious efforts for abolition as the preserve of a select cadre of individuals who were "British" in origin, if not in homeland. Clarkson even goes so far as to relegate the Quakers to the second tier of "Saints" actively working for abolition. The gaps in his list reveal that "British" does not include Africans educated and "civilized" through their contact with Great Britain.[10] The construction of race,

---

[9] This two-volume study was first published in London, printed by R. Taylor and Co. for Longman, Hurst, Rees, and Orme, 1808. The same year James P. Parke published the work in Philadelphia. I have not been able to determine the print runs, although, judging from the impressive list of dedications (all of whom received a copy), the history seems to have been widely disseminated among prominent abolitionists and legislators. Other printings and locations include Wilmington, DE, in 1816, New York in 1836, and London in 1839.

[10] During the same period, the "British" in the eastern part of the empire develop the "Aryan theory" of language that transforms into a theory of race over the course of the nineteenth century. See Vasant Kaiwar's review essay, "Racism and the Writing of History," *South Asia Bulletin* 9 (1989): 32–56.

though not the virulent and "scientific" discussion of the later nineteenth century, "colored" the conception of the new and improved, moral "Briton."

Though Clarkson's "diagram" omits mention of many active abolitionists, his canonization of these men (and woman) reflects a deeper message—only "Britannia" could have produced these men. In his dedication, he attributes "the unparalleled and eternal glory of the annihilation of one of the greatest sources of crimes and sufferings, ever recorded in the annals of mankind" to the administrators who advocated on behalf of the bill. The overall intent is to inscribe a view of history that portrays Britain's engagement with the slave trade as a dangerous lapse of judgment. Having rectified this crime, Great Britain is singularly well-positioned to "instruct" both African and other European nations in the "ethic of benevolence."

The work of anti-slave-trade writers did not end with the success of their petitions and organization. By taking on the responsibility for the morality of the nation, these writers continued to publish, albeit less frequently than at the height of the debates, and remind Britons of their "superior" accomplishments. This belief in British "altruism" motivated another petitioning campaign in 1814 when 800 petitions submitted to Parliament urged the government to intervene with the newly restored French monarchy to dismantle the French slave trade.[11] In 1819, the Royal Navy established an anti-slave-trade squadron and posted it off the coast of West Africa; their purpose was to police other European trade routes and disrupt their trade. The motivation behind these interventions stemmed from the belief that Great Britain's model of abolition should be emulated by the rest of the "civilized" world. As Linda Colley summarizes, "Anti-slavery supplied the British with an epic stage upon which they could strut in an overwhelmingly attractive guise" (359).

The slave-trade debates have been undervalued with respect to their ideological and rhetorical contribution to empire and imperial activities. The nature of the trade directed conversation from the outset to the reconsideration of Britain's "dominion over the seas." While the desire for continued prosperity remained, a seemingly contradictory impulse for more "humane" and "freedom loving" form of rule also arose. I assert that the dialogue over national identity formulated a commercial and trade "ethic" that sought to reconcile the acquisition of wealth and "Christian" morality. Both regulationists and abolitionists constructed this "ethic." The image of "Britannia" as "empress of the seas" and the champion of freedom emerged from the arguments of each camp. Those who were not directly involved with the slave trade could feel a sense of accomplishment and pride in the dual capacity of abolition. Passing this law reaffirmed the freedom of Britons and granted (however spuriously) freedom to Africans. This belief in the ability of Britons to effect global change reconfigured the notion of empire that

---

[11] For a discussion of French antislavery efforts and their connection with British organizers see Lawrence Jennings' *French Anti-Slavery: The Movement for the Abolition of Slavery in France, 1802–1848*.

had previously been configured simply as the service to the mother country. The crucial factor embedded within proslavery and abolitionist arguments involved a rethinking of empire and a "new" imperialism. These debates, in defining a national character, contributed to the growing belief that the values of the mother country could project outward to regulate and guide colonial enterprise. Britons, with respect to abolition, now viewed themselves as exemplars for the rest of the world. They required little inducement to move from judging the world to owning a large part of it.

Bibliography

For the convenience of the reader, I have divided the bibliography into the categories of antislavery/abolitionist primary sources, proslavery primary sources, and secondary sources. I have chosen to list pseudonymous publications by author rather than title because my study analyzes the purpose of such conventions in publications. I have also listed the names of publishers to refer to the specific printing that was consulted. While the text may have remained unchanged over multiple printings, the pagination may differ. Unless otherwise indicated, all of the primary sources were found in the British Library and on microfilm as part of the *Goldsmiths'-Kress Library of Economic Literature*. Most sources are now available on *ECCO*.

Primary Sources

Antislavery and Abolitionist Writings

A Concise Statement of the Question Regarding the Abolition of the Slave Trade. 2nd ed. London: Printed for J. Hatchard, T. N. Longman, O. Rees, 1804.
A Letter from Capt. J. S. Smith to the Rev. Mr. Hill on the State of the Negroe Slaves. To which are added an intro. and Remarks on Free Negroes, &c. London: Printed and Sold by J. Phillips, 1786.
Am I Not a Man and a Brother? With all humility addressed to the British Legislature. Cambridge: Printed by J. Archdeacon, Sold by J. & J. Merrill, T. Payne, J. & J. Fletcher, 1788.
An Abstract of the Evidence delivered before a select committee of the House of Commons in the Years 1790, and 1791; on the part of the petitioners for the abolition of the slave-trade. London: Printed by James Phillips, 1791.
An Address to Her Royal Highness the Duchess of York, against the use of sugar. London, 1792.
An Address to the inhabitants of Glasgow, Paisley, and the neighbourhood, concerning the African slave trade. By a Society in Glasgow. Society for the Abolition of the African Slave Trade, Glasgow. Glasgow: Printed by Alex. Adam, 1791.
An Authentic Account of the conversion and experience of a negro: extracted from a letter, written by a gentlemen who was secretary to Lord H—, during part of the late American war. Whitchurch: Printed by J. Wright, 1790.
An Exhortation and Caution to Friends Concerning Buying or Keeping Negroes. New York, 1693.

Benezet, Anthony. *Observations on the Enslaving, importing and purchasing of Negroes*. Germantown, PA, 1759.

—. *A Short Account of that part of Africa Inhabited by the Negroes*. 2nd ed. with amendments. Philadelphia: Printed by W. Dunlap, 1762.

—. *A Caution to Great Britain and her Colonies, in a short representation of the calamitous state of the enslaved Negroes in the British dominions*. Philadelphia: Printed by D. Hall and W. Sellers, 1767.

—. *Some Historical Account of Guinea*. London: Printed by W. Owen and E. and C. Dilly, 1772.

—. *The Case of our Fellow-Creatures, the Oppressed Africans, respectfully recommended to the serious consideration of the Legislature of Great-Britain, by the people called the Quakers*. London: Printed by James Phillips, 1783.

Birkett, Mary. *A Poem on the African Slave Trade in two parts. Addressed to her own Sex, by M. Birkett*. Dublin: Printed by W. Corbet for J. Jones, 1792.

Bradburn, Samuel. *An Address to the People called Methodists; concerning the evil of encouraging the Slave Trade*. Manchester: Printed by J. Harper, 1792.

Bradshaw, Thomas. *The Slave Trade inconsistent with Reason and Religion. A sermon preached in the parish-church of Tottenham Middle-Sex on Sunday, March 16, 1788*. London: Printed and Sold by W. Richardson, 1788.

Burgess, Thomas. *Considerations on the Abolition of Slavery and the Slave Trade upon grounds of Natural, religious, and political duty*. Oxford: Sold by D. Princes & J. Cooke; J. & J. Fletcher; and by Elmsly, White, Payne, Cadell. London, 1789.

The Claim for fresh evidence on the subject of the Slave Trade considered. London: Printed by Phillips and Fardon, 1807.

Clarke, Thomas. *A Letter to Mr. Cobbett on His Opinions Respecting the Slave-Trade*. London: Printed for J. Hatchard, 1806.

Clarkson, Thomas. *An Essay on the Slavery and Commerce of the Human Species, particularly the African, translated from a Latin dissertation which was honoured with the first prize in the University of Cambridge for the Year 1785, with Additions*. London: Printed by J. Phillips and Sold by T. Cadell and J. Phillips, 1786; reprinted in Philadelphia by Joseph Crukshank, 1786.

—. *An Essay on the Impolicy of the African Slave Trade in two parts*. London: Printed by J. Phillips, 1788.

—. *An Essay on the Comparative Efficiency of regulations or Abolition, as applied to Slave Trade shewing that the latter only can remove the evils to be found in that commerce*. London: Printed by James Phillips, 1789.

—. *Letters on the Slave-Trade, and the State of the Natives in those parts of Africa which are contiguous to Fort St. Louis and Goree, written at Paris in December 1789 and January 1790*. London: Printed and Sold by James Phillips, 1791.

—. *The History of the Rise, Progress and Accomplishment of the Abolition of the African Slave-Trade by the British Parliament*. 2 vols. London: Printed by R. Taylor and Co. for Longman, Hurst, Rees, and Orme, 1808.

Coleridge, Samuel Taylor. "On the Slave Trade." *The Watchman* no. IV, 25 March 1796.

Cooper, David. *A mite cast into the treasury: or, observations on slave-keeping.* Philadelphia, 1772.

Cooper, Thomas. *Letters on the slave trade, First published in* Wheeler's Manchester Chronicle; *and since reprinted with additions and alterations, by Thomas Cooper, Esq.* Manchester: Printed by C. Wheeler, 1787.

—. *Considerations on the Slave Trade; and the Consumption of West Indian Produce.* London: Printed and Sold by Darton and Harvey, J. Carter, and J. Parsons, 1791.

Crafton, William Bell. *A Short Sketch of the Evidence, for the Abolition of the Slave Trade.* London: Printed in the year 1792.

Cugoano, Quobna Ottobah. *Thoughts and Sentiments on the Evil of Slavery.* Ed. Vincent Carretta. New York: Penguin Books, 1999.

Dannett, Henry. *A Particular examination of Mr. Harris's Scriptural researches on the licitness of the slave trade.* London: Printed and Sold by T. Payne; Oxford: D. Prince and Cooke, 1788.

The Debate on a Motion for the Abolition of the Slave-Trade, in the House of Commons, on Monday and Tuesday, April 18 and 19, 1791, reported in detail. London: Printed by and for W. Woodfall, and sold at the printing-office of the diary, 1791.

Dore, James. *A Sermon on the African Slave Trade, preached at Maze-Pond, Southwark, Lord's day afternoon, November 30, 1788.* London: Printed by R. Wayland and Sold by J. Buckland, C. Dilly, M. Curney, and W. Button, 1789.

Dundas, Henry. *Speech of the Right Honourable Henry Dundas, delegate in the House of Commons, The 15th of March 1796 on the farther consideration of the report of the committee, upon the bill for the abolition of the Slave Trade.* London, 1796.

Edwards, Jonathan. *The Injustice and Impolicy of the Slave Trade, and of the Slavery of the Africans: illustrated in a sermon preached before the Connecticut society for the Promotion of Freedom, and for the Relief of persons unlawfully holden in bondage, at their annual meeting in New-Haven, September 15, 1791.* New Haven: Printed by Thomas and Samuel Green, 1791.

Equiano, Olaudah. *The Interesting Narrative and Other Writings.* Ed. Vincent Carretta. New York: Penguin Books, 1995.

Falconbridge, Alexander. *An Account of the Slave Trade on the Coast of Africa.* London: Printed by J. Phillips, 1788.

Fox, William. *An Address to the People of Great Britain, on the Propriety of Abstaining from West India Sugar and Rum.* London: Printed by M. Gurney, 1791.

G. C. P. *Reflections on the Slave Trade, with Remarks on the Policy of its Abolition. In a Letter to a Clergyman in the County of Suffolk.* Bury: Printed for the author by P. Gedge, for J. H. Riley, Sudbury; and Sold by the printer and publisher;

also by Shave and Jackson, and Jermyn, Ipswich; Leatherdale, Hadleigh; Keymer, Colchester; Clachar, Chelmsford; and by T. Knott, London, 1791.

Gisborne, Thomas. *Remarks on the Late Decision of The House of Commons respecting the abolition of the slave trade*. London: Printed for B. White and sons, 1792.

Gronniosaw, James Albert Ukawsaw. *A Narrative of the Most Remarkable Particulars in the Life of James Albert Ukawsaw Gronniosaw, An African Prince, as Related by Himself.* Bath: Printed by W. Gye, 1770.

Hargrave, Francis. *An Argument in the Case of James Sommersett A Negro, lately determined by the Court of King's Bench*. London: Printed for the author, 1772.

Harrison, George. *An Address to the Right Reverend The Prelates of England and Wales, on the Subject of the Slave Trade*. London: Printed and Sold by J. Parsons, 1792.

Heron, Robert. *A Letter to William Wilberforce, Esq, MP on the justice and expediency of slavery and the Slave-Trade, and on the best means to improve the manners and conditions of the Negroes in the West Indies*. London: Printed for Jordon & Maxwell, 1806.

Hints for a specific plan for an abolition of the Slave Trade, and for relief of the Negroes in the British West Indies. By a translator of Cicero's Orations against Verres (attributed to James White). London: Printed for J. Debbrett, 1788.

Hughes, W. *An Answer to the Reverend Mr Harris's "Scriptural Researches on the Licitness of the Slave Trade" By W. Hughes*. London: Printed for T. Cadell, 1788.

Johnson, Samuel. *Taxation no tyranny: an answer to the resolutions and address of the American Congress*. London: Printed for T. Cadell, 1775.

Kilner, Dorothy. *The Rotchford's; or the Friendly Counsellor*. London: Printed and Sold by John Marshall, 1786.

Lay, Benjamin. *All Slave-Keepers, That Keep the Innocent in Bondage, Apostates*. Philadelphia, 1737.

Layman, Captain. *Outline of a plan for cultivation, security, or defence of the British West Indies: being the original suggestion for providing an effectual substitute for the African Slave Trade*. London: Printed for and Sold by Black, Parry, & Kingsbury, 1807.

Long, Edward. *Candid Reflections upon the Judgment lately award by The Court of King's Bench*. London: Printed for T. Lowndes, 1722.

Maxwell, James. *On the Prolongation of the Slave Trade. A Moral Essay set forth in the following Dialogue*. London, 1785 (?).

[Morgann, Maurice]. *A Plan for the Abolition of Slavery in the West Indies*. London: William Griffin, 1772.

Newton, John. *Thoughts Upon the African Slave Trade*. London: Printed for J. Buckland and J. Johnson, 1788.

Poems on the abolition of the slave trade; written by James Montgomery, James Grahame, and E. Benger. Embellished with Engravings from pictures painted by R. Smirke, Esq. R.A. London: Printed for R. Bowyer, 1809.

Ramsay, James. *An Essay on the Treatment and Conversion of African Slaves in the British Sugar Colonies.* London: Printed and Sold by James Phillips, 1784.

—. *An Inquiry into the Effects of putting a stop to the African Slave Trade, and of granting liberty to the slave in the BRITISH SUGAR COLONIES.* London: Printed and Sold by James Phillips, 1784.

—. *A Reply to the Personal Invectives and Objections contained in two answers, published by certain anonymous persons, to An Essay. By James Ramsay, MA Vicar of Teston.* London: Printed and Sold by James Phillips, 1785.

—. *A Letter to James Tobin, Esq., late member of His Majesty's council in the Island of Nevis. From James Ramsay, AM, Vicar of Teston.* London: Printed and Sold by James Phillips, 1787.

Randolph, F. *A Letter to the Right Honourable William Pitt on the proposed abolition of the African Slave Trade.* London: Printed for J. Cadell, 1788.

Remarks on the African Slave Trade (also printed as *An Essay on the African Slave Trade*). London: C. Dilly, 1790.

Roscoe, William. *A scriptural refutation of a pamphlet, lately published by the Rev. Raymund Harris, intitled, "Scriptural Researches on the licitness of the slave trade" In four letters from the author to a friend.* London: Printed for J. Phillips, 1788; Printed for B. Law, 1788.

Rush, Benjamin. *An Address to the Inhabitants of the British Settlements in America, upon slave-keeping.* Philadelphia: Printed and Sold by J. Dunlap, 1773.

Sancho, Ignatius. *Letters of the Late Ignatius Sancho, An African.* 1782. Ed. Vincent Carretta. New York: Penguin Books, 1998.

Scripture the Friend of Freedom; exemplified by a refutation of the arguments offered in defence of slavery, in a tract entitled, Scriptural Researches on the Licitness of the Slave Trade. London: Printed by W. Smith, Sold by J. Phillips and J. Debrett, 1789.

Sharp, Granville. *A Representation of the Injustice and Dangerous Tendency of Tolerating Slavery.* London: Printed for Benjamin White and Robert Horsfield, 1769.

—. *An Essay on Slavery.* Burlington, NJ: Printed and sold by Isaac Collins, 1773.

—. *The Law of Retribution; or, A Serious warning to Great Britain and her colonies founded on unquestionable examples of God's temporal vengeance against tyrants, slave holders, and oppressors.* London, 1776.

—. *The Just Limitation of Slavery in the Laws of God.* London, 1776.

—. *The Law of Passive Obedience.* London, 1776.

—. *The Law of Liberty, or, Royal Law.* London, 1776.

Speeches in Parliament respecting the abolition of the African Slave Trade. Edinburgh: Printed by D. Willison for the Edinburgh Antislavery Society, 1789.

Stedman, John Gabriel. *Narrative of a Five Years' Expedition against the Revolted Negroes of Surinam.* 2 vols. London: Printed by J. Johnson and J. Edwards, 1796.

Sterne, Laurence. *The Letters of Laurence Sterne.* Ed. Lewis Perry Curtis. Oxford: Clarendon Press, 1935.

Two of the Petitions from Scotland, which were presented to the Last Parliament, praying the Abolition of the African Slave Trade. Edinburgh: Printed by the order of the Society established at Edinburgh, for Effecting the Abolition of the African Slave Trade, 1790.

Vindex. *Old Truths and Established Facts, being an answer to A Very New Pamphlet indeed!* London, 1792 (?).

Wesley, John. *Thoughts upon Slavery.* London, 1774.

—. *A serious address to the people of England with regard to the state of the nation.* London: R. Hawes, 1778.

Wheatley, Phillis. *Complete Writings.* Ed. Vincent Carretta. New York: Penguin Books, 2001.

Wilberforce, William. *The Speech of William Wilberforce, Esq. Representative for the County of York, on Wednesday the 13th of May, 1789, on the question of the ABOLITION OF THE SLAVE TRADE. To which are added, the RESOLUTIONS THEN MOVED, and a short sketch of the SPEECHES OF OTHER MEMBERS.* London: Printed at the Logographic Press, and Sold by J. Walter, C. Stalker, and W. Richardson, 1789.

Wollstonecraft, Mary. *A Vindication of the Rights of Woman.* Ed. Miriam Brody. London: Penguin Classics, 1992.

Proslavery Writings

A Country Gentleman's Reasons for voting against Mr. Wilberforce's motion for a bill to prohibit the importation of African Negroes into the Colonies. London: Printed for J. Debrett, 1791.

A Friend to commerce and humanity. *Thoughts on Civilization, and the Gradual Abolition of Slavery in Africa and the West Indies.* London: Printed for J. Sewell, 1789.

A very New Pamphlet indeed! Being the truth: addressed to the people at large containing some Strictures on the English Jacobins, and the Evidence of Lord McCartney, and others, Before the House of Lords, respecting the Slave Trade. London, 1792.

A West-India Planter. *Consideration on the Emancipation of Negroes and on the Abolition of the Slave-Trade.* London: Printed for J. Johnson and J. Debrett, 1788.

Adair, James MacKittrick. *Unanswerable Arguments against the Abolition of the Slave Trade with a Defence of the Proprietors of the British Sugar Colonies, Against certain malignant Charges contained in Letters published by a Sailor, and by Luffman, Newton, &c.* London: Sold by J. P. Bateman, 1790.

Adams, Thomas Maxwell. *A Cool Address to the People of England on the Slave Trade.* London: R. Faulder & J. Stockdale, 1788.

An African Merchant. *A Treatise upon the Trade from Great-Britain to Africa; Humbly recommended to the Attention of the Government.* London: Printed for R. Baldwin, 1772.

An Answer to the Reverend James Ramsay's Essay, on The Treatement and Conversion of Slaves, in the British Sugar Colonies, By some Gentlemen of St. Christopher. Basseterre in St. Christopher: Printed by Edward L. Low, 1784.

An apology for Slavery or, Six Cogent Arguments against the immediate Abolition of the Slave Trade. London: J. Johnson & R. Faulder, 1792.

An appeal to the Candour and Justice of the People of England in behalf of the West India Merchants and Planters founded on plain facts and incontrovertible arguments. London: Printed for and published by J. Debrett, 1792.

An inquiry into the Origin, Progress, and Present State of Slavery with a plan for the gradual, reasonable, and secure Emancipation of slaves. By a member of the Society of universal goodwill in London and Norwich. Printed for John Murray, 1789.

An Old Member of Parliament. *Doubts on the Abolition of the Slave Trade.* London: Printed for John Stockdale, 1790.

Baillie, James. *The Speech of James Baillie, Esq. Agent for Grenada in the House of Commons, on the Question for the Abolition of the Slave Trade on Monday April 2, 1792.* London: W. Woodfall, 1792.

Beckford, William. *Remarks upon the situation of the Negroes in Jamaica, impartially made from a local Experience of nearly Thirteen Years in that Island.* London: Printed for T. & J. Egerton, 1788.

Bissett, Dr. *Essays on the Slave Trade.* London: W. McDowall, 1805. [Name and date attributed by hand at the top of first page; part of Lord Sheffield's collection.]

Boswell, James. *No Abolition of Slavery; or the Universal Empire of Love: A Poem.* London: Printed for R. Faulder, 1791.

Candidus. *A Letter to Philo Africanus upon Slavery in answer to his of the 22nd November, In the* General Evening Post; *together with the Opinions of Sir John Strange, and other eminent lawyers upon this subject, with the Sentence of Lord Mansfield, in the case of Somerset and Knowles, 1772, with his Lordship's explanation of that opinion in 1786.* London: Printed for W. Brown, 1788.

Commercial Reasons for the Non-Abolition of the Slave Trade, in the West-India Islands, by a Planter, and Merchant of many Years Residence in the West-Indies. London: Printed for W. Lane, 1789.

Considerations and Remarks on the Present state of the Trade to Africa; with Some Account of the British Settlements in that Country, and the Intrigues of the Natives since the Peace; candidly stated and considered. In a Letter Addressed to the People in Power more particularly the Nation in general. By a Gentleman, who resided upwards of Fifteen Years in that Country. Lonnon [*sic*]: Printed for and Sold by Mess. Robinson and Roberts, 1771.

Considerations upon the fatal consequences of abolishing the slave trade, in the present situation of Great Britain. London: Printed for J. Debbrett, 1789.

Cotton, Rowland. *Extracts from an account of the state of British forts, on the Gold Coast of Africa, taken by Capt. Cotton in 1777.* London: Printed for J. Bew, 1778.

Edwards, Bryan. *A Speech delivered at a free conference between the Honourable Council and Assembly of Jamaica, held the 19th November, 1789, on the subject of Mr. Wilberforce's propositions in the House of Commons, concerning the Slave-Trade.* Kingston, Jamaica: Printed by Alexander Aikman, 1789. 2nd ed. with appendix printed in 1790; reprinted in London for J. Debrett, 1790.

——. *The History, Civil and Commercial, of the British Colonies in the West Indies in 2 volumes.* London: Printed for J. Stockdale, 1793.

Ellis, George (?). *A Letter to William Wilberforce, Esq. By Philo-Africanus.* London: Printed for J. Debrett, 1790.

Estwick, Samuel. *Considerations on the Negroe Cause commonly so called, addressed to the Right Honourable Lord Mansfield, Lord Chief Justice of the Court of King's Bench, &c., by a West Indian.* London: Printed for J. Dodsley, 1772.

Foot, Jesse. *A Defence of the Planters in the West-Indies; composed in four arguments on comparative humanity, on comparative slavery, on the African Slave Trade, and on the condition of the Negroes in the West-Indies.* London: Printed for J. Debrett, 1792.

Francklyn, Gilbert. *Observations, occasioned by the attempts made in England to effect the abolition of the Slave Trade; shewing the manner in which Negroes are treated in the British colonies in the West-Indies: and also, some particular remarks addressed to the Treasurer of the Society for effecting such abolition from the Reverend Robert Boucher Nicolls.* London: Sold by J. Waster, C. Stalker, and W. Richardson, 1789. Originally published in Kingston, Jamaica.

Geddes, Alexander. *An Apology for Slavery; or, six cogent arguments against the immediate abolition of the slave-trade.* London: Printed for J. Johnson and R. Faulder, 1792.

Harris, Raymund. *Scriptural Researches on the Licitness of the Slave Trade, shewing its conformity with the principles of natural and revealed religion, delineated in the sacred writings of the Word of God.* London: John Stockdale, 1788.

Hill, Anthony. *Afer Baptizatus: or, the negro turn'd Christian.* London, 1702.

Innes, William. A Letter to the Members of Parliament who have presented petitions to the honourable House of Commons for the Abolition of the Slave Trade. London: Sold by J. Sewell, J. Murray, and J. Debrett, 1792.

Knox, William. *A Letter from W. K., Esq. To William Wilberforce, Esq.* London: Printed for J. Debrett, 1790.

Long, Edward. *The History of Jamaica: or, a general survey of the ancient and modern state of that Island with reflections on its situation, settlements inhabitants, climate, etc.* London, 1774.

Matthews, John. *A Voyage to the River Sierra-Leone on the Coast of Africa with an additional letter on the subject of the African Slave Trade.* London: Printed for B. White and Son, 1788.

Mercator. *Letters Concerning the Abolition of the Slave-Trade and other West-India Affairs.* London: Printed by C. & W. Galabin, 1807.

—. *Third Letter on the Abolition of the Slave-Trade and other West India Affairs.* London: C. & W. Galabin, 1807.

Nisbet, Richard. *Slavery Not Forbidden by Scripture or a Defence of the West-India Planters, From the Aspersions thrown out against them, by the author of a pamphlet, entitled, "An Address to the inhabitants of the British settlements in America, upon Slave-Keeping,"* By a West Indian. Philadelphia, 1773.

—. *The Capacity of Negroes for Religious and Moral Improvement Considered: with cursory hints, to proprietors and to government for the immediate melioration of the condition of slaves in the sugar colonies.* London, 1789. Reprinted Westport, CT: Negro Universities Press, 1970.

NO ABOLITION; or, An Attempt to prove to the conviction of every rational British subject, that the Abolition of the British Trade with AFRICA FOR NEGROES, WOULD BE A MEASURE AS UNJUST AS IMPOLITIC, FATAL TO THE INTERESTS OF THIS NATION, RUINOUS TO ITS SUGAR COLONIES, AND MORE OR LESS PERNICIOUS IN ITS CONSEQUENCES TO EVERY DESCRIPTION OF THE PEOPLE. In the course of which are inserted IMPORTANT EXTRACTS FROM THE REPORT OF THE RIGHT HONOURABLE COMMITTEE OF PRIVY COUNCIL. London: P. for J. Debrett, 1789.

Norris, Robert. *A Short Account of the African Slave Trade collected from local knowledge from evidence given at the bar of both Houses of Parliament, and from tracts written upon that subject.* Liverpool: Printed at Ann Smith's Navigation Shop, 1788.

Observations on the evidence given before the Committees of the Privy Council and House of Commons in support of the Bill for abolishing the slave trade. London: Printed for John Stockdale, 1791.

Plumer. *The Speech of Mr. Plumer at the bar of the House of Lords, on the 2nd reading of the bill for the abolition of the Slave Trade, in support of the petition of the West India planters and merchants against that measure.* London: Printed by C. & W. Galabin, 1807.

Remarks on a Pamphlet written by the Reverend James Ramsay under the title of Thoughts on the Slavery of Negroes in the American colonies. London: Printed for and Sold by J. P. Batemen, 1784.

Remarks on the New Sugar-Bill, and on the national compacts respecting the sugar-trade and slave-trade. London: Printed for J. Johnson and J. Debrett, 1792.

Remarks upon the evidence given by Thomas Irving, Esq., Inspector General of the Exports and Imports of Great Britain, before the Select Committee appointed to take the examination of witnesses on the slave-trade. London, 1791.

Roberts, John. *Extracts from an account of the state of British forts, on the Gold Coast of Africa, taken by Captain. Cotton, of His Majesty's ship, Pallas, in May and June, 1777. To which are added, observations by John Roberts, governor of Cape Coast Castle.* London: Printed for J. Bew, 1778.

Schaw, Janet. *Journal of a Lady of Quality; Being the narrative of a journey from Scotland to the West Indies, North Carolina, and Portugal in the years 1774–1776.* Ed. Evangeline Walker Andrews and Charles McLean Andrews. New Haven: Yale University Press, 1921.

Sheffield, Lord. *Observations on the Project for Abolishing the Slave Trade, and on the reasonableness of attempting some practicable mode of relieving the Negroes.* 2nd ed. with additions. London: Printed by J. Cooper for J. Debrett. 1791.

Substance of a Speech intended to have been made on Mr. Wilberforce's motion for the Abolition of the Slave Trade, on Tuesday, April 3, 1792. London: Printed for J. Owen, 1792.

Thompson, Reverend Thomas. *The African Trade for Negro slaves shewn to be consistent with principles of humanity and with the laws of revealed religion.* Canterbury: Printed and Sold by Simmons and Kirby, Sold also by Robert Baldwin, London, [1772?].

Thorkelin, Grime Johnson. *An essay on the Slave Trade.* London: Printed for G. Nicol, bookseller to His Majesty, 1788. Note on inside cover of text indicates author was "professor of Northern Antiquities in the Danish Academy, when he had been only about three months in England—The title page has been altered since the first publication, and now is: *An Essay on the Slave Trade among the Ancients, particularly the Northern Nations.*"

Tobin, James. *Cursory Remarks upon the Reverend Mr. Ramsay's Essay on the Treatment and Conversion of African Slaves in the Sugar Colonies.* London: Printed for G. and T. Wilkie, London; E. Easton, Salisbury, and J.B. Becket, Bristol, 1785.

—. *A Short Rejoinder to the Rev. Mr. Ramsay's Reply: w/ a word or two on some other publications of the same tendency.* London: Printed for G. & T. Wilkie and J. B. Becket, Bristol, 1787.

—. *A Farewell Address to the Rev. Mr. James Ramsay; from James Tobin, Esq. To which is added a letter from the Society for Propagating the Gospel, to Mr. Anthony Benezet of Philadelphia.* G. and T. Wilkie, London; E. Easton, Salisbury; and J. B. Becket, Bristol, 1788.

Turnbull, Gordon. *An Apology for Negro Slavery: or, the West India planters vindicated from the charge of Inhumanity. By the author of Letters to a Young*

Planter. 2nd printing with additions. London: Printed by J. Stevenson for J. Strachan, R. Faulder, W. Richardson, 1786.

Young, Sir William. *The speech of Sir William Young, Bart. On the subject of the Slave-Trade, April 19, 1791.* London: John Stockdale, 1791.

Secondary Sources

Anderson, Benedict. *Imagined Communities: Reflections on the Origin and Spread of Nationalism.* 1983. London: Verso, 1991.

Anstey, Roger. *The Atlantic Slave Trade and British Abolition, 1760–1810.* Atlantic Highlands, NJ: Humanities Press, 1975.

Aravamudan, Srinivas. *Tropicopolitans: Colonialism and Agency, 1688–1804.* Durham, NC: Duke University Press, 1999.

Armitage, David. *The Ideological Origins of the British Empire.* Cambridge: Cambridge University Press, 2000.

—. "John Locke, Carolina, and *Two Treatises of Government.*" *Political Theory* 32.5 (2004): 602–627.

Armistead, Wilson. *Anthony Benezet. From the original memoir: Revised with additions.* London: A. W. Bennett, 1859. Reprinted Freeport, NY: Books for Libraries Press, 1971.

Bacon, Jacqueline. *The Humblest May Stand Forth: Rhetoric, Empowerment, and Abolition.* Columbia: University of South Carolina Press, 2002.

Bacon, Jacqueline and Glen McClish. "Reinventing the Master's Tools: Nineteenth-Century African-American Literary Societies of Philadelphia and Rhetorical Education." *Rhetoric Society Quarterly* 30.4 (2000): 19–47.

—. "Descendents of Africa, Sons of '76: Exploring Early African-American Rhetoric." *Rhetoric Society Quarterly* 36 (2006): 1–29.

Bass, Jeff D. "An Efficient Humanitarianism: The British Slave-trade debates, 1791–1792." *Quarterly Journal of Speech* 75 (1989): 152–165.

Baum, Joan. *Mind-Forg'd Manacles: Slavery and the English Romantic Poets.* North Haven, CN: Archon Books, 1994.

Beckles, Hilary. *White Servitude and Black Slavery in Barbados, 1627–1715.* Knoxville: The University of Tennessee Press, 1989.

Bender, Thomas, ed. *The Antislavery Debate: Capitalism and Abolitionism as a Problem in Historical Interpretation.* Berkeley: University of California Press, 1992.

Berlin, Isaiah. *Four Essays on Liberty.* Oxford: Oxford University Press, 1969.

Bernstein, Jeremy. *Dawning of the Raj: The Life and Trials of Warren Hastings.* Chicago: Ivan R. Dee, 2000.

Blackburn, Robin. *The Overthrow of Colonial Slavery: 1776–1848.* London: Verso, 1988.

—. *The Making of New World Slavery.* London: Verso, 1997.

Bohls, Elizabeth A. "The gentleman planter and the metropole: Long's *History of Jamaica*." *The Country and the City Revisited: England and the Politics of Culture, 1550–1850*. Ed. Gerald MacLean, Donna Landry, and Joseph P. Ward. Cambridge: Cambridge University Press, 1999.

Bolt, Christine and Seymour Drescher, eds. *Anti-slavery, Religion and Reform: Essays in Memory of Roger Anstey*. Folkestone, Kent: W. Dawson & Sons Ltd, 1980.

Braude, Benjamin. "The Sons of Noah and the Construction of Ethnic and Geographical Identities in the Medieval and Early Modern Periods." *William and Mary Quarterly* 54 (1997): 103–142.

Brewer, John. *Party Ideology and Popular Politics at the Accession of George III*. Cambridge: Cambridge University Press, 1976.

Brooke, John. *The House of Commons 1754–1790: Introductory Survey*. Oxford: Oxford University Press, 1964.

Brookes, George S. *Friend Anthony Benezet*. Philadelphia: University of Pennsylvania Press, 1937.

Brown, Christopher Leslie. *Moral Capital: Foundations of British Abolitionism*. Chapel Hill: University of North Carolina Press, 2006.

Burke, Kenneth. *A Grammar of Motives*. 1945. Berkeley: University of California Press, 1969.

Butler, Marilyn. *Romantics, Rebels and Reactionaries: English Literature and its Background, 1760–1830*. Oxford: Oxford University Press, 1982.

Calhoun, Craig. *Nationalism*. Buckingham: Open University Press, 1997.

Carey, Brycchan. *British Abolitionism and the Rhetoric of Sensibility: Writing, Sentiment, and Slavery, 1760–1807*. New York: Palgrave Macmillan, 2005.

Carey-Webb, Allen. *Making Subject(s): Literature and the Emergence of National Identity*. New York: Garland Publications, 1998.

Carretta, Vincent, ed. *Unchained Voices: An Anthology of Black Authors in the English-Speaking World of the 18th Century*. Lexington: The University Press of Kentucky, 1996.

—. "Olaudah Equiano or Gustavus Vassa? New Light on an Eighteenth-Century Question of Identity." *Slavery and Abolition*. 20.3 (1999): 96–105.

—. *Equiano the African: Biography of a Self-Made Man*. Athens: University of Georgia Press, 2005.

Carretta, Vincent, and Philip Gould, eds. *Genius in Bondage Literature of the Early Black Atlantic*. Lexington: The University Press of Kentucky, 2001.

Coleman, Dierdre. "Conspicuous Consumption: White Abolitionism and English Women's Protest Writing in the 1790s." *English Literary History* 61.2 (1994): 341–362.

—. *Romantic Colonization and British Anti-Slavery*. Cambridge: Cambridge University Press, 2005.

Colley, Linda. *Britons: Forging the Nation, 1707–1837*. New Haven: Yale University Press, 1992.

Craton, Michael. *Sinews of Empire: A Short History of British Slavery.* Garden City, NY: Anchor Books, 1974.

—. "Reluctant Creoles: The Planters' World in the British West Indies," *Strangers within the Realm: Cultural Margins of the first British Empire.* Ed. Bernard Bailyn and Philip D. Morgan. Chapel Hill: University of North Carolina Press, 1991. 314–362.

Dabydeen, David. *The Black Presence in English Literature.* Manchester: Manchester University Press, 1985.

—. *Hogarth's Blacks: Images of Blacks in Eighteenth Century English Art.* Mundelstrup, Denmark: Dangaroo Press, 1985.

d'Anjou, Leo. *Social Movements and Cultural Change: The First Abolition Campaign Revisited.* New York: Aldine de Gruyter, 1996.

Davis, David Brion. *The Problem of Slavery in Western Culture.* Ithaca: Cornell University Press, 1973.

—. *The Problem of Slavery in the Age of Revolution 1770–1823.* Ithaca: Cornell University Press, 1975.

—. *Slavery and Human Progress.* Oxford: Oxford University Press, 1984.

—. *Inhuman Bondage: The Rise and Fall of Slavery in the New World.* Oxford: Oxford University Press, 2006.

Dibdin, Edward Rimbault Dibdin. "The Bi-Centenary of 'Rule Britannia.'" *Music and Letters* 21.3 (1940): 275–290.

Drescher, Seymour. *Econocide: British Slavery in the Era of Abolition.* Pittsburgh: University of Pittsburgh Press, 1977.

—. *Capitalism and Antislavery: British Mobilization in the Era of Abolition.* Oxford: Oxford University Press, 1987.

—. "People and Parliament: The Rhetoric of the British Slave Trade." *Journal of Interdisciplinary History* 21.2 (1990): 245–260.

—. "Whose Abolition? Popular Pressure and the Ending of the British Slave Trade." *Past and Present: A Journal of Historical Studies* 143 (1994): 136–166.

Dunn, Richard S. *Sugar and Slaves: The Rise of the Planter Class in the English West Indies, 1624–1713.* New York: W. W. Norton & Co., 1973.

Edwards, Paul and David Dabydeen, eds. *Black Writers in Britain, 1760–1890.* Edinburgh: Edinburgh University Press, 1991.

Ellis, Markman. *The Politics of Sensibility: Race, Gender and Commerce in the Sentimental Novel.* Cambridge: Cambridge University Press, 1996.

Eltis, David, and James Walvin, eds. *The Abolition of the Atlantic Slave Trade: Origins and Effects in Europe, Africa, and the Americas.* Madison: The University of Wisconsin Press, 1981.

Eltis, David. *Economic Growth and the Ending of the Transatlantic Slave Trade.* Oxford: Oxford University Press, 1987.

—. "Was the Slave Trade Dominated by Men?" *Journal of Interdisciplinary History* 23 (1992): 237–257.

—. *The Rise of African Slavery in the Americas.* Cambridge: Cambridge University Press, 2000.

Emmer, P. C., ed. *Colonialism and Migration: Indentured Labour Before and After Slavery*. Dordrecht, The Netherlands: Martinus Nijhoff Publishers, 1986.

Ericson, David F. *The Debate over Slavery: Antislavery and Proslavery Liberalism in Antebellum America*. New York: New York University Press, 2000.

Felsenstein, Frank. *English Trader, Indian Maid: Representing Gender, Race, and Slavery in the New World, An Inkle and Yarico Reader*. Baltimore: The Johns Hopkins University Press, 1999.

Ferguson, Moira. *Subject to Others: British Women Writers and Colonial Slavery, 1670–1834*. New York: Routledge, 1992.

Finkelman, Paul. *Proslavery Thought, Ideology, and Politics*. Vol. 12. New York: Garland, 1989.

Fladeland, Betty. *Men and Brothers: Anglo-American Antislavery Cooperation*. Urbana: University of Illinois Press, 1972.

—. *Abolitionists and Working-Class Problems in the Age of Industrialization*. Baton Rouge: Louisiana State University Press, 1984.

"Forum: Teaching Equiano's *Interesting Narrative*." *Eighteenth-Century Studies* 34 (Summer 2001): 601–624.

Fox-Genovese, Elizabeth and Eugene D. Genovese. *Fruits of Merchant Capital: Slavery and Bourgeois Property in the Rise and Expansion of Capitalism*. Oxford: Oxford University Press, 1983.

Fryer, Peter. *Staying Power: The History of Black People in Britain*. London: Pluto Press, 1984.

Galenson, David W. *Traders, Planters, and Slaves: Market Behavior in Early English America*. Cambridge: Cambridge University Press, 1986.

Gellner, Ernest. *Nationalism*. New York: New York University Press, 1997.

Gemery, Henry A. "Markets for Migrants: English Indentured Servitude and Emigration in Seventeenth and Eighteenth Centuries." *Colonialism and Migration; Indentured Labour before and after Slavery*. Ed. P. C. Emmer. Dordrecht, The Netherlands: Martinus Nijhoff Publishers, 1986.

Genovese, Eugene. *The World the Slaveholders Made: Two Essays in Interpretation*. New York: Pantheon Books, 1969.

—. *Roll, Jordan, Roll: The World the Slaves Made*. New York: Pantheon Books, 1974.

Gerzina, Gretchen. *Black London: Life before Emancipation*. Brunswick, NJ: Rutgers University Press, 1995.

Gilroy, Paul. *The Black Atlantic: Modernity and Double Consciousness*. Cambridge: Harvard University Press, 1993.

Goldberg, David Theo, ed. *Anatomy of Racism*. Minneapolis: University of Minnesota Press, 1990.

—. *Racist Culture: Philosophy and the Politics of Meaning*. Cambridge, MA: Blackwell Publishers, 1993.

—. *The Racial State*. Malden, MA: Blackwell Publishers, 2002.

Gould, Philip. *Barbaric Traffic: Commerce and Antislavery in the Eighteenth Century Atlantic World*. Cambridge, MA: Harvard University Press, 2003.

Gratus, Jack. *The Great White Lie: Slavery, Emancipation and Changing Racial Attitudes*. New York: Monthly Review Press, 1973.

Grimsted, David. "Anglo-American Racism and Phillis Wheatley's 'Sable Veil,' Length'ned Chain,' and 'Knitted Heart.'" *Women in the Age of the American Revolution*. Ed. Ronald Hoffman and Peter J. Albert. Charlottesville: University Press of Virginia, 1989. 338–444.

Gundara, Jagdish S. and Ian Duffield, eds. *Essays on the History of Blacks in Britain*. Brookfield, VT: Ashgate, 1992.

Hannaford, Ivan. *Race: The History of an Idea in the West*. Baltimore: The Johns Hopkins University Press, 1996.

Hawes, Clement. *Mania and Literary Style: The Rhetoric of Enthusiasm from the Ranters to Christopher Smart*. Cambridge: Cambridge University Press, 1996.

Holt, Thomas. *The Problem of Freedom: Race, Labor, and Politics in Jamaica and Britain*. Baltimore: The Johns Hopkins University Press, 1992.

Howell, Thomas Bayley. *A Complete collection of state trials and proceedings for high treason and other crimes and misdemeanors from the earliest period to the year 1783*. Volume 18. London: Printed by T. C. Hansard for Longman, Hurst, Rees, Orme, and Browne, 1816–26.

Hudson, Nicholas. "'Britons Never Will Be Slaves': National Myth, Conservatism, and the Beginnings of British Antislavery." *Eighteenth-Century Studies* 34.4 (2001): 559–576.

Hughes, Derek. *Versions of Blackness: Key Texts on Slavery from the 17th Century*. Cambridge: Cambridge University Press, 2007.

Hume, Robert D. *Reconstructing Contexts: The Aims and Principles of Archaeo-Historicism*. Oxford: Oxford University Press, 1999.

Hunt, Margaret. *The Middling Sort: Commerce, Gender, and the Family in England, 1680–1780*. Berkeley: University of California Press, 1996.

James, C. L. R. *Black Jacobins: Toussaint L'Ouverture and the San Domingo Revolution*. 2nd ed., revised. New York: Vintage Books, 1989.

Jennings, Judith. *The Business of Abolishing the Slave Trade, 1783–1807*. London: Frank Cass, 1997.

Jennings, Lawrence C. *French Anti-Slavery: The Movement for the Abolition of Slavery in France, 1802–1848*. Cambridge: Cambridge University Press, 2000.

Kaiwar, Vasant. "Racism and the Writing of History." *South Asia Bulletin* 9 (1989): 32–56.

Kaul, Suvir. *Poems of Nation, Anthems of Empire: English Verse in the Long Eighteenth Century*. Charlottesville: University Press of Virginia, 2000.

Kennedy, Deborah. *Helen Maria Williams and the Age of Revolution*. Lewisburg, PA: Bucknell University Press, 2002.

Klein, Herbert S. *The Atlantic Slave Trade*. Cambridge: Cambridge University Press, 1999.

Klingberg, Frank J. *The Anti-Slavery Movement in England: A Study in English Humanitarianism*. Yale University Press, 1926. Reprinted Archon Books, 1968.
Kitson, Peter J. and Debbie Lee, gen. eds. *Slavery, Abolition and Emancipation: Writings in the British Romantic Period*. London: Pickering & Chatto, 1999.
  Volume 1, *Black Writers*. Ed. Sukhdev Sandhu and David Dabydeen
  Volume 2, *The Abolition Debate*. Ed. Peter J. Kitson
  Volume 4, *Verse*. Ed. Alan Richardson
  Volume 6, *Fiction*. Ed. Srinivas Aravamudan
  Volume 8, *Theories of Race*. Ed. Peter J. Kitson
Lascelles, E. C. P. *Granville Sharp and the Freedom of Slaves in England*. 1928. Reprinted: New York: Negro Universities Press, 1969.
Lee, Debbie. *Slavery and the Romantic Imagination*. Philadelphia: University of Pennsylvania Press, 2002.
Linebaugh, Peter, and Marcu Rediker. *The Many-Headed Hydra: Sailors, Slaves, Commoners, and the Hidden History of the Revolutionary Atlantic*. London and New York: Verso, 2000.
Locke, John. "An Essay Concerning the *True Original, Extent, and End* of Civil Government." *Two Treatises of Government*. Ed. Peter Laslett. Cambridge: Cambridge University Press, 1967.
Lovejoy, Paul E. "The Impact of the Atlantic Slave Trade on Africa: A Review of the Literature." *Journal of African History* 30 (1989): 365–394.
Malik, Kenan. *The Meaning of Race: Race, History and Culture in Western Society*. New York: New York University Press, 1996.
Marshall, Prince J. *The Impeachment of Warren Hastings*. London: Oxford University Press, 1965.
McCalman, Iain. *Radical Underworld: Prophets, Revolutionaries and Pornographers in London, 1795–1840*. Cambridge: Cambridge University Press, 1988.
McCann, Andrew. *Cultural Politics in the 1790s: Literature, Radicalism and the Public Sphere*. New York: St. Martin's Press, 1999.
Meaders, Daniel. *Dead or Alive: Fugitive Slaves and White Indentured Servants before 1830*. New York: Garland Publishing, Inc., 1993.
Midgley, Clare. *Women Against Slavery: The British Campaigns 1780–1870*. London and New York: Routledge, 1992.
Miers, Suzanne. *Britain and the Ending of the Slave Trade*. New York: Africana Publishing Company, 1975.
Mintz, Sidney W. *Sweetness and Power: The Place of Sugar in Modern History*. New York: Viking, 1985.
Ogude, S. E. *Genius in Bondage: A Study of the Origins of African Literature in English*. Ife-Ife, Nigeria: University of Ife Press, 1983.
Oldfield, J. R. *Popular Politics and British Anti-Slavery: The Mobilisation of Public Opinion Against the Slave Trade, 1787–1807*. Manchester: Manchester University Press, 1995.

—. "The London Committee and the Mobilization of Public Opinion Against the Slave Trade." *Historical Journal* 35 (1992): 331–343.
Patterson, Orlando. *Slavery and Social Death: A Comparative Study.* Cambridge: Harvard University Press, 1982.
Pura, Murray. *Am I not a man and a brother?: The Life and Spirituality of William Wilberforce.* Toronto: Clements Press, 2002.
Rawley, James A. *The Transatlantic Slave Trade: A History.* New York: W.W. Norton, & Company, 1981.
—. *London, Metropolis of the Slave Trade.* Columbia: University of Missouri Press, 2003.
Richardson, David, ed. *Abolition and Its Aftermath: The Historical Context, 1790–1916.* London: Frank Cass, 1985.
Richardson, Ronald Kent. *Moral Imperium: Afro-Caribbeans and the Transformation of British Rule, 1776–1838.* Westport, CT: Greenwood Press, 1987.
Roberts-Miller, Patricia. "Robert Montgomery Bird and the Rhetoric of Improbable Cause." *Rhetoric Society Quarterly* 35 (Winter 2005): 73–90.
Rodgers, Nini. *Ireland, Slavery, and Antislavery: 1612–1865.* New York: Palgrave Macmillan, 2007.
Rogers, Nicholas. "Vagrancy, Impressment and the Regulation of Labour in Eighteenth-Century Britain." *Unfree Labour in the Development of the Atlantic World.* Ed. Paul Lovejoy and Nicholas Rogers. Portland: Frank Cass & Co., 1994. 102–113.
Rothschild, Emma. "Globalization and the Return to History." *Foreign Policy* 115 (1999): 106–116.
Sandiford, Keith A. *Measuring the Moment: Strategies of Protest in Eighteenth-Century Afro-English Writing.* Selinsgrove, PA: Susquehanna University Press, 1988.
—. *The Cultural Politics of Sugar: Caribbean Slavery and the Narratives of Colonialism.* Cambridge: Cambridge University Press, 2000.
Semmel, Bernard. *The Methodist Revolution.* New York: Basic Books, Inc., 1973.
Sheridan, Richard B. *Sugar and Slavery: An Economic History of the British West Indies, 1623–1775.* Barbados: Caribbean Universities Press, 1974.
Sherwood, Marika. *After Abolition: Britain and the Slave Trade Since 1807.* London and New York: I. B. Tauris and Co., 2007.
Shyllon, F. O. *Black Slaves in Britain.* London: Oxford University Press, 1974.
—. *Black People in Britain, 1555–1833.* London: Oxford University Press, 1977
—. *James Ramsay: The Unknown Abolitionist.* Edinburgh: Canongate, 1977.
Simmons, Herbert W., and Trevor Melia, eds. *The Legacy of Kenneth Burke.* Madison: The University of Wisconsin Press, 1989.
Smallwood, Stephanie E. *Saltwater Slavery: A Middle Passage from Africa to American Diaspora.* Cambridge, MA: Harvard University Press, 2007.

Smith, Adam. *The Theory of Moral Sentiments*. 1759. Amherst, NY: Prometheus Books, 2000.

—. *An Inquiry into the Nature and Causes of the Wealth of Nations*. 1776. Ed. Andrew Skinner. London: Penguin Books, 1999.

Soderlund, Jean R. *Quakers and Slavery: A Divided Spirit*. Princeton: Princeton University Press, 1985.

Solow, Barbara L., and Stanley Engerman, eds. *British Capitalism and Caribbean Slavery*. Cambridge: Cambridge University Press, 1987.

Sorensen, Janet. *The Grammar of Empire in Eighteenth-Century British Writing*. Cambridge: Cambridge University Press, 2000.

Spadafora, David. *The Idea of Progress in Eighteenth-Century Britain*. New Haven: Yale University Press, 1990.

Sussman, Charlotte. *Consuming Anxieties: Consumer Protest, Gender, and British Slavery, 1713–1833*. Stanford: Stanford University Press, 2000.

Swaminathan, Srividhya. "Developing the West Indian Proslavery Position after the Somerset Decision," *Slavery and Abolition* 24.3 (2003): 40–60.

—. "'That Creature of Propaganda': Anthony Benezet's Depictions of African Oppression." *British Journal of Eighteenth Century Studies* 29 (2006): 115–130.

Sypher, Wylie. *Guinea's Captive Kings: British Anti-Slavery Literature of the XVIIIth Century*. New York: Octagon Books, 1969.

Temperley, Howard. "Anti-Slavery as a Form of Cultural Imperialism." *Antislavery, Religion, and Reform: Essays in Memory of Roger Anstey*. Ed. Christine Bolt and Seymour Drescher. Folkestone, Kent: W. Dawson & Sons, 1980. 335–350.

Thomas, Helen. *Romanticism and Slave Narratives: Transatlantic Testimonies*. Cambridge: Cambridge University Press, 2000.

Thomas, Hugh. *The Slave Trade: The Story of the Atlantic Slave Trade, 1440–1870*. New York: Simon and Schuster, 1997.

Thompson, E. P. *The Making of the English Working Class*. New York: Pantheon Books, 1964.

Tise, Larry. *Proslavery: A History of the Defense of Slavery in America, 1701–1840*. Athens: The University of Georgia Press, 1987.

Trautmann, Thomas R. *Aryans in British India*. Berkeley: University of California Press, 1997.

Turley, David. *The Culture of English Antislavery, 1780–1860*. New York: Routledge, 1991.

Turley, David, and Nicholas Rogers, eds. *Unfree Labour in the Development of the Atlantic World*. Portland, OR: Frank Cass, 1994.

Walvin, James, ed. *Slavery and British Society, 1776–1846*. Baton Rouge: Louisiana State University Press, 1982.

—. *Black Ivory: A History of British Slavery*. London: HarperCollins, 1992.

—. *Slaves and Slavery: The British Colonial Experience*. New York: St. Martin's Press, 1992.

—. *Questioning Slavery*. New York: Routledge, 1996.

—. *An African's Life: The Life and Times of Olaudah Equiano, 1745–1797*. London: Cassell, 1998.

Wess, Robert. *Kenneth Burke: Rhetoric, Subjectivity, and Postmodernism*. Cambridge: Cambridge University Press, 1996.

Wheeler, Roxann. *The Complexion of Race: Categories of Difference in Eighteenth-Century British Culture*. Philadelphia: University of Pennsylvania Press, 2000.

Williams, Eric. *Capitalism and Slavery*. 1944. Chapel Hill: University of North Carolina, 1994.

Williams, Raymond. *The Long Revolution*. New York: Columbia University Press, 1961.

Wilson, Kathleen. *The Sense of the People: Politics, Culture and Imperialism in England, 1715–1785*. Cambridge: Cambridge University Press, 1995.

Wise, Steven M. *Though the Heavens May Fall: The Landmark Trial that Led to the End of Human Slavery*. New York: Da Capo Press, 2005.

Wood, Marcus. *Blind Memory: Visual Representations of Slavery in England and America, 1780–1805*. New York: Routledge, 2000.

—. *Slavery, Empathy, and Pornography*. Oxford: Oxford University Press, 2002.

Woodard, Helena. *African-British Writings in the Eighteenth Century: The Politics of Race and Reason*. Westport, CT: Greenwood Press, 1993.

Worrall, David. *Radical Culture*. Detroit: Wayne State University Press, 1992.

Young, Robert C. *Colonial Desire: Hybridity in Theory, Culture and Race*. London: Routledge, 1995.

Index

abolition
  and 1807 169, 172n, 173, 175, 178, 203–214
  and class 8, 14, 15, 17, 22, 28, 32, 40, 43, 45, 82, 102, 111n, 124, 127, 138, 171, 179, 189n, 192, 196, 199, 207, 215
  and gender 8, 17, 28, 32, 43, 45, 82, 102, 124, 172n, 189–191, 207
  and Parliament 6, 15, 26, 29, 40–42, 50, 53, 72, 75, 80n, 86, 91, 94, 100n, 135, 137, 139, 141–143, 160, 169, 174, 178, 181, 187, 192, 195–197, 199, 202–206, 211–212, 215, 216
  history of 2–9, 16–18
  see also abolitionist; Dolben's bill; London Abolitionist Society; Quakers, race
abolitionist 2–3, 38, 89n, 95, 96, 98, 128, 146, 161, 207–210
  campaign 7–9, 11–13, 29, 33, 35n, 39–49, 76–77, 104, 108, 110n, 161, 165, 176–178, 191–192
  literature 3–4, 8–9, 101, 102n, 111, 112n, 116, 135, 137n, 194–197, 199
  rhetoric 6, 22–25, 32, 50–51, 58, 85, 107, 142, 171, 180–191, 202–205, 212, 215
  society 83, 89, 94, 103, 131, 172–173, 175, 178–180, 207
  usage of term 13–14, 95n, 215
  see also abolition; Clarkson, Thomas; Equiano, Olaudah; Sharp, Granville
act 43–45, 52–57, 68, 95–96, 99, 131, 147–151, 176–178
  see also Burke, Kenneth
Act of Union 1–2
Adair, James MacKittrick 155n, 156 Fig. 4.2, 197–199

Adventures of Jonathan Corncob 109
Africans 5, 7, 29, 30, 31, 35, 36, 45, 47, 52n, 61, 62, 65, 79, 95–96, 98, 101, 102, 109, 110, 111n, 112, 118–124, 127, 131, 133, 134, 146, 157, 165–166, 177, 195, 198n, 200, 206, 209, 211, 216
  and Christianity 16, 31, 34, 51, 62, 74, 76, 158n, 182, 184
  and poetry 105–108, 115–116, 142–143, 190
  and race 8, 34, 51, 59, 60, 84n, 96, 167–169, 185–187
  as traders 43, 56, 60, 138, 161n, 162 Fig. 4.3, 163
  in Great Britain 15, 63n, 68–69, 113, 138–139
  see also Cugoano, Ottabah; Equiano, Olaudah; Gronniosaw, James; Royal African Company; Sancho, Ignatius; Wheatley, Phillis; Williams, Francis
African-American 3n, 111, 112n
African slave trade 61, 72, 74, 75, 98, 99n, 101, 146, 148, 150, 153n, 160, 167, 185, 190, 192, 200n, 202n, 211n, 215
  history of xi–xiii, 2–3
African slavery 1, 4, 16, 30, 47, 61n, 62, 65, 74, 76, 86, 88, 106n, 127n, 133
Afro-British 111–115, 117–124, 131, 215
  see also African-American
agency 43, 44, 56, 68, 95, 117, 143
  see also Burke, Kenneth
agent 43–45, 52, 55, 56, 68, 95, 99, 145, 147, 150, 158
  see also Burke, Kenneth
American colonies 7, 16, 19, 25–27, 32–34, 37, 45, 48–50, 58–61, 72n, 73–78, 80–81, 91–94, 112, 130–135, 144, 154, 159n, 174–176, 206

American proslavery 130n, 133n, 172n
American Revolution *see* revolution
American slavery 2, 144, 172n
An Address to Her Royal Highness the Duchess of York, against the use of sugar 189
Anderson, Benedict 12, 43
    imagined communities 43
    print culture 12, 19, 32–33
    see also nation, national identity, nationalism
Anglican Church 61, 81n
antislavery
    antislavery/abolitionist 6, 13, 32, 38, 40, 43, 58, 135, 173
    arguments 14, 16, 23, 47, 49, 60, 61, 64, 83, 85, 93, 107, 119, 146, 159, 176n, 192
    in pamphlet literature 86, 88
Aristotelian 84
    modes of rhetoric 6
    ethos 6, 55, 110, 129, 143–147, 179
    logos 6, 85–86
    pathos 6, 84, 85, 100
    see also rhetorical appeal
Armistead, Wilson 52n, 71n
Armitage, David 17n, 78n, 212–214
Arvamudan, Srinivas 2, 122

Bacon, Jacqueline 3
Barbados 29, 48n, 62n, 64, 109, 130, 135, 176n, 177n, 195
    see also West Indies
Barbauld, Anna Leticia 186
Benezet, Anthony 5, 7, 48–49, 49–61, 68, 70n, 71–72, 79–82, 83–85, 86, 94, 100–101, 143, 152, 176, 215
    A Caution to Great Britain and her Colonies 53, 54 Fig. 2.1, 58–60
    A Short Account of that part of Africa Inhabited by the Negroes 53, 56–57, 59, 71
    Observations on the Inslaving, importing and purchasing of Negroes 53, 55–57
    Some Historical Account of Guinea 71–72
    see also Sharp, Granville; Quakers

Birkett, Mary 185, 190
Blackburn, Robin 16n, 77, 83, 172n
Blake, William 103, 110
Boswell, James 212
Bradburn, Samuel 208
Braude, Benjamin 158n
Briton 1–9, 13–14, 15n, 19, 31–33, 38, 41–43, 46, 47, 56–57, 59, 74, 76, 79, 83–85, 88, 95, 99–100, 104–107, 112–214, 120–124, 129, 138–141, 152, 155–160, 163, 166, 169–170, 171–191, 199, 201, 206–210, 211–217
Brookes diagram 187, 188 Fig. 5.1
Brown, Christopher Leslie 2–3, 11n, 40, 73n, 83, 87n,
Burgess, Thomas 99–100
Burke, Edmund 20, 27–28, 191n, 214n
Burke, Kenneth 6–7, 13, 43
    circumference 6–8, 44–45, 49, 52, 68, 76, 80, 85, 89, 99, 145, 174–177
    dramatic pentad 6–7, 43–44, 45, 95
    see also Aristotelian; rhetorical appeals

capital 21, 205
    capitalism 21, 25
    capitalist 21, 24, 157
    see also commerce; merchant capital
Carey, Brycchan 2, 39, 85, 101n, 102, 148, 171n, 174n
Carretta, Vincent 111n, 112n, 113n, 117n, 118n, 120n, 121n, 122n
Catholicism 61n, 99, 183n
    in defense of slavery 183
    in Spanish colonialism 61, 183n
Christianity 41, 49n, 61, 64, 106–107, 113, 120
    as progress narrative 18, 34, 209–210, 213, 215
    Christian doctrine 18, 34, 47, 113, 183, 209
    conversion of slaves 31, 62, 114, 116–117
    in defense of slavery 30–32, 164–165, 200–202
    in opposition to slavery 57–58, 69, 98–99, 124, 136, 181–184

sons of Ham 30–31, 158n, 165, 200–201
citizen 28, 35, 73n, 74, 85, 119, 145
Clarkson, Thomas 18, 28, 34, 77n, 79n, 100, 122, 157, 159n, 175n, 176, 188 Fig. 5.1, 202, 204
   An Essay on the Slavery and Commerce of the Human Species 95–96, 101, 146, 179
   The History of the Rise, Progress and Accomplishment of the Abolition of the African Slave-Trade by the British Parliament 11, 52, 211–212, 215–216
   see also London Abolitionist Society
Code Noir 150, 152, 159
Coleman, Deirdre 2, 39, 85, 189n, 191n
Coleridge, Samuel T. 210
Colley, Linda 12, 26–27, 40–41, 77, 87n, 98, 180n, 181n, 182n, 189, 205, 212, 215–216
   see also national identity, nationalism
colonialism 13n, 35
commerce 1, 21–22, 33, 35, 41, 47, 74, 110, 119, 124, 127–141, 145–146, 152, 155, 157, 159, 161, 163, 169, 174, 187, 194–195, 202, 206–208, 212–213
   see also capital; Smith, Adam
Cooper, Thomas 146, 185
Cowper, William
   "The Negro's Complaint" 106n, 110, 184
Craton, Michael 16n, 154n, 159n
Cruikshank, Isaac
   "The Abolition of the Slave Trade" 98n, 193 Fig. 5.2
Cugoano, Quobna Ottobah 8, 112–213, 120–122

Dabydeen, David 104n, 111n
d'Anjou, Leo 42
Davis, David Brion 2, 14n, 16, 20, 28, 30, 40, 64n, 77, 83, 97n, 154n, 172n, 176, 205, 214n
Dent, William 161n
   "Abolition of the Slave Trade, or the Man the Master" 161–163, 162 Fig. 4.3

Dolben's bill 177n, 181
   see also Williams, Helen Maria
Dore, James 99
Drescher, Seymour 20, 21n, 39, 40n, 77n, 98
Dying Negro, The 101, 104

East India Company 19, 207
   see also Burke, Edmund; Hastings, Warren
Edwards, Bryan 105–107, 194n
Ellis, Markman 2, 39, 102
empire, British 1, 4, 6, 8, 9–12, 19, 39, 42, 45, 49, 59, 76, 78, 80, 86, 91, 93, 104–105, 119, 133–135, 145, 148, 155, 158, 163, 174, 180, 194, 202–217
empire, Ottoman 47n
English civil law 65–70, 86, 88, 91, 135n
Equiano, Olaudah 8, 85, 97, 113, 120, 121–124, 175n, 177n, 209, 215
Estwick, Samuel 134n, 137n, 139, 141, 146
Evangelical 34, 73n, 179, 181, 184
   Evangelical movement 61

Falconbridge, Alexander 100n, 142n
Ferguson, Moira 40n, 85n, 104n, 172n, 189–190
Foot, Jesse 200
Fox, Charles 192
Fox, George 48n
Fox, William 187, 189
Francklyn, Gilbert 194n, 198
French antislavery 28n, 216n
   see also Jennings, Lawrence
French Revolution *see* revolution
Fryer, Peter 15n, 63n, 85n, 110–111

Gellner, Ernest 13, 16
Gerzina, Gretchen 15n, 63n, 111
Gilroy, Paul 112–113
Goldberg, David Theo 45, 164, 167n, 184n, 185
   see also race
Gronniosaw, James Albert Ukawsaw 85, 113, 114–115, 120
Guinea 60

Haiti 28, 29, 37
  see also revolution
Haitian Revolution *see* revolution
Hannaford, Ivan 163–164, 167n
  see also race
Hargrave, Francis 70n, 88n, 89–91, 90 Fig. 3.1, 133, 135n
Harris, Raymund 99, 121, 182–184, 200
Hastings, Warren, trial of 20, 147n, 214n
Hawes, Clement C. 84n
Holt, Thomas 140n, 158n, 212n
Hudson, Nicholas 98n
Hume, David 164, 165, 166n
Hunt, Margaret 14n, 15

imperialism, British 6, 9, 39, 40, 46, 173n, 180n, 212n, 217
indentured servants 35, 50n, 139, 163, 168
Inkle and Yarico 62

Jacobite 27n, 62
Jamaica 29, 65, 70, 97, 105, 112, 135, 140, 150, 166, 168, 176n, 194n, 195, 203, 212n
  see also West Indies
Jennings, Judith 175n, 178
Jennings, Lawrence 28n, 216n
Johnson, Samuel 93

Kaul, Suvir 2, 39, 85, 103n
Kilner, Dorothy
  The Rotchfords 108–110
King's Bench, court of 70, 137n
Kitson, Peter 2, 39
Knox, William 194–195, 200

labor
  conditions of 17, 23, 35, 93, 127, 152–154, 168–169, 177, 200
  division of 22–23
  domestic 15–16, 63, 70, 134
  free vs. slave 21, 23–25, 34–36, 51, 53, 80, 129, 132n, 135–139, 145, 148, 157
  plantation 30, 47, 50n, 58–60, 78, 80, 131, 161

slave labor 15n, 24–25, 34–36, 47, 51, 55, 70n, 78, 80n, 127, 129, 147–148, 157, 206
  see also Smith, Adam
Lee, Debbie 2, 39
liberty 11, 20–21, 25–29, 33, 36–37, 41, 45–46, 59–60, 65, 69, 76, 79, 87–89
  concept of 25, 94–95, 98–99, 147
  discourse of 58, 93, 134
  English liberty 59, 62, 64, 89, 94, 199
  individual liberty 20, 91
  love of 85, 93, 122
  see also Sharp, Granville
Liverpool 37, 78, 80, 111n, 141n, 174, 178n, 182n, 202n
Locke, John 16–17, 19, 33
London Abolitionist Society 42, 94–95, 102n, 186
  see also abolition; abolitionist; Clarkson, Thomas; Sharp, Granville; Phillips, James
Long, Edward 101n, 112, 137–139, 146, 154, 158, 159n, 165–166, 184, 194n
  Candid Reflections 137–8
  History of Jamaica 112, 154, 159n, 165

MacKenzie, Henry
  Julia de Roubigné 108
Mansfield, William Murray, first Earl of 31, 70–71, 73, 86–91, 94, 97, 129–30, 132n, 135, 137, 141, 142
  see also Mansfield decision; Somerset, James
Mansfield decision 132n, 134–135, 137, 139–140
  see also Hargrave, Francis; Mansfield, William; Sharp, Granville; Somerset decision; Somerset, James
McClish, Glen 3
mercantilism 35, 157, 206
Mercator 139–140, 207
merchant 14, 22, 35, 37, 41, 47, 95, 100, 124–125, 129–132, 135, 138–142, 155, 165–168, 179, 206, 211
  as pseudonym 129, 136, 138, 148, 194n, 203

French 28
  representation of 146–148, 152–153, 155–163, 185–186, 192, 195–197, 201, 207–208
merchant capital 21
Methodism 81n
  see also Methodist; Wesley, John
Methodist 34, 61, 81, 98n, 181, 182, 208n
  see also Methodism; Wesley, John
middle passage 38, 79, 85, 95, 98, 142–143, 146, 177, 191, 192, 195, 202
  in abolitionist cartoons 193 Fig. 5.2
  in proslavery writing 175, 187, 194n, 200, 202
Midgley, Clare 83, 85n, 104n, 172n, 178n, 189, 190n, 202n
Montesquieu, Charles de Secondat 33, 164
Montgomery, James 211, 214
More, Hannah 107, 190
  Slavery, A Poem 102, 104–105, 106, 185–186
  Sorrows of Yamba 209–210
Morgann, Maurice 87

nabob 147, 214n
nation 9, 11–12, 15, 22, 24, 26, 33, 42–43, 47, 55–59, 68, 73–76, 82, 87, 97, 104, 106–107, 112, 124, 125, 129, 138, 140, 142, 155, 164, 169, 171–173, 195, 204, 207–211
  American nation 93–94
  British nation 20, 40, 41, 52, 56, 58, 75, 104, 125, 175, 203–205
  Christian nation 99, 120
  proslavery nation 152–159, 196
  white nation 110, 120, 199, 215
national character, British 4–5, 7–8, 20, 31–32, 41, 43, 46, 59, 82–83, 96, 104–106, 119–121, 128, 129, 140, 158, 164–165, 170, 171, 173, 180–182, 185, 187, 190, 196, 203, 206–207, 217
national identity 1, 3–6, 9, 12–13, 38, 39, 41, 43, 49, 72, 85, 87n, 88, 104, 123, 163, 170, 197, 210
  British 3, 5, 27n, 33, 40, 106, 111, 112n, 128, 172n, 181, 206, 215

  construction of 1, 45–46, 99, 123–124, 128, 165, 173–175, 180n
  counter-discourse of national identity 135, 157
  discourse of 4, 5, 31, 33, 42, 83, 119, 129, 155
nationalism 12, 41, 122n, 175, 210
native
  African 31, 34, 59–60, 114, 120, 123, 130n, 157, 209
  definition of 1–3
  natural born 89, 134, 138, 163, 169
  see also national character
Native American 35, 116, 167n
natural rights 5, 17, 28, 33–35, 45, 69, 116, 135, 138, 144, 147, 157, 160, 163–164, 167, 169, 182, 197, 205, 206
Newton, John 142n, 146, 150, 204
Newton, Richard 196n
Nisbet, Richard 91n, 134n, 144–146
nominal Christian 76, 106n
  see also Sharp, Granville
Norris, Robert 153n, 160–161, 168, 194n

Occom, Samson 115–116
Oldfield, J. R. 172n

petitions
  campaign 171, 172n
  Quaker 53
Pitt, Willam 192, 196n
  see also Wilberforce, William
planter 8, 25, 29, 35–36, 41, 69, 73n, 109, 132, 135, 137, 139, 143, 145–147, 150, 155, 168
  as pseudonym 129, 148, 167n, 194n
  discourse 158–159, 161, 163, 201, 207
  shift in terminology 95, 152–153, 195–198
Porteus, Beilby 182
"positive good" 130
positive law 88, 137, 139
  see also Somerset decision
proslavery 2–3, 5–6, 8, 13, 14n, 15, 28, 39–41, 51, 56, 63, 71, 75, 86–89, 96–100, 142–170, 206, 210, 217

arguments 25, 29, 32–38, 47, 68, 73n, 81–82, 91–92, 95, 121, 135–141, 173–188
clergy 30–31, 48, 65, 84, 127–128
rhetoric of 3, 6, 8, 41, 129, 148n, 161, 164n, 169, 173, 191–203, 205, 207
view of Africans 23, 45, 59–61, 78, 114, 121–122, 124–125
see also abolition; African; national identity; race
pseudonyms 148, 151, 198n

Quakers 64, 84n, 176, 192
American Meeting 25, 48, 50, 52–53, 56, 61, 68, 94, 133
Lay, Benjamin 51
London Meeting 53–55, 71, 76, 81, 95n, 104, 175, 178–179
The Case of our Fellow-Creatures, the Oppressed Africans 53
Phillips, James 95, 178, 192
see also Benezet, Anthony

race 8, 29, 33–34, 39, 41, 43, 45, 52, 59–60, 82, 104, 106, 107, 110–114, 117–121, 123–124, 141, 153, 155, 158, 161–164, 183
and blackness 107, 114, 120
and whiteness 84n, 107, 109, 123, 165, 167, 169, 185–186, 215
race discourse 129, 131n, 164–165
race theory 45, 59–60, 164–165, 184n, 187
see also Goldberg, David Theo; Hannaford, Ivan
Ramsay, James 96–97, 142, 148, 151–153, 157, 159, 168, 176, 204
An Essay on the Treatment and Conversion of African Slaves 96n, 148, 149 Fig. 4.1, 150
An Inquiry into the Effects of putting a stop to the African Slave Trade 98, 148, 150–151
reform 4–5, 60, 77, 79, 81–82, 84, 94, 102, 124, 153–155, 163, 177, 199, 200, 211, 213
rhetoric of 11–14, 16, 132, 145–146, 155, 169, 192, 195

reform movement 4, 11, 12, 14, 17, 29, 37, 50
regulationist 177, 192, 194–197, 199–208, 210
revolution 16, 25–27, 36–37, 96, 134
American 27–28, 40, 80, 93–94, 133n, 134, 145, 176
French 27–28, 174, 198
Haitian 28–29, 110n, 174, 203
rhetoric *see* Burke, Kenneth; rhetorical appeal
rhetorical appeal 9, 79, 82, 84–85
ethical appeal 143, 148, 157, 191, 196–197
logical appeal 59, 69, 79, 200
pathetic appeal 43, 57, 59, 79, 81, 122, 141–142, 169, 177, 185–186, 191
see also Aristotelian; Burke, Kenneth
rhetorical terrain 3, 29, 155, 157, 171, 210
see also national identity; rhetorical appeal
Roberts-Miller, Patricia 3
Royal African Company 37, 55, 91, 132, 139, 146, 157, 194, 209
Rush, Benjamin 53n, 72, 80n, 91–92, 134n, 144, 146

St. Domingue *see* Haiti; revolution
Sancho, Ignatius 8, 102, 111, 113, 117–119, 209
correspondence with Laurence Sterne 102–103, 118
savage 56
and Africans 59–60, 95–96, 118–119, 165–166, 169
and proslavery writers 106, 185–186, 123, 146
scene 43–45, 52, 56, 58, 68, 95, 102–103, 109, 114, 116, 123, 131, 143, 145, 150
Schaw, Janet 131n
Sharp, Granville 5, 7, 8, 49, 53, 55n, 56, 60, 61–76, 79–82, 83, 84, 85, 86, 88, 91, 94, 98, 100, 113, 121n, 122, 130, 135n, 143, 152, 175, 176, 182, 187, 201n, 215
"An Essay on Slavery" 73–74

Representation of the Injustice and Dangerous Tendency of Tolerating Slavery 31n, 64n, 66–67 Fig. 2.2a and 2.2b, 65–71, 89, 101n, 106n, 138–139
  The Just Limitation of Slavery in the Laws of God 75
  The Law of Liberty, or, Royal Law 75–76
  The Law of Passive Obedience 75–76
  The Law of Retribution 74–75
Sheffield, Lord John 194n, 196, 198n, 205n
Sherwood, Marika 172n
Shyllon, F. O. 97n, 110, 111n, 148n
Sierra Leone 201n
slave holder *see* planter
  see also abolition
slavery *see* African slavery; African slave trade
Smith, Adam 21–25, 215
  see also capital; commerce; labor
social movement 3, 5, 32, 39, 42–43, 46, 171, 214
Society for Effecting the Abolition of the Slave Trade, *see* London Abolitionist Society
Society for the Propagation of the Gospel in Foreign Parts 30, 152n, 177n
Soderlund, Jean R 50n, 51n
Somerset decision 63n, 73, 75n, 85, 88, 89, 91–92, 129, 131, 133, 134n, 135
  see also Mansfield decision; Somerset, James
Somerset, James 63, 70–71, 73, 86–88, 97, 130, 136–138, 140
Sterne, Laurence
  correspondence with Ignatius Sancho 102
  Tristram Shandy 102–103
Strong, Jonathan 64–65, 70, 135n
subject 15, 19, 29, 38, 40, 48, 55, 57, 60, 68, 69–70, 76, 94, 113, 115, 116–117, 120, 124, 134, 138–143, 151, 153, 155, 159, 160, 165, 168, 174, 177, 180, 181, 187, 189, 192n, 202, 205–206, 214
sugar 21, 25, 28, 34, 35–36, 58n, 92, 96, 98, 127, 131, 145, 148, 151, 163, 168, 188–190, 194n, 212
  boycotts 35–36, 80n, 187–190

Swift, Jonathan 106n
Sypher, Wylie 100n, 103

Thompson, Reverend Thomas 73–74, 142
Thomson, James 1
Tise, Larry 128, 130n, 133n, 183n
Tobin, James 146, 147–148, 151–152, 168
topos 3, 49, 167, *see* national identity
trader *see* merchant
transformation 6–7, 9, 11–12, 13–14, 16, 29, 32–33, 43–45, 47, 49, 59, 76–77, 94, 113n, 115n, 128, 143, 145, 158n, 163, 175, 180, 191, 205, 213
travel narratives 59, 101n, 110, 122n, 131n
Turley, David 77, 83
Turnbull, Gordon 153–154

villeinage 71–72, 88n, 91n, 133n
  see also Hargrave, Francis; Sharp, Granville

Walvin, James 16n, 97n, 205
Wedgewood, Josiah 100n
Wedgewood medallion 161, 186, 190
Wesley, John 18, 34, 72, 79n, 101
  A serious address to the people of England 92
  Thoughts Upon Slavery 81–82, 143
West Indies 8, 50n, 56, 58, 64, 87, 92–96, 101, 109, 110, 122–123, 128–132, 134–136, 142–160, 166, 168, 176n, 177, 184–186, 189, 192, 194n, 193–198, 200–201, 206–210
  "The West Indies" 211, 214
Wheatley, Phillis 8, 111–112, 113, 115–117, 119–120, 209
Wheeler, Roxann 102n, 107, 110, 167
Wilberforce, William 174–175, 178–182, 186, 192, 195, 197–199, 204, 215
Williams, Eric 21n, 25n, 39, 157n
Williams, Francis 112, 166
Williams, Helen Maria 107–108, 181
Wilson, Kathleen 12n, 15, 212–213
Wood, Marcus 186n, 187, 195n, 196n

Yearsley, Ann 104–105, 107, 186–187

Zong incident 97–98, 194